The American Film Industry

edited by

Tino Balio

The University of Wisconsin Press

Published 1976
The University of Wisconsin Press
Box 1379, Madison, Wisconsin 53701

The University of Wisconsin Press, Ltd.
70 Great Russell Street, London

First printing

Printed in the United States of America
For LC CIP information see the colophon

ISBN 0-299-07000-X cloth; 0-299-07004-2 paper

Contents

Preface

This book, comprising original papers and previously published materials, is designed primarily as a collateral text for undergraduate courses dealing with the development of American film. My goal in bringing together these readings is to present a systematic survey of the history of the industry, allowing the individual materials to suggest to the reader ways in which the realities of economics, changing legal restraints, technological advances, studio organization and procedures, financing, distribution trade practices, and exhibitor preferences have influenced the form and content of the movies. No other American art form, including theater, dance, music, and fine arts, has been subjected to so many constraints, nor has any other art been influenced so heavily by the predilections of the business world.

The organization of the book delineates the development of the industry in terms of its economic structure. It is divided into four parts, each of which is preceded by an introduction presenting an overview of the period as an aid to the reader in placing the readings in context.

Part I (1894-1908) describes the period when motion pictures changed from a novelty into a business enterprise. Inventors gave way to aggressive entrepreneurs who exploited inventions to make quick profits, meanwhile increasing the public's appetite for this new entertainment form. The industry separated into three branches: production, distribution, and exhibition. Each functioned separately and the growth of each was encouraged because of its small investment requirements. Hundreds of small businesses were formed in this early era of near-perfect competition.

The period covered by Part II (1908-1930) is characterized by the growth of the industry into a mature oligopoly. Struggles for control of the business began with the establishment of the Motion Picture Patents Company, a monopoly based on patent rights, and continued with the attempts of other companies to gain dominant economic power in the marketplace through various means—the exploitation of the star system, the supplanting of one- and two-reelers by feature films, and the vigorous acquisition of motion picture theaters. During this struggle, the strong survived and grew. More and more power fell into the hands of fewer and fewer companies, as they merged production, distribution, and exhibition efforts. The advent of sound, which might be expected to have revolutionized the industry's structure, merely served to hasten this vertical integration.

Part III (1930-1948) describes the behavior and organization of the oligopoly. The period of struggle was essentially over, and the industry, then dominated by five giant companies, entered an era of cooperation as a means of preserving the structure, protecting itself from governmental and civic regulation, and maximizing profits. Earnings plunged during the Depression, but the major companies capitalized on an opportunity granted them by the National Industrial Relations Act to tighten their grip on the marketplace. The industry emerged from the Depression unscathed, soared to new heights during World War II, and enjoyed unbridled prosperity until 1948, when television and an important Supreme Court antitrust decision brought this rosy era to a close.

Part IV (1948 to the present) describes the profound effects of the Supreme Court's *Paramount* decision on the industry. The Court's decrees forced the integrated companies to divorce their exhibition branches from their production and distribution operations and outlawed several trade practices upon which the industry had depended to preserve the status quo. In adjusting to the forced reorganization of its entire business structure, the industry also had to confront the competition of television, increasing resistance to the export of its product by foreign governments, and the witch hunts of the House Committee on Un-American Activities. The industry adjusted surprisingly well to these major tremors, and today a relatively small number of firms, some of which are part of huge multinational conglomerates, still control the bulk of the business.

The previously published articles selected for inclusion were drawn from bibliographies prepared for two graduate research seminars that I teach on the economics of the motion picture industry. These bibliographies also served as a guide to background literature in the preparation of my *United Artists: The Company Built by the Stars* (University of Wisconsin Press, 1975). In turn, my own contribution to this collection was suggested and formed by the research that I conducted for that book. Several publications and chapters from book-length studies have been specially adapted, with the cooperation of their authors, for inclusion in this collection (see chapters 1, 2, 6, and 16). The Mae D. Huettig reading (11) is a condensation of a chapter from her book, edited with permission from the present copyright holder. Four original papers, in addition to my own, were commissioned for the book.

All illustrations appearing in the book have been especially gathered from the following sources: the British Film Institute National Film Archive/Stills Library; the Bruce Torrence Historical Collection, c/o First Federal of Hollywood; Metro-Goldwyn-Mayer, Inc.; the United Artists

Corporation; Universal Pictures; and the Wisconsin Center for Film and Theater Research.

It is my hope that this combination of original and previously published materials forms an accurate and reasonably full survey of the industry's history, focusing upon its economic and business aspects. I hope also that, as more researchers are drawn into this little-explored field, additional original contributions in these areas will result, making revised editions of this book even more valuable to both students and scholars.

TINO BALIO

Madison, Wisconsin
January 1976

The American Film Industry

Part I

A Novelty Spawns Small Businesses: 1894-1908

On April 14, 1894, the world's first Kinetoscope parlor opened its doors at 1155 Broadway in New York City (see ch. 2). No one knows who the customers were on that day, or exactly how many of them parted with some change to satisfy their curiosity about the new picture machine—but we can be sure that they had no idea of their place in history as they gazed into the peepholes in amazement. They were the first paying customers for the motion pictures, a handful of unwitting pioneers, destined to be followed by countless millions in America's long and exciting romance with the movies. That day and that place marked the commercial beginnings of the motion picture industry in the United States.

The Kinetoscope which amused Broadway strollers was a peephole machine which showed a short filmstrip. It had been perfected by William Kennedy Laurie Dickson at Thomas Edison's laboratory in nearby West Orange, New Jersey. A syndicate headed by A. O. Tate, Thomas R. Lombard, and Erastus A. Benson was the first to see the moneymaking possibilities of the machine, and so it acquired a concession from Edison to market it.

The trial balloon, launched on Broadway, was soon followed by a veritable skyful. Within the year, the syndicate (which by then had added three new partners—Andrew M. Holland, Norman C. Raff, and Frank R. Gammon) installed Kinetoscopes in department stores, hotels, saloons, and phonograph parlors in major cities throughout the country, always with the same gratifying results—curiosity, amusement, patronage, and profits. Noting the machine's domestic success, another firm, headed by Frank Z. Maguire and Joseph D. Baucus, acquired the foreign rights and marketed America's new plaything abroad.

3

Debut of the Projector

The enthusiastic reception of the Kinetoscope ensured its
multiplication and success—and inevitably was the cause of its
decline and supplantation. The Kinetoscope, after all, had a
major limitation: it could be seen by only one viewer at a time.
What if the picture image could be projected onto a screen, so
that the small change of a large audience could be collected all
at one time? No sooner had entrepreneurs dreamed of such an
advance than technicians turned the dream into reality.
Through the work of Robert W. Paul in England, the Lumière
brothers in France, and, in America, the Lathams, Thomas
Armat, Herman Casler, Albert E. Smith, and Dickson, the
motion picture projector became a commercial reality only two
years after the unveiling of the first Kinetoscope.

Edison introduced a projector to the public on April 23,
1896, at Koster & Bial's Music Hall, Herald Square, New York
City (ch. 1). Its appearance came just in time, perhaps,
because by then the novelty of the Kinetoscope was wearing
off. Kinetoscope business, in fact, began to decline in 1895
and showed no signs of resurgence by the time the first
projector appeared. Edison himself, it appears, had limited
faith in the durability of the Kinetoscope idea, since he had not
even bothered to take out foreign patents on it.

Edison's projector was called the Vitascope, the invention of
Thomas Armat. Edison did not wait to develop a projector of
his own, since other inventors and developers were already
anticipating public demand. One projector, in fact, had
already been introduced, this by the Latham brothers, Otway
and Gray, and their father Woodville. They had devised a
projection machine based on the principle of the Kinetoscope.
It was an imperfect machine, but marketable, and others were
swiftly on the way. Edison, faced with the possibility of being
shut out of the market he himself had created, decided to get
into the swim without delay by purchasing the manufacturing
and marketing rights to Armat's projector.

Movies Come to Vaudeville

That same summer, on June 29, 1896, Edison received some
serious competition. Another New York vaudeville house,
B. F. Keith's Union Square Theatre, exhibited a Lumière

Cinématographe.This was an event of major importance in the motion picture business. Since J. Austin Fynes, manager of the Keith theater, was highly respected by vaudeville managers, his acceptance of motion pictures and of the Lumière projector was a clear signal to other vaudeville houses. The Proctor circuit and other houses soon began to include motion pictures on their cards, along with dog acts, lyric tenors, and slapstick comics. Movies had come to the stage.

Less than four months later, both the Vitascope and the Lumière Cinématographe were challenged for primacy in the field. Appearing on the scene was the Biograph projector, which was capable of showing pictures significantly larger than its precursors, and much clearer and sharper, too. It was the invention of Dickson, then a partner in the American Mutoscope Company (soon to be called the American Mutoscope and Biograph Company). Dickson's Biograph made its "regular" debut on October 12, 1896, at Hammerstein's Opera House in New York. It was an instant success, making its competitors obsolete in short order. The Biograph moved to the Union Square Theater on January 18, 1897, and, with only a four-month hiatus, closed on July 15, 1905, after eight and a half years—"an incomparably long run in the history of the American theatre to that date," in the words of Gordon Hendricks.[1]

In introducing motion pictures to vaudeville, it was only natural for managers to include them as one turn in the series of acts. A vaudeville turn lasted approximately fifteen minutes, and since the early films were around fifty feet in length, it was necessary to string a minimum of ten subjects together to fill a time slot. At Koster & Bial's, for example, the Vitascope program consisted of twelve subjects and was one of eight acts given before the first intermission. The films were no doubt accompanied by music—in the large houses by the versatile pit orchestras, and in the smaller ones by a piano.

Until 1896, theater owners who wanted to book a projector could do so with a certain measure of protection, which came in the form of exclusive exhibition rights to carefully defined geographical areas.[2] But in 1896, Edison brought out a

1. Gordon Hendricks, *Beginnings of the Biograph* (New York, 1964), p. 51.
2. Vitascope sales were handled by Raff and Gammon's Kinetoscope Company; the Cinématographe by Lumière's American representative, W. B. Hurd; and the Biograph directly by the American Mutoscope Company.

projector of his own devising, the Edison Projecting
Kinetoscope, and placed it on the open market with no
geographical restrictions attached. Anyone could buy the
Edison and use it for commercial showings wherever the traffic
would allow. Edison's bold marketing move probably made
more than a few theater operators uncomfortable, but its
success soon forced other companies to adopt similar policies.
Sales of the projectors, thus unbridled, increased dramatically,
giving a significant stimulus to the entire motion picture
industry in the United States.

Motion Picture Exhibitions on the Road

While films were finding a ready place in metropolitan
vaudeville houses, they had also taken to the road (ch. 3).
Lumière showmen began the first of their long tours in the
summer of 1895. That same summer, LeRoy Latham (nephew
of Woodville) purchased the territorial rights to the Latham
Pantopticon for the state of Virginia. Latham's venture was
short-lived, largely because of the inferior quality of the
projector itself, but he obviously had the right idea. Where the
pioneer Latham failed, other entrepreneurs succeeded, among
them William T. Rock, who took the Raff & Gammon
projector to Louisiana, a state that the Kinetoscope Company
was happy to relinquish for $1,500. Rock opened a motion
picture "store" in New Orleans on June 28, 1896. After three
months, his meager supply of films exhausted the market,
forcing him to take the show into smaller cities.
    Soon after, in August 1896, Thomas L. Tally opened a
"Phonograph and Vitascope Parlor" in Los Angeles. Although
he, too, was plagued by a scarcity of films, he survived by
making the broadest possible use of the various machines on
the market: he offered customers not only the Kinetoscope, but
also the Vitascope, the phonograph, and the Mutoscope, a
peephole machine which flipped printed cards before the
viewer's eyes, giving the illusion of motion.
    Other traveling showmen brought the movies to small-town
America, wherever there were enough people in one place with
money in their pockets and adventure in their hearts. In New
England, audiences packed amusement parks, club halls, and
vacant storefronts on Sundays when legitimate theaters were
closed. Harry and Herbert Miles lugged a projector all the way

to Juneau, Alaska, where they played the gold camps on the
outskirts of town. All of these showmen traversed rural
America for reasons of their own: the promise of financial
reward, the lure of the open road, the excitement of "show
business." But together they performed an invaluable service
for the future of the entire industry, for they helped to create a
public taste for motion pictures on a national level, and by
doing so they laid the broad foundation for the modern movie
theater. The creation of such a theater, however, had to wait
until large and efficient production and distribution companies
could provide a regular supply of films at low cost.

Motion Picture Production, 1895-1903

The average length of motion pictures before the turn of the
century was about fifty feet. The most common subjects were
those that took the viewer beyond his day-to-day experiences:
scenic pictures of faraway places, little dramatic incidents,
comedies, trick films, and vaudeville turns. Audiences were
thrilled most, however, by swirling and powerful movement—
onrushing trains, careening fire trucks, exotic dancers, and
stirring parades were among the favorites.

Nearly all of the early films were supplied by three major
producers—Edison, Biograph, and Vitagraph. These
companies made the bulk of their profits not on films,
however, but on projecting equipment, on which they each
held key patents. They produced films more out of economic
necessity than anything else, to maintain and increase the
demand for equipment. The price charged for Kinetoscope
subjects, as seen in the Raff & Gammon 1894 catalog, ranged
from ten to fifteen dollars a reel. After the introduction of the
projector, however, film prices dropped. They were sold
outright at about ten to twelve cents a foot, regardless of
quality or subject matter, bringing the cost of an average-
length reel to between five and six dollars.

Making films did not require a large capital investment, and
soon many producers and manufacturers found their way into
the trade. Some imported cameras from Europe, while others
bootlegged cameras by copying or modifying American
inventions and selling them as their own. To squelch these
interlopers and to cement the entire market for himself, Edison
instituted a series of patent infringement suits in December

1897 against nearly every organization and individual of
consequence that had entered the business. In pressing the
cases, his lawyers insisted that all inventors and manufacturers
of motion picture equipment, and all producers in the United
States, were operating in violation of the patent rights that
Edison had secured on his Kinetoscope. The main targets of
Edison's legal attack—the American Mutoscope and Biograph
Company and the Vitagraph Company—stood and fought by
entering counterclaims. The fly-by-night and small-time
operators scattered quickly, rather than become involved in
costly litigation against the giant Edison, but no sooner
had any three disappeared than three or four came to
take their place.

Development of the Studio

Scenic and topical films were routinely shot on location
throughout the world. The Lumières were preeminent in this
field, aided by their compact and highly portable camera.
Vaudeville turns and staged scenes, however, were usually
filmed in studios, where most producers preferred to do their
work. The precedent for photographing in studios had been
established by Dickson, who found it easier to bring subjects to
the "Black Maria," a frame, tar-paper-covered studio, than to
take the heavy and awkward Kinetograph camera to meet the
subjects. The studios of Biograph and Vitagraph were open-air
stages situated on the roofs of their buildings in New York.
Although studio productions necessitated props, scenery,
costumes, and actors, this method eliminated the uncertainties
of location shooting and allowed producers to approach a
mechanical and dependable regularity in their work. With the
perfection of artificial lighting, production work came off the
rooftops and into the buildings, thus avoiding the vagaries of
weather. Ironically, Edison, the developer of the incandescent
bulb, preferred natural lighting and built a $100,000 glassed-in
studio in the Bronx in 1905.

By 1898, projected motion pictures had lost much of their
novelty, just as peep shows had before them. In vaudeville
houses, they were being relegated to the position of "chasers,"
signaling to the audience that the show was over and that it
was time to clear the house for the next performance. Movie
patrons of dime museums and arcades still seemed willing to
satisfy an apparently insatiable appetite for the entertainment
provided them, but producers realized that the larger public

would soon have to be offered films of greater impact if the business was to survive and grow.

The obvious route to improvement of the product was in lengthening the films, thus providing time for more complete dramas. Shortly after 1900, therefore, films from 250 to 400 feet in length, embodying slight themes, began to appear on the market.[3] During 1902 and 1903, films 300 to 600 feet in length were regularly produced. Most offered simple stories, typical of which was *The Adventures of Sandy McGregor,* described by its producer as "a very humorous subject showing the adventures of Sandy who is caught by two young ladies on a lonely beach while preparing to take his bath."[4]

Impact of *The Great Train Robbery*

In 1903, just when the movie industry seemed to be heading for the special and ignominious fate reserved for all social fads, a major event occurred that brought the public swarming back to the theaters—this time, as it turned out, for good.

The event was the production of Edwin S. Porter's *The Great Train Robbery,* an exciting film of extraordinary length (1,100 feet). But it was not the length of the film that endeared it to audiences, but the way in which it was put together. Porter, with this film, had invented the principle of editing. Instead of merely presenting a series of short clips strung together, he was able to tell a compelling and dramatic story with a daring train holdup, a brave and desperate pursuit, and a thrilling last-minute capture. According to Lewis Jacobs, *The Great Train Robbery* "was the nickelodeon's most widely exhibited picture, and it is said to have insured the permanence of the movies. It became the bible for all film makers until Griffith's films further developed Porter's editing principle. The efforts of all movie makers to imitate its form and content stimulated the industry as nothing—not even Méliès' films—had ever done before."[5]

3. At least two longer films had been made before this time—the Enoch Rector film of the Corbett-Fitzsimmons prize fight in 1897 and a production of a Passion Play in 1898—but these were independent ventures and apparently had little impact on either the public or the major companies.

4. Benjamin B. Hampton, *A History of the Movies* (New York, 1931), p. 38.

5. Lewis Jacobs, "Edwin S. Porter and the Editing Principle," in Jacobs (ed.), *The Emergence of Film Art* (New York, 1969), p. 27.

The Mutograph photographing the Pennsylvania Limited running sixty miles an hour

An Open-Air Studio: The American Mutoscope Company

The American Mutoscope Company, founded on December 27, 1895, by Herman Casler, Harry Marvin, W. K. L. Dickson, and Elias Koopman, rested on the invention of the Mutoscope, a peephole device that flipped printed cards before the viewer's eye, riffle fashion, creating an illusion of motion. It differed in this way from the Kinetoscope, which used a continuous band of film. The Mutoscope was conceived by Dickson but brought to fruition by Casler, who applied for the patent—wisely so, since Dickson's contribution to the machine was made while he was an employee of Edison (he left on April 2, 1895).

American Mutoscope's headquarters were established at 841 Broadway, New York, in January 1896. Dickson again put his considerable talents to work in designing the roof stage and laboratory facilities, which were described fully in the *Scientific American* of April 17, 1897. These facilities are full testament to Dickson's ingenuity. The open-air stage was

Drying and retouching room, Mutoscope shown in the foreground

mounted on wheels and revolved on tracks. The camera, also mounted on wheels, could be tracked back and forth at right angles from the stage. The film processing rooms were large, well equipped, and designed for efficiency of operation.

The novelty of Edison's Kinetoscope began to wear off after the autumn of 1895, especially as screen projection became more common. American Mutoscope, reacting to the winds of change, postponed any further development and promotion of its peephole machine and concentrated its efforts on perfecting a projector. The result was Mutoscope's greatest triumph—the famous Biograph, which showed pictures larger and photographically superior to those of any other projector. Again, Dickson and Mutoscope had out-Edisoned Edison himself. As this projector outstripped the competition in popularity, cameramen turned out subjects weekly to satisfy the eager and growing public demand. By this time, "Biograph" had proudly been added to the American Mutoscope name.

The dark room and reel for drying films

Interior of the Mutoscope

The Biograph at work in a New York theater

12

Movable stage for photographing scenes with the Mutograph

13

The Organization of Exchanges

The development of the story film and its enthusiastic acceptance by audiences set the stage for the expansion of the industry into a big business. The problem of distribution, however, remained an inhibiting factor. As mentioned earlier, films were sold outright by the foot. Pictures were ordered by mail from a catalog and as they grew in length, their prices rose accordingly. A showman paid anywhere from $50 to more than $100 for a picture which he exhibited until it had saturated the market. This method of distribution, obviously, did little to encourage the expansion of the industry, since the costs of films remained relatively high in comparison to their potential for producing income. Many independent exhibitors began to appear after 1903 and these small operators could scarcely afford to keep on buying films, laying each aside after a short run. This disability became even more pronounced as audiences became more sophisticated and selective. Exhibitors realized that in order to operate a show successfully, they required from three to five one-reel pictures on their programs —and the program might have to change several times a week, if decent-sized audiences were to be attracted. Exhibitors also wanted new pictures. Then, as today, the first showing of a picture had the greatest drawing power.

Exhibitors sought a solution to the problem by trading films among themselves, but the distribution problem was not really solved until the establishment of motion picture exchanges. The first such exchange appeared in San Francisco in 1902. It was organized by Harry and Herbert Miles, who purchased films from producers and rented them to exhibitors at one-fourth the purchase price. The idea worked to everyone's satisfaction. By 1907, between 125 and 150 such exchanges were in operation, serving all areas of the country. The evolution of this method of distribution pleased producers because they could then deal with a few large exchanges instead of thousands of small exhibitors. Each exchange agreed to buy most of their output, usually at good prices. The idea pleased exhibitors because it cut their costs, enabled them to change their programs more frequently, and did much to stimulate movie attendance. Perhaps most of all it pleased the exchange operators, who could continue to rent out films long after their purchase costs had been recovered.

The Nickelodeon Theater

With films available on a rental basis, the establishment of
theaters devoted primarily to the showing of motion pictures
became a sound business enterprise. Harry Davis and John P.
Harris of Pittsburgh demonstrated this soundness in
spectacular fashion in 1905. Davis and Harris were real estate
operators who turned a vacant storeroom into a motion picture
theater by the simple expedient of adding decorations
discarded from the Grand Opera House and installing a
projector, piano, and about a hundred seats. Because the
admission charge would be five cents, they called their theater
"Nickelodeon." Some say that it opened with *The Great Train
Robbery*. The title of the film, though, is less important than
the successful demonstration of this new exhibition concept.
After two weeks, the partners' films had played to
near-capacity houses, with screenings from eight in the morning
until midnight. Davis and Harris made profits of $1,000
a week.

The spectacular financial success of the Davis-Harris venture
made a tremendous impression on showmen. It was clear that
anyone who could rent a storefront, dance hall, or restaurant,
buy a projector, and set up a few chairs could strike a
bonanza. Within a year, a thousand or more nickelodeons had
sprung up across the country, and by 1910 there were ten
thousand. Their concentrations were mainly in the industrial
cities with large populations of blue-collar workers. Pittsburgh,
for example, with its burgeoning coal and steel industries,
supported a hundred of these theaters. Movies presented no
language barriers to the throngs of immigrants, and for the
urban worker in general they were an inexpensive and exciting
release from long hours of menial labor.

Movies, however, did not long remain the province of the
working class. As Russell Merritt demonstrates, nickelodeon
operators from the beginning reached out to capture the more
affluent middle-class audience (ch. 4).

Within a decade, "ten million—maybe twenty million . . .
new entertainment buyers had suddenly appeared in all parts
of America, and were pouring their nickels into the
ticket-windows. The small coins of the masses had created . . .
a business larger in volume than that of all spoken-drama
theatres,dime museums, variety houses, lecture bureaus,

concert halls, circuses, and street carnivals combined. Experienced purveyors of entertainment and amusement were dazed. There were no precedents by which such an extensive public movement could be appraised. Not only were movies new to the world, but this surge of millions of people to ticket windows was something incomprehensible, incredible, fantastic."[6]

Corporate Struggle for Industry Control

Simultaneously with the growth of the nickelodeons and motion picture exchanges, the industry accommodated itself to mass production. Although the industry remained a legal battlefield as Edison sustained his attacks to establish the priority of his patents, there had been no final adjudication by the courts. In the suit against the American Mutoscope and Biograph Company, the court, while ruling that Edison was not the sole inventor of motion picture film, allowed his camera patent. At the same time, however, it also allowed the Biograph camera. Although the history of patent litigation reveals that virtually hundreds of legal actions would eventually be filed, creating chaotic conditions in the industry, the lure of profits was so great after 1903 that scores of new companies were formed. There were only about ten well-established concerns, however, each of which held letters patent. In addition to Edison, Biograph, and Vitagraph, there were Selig, Kalem, Essanay, and Lubin. Still others, notably George Kleine, supplied pictures by importing them from Europe.

In this warlike atmosphere of patent litigation, every studio became a guarded stronghold. Producers, who spent much of their time acting as litigants, fortified their studios to conceal their production methods, in fear either of having their own legitimate inventions stolen, or of being caught in a patent infringement against someone else.

Production was centered mainly in New York, Chicago, and Philadelphia. The migration west was a few years away, but because sunshine was at a premium in eastern cities during the winter months, producers began to explore Florida, Cuba, and Southern California. The Chicago-based Selig company, for

6. Hampton, *A History of the Movies,* p. 57.

instance, sent a unit to Los Angeles to complete the shooting of *The Count of Monte Cristo* as early as 1907.

By 1905, the standard length of movies became one reel, which held from 800 to 1,000 feet of film, taking about fourteen minutes of screen time. This gave producers sufficient time to present a little drama complete with a beginning, middle, and end. Short subjects 300 to 500 feet in length were still being made, but mostly by the smaller and less established outfits.

Since public demand for pictures was constantly running ahead of the supply, speed of output was essential. Companies churned out hundreds of pictures with lightning speed and minimum costs, ranging from $400 to $500 for one-reelers and around $200 for shorts. Anywhere from fifty to a hundred copies of a picture were printed in laboratories, packed in cans, and shipped to all parts of the globe to thousands of theaters. This widening distribution kept box-office prices low—from ten to twenty-five cents in most American cities.

Mass production of films soon necessitated a division of labor for increased efficiency. Directing, acting, writing, photography, and laboratory work all became separate crafts. Scenery had to be built and painted. There had to be dressing rooms for players, offices for directors and executives, and laboratories where negatives could be developed and prints made. The increased quantity of work could now support such specialists, thus encouraging and improving their expertise. This natural economic development—the studio system—would have profound effects on the course of the industry from that point onward.

Production work centered on the director. Using a scenario of his own devising, or more often that of a writer, he would plot the action, choose a cast, advise the technical crew, and decide on the locations; during the actual shooting he coached the actors and supervised the cameraman. Pictures were commonly shot in a single day. Finally, the director edited the finished film, bringing it down to the desired length.

Professional actors were in great demand by movie producers, but nearly all "legitimate" actors shunned the movies, which they considered to be beneath their talent and dignity. Still, Vitagraph (see ch. 5) succeeded in luring actors from the legitimate stage by forming a stock company, offering steady work, and paying top wages—up to forty dollars a week.

Other companies contented themselves with hiring an occasional professional who was out of work and hungry. Other actors found movie work a convenient way to pick up some extra money between stage appearances. For a day's labor, a leading player might be paid ten dollars; the rank-and-file player got five dollars; and extras from two to three dollars.

Story films meant that special attention had to be given to scenarios. Plots were appropriated from short stories, novels, and stage plays. And since copyright laws had not anticipated motion pictures, authors of the original works received no compensation. Screen writing attracted newspapermen or fledgling playwrights who wanted to supplement their incomes with the ten to twenty-five dollars producers paid per scenario.

Burgeoning Infancy

In a scant fourteen years, then, the movie industry had expanded nationally on three fronts: production, distribution, and exhibition. There were a dozen well-established producers with large studios, and scores of smaller operators producing their own pictures or importing them from abroad. An exchange system had been established, enabling theater operators to rent rather than buy both domestic and foreign films, and marketing practices had gone far toward standardization. Exhibition had grown to become the largest branch of the industry in terms of capital investment. Despite protests from ministers, social reformers, and theater critics, the demand for movies continued unabated and movies became a regular and important form of entertainment for millions of Americans. The movies had ceased to be just another novelty touted by a handful of showmen, but had grown into a genuine industry. The potentialities of that industry were recognized in full when, in 1908, the Motion Picture Patents Company was formed for the purpose of capturing monopolistic control.

1

A. R. FULTON

The Machine

Although the attempt to represent the illusion of motion by pictures is older than civilization, the art of the motion pictures was not created until the twentieth century. From that prehistoric day when an artist drew a many-legged boar on the wall of a cave in Altamira, Spain, down through the ages, during which time various other devices were originated to depict motion, man had to wait until modern times before the motion pictures could be born. This waiting was necessary because the motion pictures depend, to a greater extent than any other art, upon machinery. The motion pictures, the newest of the arts, the only art to originate in the twentieth century, are a product of the Machine Age.

The motion pictures did not originate as art but as a machine. They were invented. That is, the machinery that makes the pictures, and that makes them motion pictures, was invented. Thus the term *motion pictures* means the device as well as the art.

If one were to hold a piece of motion-picture film up to the light, he would see that it is a series of little pictures arranged crosswise to the length of the film. Each picture, or frame, is approximately four-fifths of an inch wide and three-fifths of an inch high. Examining the frames in relation to one another, one notices that, although each frame may be a picture of the same scene, the position of the objects in each frame is

From *Motion Pictures: The Development of an Art from Silent Pictures to the Age of Television* (Norman, Okla., 1960), pp. 3-18.

19

slightly different. When the film, which contains sixteen frames to each foot of film, is run through the motion-picture projector at the rate of twenty-four frames per second, enlarged images of the frames are cast in corresponding succession onto the screen.

The projector operates on the principle of that old toy the magic lantern (and of its modern counterpart, the slide projector). When a glass slide was inserted in the lantern, an image of the slide was cast upon the screen by means of a light directed through the slide and, to enlarge the image, through a magnifying lens. The frames in the film are comparable to the slides in the magic lantern. The images of the frames as they are cast upon the screen do not move any more than the images of the magic-lantern slides moved. The term *motion pictures* is therefore misleading. The pictures do not move but only seem to.

The illusion of motion is caused partly by persistence of vision, the optical fact—said to have been discovered by the astronomer Ptolemy in the second century—that it takes the eye a fraction of a second to record the impression of an image and transmit it to the brain and that, having received the impression, the eye retains it one-twentieth to one-tenth of one second after the image itself has disappeared. Accordingly, the motion-picture projector includes a mechanism which draws the film between the light and the lens in a stop-and-go motion, the film pausing long enough at each frame to allow the eye to take in the picture; then, as a shutter closes and the eye retains the image, the mechanism propels the film ahead to the next frame. The perforations along the edge of the film enable the teeth of the driving mechanism to engage the film and not only to move it along from one frame to the next but also to hold it steady. The stop-and-go motion gives the illusion of a continuous picture. If the film did not pause at each frame, the impression that the eye receives would be blurred.

The illusion that motion pictures move depends also on the imagination of the spectator. Watching a succession of pictures, each one representing a change in the position of the image from that of the preceding one, the spectator imagines that the image is moving because he associates it with a corresponding object that he has seen actually moving. Furthermore, he imagines that he sees more of the picture than the camera has recorded. A film moves through the camera at the rate of twenty-four frames per second. Every second, then, the camera takes twenty-four individual snapshots, each exposed in 1/48th of a second. Like the projector, the camera operates with a stop-and-go motion, the shutter opening for 1/48th of a second to allow the exposure and then closing for the film to move ahead to the next frame. Because the shutter is closed half the time, the camera photographs only half of what happens. But when the film is projected onto the screen, persistence of vision compensates for the missing action. Accordingly the spectator has the illusion not only that the pictures are moving but that he is seeing twice as much as he actually sees.

Principles of vision and the manufacture of film, camera, and projector—these matters of optics, chemistry, and machinery are inherent in the motion pictures as a device. The art of the motion pictures, depending on the instrument, had to wait for the invention of the device. The machine, however, was not invented to make the art possible. It was originated merely as a device—a device to record and depict motion.

Some of the principles of motion-picture machinery were understood long before the device was perfected, and crude variations of it were devised. Apart from such early devices as Leonardo da Vinci's *camera obscura,* its origin is the magic lantern, invented by the Dutch scientist Christian Huygens about 1655.[1] Almost two centuries later, in 1832, Simon Ritter von Stampfer, of Vienna, made a device he called the Stroboscope, whereby drawings on the rim of a disc viewed through slits in a second disc simulated motion. Then, in 1853, another Viennese, Franz von Uchatius, used a magic lantern to project the Stroboscope pictures onto a wall. One of the most popular early versions of the motion-picture machine was the Zoetrope, or wheel of life. Devised in 1833 by an Englishman, William George Horner, as the Daedalum, or wheel of the devil—because its first pictures were of the devil—it consisted of a shallow cylinder about one foot in diameter with vertical slots in the edge and, on the inside, a series of pictures which, seen through the slots, seemed to move when the wheel was turned. Another kind of wheel machine, patented in 1861 by Coleman Sellers, a Philadelphia machinist, was an arrangement whereby photographs were mounted on paddles. Sellers called his paddle-wheel machine the Kinematoscope. Such were the early gropings toward the motion pictures. They were, however, gropings primarily in the direction of motion-picture projection. The motion-picture camera had to wait for the invention not only of photography but also of photographic film.

Photography came first, when in 1837 the Frenchman Louis Daguerre invented a process whereby a photograph could be exposed on a chemically coated plate. Although the sitter for a daguerreotype had to remain motionless for the several minutes it took the plate to become exposed, refinements in the process decreased the length of this time. In 1872, it occurred to Governor Leland Stanford of California that photography might be the means whereby he could prove his contention—and win a bet of $25,000—

1. Kenneth Macgowan explains why Athanasius Kirchener's claim to have invented the magic lantern is untenable in *Behind the Screen: The History and Techniques of the Motion Picture* (New York: 1965), p. 27.

that a running horse takes all four feet off the ground simultaneously. Accordingly, he employed a San Francisco photographer, Eadweard Muybridge, to take pictures at the Stanford race track at Sacramento. The result was unsatisfactory: the pictures were too much blurred to settle the question. Five years later, however, Muybridge tried again. He arranged a battery of twenty-four cameras—their lenses one foot apart— along a track at Palo Alto and, by an electric device which set the cameras in successive operation as the horse went by, got some pictures that were clear enough to prove the Governor right. In 1879, Muybridge was granted a patent on "a method and apparatus for photographing objects in motion." Three years later, in Paris, Muybridge's photographs were projected in the Praxinoscope, a machine devised by Émile Reynaud to project pictures from behind a screen.

Another step toward motion-picture photography was the photographic gun, which Étienne Jules Marey invented, in 1882, to photograph the flight of birds. Marey devised his gun on the principle of the revolver, the chambers containing photographic plates which recorded pictures when the trigger was released.

Thomas Edison has been given credit for inventing the motion pictures. It would be more nearly accurate to say that Edison, coordinating the ideas of other inventors, promoted in his laboratory the building of both a motion-picture camera and a motion-picture projector. Edison was an inventor aware of the importance of patents on devices that could be manufactured for profit. Since he saw no commercial value in the motion pictures, it is remarkable that he concerned himself with them at all. But he was trying to perfect his phonograph, and he said that in 1887 the idea occurred to him that "it was possible to devise an instrument which should do for the eye what the phonograph does for the ear, and that by a combination of the two, all motion and sound could be recorded and reproduced simultaneously."[2] However, he investigated the idea so desultorily that nine years elapsed before the projection of motion pictures onto a screen became a practical reality. He assigned one of his assistants, William Kennedy Laurie Dickson, to the project.

Edison said years later that he had only one fact to guide him, "the principle of optics technically called the persistence of vision."[3] But he and Dickson were also familiar with the Zoetrope, and they knew about Muybridge's horse pictures and Marey's photographic gun. In fact, Edison said that the germ of his idea came from the Zoetrope and the

2. Foreword to article by Antonia and William Kennedy Laurie Dickson, "Edison's Invention of the Kinetophonograph," *Century Magazine* 48 (June 1894): 206.
3. *The Diary and Sundry Observations of Thomas Alva Edison,* ed. Dagobert D. Runes (New York, 1948), p. 71.

work of Muybridge, Marey, and others. Dickson started with the Zoetrope. Since Edison had already invented a phonograph record and since the purpose was to give eyes to the phonograph, Dickson built a device that seemed to incorporate both Zoetrope and record. It was a cylinder somewhat larger than the phonograph cylinder and containing microscopic photographs. Dickson placed it and a phonograph cylinder side by side on a shaft and recorded sound on the phonograph cylinder as synchronously as possible with the photographs. But the pictures were less satisfactory than the sound, and Dickson tried something different.

Incorporating in his camera a stop-motion device, he took pictures on sheets of sensitized Celluloid—pictures so small that he recorded about two hundred of them in a spiral arrangement around a single cylinder. After developing and fixing the Celluloid, he placed it on a transparent drum. When the drum was turned, a device lighted up each image from the inside. Here, gropingly but unerringly, he had established an important principle—that the motion pictures depend on light passing through the frame, whether the frame is projected onto a screen or viewed directly. But the curvature of the cylinder brought only the center of each picture into focus. Dickson took another step.

Abandoning the idea of the cylinder, he cemented together sheets of emulsion-covered Celluloid to form a strip half an inch wide. Then, because this area proved too narrow, he substituted a one-and-one-half-inch strip, which allowed for one-inch pictures and additional space for perforations along the edge. The perforations enabled the teeth of a locking device to hold the strip of sheets steady as it moved, by a stop-motion device, through the camera. The year was 1891; Dickson had discovered motion-picture film and recorded a motion picture on it.

From the negative Dickson made a positive print which he placed in a boxlike structure, about four feet high and two feet square, containing a battery-run motor. Propelled by the motor, the strip ran on a loop between an electric lamp and a shutter. The pictures were visible by flashes under a magnifying lens as the viewer looked through a slit in the top of the box. The little viewing machine was called the Kinetoscope, the camera the Kinetograph.

Like the original phonograph—an apparatus equipped with earphones—the Kinetoscope was a device for the individual, not the group, although there is evidence that at the time Dickson was experimenting with the Kinetoscope he succeeded in projecting pictures onto a screen. Keeping Edison's purpose in mind, Dickson had designed the Kinetograph and the Kinetoscope so that pictures and sound could be recorded simultaneously and, by a simple mechanism, could also be reproduced simultaneously. [Hendricks asserts that Dickson abandoned simultaneous talking and

Cripple Creek Barroom (Edison, 1898), shot in the Black Maria Studio

recording experiments as fruitless (ch. 2).—Ed.] But the pictures, which were to have been only an adjunct to the phonograph, now took precedence, and it was years before pictures and sound were linked again.

In 1891, Edison applied for patents on his camera and on "an apparatus for exhibiting photographs of moving objects." The patents were granted in the spring of 1893, and Edison contracted to manufacture Kinetoscopes for Raff & Gammon, a firm organized expressly to sell them. Raff & Gammon would pay Edison $200 apiece for the Kineto-scopes and retail them for $300 to $350. [According to Hendricks (ch. 2), Edison signed his first sales contract for the Kinetoscope in 1892 and agreed to sell the machines for $250 apiece. The distributor was a syndicate that took the name Kinetoscope Company in 1894. Raff and Gammon managed the firm and apparently acquired the assets of the failing business in 1896 to organize the Raff & Gammon company for the purpose of marketing Edison's Vitascope projector.—Ed.] Thus on April 14, 1894, Andrew M. Holland, a Canadian, opened a Kinetoscope parlor at 1155 Broadway in New York City. The scene was a shoe store which Holland had converted for the purpose and in which he had set up ten Kinetoscopes. Each of the machines contained a fifty-foot film made with the Kinetograph at the Edison plant in West Orange, New Jersey.

The year before, a building for the taking of motion pictures had been put up at the Edison plant. Designed by Dickson, it was forty-eight feet long by fourteen feet wide—ten feet wide by eighteen feet long at the end where the camera was housed—and so constructed that a fifteen-by-fourteen-foot section of the roof, about midway, could be opened—shutterlike—to admit light. Any desired angle to the rays of the sun could be obtained, for the whole building was swung on a graphited center in the manner of a swinging bridge, the ends being supported by iron rods extending from center posts. The structure was covered with tar paper on the outside and painted black inside, to bring the actors into sharp relief. Dickson called it the kinetographic theater, but it was familiarly known as the Black Maria.

Dickson was soon filming bits of current variety-show acts—dancers, acrobats, contortionists, trained animals—and each act was abridged to be photographed on not more than fifty feet of film. Sandow the Strong Man appeared before the Kinetograph, as did Annie Oakley, Buffalo Bill, and Ruth St. Denis. One film represented part of a scene from a popular farce of the day, Charles Hoyt's *A Milk White Flag*. The repertoire included reenacted scenes such as *The Execution of Mary Queen of Scots,* which, however, was not filmed in the Black Maria but outdoors. This little film was one of the first to incorporate trick photography; in it the beheading of the unfortunate lady leaves nothing to the imagination.

Not long after the Kinetoscope parlor opened, it attracted the attention of Otway and Gray Latham, two young southerners visiting in New York. It occurred to the Latham brothers that this new toy might be a means of making money if it were used to present pictures of prize fights. Accordingly, with Samuel J. Tilden, Jr., and Enoch Rector they formed the Kinetoscope Exhibition Company, and in August 1894, they opened a parlor at 83 Nassau Street, in New York. The films they offered the public for the occasion were of a six-round fight between Michael Leonard and Jack Cushing, photographed in a ten-foot ring in the Black Maria. The capacity of the Kinetoscope had been increased for the occasion from 50 to 150 feet of film, and each of the six enlarged Kinetoscopes presented a short round of the fight. About 950 feet in length, this was the longest motion picture that had yet been made. Shortly thereafter, when Colonel Woodville Latham, the father of Otway and Gray, visited the parlor, Otway asked him whether the films they were showing in the Kinetoscopes could be projected onto a screen. The answer was yes.

The Lathams set about devising a projection machine as well as a motion-picture camera. Because their projector—for which, incidentally, they received suggestions from William Kennedy Laurie Dickson—only copied the principle of the Kinetoscope, it was of less significance than their camera. In the Kinetograph, the film was wound and unwound directly from one reel to another. Since the resulting strain of more than forty or fifty feet of film would break the film, the Kinetograph could not take a continuous picture of more than about fifteen seconds in length. Enoch Rector devised a sprocket which slackened off enough film in a loop to prevent the stop-and-go motion from tugging at the unwinding reel. Allowing the camera to take as long a film as a reel would hold, this little device—called the Latham Loop—was an important contribution to the motion pictures.[4]

At the time Edison applied for a United States patent on the Kineto- scope, he was asked whether he wished to take out foreign patents on it as well. When told that foreign patents would cost $150 more, Edison is said to have replied, "It isn't worth it." Thus, when Robert W. Paul, a London manufacturer of scientific instruments, was asked, in 1894, to duplicate the Kinetoscope, he not only did so but—finding to his amazement that it was not patented in England—manufactured and sold, within the next two years, about sixty of the machines. Then, to supply his customers with films, he built a camera which not only incorporated a stop-motion device similar to that originated by Edison and Dickson but was portable. He also built a projector—the Bioscope—which took into account the all- important principle of persistence of vision and thus effected the necessary intermittent motion. As the film passed through the projector, it was made to pause longer at each frame than between frames and thereby allowed the eye time to "take in" each picture. He demonstrated this machine, for the first time, at Finsbury Technical College, in February 1896.

Meanwhile, in Germany, Max Skladanowski had built and patented a motion-picture machine which he modeled, like Paul's, after the Kineto- scope and which he also called the Bioscope. In November 1895, Sklada- nowski demonstrated it as the concluding number on a variety bill at the Wintergarten in Berlin. The showing consisted of two films of about forty-eight frames each.

In France, the Lumière brothers—Auguste and Louis—manufacturers of photographic equipment, had also been experimenting with motion pictures. Beginning, as Paul did, with the Kinetoscope, which was shown in France for the first time in 1894—only a few months after it had been introduced in the United States—they found out that the continuous motion in the Kinetoscope would not do for a projection machine. Accordingly, they built a stop-motion device. They also built a camera, which differed from Edison's Kinetograph in the speed at which the film was fed through it, that is, in the number of pictures, or frames, it

4. Gordon Hendricks finds evidence, however, that an apparatus which Marey described to the French Academy of Sciences in 1888 contained a loop (*The Edison Motion Picture Myth* [Berkeley and Los Angeles, 1961], pp. 169-70).

recorded each second. Whereas the Kinetograph took forty-eight frames per second, the Lumières decided on sixteen as the proper rate.[5] By early 1895, they had completed both projector and camera and had taken some pictures, and on March 22, at their factory in Lyons, they demonstrated their accomplishment. They called their projector the Cinématographe, a name reminiscent of Sellers' paddle-wheel machine and anticipating the universal word for the motion pictures—cinema (Gr. *kinema, kinematos,* motion).

The Lumières decided to open an establishment in Paris for showing films. The enterprise was under the direction of their father, Antoine Lumière, who had given up the management of the Lyons factory. A basement room in the Grand Café on the Boulevard des Capucines was rented for the occasion, and here, on December 28, 1895, the showing took place. Each film, like Edison's, was fifty feet long, and there were about ten films. Included were *Lunch Hour at the Lumière Factory,* which shows workers leaving the plant at Lyons; *Arrival of a Train at a Station,* in which the oncoming locomotive is said to have terrified the spectators; *A Game of Cards,* in which the players are Antoine Lumière, the conjurer Trewey, who sits opposite him and is the dealer, and Louis Lumière's father-in-law, Winckler, the Lyons brewer, who pours out some beer; *Baby's Lunch,* a picture which Louis Lumière had taken of Auguste and Mme Lumière with their infant daughter on the walk beside the Lumière house; *Blacksmiths; The Rue de la République,* a Lyons traffic scene; and *Bathing Beach,* in which the waves break on the shore. Admission was one franc, and the receipts on that opening day were thirty-five francs. The essential principles of motion-picture photography and projection having at last been applied in a commercial enterprise, the motion pictures were born.

The idea that Edison had begun investigating eight years before had thus become a reality. Edison originated the idea, which, by the ingenious work of Dickson, took the form of the Kinetoscope; but the Kinetoscope became the motion pictures independently of Edison, in a way that he had not originally intended and over a course that he could not have foreseen. Even the Kinetoscope was not Edison's invention. First, there was Dickson; and besides Dickson, other inventors contributed to the progress which led deviously from the laboratory in West Orange, New Jersey, to the Grand Café in Paris, from the peep-show box to the motion pictures.

Then there were those who, although they were off the path of this progress, were experimenting with motion pictures at the time. There was, for example, William Friese-Greene, a photographer of Bath, England.

5. The standard rate has since been established as twenty-four.

Friese-Greene's epitaph describes him as "The Inventor of Cinematography," and attempts have been made to support this claim. Together with John Rudge, an optician, and Mortimer Evans, a civil engineer, Friese-Greene built a motion-picture camera and applied for a patent on it in 1889; but it has not been established that he effected the successful projection of motion pictures onto a screen. Although Friese-Greene apparently wrote to Edison suggesting that the motion pictures might be made a part of the phonograph—after Edison already had this idea—he neither completed a machine for this purpose nor directly contributed to the course leading from the Kinetoscope to the motion pictures as perfected by the Lumières.

The tendency to simplify has given Edison credit as the inventor of the motion pictures. To point out that he was not, that in fact no one individual may be said to have been the sole inventor, is not to minimize the importance of his idea or even of the Kinetoscope. That it was the Lumières who first built a machine incorporating the progress made by other inventors, who improved the rate of speed at which a film should pass through a camera, and who first demonstrated the completed machine as a commercial reality is a fact that those who would simplify cannot disregard. Ironically, however, if the première at the Grand Café late in 1895 had been delayed only four months, Edison would have had the distinction not only of originating the idea that led to the motion pictures but also of introducing the motion-picture machine to the world. As it was, on April 23, 1896, he introduced the device to the United States.

Even though, at the time he was working on the Kinetoscope, Dickson had effected the projection of a motion picture onto a screen, Edison had refused to put projection machines on the market. When Norman Raff proposed that they do so, Edison is reported to have replied that the company was selling Kinetoscopes for $300 to $350 apiece and making money and that if they sold machines which would enable a large group of people to see the films simultaneously, there would be use for only about ten of them in all the United States. But now the Lathams had a projector, which, as the Pantopticon, they demonstrated publicly on May 20, 1895, in New York City. The Pantopticon operated on the principle of the Kinetoscope—that is, in its continuous motion—but it projected a four-minute film of a boxing match which Otway Latham had directed on the roof of Madison Square Garden. Here was competition. Edison assigned one of his assistants, Charles H. Kayser, to the project of building a machine that would be better than the Lathams'. Meanwhile, however, Thomas Armat, of Washington, one of those inventors who were also experimenting with the motion pictures, had constructed a stop-motion mechanism for a projector, which he demonstrated at the Cotton

States Exposition in Atlanta, Georgia, in September 1895. Edison was informed of Armat's invention, and, early in 1896, an agreement was reached whereby Edison would manufacture a projection machine incorporating Armat's device. The machine would be marketed under the Edison name but would be labeled "Armat designed." The name chosen for the new machine was Vitascope.

On April 14, 1896, under the ambiguous headline "Edison's Latest Triumph," the *New York Times* reported:

Thomas A. Edison and Albert Bial have perfected arrangements by which Edison's latest invention, the vitascope, will be exhibited for the first time anywhere at Koster & Bial's Music Hall. Edison has been at work on the vitascope for several years.

The vitascope projects upon a large area of canvas groups that appear to stand forth from the canvas, and move with great facility and agility, as though actuated by separate impulses. In this way the bare canvas before the audience becomes instantly a stage upon which living beings move about.

Mr. Bial said yesterday: "I propose to reproduce in this way at Koster & Bial's scenes from various successful plays and operas of the season, and well-known statesmen and celebrities will be represented as, for instance, making a speech or performing some important act or series of acts with which their names are identified. No other manager in this city will have the right to exhibit the vitascope."

Five days later, the first newspaper advertisement of a moving picture appeared in the *Times*. At the foot of Koster & Bial's theater announcement of their current attraction—the monologuist Albert Chevalier "together with all the other Great Foreign Stars"—could be read: "Extra—Due notice will be given of the first public exhibition of Edison's latest marvel, THE VITASCOPE." The "due notice," appearing two days later,

Raff & Gammon advertisement

gave the date of the première—April 23—and on that morning the Koster
& Bial advertisement gave the Vitascope top billing, Chevalier and the
"Great Foreign Stars" being summarily relegated to second place.

The première of the Vitascope was more auspicious than that of the
Cinématographe on that winter afternoon four months before in the
basement room on the Boulevard des Capucines. Koster & Bial's, in
Herald Square, was one of New York City's popular music halls. Edison
himself came over from New Jersey for the occasion and occupied a box
seat. Armat was there, too, taking charge in the projection booth, set up
in the second balcony.

The next morning, the *Times* reported as follows:

The new thing at Koster & Bial's last night was Edison's vitascope, exhibited for
the first time. The ingenious inventor's latest toy is a projection of his kinetoscope
figures in stereopticon fashion, upon a white screen in a darkened hall. In the
center of the balcony of the big music hall is a curious object, which looks from
below like the double turret of a big monitor. In the front of each half of it are two
oblong holes. The turret is neatly covered with the blue velvet brocade which is the
favorite decorative material in this house. The white screen used on the stage is
framed like a picture. The moving figures are about half life size.

When the hall was darkened last night a buzzing and roaring were heard in the
turret, and an unusually bright light fell upon the screen. Then came into view two
precious blonde young persons of the variety stage, in pink and blue dresses, doing
the umbrella dance with commendable celerity. Their motions were all clearly
defined. When they vanished, a view of an angry surf breaking on a sandy beach
near a stone pier amazed the spectators. The waves tumbled in furiously and the
foam of the breakers flew high in the air. A burlesque boxing match between a
tall, thin comedian and a short, fat one, a comic allegory called "The Monroe
Doctrine," an instant of motion in Hoyt's farce, "A Milk White Flag," repeated
over and over again, and a skirt dance by a tall blonde completed the views, which
were all wonderfully real and singularly exhilarating. For the spectator's imagination filled the atmosphere with electricity, as sparks crackled around the moving
lifelike figures.

So enthusiastic was the appreciation of the crowd long before the extraordinary
exhibition was finished that vociferous cheering was heard. There were loud calls
for Mr. Edison, but he made no response.

Of the films included in that first showing of the Vitascope, it was, the
Times reported in its Sunday edition two days later,

the waves tumbling in on a beach and about a stone pier that caused the spectators
to cheer and marvel most of all. Big rollers broke on the beach, foam flew high,
and weakened waters poured far up on the beach. Then great combers arose and
pushed each other shoreward, one mounting above the other, and they seemed to
fall with mighty force and all together on the shifty sand, whose yellow receding
motion could be plainly seen.

Edison apparently realized, however, that the use of motion pictures to provide entertainment by the sheer novelty of the device itself could not be exploited for long. The *Times* announced:

Mr. Edison is working hard for the absolute perfection of his machine, and at the same time is arranging for the securing of pictures the like of which, in other than inertness, the public has never seen.

He has bought, for about $5000, two ancient, but still serviceable locomotives and several dozen flat cars. He has built about a quarter of a mile of railroad track in a secluded spot, not far from his laboratory. In a few weeks he will start a train from each end of the track, and will run them to a crash. The engines and cars will be manned, just as trains are in active service, and all the incidents of a train wreck will be caught by machines stationed at short intervals near the track.

Machines have been sent to Rome, and in a short while the entire stage at Koster & Bial's will be occupied by a realistic representation of Pope Leo XIII, saying mass in the Sistine Chapel.[6]

This kind of use of the motion pictures had, in fact, been predicted a year before. After the Lathams had publicly projected their boxing-match picture, Howard B. Hackett wrote in the *New York World:*

You will sit comfortably and see fighters hammering each other, circuses, suicides, hangings, electrocutions, shipwrecks, scenes on the exchanges, street scenes, horse races, football games—almost anything in fact in which there is action, as if you were on the spot during the actual event.[7]

Hackett's prediction was coming true. In 1896, when the motion pictures had become a practical reality, when they had evolved into the device essentially as it was to remain—the device for recording and projecting a film of sufficient magnitude to constitute art—their future lay, it seemed, in providing entertainment by presenting scenes of actuality.

On the other hand, Charles Frohman, the theatrical producer, saw how this use might be extended to the theater. After attending that first showing of the Vitascope, he declared:

That settles scenery. Painted trees that do not move, waves that get up a few feet and stay there, everything in scenery we simulate on our stages will have to go. When art can make us believe that we see actual living nature, the dead things of the stage must go.

And think what can be done with this invention! For instance, Chevalier comes on the screen. The audience would get all the pantomime of his coster songs. The singing, words fitted to gestures and movements, could be done from the wings or

6. *New York Times,* April 26, 1896, p. 10.

7. Quoted by Terry Ramsaye, *A Million and One Nights: A History of the Motion Picture,* 2 vols. (New York, 1926), 1:134.

behind the curtain. And so we could have on the stage at any time any artist, dead or alive, who ever faced Mr. Edison's invention.[8]

Whether the invention may be called "Mr. Edison's" is—as the records show—open to question. But there is no question about the motion pictures' having originated, not as an art, but as a machine. The ingenuity and effort, not of artists, but of inventors, mechanics, photographers, engineers, and manufacturers, made the machine possible. The purpose of these men—from Muybridge with his pictures of Leland Stanford's horses to Edison with his Vitascope—was not artistic, but utilitarian—to perfect a machine that would have a use. The machine is still being perfected, but in Edison's Vitascope, or in the Lumières' Cinématographe, the invention culminated. Appropriately, the first motion-picture shows were billed as machines: at the Grand Café, "LE CINÉMATOGRAPHE" ("*Cet appareil,*" the announcement began) and at Koster & Bial's, "Edison's latest marvel, THE VITASCOPE."

8. *New York Times,* April 26, 1896, p. 10.

2

GORDON HENDRICKS

The History of the Kinetoscope

Early in 1894 there appeared in the American market place a peephole picture machine known as the Kinetoscope. It stood on the floor to a height of four feet. Through an eyepiece on the top a customer could, upon application of the coin of the realm, cause the machine to whirr briskly and show motion pictures of dancing girls, performing animals, etc. The vast majority of these customers were enormously excited by the exhibition, came back again and again to see it, and told their friends about the new wonder. Some were impelled to build machines of their own; others, more significantly, devoted themselves to the task of projecting the pictures on a screen, so that many more than one viewer at a time could see the show. From the work of these latter came America's first projectors and the subsequent rich burgeoning of the industry in 1896 and afterward.

The Kinetoscope was the source of their inspiration, and at the same time supplied them, by stimulating public interest, with a market. It must therefore be given more than a small share of credit for the beginnings of the American motion picture industry. By 1895, the Kinetoscope was losing its lustre, however, and the camera was beginning to furnish motion picture subjects for the screen.

To West Orange, New Jersey, in 1887 came a young Scotsman, named W. K. L. Dickson, whose contribution to this work has been over-

Adapted by the editor from *The Kinetoscope: America's First Commercially Successful Motion Picture Exhibition* (New York, 1966).

33

Shooting an Annabelle Serpentine dance in the Black Maria Studio. From *Frank Leslie's Popular Monthly,* February 1895. The figure at the left is apparently meant to be Dickson. Note the "MB" in monogram at stage left (indicating a Maguire and Baucus production), the door at the left, the power line to the outside, the track for the camera, the counter on the camera, and the handle for starting and stopping the phonograph.

shadowed by the illustriousness and aggressiveness of his employer, Thomas Alva Edison. Dickson was much interested in photography, and brought this interest—and the excellent facilities of the Edison laboratory —to bear upon the problem of a camera and the Kinetoscope. By the end of 1892 he had produced both.[1]

The Kinetograph Camera

The camera (named the Kinetograph) was the fountainhead from which flowed all West Orange motion pictures. Every subject known to us up to

1. For an account of the development of the camera and Kinetoscope, see Gordon Hendricks, *The Edison Motion Picture Myth* (Berkeley and Los Angeles, 1961).

May 1896 was shot by this instrument—and many of those afterward. It was probably with this camera that Edison reentered the motion-picture-taking business in the fall of 1896, and with its patent specifications tied up the whole industry for years. It is thus as important as any other camera in the history of the business.

For all this significance, however, the details of its construction are not clear. Patent specifications are frequently ambiguous and conflicting claims profuse. Its average rate of taking pictures was thirty-eight to forty frames a second. The sketch from *Frank Leslie's Popular Monthly* (February 1895), which is here reproduced and was first brought to public attention in *The Kinetoscope,* gives a good idea of at least the external appearance of the camera.

The Kinetoscope

The Kinetoscope's overall dimensions were 18" x 27" x 48½", including the base and the eyepiece. A clear and authoritative description of the Kinetoscope's operation has been provided by Herman Casler in a lecture delivered around 1909 in Syracuse, New York:

A ribbon of transparent film carrying the pictures is laced up and down over idle spools at the lower part of the case. The ends of the film are joined, forming an endless band passing over two guide drums near the top of the case. One of these drums is driven by motor and feeds the film along by means of sprocket teeth which engage with perforations along the edges of the film. Just above the film is a shutter wheel having five spokes and a very small rectangular opening in the rim directly over the film. An incandescent lamp . . . is placed below the film between the two guide drums, and the light passes up through the film, shutter opening, and magnifying lens . . . to the eye of the observer placed at the opening in the top of the case.

The film had a continuous motion, and, I believe, showed the pictures at the rate of forty per second. The shutter was probably about 10" in diameter and, judging from the photograph, the opening must be about ¾" wide. As the shutter made one revolution for each picture, the length of exposure would be between 1/1600 and 1/1700 part of one second.[2]

The length of the film used varied from twenty-five to thirty feet in the earliest Kinetoscope to forty-two to forty-eight feet in the later ones.

The Black Maria

Granting the existence of an effective camera and an effective device for the exhibition of the product of that camera, the first substantial step in

2. Original transcript in the collection of Gordon Hendricks, New York.

the establishment of the American motion picture industry was a proposal to Edison on October 31, 1892. . . . This proposal was for the exploitation of the Kinetoscope at the World's Columbian Exposition in Chicago and was made by a syndicate consisting of the following: A. O. Tate, Edison's private secretary; Thomas R. Lombard, a partner in a firm that marketed the Edison phonograph as a dictating machine; and Erastus A. Benson, an Omaha banker and president of the Chicago Central Phonograph Company, which distributed the Edison phonograph in Chicago. The deal called for Edison to sell the syndicate 150 Kinetoscopes for use at the Exposition. The first proceeds were to go to Edison in payment for the machines, after which he was to split the profits with the three others.

"The Black Maria" was felt to be necessary as soon as motion picture plans for the Fair began to outgrow the 1889 photograph building. The stage area of that building was small and the skylight lighting insufficient. So Dickson set about designing a larger, lighter, more flexible stage. Many new subjects would have to be taken to supply the Fair Kinetoscopes, and they would have to be taken quickly. A new studio was needed.

The Black Maria was presumably 48' x 10' by 14' x 18'; certain contemporary records are vague. It was lined at least partially with black tar paper, although it was said more than once to have been painted black inside. The lining was not entire. It covered, so far as I have been able to determine, that part of the Maria surrounding the shooting area or stage. This area, the outer confines of which were somewhat altered to conform with the late-1894 alterations, was delineated at first by a raised platform and later by chalk marks, wooden barriers, or otherwise limned space.

The Black Maria swung suspended on a central vertical axis over a graphite pivot to accommodate the need for sunshine, even though as a matter of practice nearly all Maria subjects seem to have been shot close to noon, which would have made the pivoting less important.

The Maria was further supported by rollers, used less and less as time went on. The rollers were necessary, along with the iron trusses, to support the Maria's considerable end weight.

The Black Maria camera was mounted on steel tracks. It was drawn in and out of the small room facing the stage for loading and reloading.

This "revolving photograph building" was under construction from December 1892 to January 1893, and cost $637.67. It has often been called the world's first motion picture studio, but this is incorrect: the 1889 photograph building at the West Orange laboratory, if no other, predated it considerably. If we were to call the Black Maria the world's first studio specifically built for motion picture production, we would be on firm ground; I have found no earlier.

Building the First Model

The Black Maria was no more than fairly completed when Dickson had a nervous breakdown and went south for a ten weeks' rest. Delays in manufacture, largely brought about by Edison's continuing preoccupation with ore milling and his lack of interest in nearly anything which was not money making, prevented its introduction to the general public until April 1894. Plans to have Kinetoscopes ready for the Exposition opening had to be abandoned in April 1893, and the syndicate surrendered the Kineto-scope concession. Nonetheless, it had hopes of installing at least a few Kinetoscopes before the Fair closed in November and placed an order for twenty-five machines.

The manufacturer's model of the Kinetoscope was given its first "official" demonstration on May 9, 1893, at the annual meeting of the Department of Physics of the Brooklyn Institute of Arts and Sciences. This meeting was said by the Institute to be "the first time that a Kinetograph [that is, a Kinetoscope] had been exhibited outside of the Edison laboratory . . . where it was invented and manufactured."

In spite of persistent, poignant cries, Tate and his associates never got their World's Fair Kinetoscopes. Nevertheless, one machine apparently made its way to the Fair, and before the season closed, was installed in the second floor of the Electricity Building for all and sundry to see.

Drawing of the parlor at 1155 Broadway, New York. From William Kennedy Laurie Dickson and Antonia Dickson, *History of the Kinetograph, Kinetoscope and Kinetophonograph* (1895). The Dicksons wanted to give the effect of elegance and added palms, carpets, and waxed floors, none of which may have been there. It is also difficult to credit the genteel patronage shown here. Note the incandescent dragons at right and left and the bronzed bust of Edison in the foreground.

The First Kinetoscope Parlors

The Tate-Lombard-Benson order for twenty-five Kinetoscopes was not
filled until April 1894. The syndicate now had three more names
associated with it: Andrew M. Holland, Norman C. Raff, and Frank R.
Gammon. It hoped to acquire the exclusive marketing rights to the
Kinetoscope, but Edison's plan at the time was to sell the machine on the
open market. As a result, the syndicate contented itself with operating
parlors to exhibit the Kinetoscope.

On April 6, 1894, ten of the twenty-five Kinetoscopes then in existence
were shipped to Andrew M. Holland at 1155 Broadway, New York. The
machines cost $250 apiece. Sometime between April 6 and April 14
Dickson personally delivered the ten films for the debut, one film for each
of ten machines: *Sandow, Horse Shoeing, Barber Shop, Bertholdi* (*Mouth
Support*), *Wrestling, Bertholdi* (*Table Contortion*), *Blacksmiths, Highland
Dance, Trapeze,* and *Roosters.* They were charged at $10 each and were
paid for on the day of the opening.[3]

Tate offers an eyewitness account of the commercial debut of the
Kinetoscope:

We then decided to install ten of these [the original 25] in New York. . . . in
preparation for this I leased a small store, formerly a shoe shop, No. 1155
Broadway, on the west side near Twenty-seventh Street. . . . Here the ten machines
were placed in the center of the room in two rows of five each, enclosed by a metal
railing for the spectators to lean against when viewing the animated picture. One
ticket, at the price of twenty-five cents, entitled the holder to view one row of five
machines. If he wanted to see both rows he bought two tickets. On the right of the
entrance door a ticket booth was erected. At the back of the exhibition room was a
smaller room for use as an office and for repairing the films. In the window there
was a printed announcement or advertisement whose legend I cannot now recall,
and a plaster bust of Edison painted to simulate bronze. It was an excellent
portrait but a few weeks later I received a message from Edison asking me to
remove it. He thought its display undignified.

By noon on Saturday, the 14th day of April, 1894, everything was ready for the
opening of the exhibit to the public on the following Monday. My brother, the late
Bertram M. Tate, was to act as manager, and a mechanic to supervise the
machines and an attractive young woman to preside over the ticket booth were to
report for duty at nine o'clock in the morning of that day. At one o'clock on this
notable Saturday afternoon, after locking the street door, Lombard, my brother
and I went to lunch. Returning at two o'clock, I locked the door on the inside and
we all retired to the office in the rear to smoke and engage in general conversation.

3. According to Terry Ramsaye, *A Million and One Nights* (New York, 1926), p. 88,
Edison spent "a total of precisely $24,118.04 in the motion picture business, between 1887
and April 1, 1894."

We had planned to have an especially elaborate dinner at Delmonico's, then flourishing on the south east corner of Broadway and Twenty-sixth Street, to celebrate the initiation of the Kinetoscope enterprise. From where I sat I could see the display window and the groups who stopped to gaze at the bust of Edison. And a brilliant idea occurred to me.

"Look here," I said, pointing towards the window, "Why shouldn't we make that crowd out there pay for our dinner tonight?"

They both looked and observed the group before the window as it dissolved and renewed itself.

"What's your scheme?" asked Lombard with a grin.

"Bert," I said to my brother, "you take charge of the machines. I'll sell the tickets and," turning to Lombard, "you stand near the door and act as a reception committee. We can run till six o'clock and by that time we ought to have dinner money."

We all thought it a good joke. Lombard stationed himself at the head of the row of machines, my brother stood ready to supervise them, and I unlocked and opened the door and then entered the ticket booth where printed tickets like those now in use were ready to be passed out. And then the procession started.

I wish now that I had recorded the name of the person to whom I sold the first ticket. I cannot recall even a face. I was kept too busy passing out tickets and taking in money. It was a good joke all right, but the joke was on us. If we had wanted to close the place at six o'clock it would have been necessary to engage a squad of policemen. We got no dinner. At one o'clock in the morning I locked the door and we went to an all-night restaurant to regale ourselves on broiled lobsters, enriched by the sum of about one hundred and twenty dollars.[4]

Since tickets to the Kinetoscope parlor cost twenty-five cents each, it would be fair to estimate that about 480 people saw the Kinetoscope during the debut. Tate's picture of congestion is thus, to put it mildly, somewhat overdrawn, and his "squad of police," hyperbole. By the end of May, though, the parlor was staying open on Sunday to accommodate the crowds.

In May, the syndicate opened a second parlor, in Chicago, at 148 State Street. Ten machines were installed at that address. In June, it installed the remaining five machines at a third parlor, at 946 Market Street in San Francisco, under the management of Peter Bacigalupi.

As additional Kinetoscopes were manufactured, the syndicate, in association with the Columbia Phonograph Company, opened a parlor in Atlantic City on the Boardwalk and began to wholesale the machines to other concerns.

Within four months of its public debut, the Kinetoscope had thus captured the vaudeville public, whose taste had been catered to from the

4. *Edison's Open Door* (New York, 1938), pp. 285-87.

first by the Kinetoscope subjects comprised almost exclusively of vaudeville turns.

Before the American motion picture had ended its first months of exhibition, it had also had its first brushes with the law. The earliest of these
was with Senator James A. Bradley, the well-known founder of Asbury
Park, New Jersey. The *Newark Evening News* (July 17, 1894) printed the
following account:

> Senator Bradley has been shocked again, this time by the display of Carmen-
> cita's ankles in one of the series of pictures shown by the aid of "Wizard" Edison's
> latest invention, the kinetoscope. . . . Founder Bradley said he would have to have
> a look at the pictures to see if they were the proper views for the people sojourning
> in the twin cities by the sea to witness without causing blushes to mount to their
> cheeks. . . . on the night of the first day Founder Bradley and Mayor Ten Broeck
> went to the pavilion and proceeded to pass judgement on the pictures that Inventor
> Edison had so carefully prepared. The first picture shown the Senator and Mayor
> was that of the barroom and fight, and it was decided that the supremacy of the
> law over the rougher element had a good moral tone. . . .
> Then the exhibitor, pleased with his success as pleasing the powers that be [sic],
> thought that he would spring a great surprise upon the founder and the Mayor. He
> took a little tin can from a grip that he carried and placed a celluloid roll of
> pictures in the machine, at the same time remarking to the Senator, who had his
> eyes glued to the peep-hole: "Now you will be surprised, Senator. This is one of the
> best pictures in the collection."
> And the Senator was surprised, but not in the way . . . intended. . . . The view
> was that of Carmencita in her famous butterfly dance, and the Senator watched
> the graceful gyrations of the lovely Spanish dancer with interest that was ill-
> concealed. But near the end of the series of pictures the Spanish beauty gives the
> least little bit of a kick, which raises her silken draperies so that her well-turned
> ankles peep out and there is a background of white lace.
> That kick settled it. The Senator left the peep-hole with a stern look on his face. . . .
> While he was trying to collect his scattered thoughts sufficiently to give full swing
> to his wrath Mayor Ten Broeck applied his eye to the peephole. . . . The Mayor
> also was greatly shocked and agreed with the Founder that the picture was not
> fitted for the entertainment of the average summer boarder, and the exhibitor was
> told he would have to send for some new views or shut up shop.

The Latham Kinetoscope Parlor

After seeing the Kinetoscope machines in operation in the 1155
Broadway parlor and at the West Orange laboratory, Otway and Gray
Latham made their first important contribution to Kinetoscope history.
They proposed the exhibition of prizefight films in an enlarged machine.
Such films would enforce a considerably longer period of action than the
customary ten- or twenty-second films in the regulation Kinetoscope. And

the perfectly obvious recourse—to enlarge the capacity of the camera and the Kinetoscope—was an important step forward in Kinetoscope fortunes.

The enlargement of the Kinetoscope appears to have involved little more than the addition of spools to the spool bank. If the motor was thought to have needed additional strength, perhaps the Kinetoscope motor ordered on June 1 was the answer. But whatever was needed was supplied, and on June 14, the first prizefight (between Jack Cushing and Mike Leonard) for the new 150-foot machine was filmed.

With Enoch Rector and Samuel J. Tilden, Jr., the Latham brothers formed the Kinetoscope Exhibition Company for the express purpose of exploiting special peepshows with prizefight pictures. In August 1894 they opened a parlor at 83 Nassau Street in downtown New York. Each of the six special Kinetoscopes contained a round of the fight. A sign in the window and a barker at the door proclaimed the wonders of "the living pictures of the great prize fight."

Then on September 8, 1894, the anniversary of Corbett's fight with Sullivan (as a result of which he had become heavyweight champion of the world), Corbett met Pete Courtney, a Trenton heavyweight who was said to have "stood up against" Fitzsimmons for some rounds. They met in the Black Maria for six rounds of 1.16, 1.24, 1.12, 1.29, 1.23, and 50 seconds, appropriate lengths for the Latham enlarged Kinetoscope. This fight served to focus national attention on the Kinetoscope and the motion picture as no other event had yet done.

The Kinetoscope Company

By the summer of 1894, the commercial potential of the Kinetoscope had made an impression on Edison. He signed a contract on August 18, effective on September 1, assigning the exclusive domestic marketing rights to the Kinetoscope Company, formed by Norman C. Raff and Frank R. Gammon and having as stockholders the members of the syndicate earlier alluded to. The Kinetoscope Company thereupon went into business selling the territorial rights on the business of the Kineto-scopes, following the same merchandising pattern of the Edison phono-graph. According to a Kinetoscope Company financial statement dated March 15, 1895, reprinted in Ramsaye,[5] stockholders invested $17,940 to capitalize the company, $10,000 of which may have been paid to Edison as a cash bonus in consideration of his signing the contract. One can surmise that the Kinetoscope Company assumed the production costs for Kineto-scope films and that it paid Edison a royalty for the use of the camera.

5. *A Million and One Nights*, pp. 835-37.

As far as production costs were concerned, a subject like the "oriental dance" of October 1, costing $25, was relatively expensive. The money paid for it was two and a half times the amount paid the lady fencers and equal to the amount paid a prominent vaudeville act like Walton and Slavin.

The first Raff and Gammon film catalog, dated 1895, listed over fifty titles, most of which sold for from $10 to $15 each.[6]

Some of the titles and accompanying advertising are:

1. *Bertholdi,* The Marvellous Lady Contortionist
2. *Annie Oakley,* The "Little Sure Shot" of the "Wild West," Exhibition of Rifle Shooting at Glass Balls, etc.
3. *Finale of 1st Act Hoyt's "Milk White Flag."* Showing 34 Persons in Costume. The largest number ever shown as one subject in the Kinetoscope
4. *Robetta and Doretto.* Chinese Opium Den
5. *Professor Attilla.* The World Famous Athlete and Strong Man Trainer

The Kinetoscope Company by the end of 1894 had installed machines in over sixty parlors, department stores, drugstores, hotels, barrooms, and phonograph parlors in major cities throughout the country. A typical response to the machine was printed in *The Port Jervis Union* on December 14. The story sang the praises of the machine, its inventor, and the enterprising local citizen who had brought "the greatest marvel of the age" to town:

The Kinetoscope at the Clarendon Hotel

The greatest of modern inventions is on exhibition at the Clarendon Hotel in this village. We refer to Edison's far-famed and marvelous kinetoscope. This wonderful mechanism is worth going a thousand miles to see, but the enterprise of Mr. James Joyce, the proprietor of the Clarendon, has made that sacrifice of time and money unnecessary by purchasing one of the machines and placing it on exhibit at his hotel where it may be seen by everybody for the small price of ten cents. The scene which is displayed in Mr. Joyce's kinetoscope is that of three blacksmiths working at an anvil. It is perfectly natural and life-like in every respect. Mr. Joyce has another series representing two boxers in a four round contest which will be placed on exhibition in due time. Two years ago the pictorial representation of motion would have been scouted as the wildest of impossibilities, the crazy emanation of a disordered brain.

This seeming impossibility has been converted into a reality by the wizard genius

6. Ramsaye, p. 837, dates the catalog 1894, although *Professor Attila* was not produced until spring 1895. The list that follows comes from the Raff and Gammon catalog reprinted in Ramsaye.

of Edison. As we remarked before the greatest marvel of the age is now on exhibition at the Clarendon Hotel.

Net profits of the Kinetoscope Company's first month of operation (September 1 to October 1) came to $8,377.13. An interesting abstract of the company's September 1 to October 16, 1894, finances is in the Baker Library collection. It lists office expenses, cash transactions, purchases from Edison, all film expenses in which the Hollands were involved, etc., and contains the following essential facts: (1) As of October 16, 1894 the Kinetoscope Company had paid Edison $7,940 for Kinetoscopes and $369.35 for film subjects; and (2) As of October 16, 1894 the Kinetoscope Company had received $15,878.56 from customers.

With the close of 1894 the Kinetoscope business was not working out in the way Raff and Gammon had expected. Business was good for the first six months after public exhibition began, but they did not enter the field until September, and although the fall sustained itself, the end of the year brought difficulties.

Maguire and Baucus

To market the Kinetoscope abroad, Edison contracted with a firm headed by Frank Z. Maguire and Joseph D. Baucus.

By September 10, 1894, according to corporation records in the New York City Hall of Records, Maguire and Baucus set up the Continental Commerce Company at their 44 Pine Street office, and laid plans for Kinetoscope parlor openings in London and in Paris.

A November 9 letter from Maguire at the London office of the Continental Commerce Company at 70 Oxford Street (which was also a Kinetoscope parlor) gives a first ominous sound of the foreign competition that Edison failed to inhibit.

George Georgiades and George Trajedes, having bought Kinetoscopes from the Holland Brothers and having taken them to England, entered into an arrangement with Robert W. Paul to copy the Edison-manufactured Kinetoscope for European sale, free of Edison restriction.

So far as I have found, nothing was done to help Edison's European agents in their efforts to stop "the pirate who is infringing and making bogus Kinetoscopes in Europe." Edison may have felt that such attempts would have been useless, since there was no patent protection in England for the Kinetoscope.

I have found no documentary evidence that Edison's reasons for not taking out foreign patents was a disinclination to waste money, though Ramsaye, with his ease at quoting conversation after the lapse of years, has remarked that this exchange took place: "How much will it cost?" Edison asked casually. "Oh, about $150." . . . "It isn't worth it!" . . .

Maguire and Baucus, long eager to become associated with Edison, had succeeded in doing so, and remained some months stormily connected. But when Kinetoscope sales fell off in the spring of 1895 their business fell off, too. For much of the crucial early period of the motion picture business in America, however, they worked hard to gain a foreign market for the Kinetoscope and its film. They gained this market, and have thus earned a place in this record.

The Kinetophone

For years Edison thought of many new products of his laboratory as being only "improvements" on his phonograph. The motion picture camera was no exception. The Edison encounter with the motion picture problem was only an urge to improve his beloved phonograph:

> I am experimenting upon an instrument which does for the Eye what the phonograph does for the Ear, which is the recording and reproduction of things in motion, and in such a form as to be both Cheap practical and convenient.[7]

On June 16 *The Electrical World* stated the situation as of June 1894 neatly:

> While the kineto-phonograph has not been brought to a sufficiently practical form for public exhibition, as has the kinetoscope, the experiments in the inventor's laboratory have been so successful that it is regarded only as a question of time, by those engaged in the work, when the apparatus will be perfected.

But such simultaneous talking and recording experiments were abandoned as fruitless, and it was decided to insert a slightly altered model of the phonograph in the Kinetoscope case, and use sound as nonsynchronized accompaniment to, rather than illustration of, action. This consisted in playing dance or band records while a performer was seen in the film, and attaching ear tubes for listening. Synchronization was abandoned. So far as speech or other nonmusical sounds were concerned they were never seriously considered.

Only forty-five Kinetophones were made and sold, and, like Kinetoscopes, are correspondingly rare.

The Kinetophone's claim to distinction was its compactness: the picture and the accompaniment were in the same box. The Kinetophone was thus

---

7. From Edison's Motion Picture Caveat I, dated October 8, 1888, reproduced in Hendricks, *The Edison Motion Picture Myth*, pp. 158-61.

an aesthetic as well as a technical advance in the history of the motion picture.

Business Falls Off

By the close of 1894, it was evident that Kinetoscope business was not as successful as had been hoped. For one thing, there was competition between Raff and Gammon's business and the Latham group. For another, public enthusiasm had waned. At the close of business on March 15, 1895, the assets of the Kinetoscope Company totalled $31,379.37. Against this there was balanced a "Dividend #1" for $5,000, a $25,794.31 gross profit on Kinetoscopes, $2870.91 on films, and $602.40 on batteries. Operating expenses to date had been $7283.37 and bills payable $6305.87. Stock on hand—Kinetoscopes, batteries, etc.—was valued at $8089.25. The stockholders were told on March 20: "Our business at this time is rather quiet, but we have considerable confidence in the Spring and Summer trade."

By fall, 1895, business had deteriorated to the point where only seventeen Kinetoscopes were made in September, two in October, nine in November, and two in December. Raff and Gammon had been thinking about going into another business for some time, and now they were giving it additional thought. They were also trying to sell the Kinetoscope business, and were guilty of the usual colossal exaggerations in the process: "[The Kinetoscope business] has earned in the neighborhood of $50,000.00 . . . of net profits in but little over 1½ years. . . ."

Then shortly before December 8, 1895, a momentous event occurred. A Washingtonian named Thomas Armat announced that he had a new projector. Raff and Gammon saw it and it worked.

C. Francis Jenkins had developed a workable projector, and Armat, a Washington real estate operator, had gotten an interest in the new machine and was now representing to Raff and Gammon and sundry that it was his own. Before the season was out, the Vitascope (as the new projector was to be called) had a sensational opening in New York, and the Kinetoscope, America's first commercially successful motion picture exhibitor, was delivered its death blow.

In the next few years fewer and fewer Kinetoscopes were manufactured. Laboratory records show that as of the time of the Vitascope debut of April 23, 1896, there had been 905 manufactured. As of December 8, 1899, there had been 973 Kinetoscopes manufactured. By the end of the century, after only six years of business, Kinetoscopes had all but passed from the American scene.

3

GEORGE PRATT

"No Magic, No Mystery, No Sleight of Hand"

In 1896 motion pictures were new. New York, London, Paris flocked to see the latest filmed views, the latest projecting devices. The Eidoloscope, the Kinematographe, the Cinématographe, the Bioscope, the Veriscope, the Vitascope, and other "scopes" shot forth their pictures onto screens to flabbergast audiences.

Rivalry between nations for honors of priority in invention ran high. Stinging accusations crossed the Atlantic. Quarrels flared within the borders of countries.

New York City was the chief showcase in America for the newest developments in films and projectors. But everywhere enthusiasm surged up, as we can judge by the impact of motion pictures in such a city as Rochester, New York. Consider Rochester: in 1896 it was seven hours by train from New York City; its population was around 160,000; it was then, as now, third largest city in the state. Although a great photographic center, its delight in the novel medium of *moving* photographs can surely stand as typical of cities of similar size throughout all the country.

Rochester was a tardy host to the motion picture devices which emanated from the workshops of America and Europe. Its welcome may have come late, months after the huzzahs of New York City had died into history, but when it came it was wonderfully thorough. Fragile brown

Image 8 (December 1959): 192-211.

newspaper files spill out detailed advance notices and reviews to shame the skimpy lines in Manhattan dailies.

There was virtue in the circumstance that Rochester's entertainment world sparkled in only a handful of theaters. This meant less competition from opera, orchestras, legitimate theater, even from vaudeville itself (with its prancing dogs, its monologuists, its song-shouters, and its cake-walking clowns), to crowd motion pictures down to a mere mention. The motion picture's relation to vaudeville was extraordinarily close at the beginning. It shared the same bill as one more item in the parade of talent. In Rochester, as in most other cities, motion pictures rode the flying coattails of vaudeville for the first ten years of their existence.

The Rochester story begins in January 1896, when those who skimmed the Saturday newspapers with a weather eye to coming attractions at Wonderland Theater were most gratified to learn that a miraculous mechanism was about to visit their midst, for their amusement and mystification.

"First production in Rochester of . . . [the] wonderful Eidoloscope," announced the Wonderland advertisement on January 18, with restraint peculiar for show business. "An improvement on the [Edison] Kineto-scope, showing life size figures thrown on canvas of Prize Fights, Wrestling Matches, and Horse Races, without the attendant brutality. Worth three times the price of admission to see this novelty alone." On another page it was further explained that the Eidoloscope was the brainchild of the American inventor Woodville Latham, who had already exhibited his wonder in New York City.

The following historic Monday, when the new vaudeville bill commenced for the week, Rochesterians pressed into Wonderland to witness on a program otherwise devoted to "live" diversion their first projected motion pictures, as distinct from those they had previously seen in the Edison Kinetoscope, a boxed peep-show device capable of entertaining only one viewer at a time.

The experience is best described by the Rochester *Democrat & Chronicle,* which adds a touch of prophecy and also informs us that rear projection was in use: "Eidoloscope pictures, like magic lantern pictures, increase in size in proportion to the distance of the lens from the screen, and the stage of Wonderland is so shallow that the moving figures in Eidoloscope pictures shown there cannot be made more than a foot or so in height. Sometimes, too, slight alterations in the focal distance momentarily dim the image. Nevertheless, the exhibition is most remarkable and to those who have never seen a Kinetoscope must be a really startling novelty. A magic lantern picture of a four-round bout with the gloves which faithfully reproduces every minutest movement of principals, referee and spectators is a rather marvelous thing, when you come to think of it. When color photography is a commonplace, as it soon will be, and the details of the Eidoloscope are perfected, the drama is going to have a formidable rival fifty years hence in the lifelike reproductions of the most stirring events of present history that can then be shown to posterity exactly as they occurred. . . .'' The participants in the fight were Young Griffo and Barnett. There was also a filmed skirt dance by the Nichols sisters.

Encouraged by audience reaction, the manager of Wonderland booked the Eidoloscope for a second week, featuring its reproduction of "the great wrestling match between Donald C. Ross and Ernest Roeber," but adding a skirt dance and "a small portion of a horse race."

These displays at Wonderland, wondrous and unaccountable as an Arabian Night's adventure, flung open the doors to the first decade of motion pictures in Rochester, extending from 1896 through 1905. By 1906 the city could drop in on its first nickelodeon, the Bijou Dream, which gave films a white-façade theater all to themselves and marked off another chapter in local film history by indicating the impending divorce of films from vaudeville.

The pioneer decade divides quite naturally into two shorter periods, the first of them expiring in 1901—and that last verb is exactly chosen. For five years there was rarely direct competition: on only twenty-six days were films available in more than one theater at once. Competition of a subtler kind prevailed—between France and America. First one performed, then the other—in unconflicting engagements, with one exception. The opening half of the decade determined whether the field was to be seized by the French producing firm Lumière Brothers, which invaded confidently on three occasions, or by American Mutoscope and Biograph Company (Biograph), late in appearing. Two nations seemed to stake their reputations on the outcome.

For five years Rochester thronged to the theater to enjoy the yields of the struggle in a broad variety of films, often made in distant parts of the world, with novelty at a premium. Flirtations with sound, color, and big screen remind us that tentative gestures sixty years ago underlie the thundering pageant-frescoes of the motion picture today.

After the Eidoloscope showing in January 1896, some months passed before Rochesterians viewed motion pictures again. This privilege beckoned to those who journeyed out six miles by electric or steam cars or whatever, to the shores of Lake Ontario where Ontario Beach Park spread an enticing array of pavilions, rides, and sideshows. The summer of 1896 was not profitable for the park (perhaps word had gotten around about the numerous shell games conducted by the "Big Mitt" gang), and the

Vitascope, which was playing there, may have been introduced in the desperate hope of brightening the closing days of the season. If so, why wasn't it advertised?

A feature article in the *Democrat & Chronicle* of September 14, 1896, tips us off to the presence of the Vitascope, a fact not disclosed in the general advertising for the park. Assuming the Vitascope was what it claimed to be, this was the invention of Thomas Armat of Washington, D.C., first publicly exhibited at Koster & Bial's Music Hall in New York City the preceding April and called "Edison's marvel." Edison, always reluctant to have his films projected, had waited too long to develop his own projector. With the world demanding to see movies projected on a screen, he purchased the right to manufacture Armat's Vitascope. These were the days of secret schemes and jealously guarded experiments: for publicity purposes, it was arranged to link Edison's name with the Armat machine.

In the feature article a fictitious pair of rubes, Sally and Billy, leave the farm to visit Ontario Beach Park and "finally brought up against the Vitascope . . . in they went." Billy becomes excited over a "picture that was thrown upon the screen which showed an indignant farmer and his son chastising a city chap for making love to the rustic daughter and sister," and even more so over a film of a female "dancer and contortionist . . . depicted on the white sheet." Sally objects to "that wild thing . . . [cutting] up all them capers in them short skirts" and wonders if "she's the bloomer girl we read so much about?" Billy breaks away from her, determined to discover "where that gal's hidin'," pushes behind the sheet and discovers the projectionist alone with his machine. (Rear projection again.) Billy is pacified with the explanation that it is only "an electric picture" but tries to buy the machine and his offer is refused. It is not for sale. He returns to Sally. "By this time the ballet dancer had given place to a scene at the beach, where the waves were rolling mountains high, and a boat was tossing helplessly about."

Early the following month Fitzhugh Hall in Rochester brought the Vitascope into town, advertising three daily performances of "The Latest Fad—Animated Pictures, as revealed by that most wonderful of all inventions, the Vitascope." Although screenings ran for three days, four papers rigorously ignored the showings, regardless of whether an advertisement had been placed in their columns or not. There were no reviews. This is our loss, as the Fitzhugh programs were undeniably the very first in town to be entirely devoted to motion pictures, without the slightest help from vaudeville.

What followed was scarcely less curious. Cook's Opera House booked "Edison's Kinematographe" for October 12 through 14, proclaiming in the billowing language of the circus barker: "There is no magic, no mystery, no sleight of hand, but a bonafide reproduction in life size, of every human emotion, every human action, every action of lower animal life, everything that 'is' be it animate or inanimate, human or beast, that can possibly be conceived. . . . The marvelous mystifying power of this invention has been acknowledged by London, Paris, and New York."

Had Cook's merely carried off the Vitascope from Fitzhugh Hall? If so, why did they advertise their prize in terms which suggested both an American and a French projector (since the Lumières were successfully featuring a "Cinématographe")? No wonder the *Rochester Herald* babbled confusedly of "the Kinematographe or Vitascope or whatever it is."

The manager of Cook's, however, claimed he had secured the Kinematographe during a July trip to Europe and the continent. "While in Paris he dropped into the Folies Bergère in search of talent. The Kinematographe was being exhibited there. He, like the rest of the audience, was dumbfounded by its revelations. . . . What was the price for America? The reply was staggering. The hesitation was but momentary and the deal was closed. . . ." Very well, why the hocus-pocus about Edison? What exactly *was* the Kinematographe?

All this aside, it was a hit, as a review of the performance testifies: "The 'Kinematographe,' Edison's great invention, depicted clearly the marvels of photography. The [railroad] station at Peekskill was shown on the canvas and in the distance could be seen a train approaching. It was coming with lightning rapidity, but the quiet working of photography did not miss a single action and the train came steadily forward, until, as it passed the station the audience could distinguish Engine 999 and the Empire State Express. Everybody applauded. Other scenes depicted . . . a tub race, the coronation of the present czar, a watermelon match, a Parisian street scene, march of the French school children." There was also a New York City street scene.

Both the Eidoloscope and the Kinematographe showings proved no more than test runs. The first really grandly triumphant campaign to establish films in Rochester was launched the week of November 2, 1896, when the Wonderland manager booked the Lumière Cinématographe for two weeks. This French invention had been astounding New York City since late June. With an allure unprecedented in the history of Rochester entertainment, chalking up the longest run of any one attraction ever presented in a place of amusement up to that time, it whirled off films at Wonderland for a full seventeen weeks!

Opening night of the Cinématographe at Wonderland was the scene of raging excitement among an audience well primed for miracles. "The

Pastime in the Family Circle (Lumière, 1896), with Mmes. Auguste and Louis Lumière and some friends

moving figures," said the *Post Express,* "render the pictures wonderfully realistic. The first scene presented last night was the unveiling of a monument in Berlin. As company after company of soldiers marched rapidly past the reviewing stand, the audience fairly went wild with delight." This view was succeeded by eleven others, including a London street scene in which "the audience plainly saw the smoke from . . . [the] cigar" of a strolling man. The three subjects on that program most familiar to film historians today are the demolition of a wall, the arrival of a French fast mail train at Ciotat, and the charge of the French Cuirassiers.

The *Rochester Herald* confided: "The films used are about one and a quarter inches wide and ninety feet long; and on every one there are about nine hundred photographs. These pass before the lens at the rate of fifteen per second, so that the whole nine hundred only occupy a minute of time in passing before the eye of the spectator."

Wonderland rejoiced in its possession of the Cinématographe for the next sixteen weeks. Normally, twelve views were shown each week on a program assembled by adding from four to six new subjects and repeating the most popular items from the week before. In this way some 115 short films reached Wonderland's screen, photographed in those exotic parts of the world to which the enterprising Lumière cameramen had traveled: Moscow, Budapest, Venice, Dresden. American views joined the repertory in December 1896, but only after a clumsy routing back through the Lumière factory in Lyons, France, for processing. Rochester now marveled at Brooklyn Bridge on the screen, Niagara Falls, Fulton Street in Boston, Michigan Avenue in Chicago.

Three items claim more than passing notice because of either unusual filming conditions or unusual manner of presentation on the program. *Scene from a Moving Train* (week of January 4, 1897), surveying the havoc of floods in Mâcon, France, is the earliest of the Lumière films shown in Rochester which indicated that the camera was mounted on a moving vehicle, presaging the more general fad several years later for photographing from a train in motion. In the final week, Wonderland screened *Blind Man's Buff*, "made more real by the voice of Mimic Royce behind the scenes." Here we have a primitive experiment with "talking" pictures. On the same program, *French Dragoons Crossing the Sâone* had nearly run its course when it was suddenly reversed and the horses began swimming backward and scrambling hind-side-fore up a steep bank. Not an accident, the reversed action had been deliberately planned and advertised in advance. The spectacle of backward motion repeatedly figures on early programs.

Not until February 1897 did the Cinématographe depart, the last three days of the prolonged engagement coinciding with showings of the rival "Edison Projectoscope" at the Central Church (for want of a downtown theater outlet). The Edison pictures exhibited "several color effects" and benefited by the presence of the State Industrial School boys' band to present stirring music during the McKinley procession scene. The Projectoscope impressed one reviewer as "steadier and free from the eye-torturing flickers" of the Cinématographe and the Vitascope.

Wonderland now, in the restless search for novelty that characterized every lively vaudeville operation, turned to an American projector, the Biograph, and to the catalogue of Biograph films. The Biograph was installed immediately at Wonderland. This machine had already played a Rochester debut at Cook's late in November 1896, a month after the New York City opening. Nine subjects, ranging from Niagara Falls through the Empire State Express and Joe Jefferson in a scene from *Rip van Winkle,* to *Major McKinley at Home,* had been advertised. Perhaps because of cautious publicity, the Biograph debut at Cook's had slipped by as a rather routine affair. The *Post Express* referred to "the Biograph, without which or something like it, no well regulated vaudeville seems able to exist."

Yet the Biograph was to sweep all competitors from the field, but before it could be shown at Wonderland in March 1897, Wonderland had to re-condition an audience to which for seventeen weeks it had extolled the

marvels of the Cinématographe. Patrons were steered toward the Biograph through the claim that "its pictures are almost completely free from
the flicker of the Cinématographe. A very much larger screen will be used
completely filling the proscenium arch . . . [because] the Biograph throws
a much larger picture than does the French machine.[1] Another point . . .
is that, being an American machine, there will be more home views. . . .
[All] ten views announced for the opening week will be American. . . .
[As] important events occur anywhere on this side of the Atlantic they
will be produced very soon afterward on the Biograph." The McKinley
inauguration, for instance.

Wonderland's first Biograph program repeated seven views already
shown at Cook's and added three fresh ones of the New York City fire
department, the American flag, and the chutes at Atlantic City. The
house was jammed long before the first performance was scheduled to
begin, "and this despite inclement weather."

Biograph stayed five weeks, the beginning of the conquering wedge of
American-made films. In the face of this foray, Lumière ventured back for
a second booking at Wonderland, retiring to leave Biograph a nearly complete victor as of December 1897. One further re-entry by Lumière
(February 1898) completes the record of their activities. On the other
hand, there were five more return engagements of Biograph through 1901.

In five years over three hundred Biograph views were screened. Every
one of those shown in Rochester in 1896-97 had been filmed on American
ground. This intensive domestic survey had proved a weapon to rout the
Lumières. But this type of chauvinism was dumped abruptly upon the
outbreak of three wars conducted on foreign soil: the Spanish-American
War (1898), the Boer War (1899-1902), and the Boxer Rebellion (1900),
scenes from all of which flashed out upon local screens under Biograph
auspices.

Audiences left no doubt as to their opinions and preferences. They expressed approval by hearty clapping, endorsing Queen Victoria during the
Boer War, although they may have disagreed with British policy in South
Africa. A Biograph film of Victoria's visit to Ireland in 1900 "was
tremendously applauded. . . . It is evident that Queen Victoria's personal
popularity among Americans has not been seriously affected by recent
events." At other times, rage lashed out, as it had once in the case of a
Lumière view of the Spanish infantry, shown late in 1896 and "greeted
with a storm of hisses, aptly illustrating the condition of the American

1. In size, Biograph films differed from both Edison and Lumière films, which were of
standard 35-mm dimensions. The images on Biograph films were roughly 2¼ inches high by
2¾ inches wide. Impressions were taken and projected at a rate of between thirty and forty
frames a second, by means of a battery-driven motor.

mind on the Cuban question." Feelings boiled into greater aggravation more than a year later during a Biograph showing in April 1898, and a Spanish warship view had to be eliminated from the program. "At first the audience hissed and with every performance there were indications of an approaching storm. Finally the gallery gods showed their disapproval with potatoes and other garden truck, and as the management did not care to start a grocery, the obnoxious picture has been permanently removed."

In May 1900, the *Democrat & Chronicle* challenged the authenticity of one of the Biograph war views as follows: ". . . [A view] . . . showing a trainload of British troops 'en route' to join Buller at Frere Camp [Boer War] is apparently genuine. As much cannot be said for the alleged picture of American troops charging a force of rebels in the Philippines. If it is what it is represented to be, the camera must have been stationed just in front of the Tagalog position and in the direct line of fire, when the picture was taken. *A Drill at Van Cortlandt Park* would probably correctly describe it."

War views did not monopolize the screen, however. There was an ample supply of comic fictional interludes, and an occasional trick film. A panoramic view of Conway, England, taken from the front of an express train prompted Cook's to advertise in October 1898, "the greatest Biograph picture ever taken. . . . The film is 750 feet long and is the longest in existence." Even at that, it lasted only three minutes on the screen. A Paris fire film topped it for length five weeks later. Audiences were properly awed.

Sensing the need to stimulate renewed interest, Biograph brought its camera to town in the fall of 1899, and this was announced in the *Democrat & Chronicle* on September 3: "Rochesterians who happened to pass the Four Corners at about the hour of noon on Saturday, August 26th, just a week ago yesterday, had their attention attracted by a queer-looking machine that seemed to be taking pictures. Many people stopped to watch it. If they visit the Cook Opera House this week they probably will find themselves the observed of all the observers, for the queer-looking machine was a biograph camera. . . ."

Other Rochester congregations passed before the Biograph camera: the fire department ("eight pieces of apparatus . . . under full speed. The run . . . was made expressly for . . . exhibition purposes"), the police on parade, employees of Eastman Kodak and Bausch & Lomb leaving work.

A program at Cook's in November 1899 constituted an important deviation from the usual formula of vaudeville-with-Biograph, for the emphasis was squarely upon films, six of which showed Pope Leo XIII in the Vatican Gardens. Also on the same program, which included miscellaneous "live" vocal and instrumental selections, were scenes of a different character, including one of pole vaulting at Columbia University, run first forward and then backward. There was no vaudeville.

Several stray engagements apart from the conquering Biograph ought to be recorded from this early time, and these are mainly concerned with the disparate subjects of Passion Plays and Prize Fights. For two weeks in February 1898, Fitzhugh Hall played Lumière's authentic version of the Passion Play as reenacted in the Bohemian village of Horitz. The print was on its way to New York City, which had already given patronage to a fake record of this sacred pageant filmed on a Manhattan rooftop and fobbed off as an import. Organ accompaniment, a descriptive lecture, and vocal selections ensured a deluxe presentation of the two-hour showing. With questionable taste a dry goods firm later in the year offered free tickets for what may have been the same film to "all customers purchasing 25 cents worth of goods or over." Screenings were held on the premises. Fitzhugh Hall's Passion Play film of January 1899, promised "34 pictures, eight of which are introductory."

Filmed prize fights were invariably controversial. Witness the August 1897 run of Veriscope pictures of the great Corbett-Fitzsimmons championship match. Had a slow count protected Fitzsimmons in the sixth round so that he could eventually win in the fourteenth? In July 1899, the season's largest crowds mobbed Ontario Beach Park where a gala vaudeville bill included films of the championship bout between Jeffries and Fitzsimmons. It was not the real thing, but a tamer re-creation to replace the photographically botched record of the actual fight. When these films played a return date at the park in August, a huge curtain was hung outside the auditorium, and on this the pictures were projected every evening for at least a week.

An eager audience at the Empire Theater in December 1899 was affronted by a fly-by-night New York company's bootleg account of the Jeffries-Sharkey fight secured on a small camera smuggled into the crowd on the evening of the fight. Except for three or four wretchedly-focused rounds, the exhibition was faked. "That is, it was merely a repetition of the same rounds run through slower or faster as the operator saw fit. . . . It did not take the spectators any great length of time to become acquainted with the fact that they were up against a legal bunco game, and when they discovered the fraud those who were posted on the fight began to call for certain incidents and name the rounds duplicated. It was a very disgusted crowd which filed out of the exits . . . , and it is safe to say that if a similar exhibition were to be given . . . [again] there would not be a corporal's guard present."

Although beaten to town by this dismal hoax, the authorized version of the same fight played three days in February 1900. Said a Rochester paper: "Though the exhibition lasts over two hours (the film being said to be over seven miles long), the pictures are so clear and the 'flickering' effect has been so modified by recent improvements in the machinery that the strain on the eyes is not great. . . ." One minute before the end, Jeffries' left glove had come off, but the camera had chosen this precise moment to die. As the traveling narrator expressed it: "One of the fuses blowed out and the critical moment was lost."

For some unstated reason, between March 1901 and January 1903, motion pictures vanished completely from Rochester theater programs. Why? Were audiences tired of them? At any rate, films were out, in utter eclipse. The situation may have been quite uncomplicated. In five years those motion pictures that reached Rochester had not really progressed. They were still, for the most part, brief, fragmentary, rudimentary. The few that have survived the dissolution of time win us now with their simplicity, but there is a limit to that sort of appeal, and Rochester audiences may have balked.

After a blank of nearly two years, on January 18, 1903, films returned, appearing on a single Sunday evening vaudeville program at Cook's "shown by the Edison Vitagraph." They were still in danger of permanent extinction, however. Their rescue came singlehandedly from the introduction and advance of the "story" film, risen from the ashes of comic skits, and comprising a series of scenes related to a central character or group of characters. Enter sustained interest and suspense.

One of the earliest of the story films to confront Rochester audiences was the famous A Trip to the Moon of the French producer Georges Méliès, shown in the summer of 1903 as a stylish sandwich between the third and fourth acts of a stock company's performance of the stage melodrama "Saved from the Sea." "The film runs for about fifteen minutes," reported a Rochester paper, "and shows the voyage of some enterprising astronomers from earth to moon and their extraordinary adventures with the Selenites. . . . [At] least fifty trained actors, acrobats, and dancers take part." Additional Méliès films arrived, including An Impossible Voyage ("a long view running 25 minutes") and The Christmas Angel. Still another French producer, Pathé Frères, sent more story films. From England came a "five-act" East Lynne (November 1903) and other narratives.

Not to be outdone by foreign fireworks, Edison was represented in the last two months of 1903 by three story films on Rochester screens: The Life of an American Fireman, Uncle Tom's Cabin, and Jack and the Beanstalk, all three celebrated in the annals of early American films. The last two were tableau affairs in the manner of Méliès, whose films the Edison Company was circulating domestically. An influential British

A Desperate Crime (Méliès, 1899)

Edwin S. Porter's *The Great Train Robbery* (Edison, 1903)

import also offered by Edison was *A Daring Daylight Burglary* (1903), photographed entirely out of doors and narrating the crime and capture of a burglar after police pursuit. With such a model on hand, the Edison Company began production of a film whose fame eventually encircled the world and provided the decisive push in the direction of the story film.

This was *The Great Train Robbery,* which burst upon the vision of Rochester audiences in January 1904 like the dawn of a new era. More than any other film it determined the power of the new screen narratives. A fever of enthusiasm over this electric example of the "chase" film demanded eight revivals in Rochester in 1904 and 1905. Cook's repeated it, recalling: ". . . [When] shown two weeks ago . . . the Kinetograph scored the biggest moving picture hit ever made in Rochester." Three weeks later, the British burglar film arrived.

Still another story film, Biograph's *Personal,* screened late in 1904, transposed the chase into the realm of comedy, illustrating the dilemma of a French count who had been so rash as to advertise for a wife, and, overwhelmed with applicants, fled with the breathless spinsters on his traces. Rochester called it back for a second week and placed it alongside *The Great Train Robbery* as one of the memorable hits in this dawn of the story film.

As these ten years drew to an end in December 1905, announcements appeared in the papers which, in spite of the fact that they were concerned with a stage play, hold a peculiar significance for us today. For they were advertising "The Clansman," to which "The Invisible Empire of the Ku Klux Klan Bids You . . . The Play That Stirred the Nation." Possibly. But they hadn't seen anything yet compared with what happened ten years later when this same play exploded onto the screen as *The Birth of a Nation,* directed by D. W. Griffith, the overpowering climax of the story film.

Back in 1906 in Rochester, the future of the film for the time being lay with the white-fronted Bijou Dream, a nickelodeon, where story films played boldly without vaudeville and where a hoarse phonograph outside the doors lured customers from the street into a darkened interior.

4

RUSSELL MERRITT

Nickelodeon Theaters 1905-1914: Building an Audience for the Movies

In its short heyday, the nickelodeon theater was a pioneer movie house, a get-rich-quick scheme, and a national institution that was quickly turned into a state of mind. Its golden age began in 1905 and lasted scarcely nine years, but during that time it provided the movies their first permanent home, established a durable pattern for nationwide distribution, and—most important—built for the motion picture an audience that would continue to support it for another forty years. Even after its decline, it survived in popular legend as a monument to movies in their age of innocence: the theater primeval that showed movies to an unspoiled and uninhibited audience of children and poor people. How the nickelodeon was portrayed in movie histories, how sharply it was believed to contrast with the postwar years of the movie palace and expensive studio production, is evident in the terms used to identify it. James Agee, for example, writing from the perspective of his own childhood, turned the nickelodeon into a populist shrine, cataloging its delights in the style of a Whitman poem. He recalled "the barefaced honky-tonk and the waltzes by Wald-teufel, slammed out in a mechanical piano; the searing redolence of peanuts and demirep perfumery, tobacco and feet, and sweat; the laughter of unrespectable people having a hell of a fine time, laughter as violent and steady and deafening as standing under a waterfall."[1]

1. James Agee, "Comedy's Greatest Era," *Life,* September 3, 1949, reprinted in Agee, *Agee on Film: Reviews and Comments* (New York, 1958), pp. 6-7.

More recently, Edward Wagenknecht in *The Movies in the Age of Innocence* painted an unblemished portrait of Chicago nickelodeons as they appeared to him in his youth, a portrait more detailed than Agee's but no less affectionate. As other histories have shown, the nickelodeon era has been the epoch of film history easiest to sentimentalize.[2]

Few historians would claim that his nostalgic view of the nickelodeon is pure fabrication. Even those who discount the innocence of the prewar years might find it hard to resist the allure of the vintage five-cent theater. The novelty was real, the appeal obvious, the popularity undeniable. But this portrait, two dimensional and static, is patently incomplete. The purpose of my inquiry is to define that theater more sharply and, more importantly, to satisfy two nagging questions. First, how did theater operators finally attract the middle-class audiences so reluctant to peer inside the early movie houses? Second, when did the industry itself, originally supported and paid for by the working class, determine to abandon that audience for the broader, more affluent white-collar trade?

No one, to my mind, has answered these questions satisfactorily, least of all those historians who suppose that the middle-class moviegoer got started with features and World War I. By 1914, the middle-class audiences were, in fact, already in the theaters waiting for the spectacles and movie stars that would follow. The seduction of the affluent occurred, I will contend, in the preceding years, between 1905 and 1912, in precisely that theater supposedly reserved for the blue-collar workers.

"Democracy's Theater"

The nickelodeon itself was a small, uncomfortable makeshift theater, usually a converted dance hall, restaurant, pawn shop, or cigar store,

2. See the introduction to Edward Wagenknecht, *The Movies in the Age of Innocence* (Norman, Okla., 1962). Other accounts of the nickelodeon can be found in the standard film histories of the silent era: Terry Ramsaye, *A Million and One Nights* (New York, 1926); Benjamin B. Hampton, *A History of the Movies* (New York, 1931); Lewis Jacobs, *The Rise of the American Film* (New York, 1939); Kenneth Macgowan, *Behind the Screen* (New York, 1965). But these sources seldom go beyond a cursory description of nickelodeon exhibition. There is no American equivalent to the detailed study of British film exhibition found in Rachel Low, *The History of the British Film: 1906-1914* (London, 1949). The nickelodeon era, for the most part, has been ignored in the current literature of film history, but two important studies have recently been made available: Garth Jowett, "Media Power and Social Control: The Motion Picture in America, 1896-1936" (Ph.D. diss., University of Pennsylvania, 1972); and Joseph H. North, *The Early Development of the Motion Picture, 1887-1909* (New York, 1973), a reprint of a 1949 doctoral dissertation. Important primary documents and contemporary descriptions of nickelodeons have been collected in George Pratt, *Spellbound in Darkness* (Rochester, N.Y., 1966).

Theatre Unique on 14th St., New York City

made over to look like a vaudeville emporium. Outside, large lurid posters pasted into the theater windows announced the playbill for the day. For ten cents—nickelodeons were seldom a nickel—the early moviegoer went inside and saw a miscellany of brief adventure, comedy, or fantasy films that lasted about an hour. Movies were always the main attraction, but enterprising managers followed the formula created by William Fox and Marcus Loew in 1906, and enhanced their programs with sing-alongs, inexpensive vaudeville acts, and illustrated lectures.

The show customarily began with a song, usually one of the popular ballads of the day—"Sunbonnet Sue," "Bicycle Built for Two," "The Way of the Cross," or perhaps "Down in Jungle Town"—or else a patriotic anthem. Hand-colored magic lantern slides illustrated scenes from the song and a final slide projecting the lyrics encouraged the

Inside a nickelodeon projection booth

audience to join in the chorus. The manager might then present his first
movie, or bring on a live comedian, a dog act, or perhaps a ventriloquist;
or else he might go straight to his most prestigious act: the illustrated
lecture. Nickelodeon lecturing became for a time a lucrative business, with
increasing care taken to recruit authentic "professors," preachers, and
world travelers with exotic stories to tell. For the movies, a large black
projector—a Vitascope Special or a Selig Polyscope if the theater were
licensed—was set up in the back, either closed off in a separate room or
enclosed inside a metal booth. Potted palms and gilded marquees were
less essential, but popular, ways of adding "class" to the common show.
   By 1910, when the nickelodeon craze had reached its peak, more than
10,000 of these theaters had sprung up across the country, creating
demands for between one hundred and two hundred reels of film every
week. "On one street in Harlem," wrote a *Harper's Weekly* journalist,
"there are as many as five nickelodeons to a block, each one capable of
showing to one thousand people an hour. They run from early morning
until midnight, and their megaphones are barking before the milkman
has made his rounds."[3]

   3. Barton Currie, "The Nickel Madness," *Harper's Weekly* 51 (August 24, 1907): 1246.
The theater statistic is from Hampton, *A History of the Movies*, p. 58. *Moving Picture World*
(hereinafter to be referred to as *MPW*), December 5, 1908, p. 523, quotes an unnamed
article by Glenmore Davis in *Success Magazine* claiming six thousand nickelodeon theaters
in existence across the country in 1908.

If we may believe the most conservative estimates, by 1910 nickelodeons were attracting some twenty-six million Americans every week, a little less than 20 per cent of the national population. In New York City alone, between 1.2 and 1.6 million people (or more than 25 per cent of the city's population) attended movies weekly, while in Chicago, the nickelodeon craze reached 0.9 million persons (an astonishing 43 per cent of that city's population). National gross receipts for that year totaled no less than $91 million.[4]

The lion's share of that audience came from the ghetto, a fact that nickelodeon commentators never tired of discovering. The label used over and over again by journalists commenting on the five-cent movie house, usually written with a delighted air of having discovered the exact phrase, was "democracy's theater." A Russell Sage survey revealed that in 1911, 78 percent of the New York audience consisted of members "from the working class" at a time when the worker had been effectively disenfranchised from the older arts. "You cannot go to any one of the picture shows in New York," wrote Mary Vorse for *The Outlook* in 1911, "without blessing the moving picture book that has brought so much into the lives of the people who work."[5] "They will stay as long as the slums stay," wrote Joseph Medill Patterson. "For in the slums they are the fittest, and must survive."[6]

The custodians of the poor took for granted that movies were made for the immigrant, the working man, children, and the unemployed. "If Tolstoi were alive today," *The Nation* claimed, "it is not unlikely that he would find in the movies a close approximation to his ideal of art. The Russian's ultimate test of a work of art was to appeal to the untutored but unspoiled peasant . . . the man who is today the nickel theater's most faithful customer." Municipal censorship of one-reelers was under constant attack by civic groups who called it class legislation, calculated to impose harsher standards on the poor man's theater than on that of his wealthier counterpart. Many welfare agencies, seeing the nickelodeon's appeal, followed the lead of Jane Addams at Hull House and used movies

4. "Moving Pictures and the National Character," *Review of Reviews* 42 (September 1910): 315-20. Michael Davis, *The Exploitation of Pleasure* (New York, 1911), pp. 8-9, is slightly more conservative. He estimates that 900,000 New Yorkers attended movies weekly in 1910.

5. Mary H. Vorse, "Some Picture Show Audiences," *The Outlook* 97 (June 24, 1911): 442. The Russell Sage survey is in Davis, *The Exploitation of Pleasure*, pp. 8-9. Garth S. Jowett, "The First Motion Picture Audiences," *Journal of Popular Film* 3 (Winter 1974): 39-54, quotes reports from social workers in Boston, Pittsburgh, and Homestead, N.Y., which also demonstrate the preponderance of working-class people in nickelodeons.

6. Joseph Medill Patterson, "The Nickelodeons: The Poor Man's Elementary Course in the Drama," *Saturday Evening Post* 180 (November 23, 1907): 38.

as part of educational and rehabilitation programs for the poor. The
United States Navy, which at that time enlisted over five thousand immigrants per year, began in September 1910 to manufacture a series of
recruiting films that played in nickel theaters throughout New York and in
recruiting stations across the country.[7]

To that audience, movies meant escape in the most literal sense. Amidst
the famous horrors of overcrowded tenement barracks, sweatshop work
that paid coolie wages, and continuing typhoid epidemics, movies were
treated as a simple refuge—a variant of the race track, the lottery, the
fortune teller's, or the saloon. Movies offered the worker a chance to come
in from the cold and sit in the dark.

He was not particularly interested in art—or in acculturation. When
D. W. Griffith started directing at the Biograph studios in 1908, his most
important competition came from heavyweight prize fights and French
chase comedies. Films such as these demanded no great power of concentration; the comedy plots—if they can be called that—were simple and
direct, uncomplicated by subtleties of character delineation or subplot.
The fast-moving action usually rose in a straight line from one climax to
another, resolving itself in a beating or an explosion. No one who leafs
through the pages of *Moving Picture World* and reads the plot descriptions of new films can overlook the incredible stress on violent slapstick
and knockabout humor. Vitagraph's *When Casey Joined the Lodge,*
reviewed July 4, 1908, features two Irishmen at a lodge initiation fighting
each other with bricks and tossing sticks of dynamite under lodge
members, cops, and innocent bystanders. Three weeks later, Vitagraph
followed up with *A Policeman's Dream* in which two boys awaken a
daydreaming patrolman by setting him on fire.[8] Neither the policeman nor
the boys are beaten, an exceptional outcome. In other comedies for July
1908: a political candidate has dirt and paste thrown over him, then his
wife beats him;[9] partygoers fall into a young man's room when a floor
caves in and they are beaten;[10] a gentleman "endeavoring to be polite to

7. "A Democratic Art," *The Nation* 97 (August 28, 1913): 193. For the anticensorship
arguments, see "Un-American Innovation," *The Independent* 86 (May 22, 1916): 265; "The
White Slave Films," *The Outlook* 106 (January 17, 1914): 121; and U.S., Congress, House,
Committee on Education, *Hearings, A Bill to Establish a Federal Motion Picture Commission,* 63d Cong., 2d sess., 1914, 2, pt. 2: 197-98. For Navy recruiting films, see "Moving
Pictures and the National Character," 317; and Arthur Dutton, "Where Will the Navy Get
Its Men?" *Overland Monthly* 53 (March 1909): 233. The statistic for 1910 immigrant naval
recruits, a figure representing 12 percent of all naval recruits, comes from "The Report of
the Bureau of Navigation," *The Annual Reports of the Navy Department,* 1911 (Washington, D.C., 1911), p. 305.
8. *MPW,* July 25, 1908.
9. *The Candidate,* Pathé-Frères.
10. *Noisy Neighbors,* Pathé-Frères.

all mankind" inadvertently wreaks havoc on a town through his awkward-
ness and receives "many an unkind blow and boost for his trouble."[11]

Later historians would claim that such films worked as part of the immigrant's acculturation to American society, entertaining guides to the
values and customs of the new world. But, in fact, few movies of this
period performed such a task. For all their popularity with American
audiences, they revealed little about America. Indeed, the majority of
them were produced in France: exports of the Pathé Frères company, who
single-handedly released more films in the United States than the major
American companies combined; *film trucs* from Georges Méliès; slap-
sticks and travelogues from Gaumont.[12] But even when they came from
the United States, one-reelers seldom worked with the particularities of
American stereotypes, landscapes, or social themes. Rather, the films
were offered as spectacles that induced the onlooker to marvel at the
unnatural, whether in the form of a slapstick chase, a comic dream, a
wondrous adventure, or an historic disaster. Those who saw them did not
learn much; it was rather the act of going to the movies that mattered
most. By perceiving what was general in their own situation, immigrants
could identify with others who shared that situation. Like the societies, the
schools, and the press, the nickelodeon was a means through which the
immigrants came to know each other.

Exhibitors Aspire to the Middle Class

But this portrait of the nickelodeon audience, like the portrait of the
nickelodeon theater, is misleading because it is drastically incomplete.
The five-cent theater may have been widely regarded as the working man's
pastime, but the less frequently reported fact was that the theater catered
to him through necessity, not through choice. The blue-collar worker and
his family may have supported the nickelodeon. The scandal was that no
one connected with the movies much wanted his support—least of all the
immigrant film exhibitors who were working their way out of the slums
with their theaters. The exhibitors' abiding complaint against nickelodeon
audiences—voiced with monotonous regularity in trade journals, personal

11. *Too Polite,* Gaumont.
12. Cf. "What Is an American Subject?" *MPW,* January 22, 1910, p. 82, in which an
anonymous reporter counted forty films released the previous week, half of which, he noted,
were produced abroad. Of those produced in the United States, he counted no more than ten
with American themes, "that is, themes 'racy of the soil' and distinctly American in
characterization, scenery, and surroundings. The other subjects were such as might have
been made in Europe." The report concluded "that the American subject, even after a year's
plugging away, does not seem to have secured a predominant part in the film program of the
moving picture theaters of the United States."

Warner Brothers' first theater, the Cascade, New Castle, Pennsylvania

correspondence, and in congressional testimony—was that moviegoers as a group lacked "class." A movie customer wearing a suit or an officer's military uniform was a momentous event; a car parked outside the theater was reason for a letter to *Moving Picture World*. By contrast, certain kinds of workers were discouraged and occasionally even banned from the movies. An extreme example is the case of the shantytown nickelodeons at the Portsmouth and Charlestown naval shipyards that favored military officers with reduced admission prices while they refused admittance to enlisted men. Writing sympathetically of this policy, a trade editor reasoned: "One way to keep trouble out of a theatre is not to admit it in the first place. . . . The roughhouse germ is present to a greater or less extent in every squad of sailors. The manager has reason to know in advance whether they are friend or foe, and therefore one cannot blame a manager in Portsmouth or any other place for using his discretionary powers, whether it involves the livery of Uncle Sam or Johnny Bull or anybody else."[13]

Not until the Secretary of the Navy threatened a naval boycott of all nickelodeons in Boston and Portsmouth and Governor Eugene Foss of Massachusetts signed a bill prohibiting discrimination against military recruits in places of amusement did the operators relent and agree to take back the enlisted men. Meanwhile, big city nickelodeon operators were cautioned against earning reputations as ethnic theaters, and given three ground rules for attracting a "mixed" house: operators should avoid booking programs heavily slanted toward any one nationality, avoid ethnic vaudeville acts, and eliminate all songs in foreign languages.[14] Embarrassed by their regulars, ambitious managers constantly sought ways to attract the larger, middle-class family trade currently the domain of vaudeville and the legitimate stage.

The thirst for affluence and respectability helps explain the curious locations of the original nickelodeons. Even when they were working-class entertainment, the most important nickelodeons were seldom built in the worker's community or in his shopping area. Instead, they customarily opened in business districts on the outer edge of the slums, fringing white-collar shopping centers, accessible to blue-collar audiences but even closer to middle-class trade.

Boston as a Case Study

A study of nickelodeon theaters in Boston will dramatize this phenomenon. While not necessarily a "typical" American metropolis, Boston offers

13. *MPW*, June 3, 1911. The shipyard nickelodeon quarrel was reported in *MPW*, June 3, 1911, p. 1246, and June 10, 1911, p. 1321.
14. *Motography* 7 (February 1912), p. 24.

a useful and convenient case study of a city that early established itself as a large and important East Coast film market. Thanks to its reputation as a theatrical crossroads (it had already become illustrious as a testing ground for New York plays, as the headquarters for B. F. Keith's vast chain of vaudeville theaters, and as the town that introduced continuous performances), its nickelodeons were reported and analyzed in unusually full detail throughout the trade press. As a consequence of these reports and the constant attention given nickel theaters by local social workers, church groups, and the city political machine, Boston provides one of the most influential and best-documented collections of nickel theaters in the nation.

Boston's movie theaters were strung out along three strategic locations in the city's downtown shopping area. At one end, seven theaters clustered around Scollay Square and Bowdoin Square—nearer expensive Beacon Hill townhouses than Italian and Irish tenements in the North End. This was Boston's original nickelodeon district, where in 1905 Mark Mitchell built Boston's first movie theater—the Theatre Comique at 14 Tremont Row—and where Boston's first movie theater chain set up its main offices.

From this point, the nickelodeons were stretched out in a long line along Tremont Row and Washington Street, where they operated side by side with the downtown B. F. Keith vaudeville houses and the major legitimate theaters. Although Washington Street commanded the highest building rentals in the city ($30,000 per year for lots ranging from twenty-five hundred to four thousand square feet), the steady flow of business made this the most prosperous and most fiercely competitive theater district in town. Shoppers coming out of C. F. Hovey's or Meyer Jonasson department stores could select from the Bijou Dream, the Pastime, the Gaiety, or the Park without having to cross the street. The Unique and the New Washington were one block away from the "elegantly appointed" Bradford Hotel and down two blocks from the stylish Hotel Touraine. Two nearby legitimate theaters—the Shubert at 265 Tremont and the Boston at 539 Washington—were constantly complaining to the New York *Dramatic Mirror* about the cheap competition luring away their theater regulars. To meet the threat, the Shuberts began to show ten-cent movies at their Globe Theatre during the slow 1909 summer months—an unheard-of practice among Boston's expensive legitimate houses and one that created a bitter nickelodeon price war at the Eliot Street corner of Washington Street.

Past the hotel district and Chinatown, down in the city's skid row, Boston's third group of nickel theaters were coiled around Castle Square and lower Washington Street where, run-down and poorly tended, they fit in with the gray South End landscape. Sandwiched in with local saloons, pool halls, and cheap hotels, these honky-tonk theaters were the principal targets of municipal reformers and the mayor's office. The working-class family trade avoided these theaters for the most part, hopscotching over them to attend the more remote but better-tended theaters in the north. Mainly, the Castle Square theaters were taken over by the flotsam residing in the dives along Tremont and Shawmut, or the transients from the local boardinghouses. Several of the nickelodeons were used as sleeping quarters; police raids on the Paradise and Dreamland were considered commonplace. [15]

As a location, the South End was notorious as a graveyard for nickelodeons, where, despite cheap building rates, the theaters suffered the poorest record of survival. Theaters in the district changed hands constantly; successful operators to the north regarded the area as a quarantine zone, preferring to expand their own movie empires to the suburbs and the wealthy Back Bay. The idea of constructing quality nickelodeons in the South End, if it was considered, was never tried. Even further from consideration was the possibility of building theaters further south, in the South Roxbury shopping districts or near the South End factories where the catchpenny exhibits, smaller vaudeville houses, and cheaper legitimate theaters stood. Like the North End, the South End was strictly off-limits for ambitious nickelodeon entrepreneurs.

What makes this statistic startling is that there was a group of theaters in the South End neighborhood which demonstrated that catering to the ethnic family trade was economically feasible. These were the South End's three venerable first-class theaters—the Columbia, the Castle Square, and the Grand Opera House—which started showing movies to fill in the days when they weren't presenting live melodrama and variety acts, and ended by switching over to movies altogether. All three theaters demonstrated that it was possible to cater to ethnic, working-class clienteles and maintain a successful business. The Columbia, for instance, at 978 Washington Street, the South End's largest and most elaborate melodrama house in 1895, was alternating between movies and vaudeville shows ten years later, and worked on the Irish family trade by featuring ethnic acts and Irish songs between films. The Castle Square, home of the South End's single opera company in the 1890s, became a movie house in 1907, but continued with Yiddish plays in the summer for the growing Jewish community along the Pleasant Street neighborhood and North Roxbury.

15. The notable exception to this rule was the Idle Hour at Castle Square. For blacks living in the Kirkland Street neighborhood, the Idle Hour was virtually the only theater in town that permitted an integrated audience on the main floor. In fall 1910, a group of local black businessmen bought the theater outright and operated it (renamed the Pekin) for a year before it went out of business.

The Automatic One Cent Vaudeville, photographed in 1909 at 48 East 14th Street, near Union Square, the heart of New York's early movie district. This was one of some four hundred nickelodeons in the city after 1905. The peep shows were one cent, but not the projected movies in the rear of the arcade.

The Stuart (originally the Unique), at 700 Washington Street—the single Boston nickelodeon to survive as a movie house

These were precisely the paths the new theater operators chose not to
follow. The new movie theaters were determined to crash the new neighborhoods and stay out of the old ones.

Their horizons were sharply limited: the choleric opposition to the
garish common shows prevented them from entering the suburbs, nor
could managers obtain licenses to build in the wealthy Back Bay area or
along Boylston Street. The exclusive Back Bay shopping thoroughfares on
Newbury Street or Huntington Avenue were also off-limits. But even so,
the most aggressive movie managers were pushing in these directions too,
and by the beginning of World War I, even these cultural havens gave in
to the onslaught of the dread Philistines.[16]

16. Theater addresses are found in the Boston *City Directory,* 1910; for remarks on the
nickelodeons, I have depended on the New England and Boston correspondent's report to
MPW which began October 1, 1910, and continued more or less weekly throughout 1910 and
1911. See also Frederic E. Hayes, "Amusements," in *The City Wilderness,* ed. Robert A.
Woods (Boston, 1899), for South End theaters. Donald C. King, "From Museum to Multi-
Cinema," *Marquee* 6 (Third Quarter 1974): 5-22, provides a useful, lavishly illustrated
history of Boston theaters from 1794 to the present.

The pattern was similar in New York City, Chicago, Philadelphia, and St. Louis.[17] Exhibitors and producers anxious to cover their investment made no major effort to advance the industry through the working class itself. Few if any films stressed ethnic ties, few chronicled adventures of immigrants—their arrival in the New World, life in tenements, or, until D. W. Griffith appeared, working conditions in shops or factories.[18] No one with prominent ethnic features was permitted in leading roles; the American blue-eyed, brown-haired beauty was required, whether playing an Italian street singer, a Sioux Indian maiden, a Spanish duenna, or a Gibson Girl. In the midst of a strange new audience, the industry clung to the vestiges of the safe old theatrical patterns.

The old world, in this case, meant the vaudeville theater. Vaudeville, decaying since 1900 in the wake of the nickelodeon's popularity, had in effect provided the unwilling model of exhibition for the energetic new rival. Just as, five years later, movie exhibitors would use the legitimate theater as a guide to learn how to exhibit feature films, so, in 1908, nickelodeon owners preyed on vaudeville houses for methods of exhibiting movie shorts. We have already seen one example of this: the nickelodeon locations we have described were determined less by proximity to their clientele than by proximity to the beaten path of vaudeville houses. Many nickelodeons were in fact converted vaudeville houses; others were built next door to them. When managers decided on mixing their short films with an illustrated song, a guest lecture, and variety acts, they were merely plotting variations of the vaudeville routine. Vaudeville's continuous performances and gingerbread architecture were also readily adapted to the new shows. Most important, when exhibitors imagined the ideal audience, they usually thought of the vaudeville audience—a cross section of urban and suburban American life. They preferred this old audience to the new,

17. For a description of New York nickelodeon locales, see Russell Merritt, "The Impact of D. W. Griffith's Moving Pictures from 1908 to 1914 on Contemporary American Culture" (Ph.D. diss., Harvard University, 1970), pp. 106-8. Contemporary accounts of nickelodeons in Philadelphia and Chicago may be found in the pages of *MPW*. Although no systematic, updated study of these theaters has yet been made, provocative essays on individual theaters and surveys of city theater history may be found in the pages of *Marquee*, the journal of the Theatre Historical Society.

18. For example, a detailed search through *MPW* film synopses published from March 9, 1907, the magazine's inaugural issue, through December 1908 revealed that of 1,056 American-produced films reviewed, a total of eight films specifically concerned the immigrant or the poor: *The Life of a Bootblack* (Essanay, 1907); *Smuggling Chinese into the U.S.A.* (Goodfellow, 1908); *The Eviction* (Selig, 1908); *The Little Match Girl* (Goodfellow, 1908); *The Rag-Picker's Christmas* (Goodfellow, 1908); *New Way to Pay Old Debts* (Lubin, 1908); *Old Isaacs, the Pawnbroker* (Biograph, 1908); and *A Mother's Crime* (Vitagraph, 1908). The two largest French companies—Pathé-Frères and Gaumont—contributed another seven films on the subject.

unfashionable audience that had discovered them. To follow the guidelines set up by vaudeville houses became the path of least resistance.

Luring the Family Trade

The problem was how to lure that affluent family trade, so near and yet
so far. The answer, at times conscious but more frequently a matter of
convenience, was through the New American Woman and her children. If
few professional men would as yet, by 1908, consider taking their families
to the nickelodeon, the woman on a shopping break, or children out from
school, provided the ideal life line to the affluent bourgeoisie. Statistically,
women and children numbered only 30 per cent of the New York
audience, even less than that during performances after 8 P.M., but they
commanded the special attention of both the industry and its censors. In a
trade hungry for respectability, the middle-class woman was respectability
incarnate. Her very presence in the theater refuted the vituperative accusations lodged against the common show's corrupting vulgarity.[19]
Theaters spared few efforts to woo her. Soon after Boston's Theatre
Premier established the policy of giving free admission tickets to women
for prenoon shows, the Olympic reacted by charging women and children
half fare at all screenings, and thereby set the precedent that virtually all
the major Boston nickelodeons adopted. By the end of 1910, women and
children were charged half fare in all of Philadelphia's nickelodeons while,
with growing frequency, exhibitors' complaints about the movies took the
form of gallant defense of the female's tender sensibilities.[20]
Women were no less venerated in the nickelodeon movies themselves.
Original screenplays in particular reveal a preoccupation with women's
stories. Female protagonists far outnumber males, dauntless whether
combatting New York gangsters, savage Indians, oversized mashers, or
"the other woman." In the best genteel tradition, audiences were spared
scenes of debauchery and criminal acts; the outdated moral code of the
Victorian era that required vice to be punished and virtue rewarded
became an inflexible law throughout this period. "Saloons and other
places of evil repute should not be shown or else shown so briefly [as] to
carry small effect," warned an early screenwriter's manual. "Keep away
from the atmosphere of crime and debauchery and avoid as much as
possible the showing of fights, burglaries, or any other infraction of the
laws. The juvenile mind is receptive and observant. . . . If you write clean

19. For the attendance of women and children, see Committee on Education, *Hearings,*
pp. 121-22. For more information on children's attendance, see *Survey* 35 (May 9, 1914).
20. Price reduction reported in *MPW,* January 21, 1911, p. 146, and March 4, 1911,
p. 728. For Philadelphia statistic, *MPW,* June 3, 1911, p. 1245.

and decent stories, you do not have to bother about the Board of Censorship. If you want to revel in crime and bloodshed you must be careful to keep the actions of your character within the unwritten law."[21]

The pressure to keep movies "popular" was thus offset by pressure to keep them "respectable." Film producers drew heavily on the literary lions—Zola, Daudet, Poe, Tolstoi, Dumas, Hugo, Twain, De Maupassant, and Shakespeare—for film "classics." At times, the tension between the two conflicting impulses yielded bizarre results. When in 1910 Vitagraph filmed Sophocles' *Elektra* in one reel, exhibitors were told to "BILL IT LIKE A CIRCUS—IT WILL DRAW BIGGER CROWDS THAN ANY FILM YOU HAVE EVER HAD."[22] In Louis B. Mayer's Orpheum, Pathé's *Passion Play*, "the life of Christ from the Annunciation to the Ascension in twenty-seven beautiful scenes," was followed the next week by *Bluebeard, the Man with Many Wives*. Both were successful.[23]

But the more sophisticated and plausible lures came from the new blood drifting into the film production studios. Although he came from a family and circumstances profoundly different from those of the theater manager, the early director and writer of dramatic films had aspirations of his own that also worked to attract the white-collar worker to the movies. Griffith's own perspective—and in this regard he is typical of such film directors as Sidney Olcott, Allan Dwan, and Frank Powell—was one of a bourgeois, native-born theater man, proud of his old American stock, comfortably living on a family income ranging from $800 to $1,000 per month when the national average was under $600 per year.[24] Film makers told the stories they knew best, and inevitably, as they became articulate, their films revealed their own middle-class background. Their perpetual quest for acceptance among their own kind provided special pressure to return to figures and motives approved by the guardians of popular culture.

For better or for worse, the five-cent movie, like the theater that housed it, was effectively dropping out of the hands of its original audience. For the immigrant, movies were becoming more and more part of his assimilation into American life. Moviemakers, like the nickelodeon operators, were out to satisfy the broader, more demanding audience of their peers.

By Fall 1913, the concerted effort had finally begun to pay dividends. As the comfortless thrills of watching movies on wooden chairs gave way to deluxe motion picture theaters and as movies lengthened from one to four

21. Epes W. Sargent, *Technique of the Photoplay* (New York, 1913), pp. 133-34.

22. Quoted in Wagenknecht, *The Movies*, p. 64.

23. Bosley Crowther, *Hollywood Rajah: The Life and Times of Louis B. Mayer* (New York, 1960), pp. 30-31.

24. Linda Arvidson, *When the Movies Were Young* (New York, 1925), p. 134. By 1910, Griffith's royalty checks averaged $900 and $1,000 per month.

reels, the movie clientele imperceptibly began to change. Journalists wrote continually—and critically—about the "new public" and the "quicker-minded audience" that had discovered the movies and forsaken the theater and library. Residential neighborhoods, militant in their resistance to nickelodeons in 1908, gradually softened to the pressure of aggressive entrepreneurs and permitted construction of nickelodeons on their main streets. The climax came in June 1914, when a ten-reel version of Giovanni Pastrone's *Cabiria* was shown at the White House to President Wilson, his family, and members of the cabinet. The President of the United States had gone to see a movie. Who could hope to hold out after that?

The movies did not lose the immigrant and blue-collar worker, but as new theaters invaded the suburbs and movies were shown in legitimate houses, the social stigma attached to the nickelodeon all but vanished. The most reliable estimates suggest that, in sheer numbers, movie attendance practically doubled during the nickelodeon era, increasing from twenty-six million persons per week in 1908 to at least forty-nine million in 1914.[25] Although women and children were still the most discussed groups of patrons, adult males statistically outnumbered both groups combined; Frederic C. Howe estimated that 75 percent of the national movie audience was adult male.[26] Make-up and size of audiences must have differed considerably from matinee to evening and from weekend to weekday (on Saturday afternoons, it was commonly conceded, school children reigned supreme in movie theaters everywhere). But among contemporary commentators, no one has been found to contradict the prevailing sentiment that movies were attracting "the better crowd." About the new audience, Walter P. Eaton in *The Atlantic* wrote:

You cannot, of course, draw any hard and fast line which will not be crossed at many points. In Atlanta, Georgia, for example, you may often see automobiles parked two deep along the curb in front of the motion picture theatre, which hardly suggests an exclusively proletarian patronage.[27]

In *The Outlook* Howe wrote:

There is scarcely a village that has not one or more motion picture houses. . . . Men now take their wives and families for an evening at the movies where formerly they went alone to the nearby saloon.[28]

25. Frederic C. Howe, "What To Do with the Motion-Picture Show: Shall It Be Censored?" *The Outlook* 100 (June 20, 1914): 412; Committee on Education, *Hearings,* p. 65; "Moving Pictures and the National Character," *Review of Reviews* 13 (September 1910): 315-20.

26. Howe, "What To Do with the Motion-Picture Show," p. 413.

27. Walter P. Eaton, "Class-Consciousness and the 'Movies,'" *The Atlantic Monthly* 115 (January 1915): 49-50.

28. Howe, "What To Do with the Motion-Picture Show," p. 413.

Boston's New Theaters

This new clientele had not arrived by chance. That it was aggressively wooed by movie entrepreneurs eager to break existent social barriers may be seen by the rapidly shifting patterns of prewar movie exhibition. The Boston theater district, which in 1910 was restricted to two downtown thoroughfares, gained considerable new ground by the outbreak of World War I. New movie theaters opened in virtually every major residential neighborhood surrounding the city. By the end of 1913, Dorchester, Roxbury, Cambridge, Sommerville, Newton, Belmont, and Watertown had all succumbed to the rising movie fever and had permitted construction of motion picture theaters on their main streets. *Moving Picture World* treated the steady flow of news reports like dispatches from advancing front lines. "For the first time in the history of the town," it reported on December 14, 1913, "the selectmen of Brookline, Mass., have decided to grant a license for a photoplay show." Several months earlier, the same correspondent reported victory in Brighton; a nickelodeon would finally open in that wealthy suburb after three years of opposition by Mayor John F. Fitzgerald. Most remarkable of all, in Boston's exclusive Back Bay community, the city's wealthiest residential district and its cultural hub, no less than three movie houses opened during the same year. The Back Bay had been kept intact through January 1913, but within eighteen months, moviegoers were watching features at the First Spiritual Temple, which the wealthy socialite Mrs. M. S. Ayer and her friends had converted into the Exeter Street Theatre; at the St. James, one block down from Boston's Symphony Hall; and at the Potter Hall, an opera house converted to movies after its 1910 opera season had failed.[29]

Meanwhile, Boston's downtown nickelodeon district, still stretched out along Washington Street and Tremont Street, grew in another direction—skyward. The movie cathedral was still several years away, but the trend toward bigger, more elaborate theaters was unmistakable to anyone reading the frequent theater reports made to the press. The Beacon, adorned with a gigantic spinning globe over the entrance that sparkled in the dark, opened its brass doors with *The Fall of Troy* on February 19, 1910, to a full house of eight hundred persons. Four years later, the same corporation built the Modern, a Gothic marvel with over one thousand seats, flying buttresses, and a door made to look like a cathedral portal. Nathan Gordon's Scollay Square Olympia opted for Florentine Eclectic. Passing under a golden statue of Victory, arms

29. Henry Archer, *MPW*'s New England correspondent, made steady reports on these new residential theaters throughout 1913 and 1914. See particularly his reports in issues dated March 14, 1914; May 2, 1914; May 16, 1914; and May 30, 1914.

rampant and belly protruding with a luminous clock, the Olympia's customer entered a vestibule decorated with Florentine murals, a ceramic tile floor, and a ticket booth resembling a Renaissance confessional. The theater claimed a seating capacity of eleven hundred, one of the largest in the city, but its special pride were the blue, gray, and gold draperies that hung from the boxes, balcony, and gallery railings, monogrammed with the letter O.[30] Not to be outdone, two Washington Street nickelodeons— the Joliette and the Park—drastically enlarged and refurbished their interiors with grandiose displays of their own.[31]

These enlarged theaters stiffened the downtown competition, but the most fearsome and far-reaching threat came from another quarter, originally indifferent to the ten-cent movies, reluctant to exhibit them, but willing to make the move when nickelodeon competition made it necessary. Driven out of the stage business by movies, several legitimate theaters had begun to show their own two- and three-reelers, and in so doing, they had diverted a considerable percentage of the audience the nickelodeons had sought for themselves. "The public," admitted a trade journalist ruefully, "evidently likes to go to a regular theatre which is playing moving pictures and vaudeville in preference to the regular photoplay theatres, even if the shows given are not better. Everyone knows that the Globe is a 'lemon' as a straight dramatic house, but reports go to state that it knocked out nearly $1,000 per week clear profit when showing the cinematographs last summer."[32]

In increasing numbers, audiences discovered that they could watch movies without going to the nickelodeon. By the end of 1913, the National, Park, and Potter Hall theaters had abandoned legitimate drama altogether in favor of two- and three-reelers, while the Tremont, the Shubert, the Cort, and Opera House included occasional feature films in their regular theatrical season. The climax came on November 23, 1914, when B. F. Keith announced that the Boston, the city's oldest, largest, and most prestigious playhouse, would henceforth become a full-time movie theater. The gala premiere, by invitation only, featured William Farnum and Tom Santschi in *The Spoilers*. Even Senator Henry Cabot Lodge was there.[33]

Altogether, the number of Boston movie theaters increased more than 30 percent during the nickelodeon years, growing from thirty-one theaters in January 1907 to forty-one theaters in January 1914. In practically every case, the new theaters, with their enlarged seating capacities and more

30. *MPW*, November 26, 1910; January 17, 1914; July 25, 1914; *Boston Globe*, April 2, 1914; July 1, 1914.
31. *MPW*, June 20, 1914; December 5, 1914; *Boston Globe*, December 3, 1914.
32. *MPW*, December 17, 1910.
33. *MPW*, December 5, 1914; *Boston Evening Transcript*, November 24, 1914.

ornate decoration, were started in more prosperous and more exclusive business areas than those of their predecessors. No instance has been found of a Boston movie theater opening between 1910 and 1914 in an area that could be described as a working-class community—Castle Square, the North End, the South End, or North Roxbury. The seduction of the affluent was taking place in thoroughfares closer to home.

Prestigious trappings for movies were nothing new. For the well-to-do, private screenings at society balls were chic novelties since the 1897 Paris Charity Bazaar which caught fire and caused the famous scandal; when Nora Saltonstall threw her annual gala at Boston's Copley Plaza Hotel, the *Globe* called the five reels of silent comedies a diverting but familiar social entertainment. Schools, charity balls, churches, and civic clubs projected movies eagerly supplied by exchange men anxious to launder the nickelodeon's shabby reputation. But, of course, this was not moviegoing in its customary sense. Society and the movie operator agreed that these were special activities, exceptional performances that created good will without interfering with the day-to-day commercial enterprise or compromising social position.

Legitimate theaters, by contrast, were seen as places where the affluent could watch movies on a regular basis, unembarrassed, at full fare. When such theaters began screening movies, they were immediately recognized as an enemy force which Boston's most important nickelodeon owners were eager to join. Marcus Loew, B. F. Keith, Nathan Gordon, and Mark Mitchell, by 1914 Boston's four most important nickelodeon owners, started systematic raids on legitimate theaters in order to bring them into their movie chains. At the same time, smaller operators who could not afford to purchase or lease legitimate theaters revamped their nickelodeons to resemble "first-class" houses in both appearance and format. Owners went out of their way to recruit managers with background in legitimate theater management, and modified the old format borrowed from vaudeville to give their shows the new look of the legitimate stage.

One important consequence of this invasion was that a social hierarchy, nonexistent among movie theaters in 1910, was rapidly developed by World War I. Patron and exhibitor alike began to rank theaters according to size and quality, discriminating between first-class theaters and the nickelodeon. The most expensive theaters worked conscientiously to disassociate themselves from the cheap theaters even as they encouraged comparisons with legitimate playhouses, while the public quickly adopted a double standard in regard to movie houses whereby films permitted in one kind of theater were not allowed in the other. When, for instance, the five-year-old National Board of Censorship was described by its chairman, Frederic C. Howe, in 1914, its jurisdiction was limited to five- and ten-cent theaters, enabling the dollar theaters to play films—like the white slavery cycle and sex education shorts—that the NBC prohibited from nickelodeons.[34] First-class theaters gained other trade advantages too, notably first-run, exclusive engagements in exchange for higher rental fees, that helped single them out from second-run, cheaper theaters which, if they played the same films, played them weeks later, frequently opposite other second-run theaters showing the same bill.

The Nickelodeon's Demise

When, during the war years, production companies of the Motion Picture Patents Company collapsed, they took the nickelodeon down with them. Frozen out by the new independent production companies who regarded one-reelers as outmoded, nickelodeons either enlarged, changed format, or died. As early as 1914, trade journals spoke of the five-cent theater as an endangered species. "We cannot close our eyes to the fact," wrote Stephen Bush, "that theatres with small capacity using mostly single reels are going out of business all around us."[35] Salvage efforts took many forms, but the most important operators saw the handwriting on the wall. Not until 1928, with the coming of sound, would there be another such massive effort to renovate, build, and dump movie houses as occurred in 1913 and 1914.

But, by then, the job of building an audience for the movies was about finished. Without feature films and refined theaters, it is unlikely that the middle-class audience would have long remained. But the nickelodeon and its one- and two-reelers had in fact performed the initial task generally credited to imported features, movie palaces, and World War I. Mostly, it was the work of immigrants who would go on to control production as they had exhibition. As film manufacturers their names—Zukor, Loew, Laemmle, Fox, Mayer, the Warners—would become nearly as famous as the stars they promoted. But even as anonymous nickelodeon operators they moved the industry in the direction that would remain unchanged for another generation.

34. Howe, "What To Do with the Motion-Picture Show," p. 414.
35. W. Stephen Bush, "The Single Reel: II," *MPW,* July 4, 1914, p. 36.

Portrait of a Pioneering Studio

The Vitagraph Company of America

Of all the early studios, the Vitagraph Company of America was the most successful and most enduring, playing a conspicuous role in the industry from the company's founding in 1900 until 1925, when it was acquired by Warner Brothers.

The origins of Vitagraph, like those of American Mutoscope, were inspired by Edison's Kinetoscope. When two young Englishmen, Albert E. Smith and J. Stuart Blackton, saw their first Kinetoscope demonstration in a New York parlor in 1895, they were partners in a floundering vaudeville team called the International Novelty Company. Smith performed sleight-of-hand tricks and Blackton drew cartoons on an easel. This act wasn't exactly wowing audiences anywhere, and the two saw in the peephole machines the potential to bolster their anemic routines. The trick, of course, was to develop a means of projecting the image onto a screen. Smith, who was mechanically inclined, set about this task of invention and, by 1896, had developed a workable projection device that he called the Vitagraph.

Smith's machine contained a framing aperture that could be adjusted while the machine was in operation to correct the alignment of the film—a neat device that would be copied on most subsequent projectors. In 1898, he improved the Vitagraph by adding a device to eliminate screen flicker. With fairly good alignment and no flicker, the resourceful Smith had removed two serious projection flaws that exasperated early audiences and inventors alike.

According to Smith, the Vitagraph made its debut at Tony Pastor's New

Fourteenth Street Theatre in New York on March 23, 1896.[1] Their contract with Pastor called for two new films each week, which they selected from Kinetoscope subjects. It soon became apparent, however, that there were too few Kinetoscope subjects to fill the bill, and so Smith and Blackton decided to make their own pictures. Returning to the drawing board, Smith set out to construct a camera, a task that he accomplished within four weeks. His camera was based on the principles of Edison's, but it was much smaller.[2]

The next problem was finding a studio. For ten dollars a month they rented a one-room office on the top floor of the Morse Building at 140 Nassau Street, New York. The office was conveniently located just below the otherwise unused roof of the building, which is where they shot their first picture, not surprisingly entitled *The Burglar on the Roof;* Blackton starred as the burglar, and Smith operated the camera.

Smith and Blackton got by largely on ingenuity and hard work during the early years, capitalizing on military events such as the sinking of the American battleship *Maine* in Havana Harbor, Teddy Roosevelt's assault on San Juan Hill, the Battle of Santiago Bay, and the British-Boer War. When Smith couldn't get to the action for real news films, the two simply faked them on the studio roof.

William T. Rock, a fifty-year-old former motion picture showman from Louisiana, joined the Smith-Blackton team in 1899 as its business manager. The next year, each of the three put up $2,000 to capitalize the Vitagraph Company of America. Rock was named president, a position he held until his death in 1916.

At the company's birth, the activities of its principals were still not very strongly directed. Smith and Blackton were still performing their acts in Lyceum bureaus, although their chief source of revenue was in putting together film projection packages for vaudeville houses. For a fee of fifty to seventy-five dollars a week, they would furnish a projector, a man to operate it, a screen, and film. After 1900, however, they decided to devote their full efforts to the production of motion pictures. Vaudeville's loss, although slight, was the film industry's gain.

They moved their studio to 116 Nassau Street, a building that offered a more spacious roof. There they built their first stage. By 1903, they outgrew even these larger quarters and moved to the "wilds of Flatbush," where they constructed the first of several glass-topped studios. It was at this point that Vitagraph lost all traces of amateurism, systematized its

1. Albert E. Smith and Phil A. Koury, *Two Reels and a Crank* (Garden City, N.Y., 1952), p. 38.
2. Ibid., p. 40.

production activities, and became a major force in the industry. No longer did Blackton and Smith act in and direct their own films. No longer were secretaries and family members pressed into unrehearsed performances before the cameras. Smith and Blackton became producers, hiring directors, actors, property men, and other professionals to perform specialized functions in a professional manner. By 1908, Vitagraph was producing eight films a week, mostly one- and two-reelers cast from the studio's stock company of four hundred players.

Among the many Vitagraph stars in its twenty-five-year history were Florence Turner, Rudolph Valentino, Anita Stewart, John Bunny, Corrine Griffith, Clara Kimball Young, and Maurice Costello. But the most illustrious was the glamorous and immensely popular Norma Talmadge, who first found success in the 1911 production of *A Tale of Two Cities*. By 1915, when she left Vitagraph for First National, she had appeared in more than 250 productions for Smith, Blackton, and Rock. In the following story, Norma Talmadge reminisces about the way things were done at Vitagraph during her brief but prolific stay there.

5

NORMA TALMADGE

Close-Ups

At the age of fourteen, my brown curls reaching almost to my waistline, my skirts just touching my knees, and my ambition soaring to the skies, I first faced a camera professionally. Not a motion-picture camera, however, but the kind that was used for taking colored slides. It was in the days when every five-and-ten-cent motion-picture theater presented, as a part of its regular program, popular sentimental ballads bawled by attenuated tenors to the accompaniment of a tin piano, and illustrated by hectic lovers down by the old mill stream under the greenest trees and bluest skies ever invented by a paintbrush.

We were very poor. My mother was busy from morning until night with household duties—cleaning, cooking, and keeping the rather worn clothes of three growing girls from looking too shabby. My father was traveling on the road selling advertising. Natalie and Constance were attending Public School Number 92 in Brooklyn, and I was struggling with algebra and French in my first year at Erasmus Hall High School.

Every penny had to be counted, and being the oldest of three sisters I had to help out the family.

At the same time Peg and Fred—we have always called our mother and father by their Christian names, and even my granddad was just plain John to us; not from any irreverence, of course, but because our family attitude has ever been one of equality, like a jolly group of sisters and

Saturday Evening Post 199 (March 12, 1927): 6-7+.

Norma Talmadge, 1913

brothers, or perhaps "friends" would be the better word—wanted me to have an education, so they hit upon my posing for advertisements and song slides in the afternoons and Saturday mornings as a means of earning a little money in a way that would not tax my strength.

One Hundred Pictures My First Week

I shall never forget that first interview with the slide photographers. They agreed to pay me three dollars each. I thought that meant three shiny greenbacks for each slide and, as I made about one hundred pictures my first week, proudly figured that I had earned three hundred dollars. Imagine my feelings when the man handed me a check for nine dollars and I learned that it meant three dollars for each song—not each slide! However, when one is fourteen and a trifle threadbare at the elbows, to say nothing of cardboard in the bottoms of one's shoes where soles are wearing thin, a dollar in the hand is worth two in the bank. So I was glad to continue at the same rate as often as they could use me.

One day quite recently I was swapping beginnings with Irving Berlin. He was telling me of his early days in the Lower East Side in New York as a singing waiter and a drugstore clerk, and I was describing my start posing for hat-and-coat advertisements and song slides. I hummed a bit of the lyric of the very first song I illustrated:

"Take me out upon that ocean called the lovable sea;
  Fry each kiss in honey and present them to me;

"Cuddle and kiss your baby,
  Anchor right at Cupid's door—
  Oh, honey, stop, stop, stop, stop,
  Don't you dare to stop——
  Come over and love me some more."

Irving added another emphatic "Stop!" Then he laughed and said, "Have a heart. I wrote that song!"

That slide work taught me something. I learned the value of expression and acquired a certain poise. Peg fairly haunted all the neighborhood makeshift theaters in Brooklyn, trying to find out where the songs for which I posed were being sung, and in this way we acquired the habit of going to the movies as frequently as possible.

Out of my meager earnings I used to treat the entire family. We would sit in a nickelodeon watching the continuous performance over and over, until one of the two ushers, or rather bouncers, as they did not have regular ushers then, would request us, none too politely, to leave and make room for newcomers. How well I remember those first five-and-ten-cent cinema theaters which were one day to develop into picture palaces. They were generally converted from stores—a long, narrow room with one aisle down the center and rows of wooden folding chairs, often rented from funeral parlors, on either side. They always reminded me of a train.

Florence Turner was my idol. I never missed a single picture in which she appeared and I would rather have touched the hem of her skirt than to have shaken hands with Saint Peter. Leaning forward in my hard chair, I was as much a part of Florence Turner as was her own reflection on the silver sheet. I laughed when she laughed, suffered when she suffered, wept when she wept. A veritable orgy of emotions for five copper pennies!

With all the pathetic ego of fourteen summers, I not only longed to express myself, but was thoroughly convinced that if only given the chance I, too, could become a great screen actress. It never occurred to me that one had to have a camera face to begin with, and as for technique—I didn't know how to spell it. But, though I knew nothing of the difficulties, I knew what I wanted, and I really believe if we want a thing badly enough and sincerely enough to go after it, the odds are four to one that it will meet us halfway. I have always remembered what Emerson says in one of his essays—I think it is the one on Friendship: "Be careful what you set your heart on, for it will surely be yours." Anyhow, I set my heart on moving pictures in preference to still pictures or song slides.

One day Peg herself suggested taking me to the Vitagraph Studios. We sat on the front porch of our old-fashioned house in Fenimore Street. It was twilight.

"Norma," Peg began, "is it true that you cut school again today?"

Cutting School to Play Theater

I am afraid I was not exactly the soul of honor as a child. I had no scruples against playing hookey, and I lied to my teachers without a blush, but it was no use lying to Peg. She is the kind who always leaps one jump ahead of you, and no one ever gets away with anything where Peg is concerned. I made a feeble explanation, but admitted my absence. I was in the habit of going to Prospect Park about once a week with a group of other truants, and when we had hidden our books in the bushes we played theater, with a lovely green knoll as our outdoor stage.

"Since you show no interest in your studies," Peg said, "and the higher your education the lower your marks, it seems to me there is not much point in our skimping and saving to keep you in school. One thing is clear to me—you will never make a teacher; so you may just as well give up high school altogether and learn to support yourself now. You have to decide upon some means of making your own living sooner or later. Have you any ideas? What would you like to do?"

Of course I didn't dare tell Peg that I longed to become a screen actress. I never dreamed that she would approve, but Peg liked the movies as well as any of us. She sat thinking silently for a few minutes; then, as I had not replied, she made a suggestion that sent me into ecstasies.

"How would you like to take up moving pictures?"

"Better than anything in the world, but how could I get a start?"

"The usual beginning for anything is to try," was Peg's laconic and characteristic response.

The very next day we boarded the Brooklyn Rapid Transit Elevated train for the Vitagraph Studio, which was on Elm Street in the very wilds of Flatbush about three miles from our house.

It was not particularly difficult to get into the studio. No letter of introduction was necessary; no photographs were required if one applied for day-to-day work; no snippy office boy glared at one for daring to come without an appointment. The canned drama of the first ten years of the twentieth century was considered too lowly and despicable a means of livelihood to attract the streams of ambitious seekers for celluloid fame and fortune which swell the population of present-day Hollywood.

The motion-picture player was looked upon almost as an illegitimate child in the profession. Consequently it was rather difficult for Vitagraph, Biograph, and other early companies to interest experienced players, and any chance comer who had fairly regular features and the courage to apply was at least interviewed, if not engaged. But all the extra people necessary had already been engaged that first day Peg and I applied, and Harry Mayo, the casting director, told us to come back another time. Before departing, however, I was duly registered—my age, height, weight, coloring, and so on, itemized on a filing card. In the space allotted for "experience" I wrote: "The leading character in many tableaux and school plays. Also have posed for song slides." We were told that they would send for us when needed, and the next day I returned to Erasmus, crushed and disappointed.

The First Lesson

The promised telephone call never came. One morning about a week later Peg decided that we had to have some new sheets and pillowcases and, as a department store was advertising a special one-day "White Sale," told me to take a day off from school and go shopping. I was to have a quarter for myself for doing a number of errands, and as my adolescent ruling passions were cinemas and sodas, planned to treat myself royally. But on second thought it occurred to me that it would be a lark to use the money for car fare to the Vitagraph, and without saying anything to Peg try again for a job on my way back from the department store. I confided in Baby, as we always called Constance when she was little, and took her with me.

I was under the impression that the reason they had not sent for me at the studio after the day I registered was because they thought me too young. So this time I borrowed a russet-colored grown-up dress and an enormous picture hat with huge red roses growing upside down over the left ear. By converting my curls into two long braids and winding them around my head under the flopping leghorn, I thought I looked quite a woman of the world. Then, growing bolder with my change of character, came a change in my plans. I would go to the studio first and attend to Peg's shopping afterward.

Approaching confidently, secure in my borrowed finery, and holding Baby by the hand, we encountered Mr. Sam Spedon, a gaunt, thin, energetic man with keen, deep-set eyes, nicknamed around the Vitagraph "the human skeleton," who looked up from his desk. Mr. Spedon had charge of the publicity department, assisted Harry Mayo with the casting, helped find stories, and was a sort of office manager. Everyone had three or four different jobs in those days.

"What can you do?" he inquired.

"I have posed for song slides, and I can recite."

"That last will help a lot," he snapped, and my heart sank to my first high-heeled shoes—borrowed shoes, at that.

Just then Mrs. Breuill, who had to do with stories, stopped to confer with Mr. Spedon, and as I waited speechlessly, she gave me a friendly nod. But I soon felt, by her amused smile, that all was not well with my borrowed clothes. While nervously adjusting the flower-laden leghorn one of my braids came tumbling down. In the midst of my mortification Mrs. Breuill removed my hat and unpinned the other braid. "There, how much better! Now you look like a human being and we can probably use you. . . . Lovely eyes," she said in an aside to Mr. Spedon.

So ended my first sophisticated rôle and so began my first lesson in being myself. Later I was to learn that being natural is the very first step toward being an actress, although that would have seemed to me a paradox my first day, had I known what a paradox meant.

Alice in Cameraland

"You may both stay today," Mrs. Breuill invited, and as soon as I could find my tongue I asked permission to telephone my mother. When Peg heard that if I didn't have to go shopping I had landed a job, needless to say the silver sheet won out over the cotton ones. She was almost as excited as were Constance and I.

Mrs. Breuill led Baby and me to the set. Constance was too young and nonchalant to be particularly thrilled, but I was trembling with excitement. Four or five different companies were working at the same time—men were flitting about in swallow-tailed evening dress, doublet and hose, or armor. Women were dragging dusty trains across the painted canvas floors. Strange people were hurrying back and forth shouting incoherent commands. Scattered here and there on desultory chairs were odd-looking persons with and without makeup. Somewhere near by a machine gave forth a curious clicking sound. It was the camera.

Clutching Baby tightly by the hand, I darted forward as someone on the sidelines yelled: "Keep moving! Keep moving!" But the order was not meant for us. It was addressed to the players in the scene, who had to keep continually passing to and fro in a small space chalked on the floor in order not to be out of the picture. A carpenter in blue overalls jerked us back. "Be careful. They're gonna shoot!" We covered our ears expecting a deafening report, but soon learned that "shoot" meant "Ready! Start grinding the camera." The director of today simply says "Camera." Alice in Wonderland was not a patch on me that first day on a set. After watching a little while we were taken out on the lot and our first work in motion pictures soon began.

Our particular picture was *The Four-Footed Pest* and dealt with the adventures of a filly that was always getting people into hot water. My bit was to be kissing a young man, whose name I forget, on a street corner, under a black cloth that was thrown over a camera, until the horse came along and lifted the cloth with her teeth. Only the back of my head was revealed, with my arms around the youth's neck. Then we had to run away. That was a sad humiliation for me—to be in the movies at last and not show my face! When I told the family that night how the business was almost entirely with my arms and feet, Natalie, in true sisterly fashion, remarked, "Since you didn't have to use your head, old dear, you will probably be a great success." But to me there was very little joke attached to that initial appearance. I was in constant terror every time we rehearsed, lest the horse, when lifting the focusing cloth between her teeth, might take my hair along with it and do a scalping act that was not in the scenario.

When Everybody Worked

We finished the whole picture in half a day! The great majority of pictures then were told in only one reel, consisting of a thousand feet, with nine hundred feet of story and titles, the remainder for winding, advertising trailer, and so on. Often little comedies were done in split reels, or five hundred feet. It was quite the usual routine to complete an entire production in from one to three days. Sometimes the story was written only the night before. How amusing this seems to me now, when we devote several weeks to mere cutting and titling, and in my own company, average from eight weeks to six months on a single production!

Constance played one of a group of little girls on the sidewalk who crowded around the camera to watch the antics of the horse. She wore her own clothes, but I was given a young girl's dress to replace my borrowed finery.

Florence Turner's mother had charge of the wardrobe department, which consisted of one long room with many poles stretched across, from which hung row after row of coats, dresses, and period gowns. Often a little group of players who were waiting around to be called would assist in the making or mending of costumes. They even helped paint the scenery, and, as personal maids were unheard-of, everybody took a turn at buttoning everybody else's clothes, assisted with each other's makeups, and dressed each other's hair.

Even Florence Turner, herself one of the most important players, lent a hand at everything. She had charge of the supers' salaries and doled out their money every evening. Also, she helped her mother with the wardrobe department.

Maurice Costello had caused the greatest upheaval at the Vitagraph by being the first actor to join the company with the express stipulation that he was never to wear a hammer in his belt and assist the carpenters, nor would he touch a paint brush.

He had come from the speaking stage, and informed A. E. Smith, one of the executives, that he was an actor, not a handy man. But even Costello dressed in a room with seven or eight others. As for me, that first day I dressed in a long room with a sort of wooden counter built against the wall as a dressing table, with a square mirror above it. We sat on stools, as at a lunch counter, and borrowed each other's powder and cold cream.

Harry Mayo, the casting man, had asked me if I knew how to make up.

"Yes, indeed," I answered, but as a matter of fact I knew nothing about it. I watched the girls on either side of me and copied everything they did with the most elaborate care. I might have spared myself all these pains had I known they were not going to use my face. It wasn't necessary for Baby to make up, as she was just a quick flash in the crowd. At the end of the day I received two dollars and fifty cents for my services and Constance was given two dollars. But more precious to me than any amount of money was the sweet smile from Miss Turner as she handed us our envelopes.

"When shall I come again?" I asked at the desk on my way out.

"When you're sent for," was the taciturn reply. "We have your address on file and will notify you by mail."

The next day Baby and I again returned to school, but I, for one, gained very little knowledge. Across the pages of my history book stepped brave knights in doublet and hose, and beautiful ladies in trailing gowns with diadems in their hair were gesticulating before a camera. During the English period the books we studied began to dramatize themselves in my mind as motion pictures. Algebra became utterly hateful because I could find no way of relating it to my brief acting experience. I had flunked in nearly all my classes because my mind was on one thing only. When would that letter come from the studio?

A week of watching and waiting for the postman went by. Every day I hurried home and dashed down the hall to the old-fashioned hat rack where Peg used to place the mail, but, alas, there was no envelope with Vitagraph Company in the upper left-hand corner.

A Daughter of the South

The second week passed and I was beginning to give up hope, when about the middle of the third week a loud whistle heralded a letter carrier, who, leaving his bicycle at the gate, trotted up the walk with a special-delivery letter in his hand. It bore the typewritten address:

>Miss Norma Talmadge
>Fenimore St.
>Brooklyn, N. Y.

My hand shook so with excitement that I could hardly open the letter, and even while I was enjoying the gorgeous thrill of suspense, Peg calmly snatched it from my fingers, and with unbelievably steady hands tore it open—as if a special delivery addressed to a fourteen-year-old girl were an everyday occurrence. All my hopes were realized, for it was a brief form letter to report for work at nine o'clock the following morning and ask for Mr. Charles Kent.

Peg accompanied me, and on arriving at the studio, imagine my joy when they told me I was to play in a Florence Turner picture! It was called *The Dixie Mother.*

Miss Turner was the Southern mother of seven sons and I was their little sister. The story told of the last call to arms, which meant that the youngest son, inclined to cowardice and afraid to go to war, must answer. In less than fifty feet the mother had to make the son, played by Carlyle

Blackwell, understand his duty to his country and march him off to join his father and brothers at the front.

Though no word was received concerning the older boys, yet news came that the youngest son had been killed, whereupon the mother, having forced her last boy to answer duty's call, became insane. Meantime there had been a love affair going on between me, a daughter of the South, and a Northern soldier, whose parents heartily disapproved. But my father, played by Charles Kent, who was also the director, arrived home on leave just in time absolutely to forbid my having any communication with a Northern family. Nevertheless, young love had its way and I eloped with the Northerner, returning to my family after the war with a child—symbolizing the union of the North and South—the child's appearance bringing about the recovery of the mother's sanity. As a grand finale the Union flag fluttered in the breeze. Never will I forget how inexpressibly thrilled I was when Miss Turner took me in her arms and hugged me close, sobbing out her forgiveness. Thus, I, who had longed to kneel at her feet, was actually in flesh-and-blood embrace with my idol.

This first picture is typical of how much story and action was crowded into nine hundred feet in 1910.

We rehearsed each scene over and over again, because footage was the all-important thing, and we had to know exactly where to stand, how many steps to take to the right, and on just what signal to start our business so as not to waste a scrap of film. We even made our entrances and exits on counts. There was a board placed exactly nine feet from the camera and a space chalk-marked on the floor about fifteen feet wide. Whether there were two or ten persons in a scene, all of them had to be within that radius of the camera; otherwise they were out of the picture entirely. The camera, of course, was stationary and only one camera was used. To have had different cameras at varied angles, such as we have today, would have been an expense unheard-of, and devices for moving the camera for long shots, medium shots, and three-foot close-ups had not yet been invented.

The Vitagraph Company did, however, have a camera with two lenses which ground two sets of pictures at slightly different angles, so that one negative could be sent abroad and the other used for the United States and Canada. Vitagraph was the only studio that had a double-lens camera, and this was considered a great step in advance of other companies.

Curiously enough, more prints were sent abroad than were circulated in America. If I remember correctly, one hundred twenty prints was the usual number struck off for international circulation. Of these about forty were retained for the States and Canada, while the remaining eighty found their way to foreign countries. It is interesting to note that Europe, although slower to turn out high-class pictures in mass production, was quicker than our own country to recognize the entertainment value of the cinema.

But to return to *The Dixie Mother*. After numerous rehearsals—we rehearsed much more then than we do now because we were allowed only a certain number of feet for each scene—we were assigned our individual places. On account of the action being so close to the camera, there was no necessity for the directors to have megaphones, as the voice carried easily.

Mr. Kent shouted, "Ready. Shoot!"

The Free-Lunch Days

This time I knew what "shoot" meant; nevertheless, as Miss Turner entered the set and I could hear the grinding and was given my signal, my feet refused to move. I stared into Miss Turner's famous soulful eyes and was so carried away with her performance that I stood glued to the floor. How incredible for poor, insignificant me to step into the hallowed chalked square with so great an actress! It seemed a bold intrusion. But all the time I hesitated film was revolving on the reel, and Charles Kent flew into a justified rage at my being the cause of several wasted feet. Someone behind pushed me unceremoniously forward. Before I knew it I was acting in earnest. When the scene was finished Miss Turner said a few kind words to me—a gracious act which is stamped indelibly on my memory.

Meantime Peg had been finding out how much salary I was to get, and though it didn't matter particularly to me, since to be in the enchanted atmosphere was all I cared about, yet five dollars for each day I worked, added to Fred's modest income, meant a great deal to her.

Much to the general rejoicing of the family, I worked in small parts every day for the next two weeks. Once a couple hundred people were needed for a big mob scene, and the casting director said to me:

"Bring your mother tomorrow and tell the kids to come over after school."

Everybody's mother and sisters, brothers, uncles, aunts, and cousins were pressed into service. The mothers of Florence Turner, Lillian Walker, and Anita Stewart, who was known as Anna then, often appeared in the same scenes with Peg. If they received a call, then were not used, they received fifty cents; if they were dressed and made up and it was then discovered that they were unnecessary that day, they received $1.50; but if they actually played they received $2.50, except on rare occasions when they might have had a bit of business for which they received $5.00.

Lunch was always included, and whether one carried a spear in the crowd or played Lady Macbeth, Juliet, or Rosalind—Shakespeare was

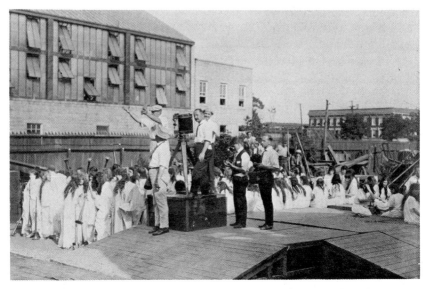

A choir of angels awaiting the call to the set. Vitagraph Studio, Brooklyn

much more popular on the screen at that time than he is now—everybody ate together, and all had the same menu: a big bowl of soup, bread and butter, choice of milk or coffee, and rice pudding, which was varied occasionally with apple pie or custard.

At the time I entered Vitagraph—November 1910—it occupied almost two city blocks, although it had started in 1900 with only a single shed about thirty by sixty feet. Some of the companies worked on the outside lot, or on location, mostly at a place called The Cedars, in Coney Island, where scenes laid everywhere from the Sahara Desert to the Canadian Rockies were made.

Other companies were operating indoors on stages Number One and Two. There were about ten directors—Bill Ranous, the first regular director Vitagraph ever had; Van Dyke Brooke, who was to prove the most important individual in my own career; Charles Kent, Larry Trimble, Bert Angeles, John Adolfi, Monsieur St. Louis, Monsieur Alberteri, Albert W. Hale, William Humphreys, Ralph Ince, and another, whose name escapes me.

There were about one hundred players in the stock company, and, with four or five exceptions, they all received pretty much the same salaries, ranging from twenty-five to thirty-five dollars a week, regardless of the relative importance or insignificance of their respective rôles. One day they would play bits and the next day they were cast as leads. Everybody reported at nine o'clock in the morning and the studio was run very much like a school, with William T. Rock, Albert E. Smith, and J. Stuart Blackton as the schoolmasters. The men's dressing rooms were all on one side and the women's on the other. Only Florence Turner was allowed the privilege of using Mr. Smith's office when she was tired. She was permitted to lie down on the couch between scenes, and to the rest of us that entrée into the sacred precincts of the executive office seemed the very height of stardom.

At first no names were used, even Florence Turner being known to the public only as "the Vitagraph Girl," just as Maurice Costello was known as "the man with the dimples," and Mary Pickford, at the Biograph Company, was referred to as "the girl with the curls." In the early publicity material designed by Sam Spedon only the names of the characters in the cast were used. The director, the names of the players, and that of the author were considered of no importance to the public. Speaking of the author, the very early Vitagraph pictures were all written by Bill Ranous, Florence Turner, Mr. Smith, and Mr. Blackton, although sometimes five dollars would be paid to an outsider for an idea.

Many members of the stock company added to their incomes by totally different work on the outside, as of course all the hundred or more on the payroll were seldom all playing at the same time. Hughie Mack, for example, a good comedian, who appeared in many of the old John Bunny pictures, was an undertaker on the side.

Albert E. Smith and J. Stuart Blackton were the only persons at Vitagraph who owned automobiles. Mr. Smith's car was a sporty little roadster and we used to gather around to watch him drive away in it. How well I remember one day when the machine absolutely refused to start, and a couple of the heavies were pressed into service to manipulate the crank. With a sudden turning over, the roadster leaped in the air and drove right through the studio wall and into J. Stuart Blackton's office. I had an awful crush on Mr. Smith in those days, chiefly, I think, because he wore silk shirts and had several sets of jeweled cuff links. Of course he never knew the secret passion I cherished for him, but now that he has retired from the picture game and has taken up ranching near Santa Barbara, we occasionally meet and always laugh about the way I used to gaze at his studs, tie pins, and cuff links. Little did I dream that the time would ever come when Mr. and Mrs. Smith would be interested in seeing my collection of jewels.

While I was still playing bits, in between scenes I used to wander about watching the work of the various members of the stock company, and in the evenings at home I would tell the stories to Peg, Nate, and Baby. We would have loads of fun dragging out all the junk in the garret from which to make costumes and props, and produced our own pictures in the dining room. I always insisted upon playing the lead, and Peg, bless her heart, was cast for the villain. Natalie, Constance, and our little friends in the neighborhood played the minor parts. While Natalie enjoyed these home performances, she was the only one who never showed any great enthusiasm for the screen. She was the most domestic member of the family and although she sometimes acted as an extra at the Vitagraph after school hours or on Saturday mornings, she did so only to earn a little money—not because her heart was in the work.

Early Worms

As for myself, I cannot remember a time when I was not keenly interested in any and every form of entertainment. I learned to speak a piece long before I could say my A B C's. While Natalie played with dolls and Constance rolled a hoop, I played theater. I greatly preferred animals to dolls, and all the stray dogs and cats in the neighborhood were dragged into service for our circus performances, which were held Friday afternoons in the cellar with five pins as the admission price. Natalie used to make funny jockeys out of old stockings, their bodies stuffed into rotundity with cotton and their faces embroidered in red and green worsted. These were perched on the dogs, which served as ponies; an old sheet was converted into a tent, a nearby butcher shop supplying the sawdust.

Constance, who could turn handsprings and hang from a trapeze by her toes, was our star acrobat. We adored dressing up like clowns, and Peg always entered into the spirit of it all and helped cut and sew our costumes.

We never regarded her as many children do their mothers—as an older person who would throw a damper on any kind of lark. On the contrary she was one of us, and her wonderful spirit of youth still prevails. She is always included with young folk at parties in Hollywood.

When our schoolmates lacked enthusiasm for our amateur theatricals or found other diversions more to their liking, we made up any deficiency in attendance by digging up angle worms and arranging them in cardboard shoe boxes to act as the audience. Our orchestra consisted of bells, frying pans, castanets, and a drum. We varied the circus performances with one-act plays which I wrote, usually adaptations of terrible Diamond Dick stories or cheap dime novels. When I was graduated from public school my diploma meant much less to me than the opportunity of dancing the minuet in costume as part of the class-day exercises.

Perhaps this early dramatic sense helped me somewhat at the Vitagraph. I was shy enough at home when it came to meeting strangers, but I suffered no stage fright at the studio. To begin with, I was too young to know self-consciousness, and besides, I was in love with the work.

All the scenery was painted on canvas. There was no Bristol board or plastering—none of the materials used today. If one slammed a door too hurriedly when making an entrance or an exit, the entire set was apt to come tumbling down like a house of cards. Once, when Florence Turner was playing Carmen and the audience in the bullring was painted on a backdrop, the entire wall crashed in on Paul Panzer, who stood there balancing the arena on his back, like Atlas with the world on his shoulders.

Speaking of Carmen reminds me of Viola, the Vitagraph cow, which was hired at twenty-five cents a day from a nearby farm. Viola was cast for the bull in Mérimée's masterpiece, and was wrapped in three coats of canvas and painted black, with the elk horns off the hat rack in Mr. Smith's office glued to her head—crêpe hair pasted between the horns. Viola, insensible to the cost of film, kept right on chewing her cud and refused to fight when the toreador stood awaiting her. Mr. Blackton ordered a shotgun to be fired behind her, but it had no effect on Viola. Finally a property man got an electric battery and a zinc plate, which was fastened to the rear of Viola. When the button was pressed Vi shot across the painted arena in great style, and kept right on going!

The same two walls that were used for the corner of a tenement room in East Houston Street on Monday would, with a can of paint and a change from kitchen chairs to secondhand blue-plush furniture, become Miss Ladada's Fifth Avenue residence on Tuesday. A large artificial plant was the trademark of all society drawing-rooms, and to dress up a set was to stick in a palm or a telephone. A couple of handsome sofa cushions and a standing lamp were other swell-society props.

Cold Cream and Powder

As for lights, we used the old Aristo arcs, now obsolete, which used to flicker and sputter and give out a terrific heat. They were as round as fish globes, with two upright carbons in the center. We depended almost entirely upon daylight for exteriors. In time the arcs were caged in boxes and placed overhead as well as on the sidelines, the sets being built within these cages of lights. Mr. Blackton was first to discover the use of backlights and I think it was the Biograph Company that was first to use Cooper-Hewitts—long mercury-vapor tubes which did not give out much heat and presented a soft, rather diffused light. By degrees the Cooper-Hewitts and improved lights have been perfected to a point where they are especially built for motion pictures.

The largest light in diameter in the old Vitagraph days was twelve inches, and for big scenes we used about seven of them. Now it is not unusual to have fifty on a set, and recently a mirror sunlight arc has been perfected, sixty inches in diameter. Cooper-Hewitts are used at present for the soft lighting, and arcs for direction. At first there were no individual spotlights to follow anyone—that is to say, not even for the leading players were there any special lights provided for faces, and of course close-ups were not introduced by D. W. Griffith until several years later.

Lighting was indifferent, and so little thought was given to photographic angles, such as full-face, profile, or other position, that we used to make up only the ears, and if I could possibly sneak out of it, I never bothered to whiten my neck. Our faces resembled whitewashed masks covering the oval with two flesh-colored ears poking out. Our eyelashes, heavily beaded, stuck out like the bristles of a toothbrush and we looked like the pictures of Rosamond in *Desperate Desmond.* I used a sort of black wax which was melted and put on the edge of the lashes with a hair-pin or toothpick. Now I merely darken the lashes slightly with mascara and pencil a thin line underneath the eyes.

The old dead whitening, which resulted from a cold-cream base with powder over it, has gone out entirely, and nowadays there are dozens of shades of grease paints to effect the smooth peach-bloom complexion of extreme youth or the sallow skin of wrinkled age. Today each player takes infinite pains with a make-up, and every time I start a new picture I first take a half-dozen individual tests with different make-ups, according to whether I am a blonde or brunette or a white-haired old lady.

Thrown Out of the Picture

I remember in one of those early Vitagraph pictures that Dorothy Kelly, now the mother of three sets of twins, Mabel Normand, and I were to play in a group of slave girls. It was a story which took place before the Civil War, and was called *The Octoroon,* and a number of Negro players were engaged for the day. Along with the colored extras, Dorothy, Mabel, and I were to be sold as slaves on the auction block, and knocked down to a sort of Simon Legree type for about fifty cents apiece.

Our pride was hurt at the small value placed on our personal charms, so we got together in a corner and deliberately decided to do everything in our power to be thrown out of the picture. We didn't dare actually refuse any parts assigned to us, but we figured if we did something that would require a retake we would be ordered home for the day, which we knew to be the punishment for wasting footage. So the three of us blackened only our faces and the front parts of our necks, and as the auction block revolved the camera registered the backs of our necks snow-white. Needless to say, we were immediately dragged off the set, bawled out in very inelegant language, and sent home that day with no pay checks.

Another time I was on the verge of being thrown out when Zeena Keefe and I did a story in which we had to chase each other around a lake. This lake was the trusty old Vitagraph tank with a few artificial ferns and evergreens. Zeena and I got into a heated argument while the camera was grinding, and to give emphasis to my views on the subject I proceeded to knock her into the water. All that saved me that day was that Zeena lied nobly for me and pretended it was an accident. From then on we became bosom friends.

At the time of which I write the old Vitagraph Company had already been in existence at the Flatbush studios for several years. The executives were William T. Rock, J. Stuart Blackton and Albert E. Smith—all three among the very first pioneers in the motion-picture field. . . .

We always referred to Mr. Rock as "Pop Rock." He was the silent partner and took very little active part at the studio. Mr. Smith became the presiding mechanical genius, Mr. Blackton the artistic director. Despite their youth, both Smith and Blackton were fatherly men to whom everybody took their troubles. If an actor's wife did not receive her husband's pay check on Saturday, she rushed to A. E. Smith for advice and consolation; if two players got into a scrap as to which was to have the blue dress or which must wear the black hat, they flew from the wardrobe department to Stuart Blackton. Their decisions were law. The same genial hospitality that pervaded the executive's office spread throughout the studio. We were like one big, happy family. No one ever thought of being ritzy or upstage. Between scenes the leading players chatted with the supers, and a wonderful spirit of democracy prevailed.

Following *The Dixie Mother,* I played everything from children's parts, with my brown braids or corkscrew curls hanging down my back, to a drunken old lady of sixty. Whenever it was necessary for me to look mature, they padded my figure and put up my hair. These were all one-reel or split-reel pictures ranging from slapstick comedy to historical drama. Sometimes we even made two pictures in one day. Retakes were unheard-of, as quality counted less than footage.

After two weeks of these varied rôles I was laid off for a few days. While waiting to be called again, I asked Peg if it would be all right for me to go down and see Mr. Smith and ask him to give me a two weeks' tryout, as a sort of probation, in the regular stock company, instead of depending

Norma Talmadge and Maurice Costello in *A Tale of Two Cities* (Vitagraph, 1911)

upon day-to-day parts. Peg always said that there was no harm in asking sensible questions, and to ask for steady work seemed just about as sensible to her as anything I could suggest. So again, we boarded the L and set out for the Vitagraph Studios, getting off at Avenue W, without waiting to be sent for.

On Probation

There was always a long line of people waiting to see Messrs. Smith and Blackton—some seeking positions, others seeking an audience to discuss their difficulties or differences—but all intent upon seeing the bosses. Peg and I brought up the rear, but I felt that I was entitled to a little extra courtesy, since I had worked there two weeks before.

So, deciding that it was a case of now or never, I cautioned Peg to hold our place, and with an attitude of importance sailed past twenty or thirty other people to the head of the line.

"I am a little late for my appointment. Would you mind letting me through? Mr. Blackton is expecting me," I said, with my sweetest smile, to the girl whose turn was next.

It worked like magic and in I went. Or course Mr. Blackton never knew that I cheated to avoid standing in line. He remembered me from my day work and was very cordial.

The upshot of the interview was that I returned to Peg with Mr. Blackton's promise of being put in stock for a two weeks' trial. If I made good I was to remain permanently.

Part II
Struggles for Control: 1908-1930

The motion picture business in its infancy was wide open and freewheeling. It took relatively little capital to enter the field, and numerous small producers, distributors, and theater owners vied to make quick profits. No single company or alliance controlled the marketplace. But this era of nearly perfect competition came to an end with the formation of the Motion Picture Patents Company in 1908.

The Motion Picture Patents Company

The MPPC was the result of a peace settlement between two hostile factions—one led by the Edison Manufacturing Company and the other by the American Mutoscope and Biograph Company—that had been fighting each other to establish the hegemony of their respective patents. Together they held all the important patents on motion picture film, cameras, and projectors and secured a stranglehold on the industry for more than three years. There were ten constituent members of the Trust, as the MPPC came to be called, including virtually every leading producer and manufacturer of equipment (see ch. 6).

The Trust issued licenses to produce pictures only to its members. Eastman Kodak colluded with the Trust in an attempt to drive all other producers out of the field by granting it the exclusive right to purchase film stock. On the distribution level, members agreed to lease pictures only to those exchanges that dealt in licensed film entirely and at stipulated prices. These exchanges in turn could rent pictures only to exhibitors using licensed projectors.

Hollywood in 1915—Hollywood Hotel on the corner of Hollywood Boulevard and Highland Avenue. Courtesy Bruce Torrence Historical Collection, c/o First Federal of Hollywood

To enforce its regulations, the Trust filed lawsuits by the hundred, employed private detectives to search for evidence of patent violations, and called upon federal marshals to arrest offenders, confiscate their equipment, and throw them in jail. Nonetheless, outlaw producers continued to make pictures and found outlets for them among exhibitors eager for new and different films. It was these independent producers who helped to establish Hollywood rather than New York as the production center of the industry. The Los Angeles area, with its temperate climate, cheap labor, and proximity to the Mexican border for quick getaways, was found to be the ideal location.

Nor did the Trust succeed in eliminating all competition among exchanges. Independent exchanges continued to operate; even the licensed exchanges, succumbing to the temptation of easy money, defied Trust regulations.

This apparent failure at total monopoly spurred the Trust to go into distribution. In 1910, it organized the General Film Company, the first vertical integration in the industry, which bought out fifty-eight exchanges nationwide. Others were driven out of business by such expedients as cutting off the supply of films, price cutting, and other forms of discrimination. Within a year, only one of the former exchanges remained, and, with this exception, General Film was the sole distributor of motion pictures in the United States. The one exception, however, was partly instrumental in the Trust's undoing. William Fox, who then operated theaters and an exchange called the Greater New York Film Rental Company, in New York City, refused to sell out. Instead, he went into film production and instituted a lawsuit against the Trust under the provisions of the Sherman Antitrust Act, charging unlawful conspiracy in restraint of trade. The suit went to trial in January 1913 and resulted in the dissolution of the MPPC by the courts five years later. By then, however, competition and other factors had long since killed it.

Resistance to the Trust

By 1912, a strong and well-organized independent movement had come into existence. Among the early producers, in addition to Fox, were the Independent Motion Picture Company (IMP), Keystone, Thanhouser, and Rex; among distributors, Mutual and Universal were the most important. By 1914, literally hundreds of new firms had entered the business.

The competition engendered by the independents had far-reaching effects on the content of the film as well as on the structure of the industry. The Trust, in attempting to regulate commerce, considered the motion picture as merchandise to be mass-produced at low cost in standard lengths of 1,000-foot reels,which were sold at rates based on theater size rather than quality of the picture, the actors, or the director. Although movie patrons were beginning to express yearnings to learn about the lives of screen actors, Trust producers did little to exploit this interest. Their thinking was that public acclaim would inspire demands for greater salaries. The objective was to manufacture an economically uniform commodity—film to fill the weekly playing schedule of theaters. That the motion picture had enormous potential as a medium of mass entertainment had yet to dawn on the Trust.

Successful Innovations—Stars and Feature Films

Independents, on the other hand, experimented freely to please the public. For example, Carl Laemmle, the head of IMP, created the first movie star in the person of Florence Lawrence. While working for Biograph, she had been known to her admirers only as "the Biograph Girl." Laemmle hired her away from the company with an offer of a larger salary, rechristened her "the Imp Girl," and in a daring publicity stunt revealed her name to the public. He planted a story in a St. Louis newspaper stating that the former Biograph player, Florence Lawrence, had died in a streetcar accident. Soon after, he took out an ad in the newspaper declaring that the story was a false rumor spread by the Trust. She was alive and well, the ad continued, and Miss Lawrence would be featured in forthcoming IMP productions.

Thus began the star system of motion picture production. Other independents followed suit by publicizing the names of their players or by turning to Broadway for a steady supply of stars and actors with established reputations. The star craze hit the industry like a storm and forced even the conservative members of the Trust to change with the times, although by then most of their promising actors had been stolen by independents.

The star system affected the economics of the industry by becoming the prime means of stabilizing production. Producers discovered that the unique personalities of certain actors could attract a large and faithful following through the use of advertising and publicity, including ballyhoo and hokum (ch. 8). A star became a production value unto himself, a trademark enhancing the prestige of his producer and an insurance policy guaranteeing success at the box office. As a result, companies competed for big names and paid out-of-this-world salaries for their services. And did the salaries skyrocket: $100, $500, $1,000, and, for the brightest and most illustrious, Mary Pickford and Charlie Chaplin, $10,000 a week! For a while, it seemed that stars could dominate the business, and, indeed, many formed their own companies. The culmination of this movement was the formation of United Artists by Pickford, Chaplin, Douglas Fairbanks, and D. W. Griffith in 1919 (ch. 7).

Another innovation of the independents was the feature film.

Before 1911, a few longer films—two, three, and even four reels in length—had been imported from Europe and enthusiastically received in the exchanges. But, once again, the Trust's standardization policies stood in the way of the production of longer films in the United States. Exhibitors had been clamoring for better and longer films, ones that told well-developed and sophisticated stories that could attract a more intelligent clientele. The Trust, though, believed that audiences did not have the mental capacity to understand, let alone appreciate, longer films.

Like other nickelodeon owners of the day, Adolph Zukor observed a growing unrest with the usual movie fare and thought that audiences would be receptive to feature films. Since there was no steady source for this kind of picture, Zukor went to the heads of the Trust to persuade them to revamp their production policy. After receiving a humiliating rebuff, Zukor decided to risk his savings on his own production. As a beginning, he experimented with the imported French film *Queen Elizabeth,* starring Sarah Bernhardt. His hunch proved correct. The longer film would go over with the public, especially if it had a star. Thus, with Daniel Frohman, one of the biggest theatrical producers, Zukor formed Famous Players in 1912 and signed up Broadway stars: first James O'Neill and James K. Hackett, then Lillie Langtry, John Barrymore, and Fannie Ward.

Zukor's pictures were distributed on a "state's rights" basis, meaning that exhibition rights to pictures were sold to distributors operating within a particular metropolitan or geographical area. A national distribution network did not yet exist to handle feature films; Mutual, Universal, and Fox still sold programs of short subjects that changed daily or every other day. Feature films required special and individual promotional effort, and the state's rights method had to suffice until a better one could be perfected.

The state's rights method of distribution involved two steps. First, the producer sold his picture to a state's rights buyer, usually at a flat fee for the exclusive right to market the picture in a specified territory. Second, the buyer leased the picture to individual theaters, either on a flat rental or percentage-of-the-gross basis. This method, in its earlier form, presented little opportunity for the producer to share in any unusual profits that might appear on the distribution level.

Lillian Gish in *The Birth of a Nation* (Epoch Producing Corporation, 1915)

Cecil B. DeMille directing *The Squaw Man* (Jesse L. Lasky Feature Play Co., 1913).
Courtesy Bruce Torrence Historical Collection, c/o First Federal of Hollywood

Later, this disadvantage was overcome by selling the distribution rights either for a limited time rather than in perpetuity or on a percentage basis.

Another distribution method used nearly from the outset was the roadshowing technique. In roadshowing his picture the producer bypassed the distributor and dealt directly with exhibitors. He would book the picture on a percentage basis or actually take over the operation of the theater for a limited period. The advantage of this method was that large and well-appointed legitimate theaters, rather than nickelodeons, could be used to show motion pictures.

D. W. Griffith and his partners perfected the roadshowing method in 1915. In distributing *The Birth of a Nation* they booked the leading legitimate theaters in America and established a whole new technique of motion picture presentation. The picture was presented in standard theatrical form, twice daily, at scheduled performances, divided like a play into two "acts" with an intermission in between, and accompanied by a symphony orchestra that played a full score. Tickets were sold in advance on a reserved-seat basis at two dollars apiece—making it the first two-dollar attraction in screen history.

Although state's rights selling and roadshowing were basically different, they were not mutually exclusive. A producer might first roadshow his picture in big cities, where most of the revenue was generated, and later sell the state's rights to the film, as was done with *The Birth of a Nation.*

The Rise of Paramount

In 1914, W. W. Hodkinson, a progressive exhibitor with overwhelming faith in quality pictures, organized Paramount Pictures Corporation, the industry's first national distributor of feature films. Paramount consisted of eleven regional state's rights buyers who joined forces to advance a steady stream of capital to producers that would enable them to make a regular supply of features. Zukor's Famous Players was brought into the scheme as well as Bosworth, Inc., Jesse L. Lasky Feature Play Co., Morosco Photo Play Company, and others. These companies signed franchise agreements granting Paramount the exclusive right to distribute their pictures for a period of years at the fee of 35 percent of the gross sales.

Paramount had geared itself to deliver two features a week. Theater owners and audiences enthusiastically endorsed the plan, which assured the company success from the start. Although negatives were now costing from $10,000 to $30,000 on the average, gross rentals soon reached the unprecedented amounts of $100,000 to $125,000 per picture. Other companies got on the bandwagon, among them Lewis Selznick's World Film Corporation, Triangle Film Corporation, Goldwyn Pictures Corporation, Metro Pictures Corporation, and Fox Film Corporation. And a wave of theater construction began in the principal cities to accommodate the growing audiences. In the midst of the feature film revolution, the Trust and General Film gradually faded away.

This tremendous expansion of the movie business convinced Zukor that Paramount and its producers should merge, not only to effect economies of scale in production but also to enable him to share more equitably in Paramount's burgeoning profits. Famous Players in its third year of existence earned over $1 million in profits and had become the mainstay of Paramount's operations. Yet, 35 percent of its revenues remained in Paramount's tills as distribution fees. Hodkinson vetoed the idea, arguing that the three branches of motion pictures—production, distribution, and exhibition—should be kept separate. In his view, better pictures, better distribution, and better theater management would result if a lively independence existed among them.

But Zukor was not to be denied. He went to work on Paramount's board of directors and persuaded a majority to see things his way, with the result that, in 1916, Hodkinson was deposed; Paramount, Famous Players, and Lasky were merged; and Adolph Zukor assumed the presidency of the $25 million Famous Players-Lasky Corporation. Paramount now became a Zukor subsidiary, marking a turning point of major significance for the industry. The independent movement that grew up in opposition to the Trust was coming to an end; the vertical integration of production, distribution, and exhibition would continue until, in the twenties, a new form of monopoly would control the motion picture business.

Zukor would not go into exhibition as long as he could maintain a strategic hold on the market with his stable of stars. He had long since abandoned his original plan to use personages from the legitimate stage. Trained primarily to use the voice rather than pantomime as the main instrument of communication, and often too old and too heavy to photograph well, theater idols had proven unsatisfactory for the silent screen. Zukor thereafter gathered together in his organization players and other artists on whom the movie public had conferred stardom. His greatest prize was Mary Pickford; others in his illustrious stable were Douglas Fairbanks, Gloria Swanson, William S. Hart, Fatty Arbuckle, Pauline Frederick, Blanche Sweet, Norma and Constance Talmadge, Nazimova, and directors Cecil B. DeMille, D. W. Griffith, and Mack Sennett. With most of the best talent in the industry under his control, Zukor could dominate the field.

Now at the reins of Paramount as well, Zukor implemented the next stage of his thinking. Before the year 1916 ended, he

Motion picture pioneers Adolph Zukor and Marcus Loew

increased film rentals sharply and introduced block booking
(i.e., selling pictures in groups) to the Paramount distribution
system. Block booking was not new to the industry, but it had
never been particularly effective until Zukor used it. Zukor had
greatly expanded his production program, so much so that by
1918 Paramount distributed 220 features, more in one year
than any one company before or since. Although
Famous Players-Lasky had the greatest array of talent around,
a major portion of its output was decidedly second-rate. But by
using the distribution practice of block booking, Zukor
ensured that these pictures would be rented to exhibitors at a
profit.

Resistance to Zukor—First National

Paramount's seasonal output was arranged in blocks of up
to 104 pictures, enough to fill the entire annual playing time
of a theater that changed its bill twice a week. Each block
would be sprinkled with a few specials containing top-name
stars and maybe even a Mary Pickford super-special. The bulk
of the block, however, consisted of pictures that, if offered
individually, would rarely find takers. Zukor's block-booking
system worked because the enormous drawing power of Mary
Pickford and his other stars virtually forced exhibitors to
accept the entire block. An exhibitor who rejected Paramount's
rental terms would likely find his patrons deserting him in
favor of a theater down the street featuring the Paramount
stars.

Exhibitor resentment toward the imperious Zukor climaxed
in 1917 with the formation of the First National Exhibitors
Circuit. This brainchild of Los Angeles theater owner Thomas
L. Tally was created to act as purchasing agent for twenty-six
of the nation's largest first-run exhibitors located in cities
where national distributors had their regional exchanges. Their
objective was to acquire outstanding pictures made by
independent producers. First National would not waste money
buying or building studios; rather, it would use its considerable
purchasing power to capture the biggest box-office names. The
twenty-six franchise holders agreed to offer financing in return
for the right to exhibit the picture and then to distribute it
among theaters in their respective territories.

First National proved its determination by plucking Charlie
Chaplin from Mutual and then Mary Pickford from

Paramount with $1 million contracts in 1918. By then, the franchise holders controlled nearly two hundred first-run houses and approximately sixty subsequent-run houses, as well as more than 350 theaters controlled under subfranchise agreements. First National was indeed becoming an aggressive opponent.

The Battle for Theaters

First National's control of the biggest theaters in the major metropolitan areas soon posed an ominous threat to the rest of the industry. These theaters were the first-run houses and their importance was enormous. Their proximity to large concentrations of population meant that they received the bulk of the business (ch. 11). No picture could earn a profit without first-run showings. Typically, a producer received up to 50 per cent of the total rental from these theaters, usually within six months after a picture's release. Further, a successful first-run showing became the greatest selling point for distributors in dealing with the thousands of small theater managers throughout the country. In short, control of these theaters meant control over access to the screen. And if First National increased production to fill the playing time of its theaters, the market for Zukor's pictures would dry up.

Zukor, as a result, went into the theater business. The fear of First National was not his sole motivation, however. He realized that of the $750 million taken in by the movies, less than $100 million reached producers. The retail branch of the business had become the steadiest earner in the industry. It was not inherently speculative like motion picture production, because the public had come to regard the movies more as a necessity than a luxury. Attendance rose steadily in this period, reaching about eighty million per week by 1929—an average of nearly one theater visit per week for every person in the United States.

Once the decision was made, Zukor moved in a big way. With $10 million in cash from a Kuhn, Loeb and Company stock flotation in 1919, Zukor terrorized First National's ranks by buying options, intimidating theater owners, and awing local bankers from New England to Texas. Zukor's roving representatives were soon dubbed "the wrecking crew" and the "dynamite gang" by theater owners. His biggest victory in a long series of battles with First National occurred in 1926,

when he acquired controlling interest of Balaban and Katz,
which operated ninety-three theaters in and around Chicago
and was First National's tower of exhibiting strength. Zukor
now owned or controlled over a thousand theaters, which he
consolidated under the name Publix Theatres Corporation.

In 1919, Zukor's company thus became the first in the
industry to be completely integrated, by adding exhibition to
its production-distribution activities. But others were soon
forced to follow suit. First National added production to its
distribution-exhibition arms by building a giant studio in
Burbank in 1922. Marcus Loew, meanwhile, who owned a
chain of a hundred theaters, had bought an impoverished
producer-distributor company called Metro in 1920. Going
deeper into production in 1924, he purchased first the
Goldwyn Pictures Corporation and then the Louis B. Mayer
unit. The trend continued. Fox Theaters Corporation, one of
the most important chains in the country, embarked on a spree
calling for the construction of thirty first-run theaters, each
seating between four and five thousand.

By the mid-twenties, the skeleton of the motion picture
industry's organizational structure that would characterize it
for the next two decades had become apparent. After having
undergone a series of major adjustments, the result of the
decline of the Trust, the industry after World War I saw the
consolidation of the production, distribution, and exhibition
branches of the business. Fewer and fewer companies had
come to assume more and more power with their studios,
national systems of distribution, and large chains of important
theaters. In 1925, Paramount, First National, Loew's, and Fox
were the major entities. The movement toward consolidation
would continue, bringing two additional companies to the
fore—Warner Brothers and RKO. The story of their arrival is
tied in with the advent of sound.

The Industry at the Apex of the Silent Era

By the twenties, the movies ranked as a major industry
(ch. 9). Its captains were an exceptional breed of showmen
who, by exploiting the star system and feature films, and by
dreaming up bold and imaginative promotion techniques,
enabled the movies to surpass every other branch of show
business. Not only did the industry make great strides at home,

it also captured the world market by supplying 80 percent of the motion pictures exhibited abroad (ch. 9). The big companies now were listed on the New York Stock Exchange. Motion picture securities publicly offered from 1924 to 1926 by

A traveling movie palace

Grauman's Chinese Theater, Hollywood

Wall Street banking houses amounted to $54 million in bonds, $81 million in stocks, and $47 million in real estate bonds— for a total of $182 million (ch.9). The total capital invested in the business came to a phenomenal $1.5 billion in 1926. Investment in theaters alone for 1925 was $250 million, bringing the number to an estimated 20,000, with a total seating capacity of eighteen million and an annual box-office intake conservatively calculated at $750 million. The industry was in a boom period and it seemed that the end of its expansion was nowhere in sight.

The Advent of the Talkies

When American Telephone and Telegraph salesmen first made the rounds of the major producers, they found no takers for their new sound equipment (ch. 10). Prudent studio chiefs were not about to tamper with a flourishing business. Producers had extensive inventories of silent pictures. Their studios were designed only for the production of such pictures, and theaters throughout the country were built and equipped for them. Actors in whom producers had made huge investments were trained in making silents. The change to sound would involve not only scrapping millions but investing corresponding amounts in sound equipment. Moreover, the Western Electric sound system of AT&T was far from perfect. But the companies soon found they had no choice.

The Warner brothers had by 1925 succeeded in establishing a prosperous production company in Hollywood. They solved the problem of distribution by purchasing Vitagraph with its nationwide system of exchanges. Business was good; profits for 1924 came to $1 million. Yet, Warner was in a precarious position. The battle for theater control had reached a climax, and Warner, now fully extended, found itself without the resources to acquire a first-run theater chain of its own.

The bulk of Warner's business was done with small independent circuits and struggling neighborhood houses. If Warner could equip these theaters with sound, they could compete with the opulent downtown movie palaces. Sound, in the form of synchronized musical accompaniments for pictures, could provide a cheaper equivalent to live, full-sized pit orchestras. What Warner decided to do then was to produce entertainment programs for smaller exhibitors

comparable in quality to those presented by the best
metropolitan theaters. Accordingly, in April 1926, Warner
formed the Vitaphone Corporation with Western Electric to
make sound motion pictures and to market
sound-reproduction equipment.

The première of *Don Juan* at the Warners' Theatre in New
York on August 6, 1926, marked the first step in Warner's
strategy. This film, starring John Barrymore, had a
synchronized musical background played by the New York
Philharmonic Orchestra. It was the eight "Vitaphone
Preludes" on the program, however, and not the feature that
caused the greatest stir. These consisted of a speech by Will
Hays and operatic and concert performances. Although the
demand for Vitaphone slowly began to build afterward, the
major companies decided in February 1927 to postpone
making the conversion for a year unless they collectively agreed
to move sooner. In the meantime, they would study the
situation.

The only exception was the Fox Film Corporation, which
had its own sound patents. Its head, William Fox, organized
the Fox-Case Corporation in 1926 to exploit the Movietone
sound system by producing sound newsreels. Fox scored his first
success in May 1927 with a Movietone newsreel showing
Charles Lindbergh's takeoff at Roosevelt Field, Long Island,
on his historic trans-Atlantic flight.

After the première of *The Jazz Singer,* on October 6, 1927,
the public reaction to sound became intense. The other
companies began wiring their studios and theaters for sound in
the spring and summer of 1928. Electrical Research Products,
Inc. (ERPI), the AT&T subsidiary that had taken over the
marketing of the sound equipment from Vitaphone, could not
fill orders fast enough and exhibitors grew frantic because of
the delays. It took a year before the majors added sound to
their pictures. In the meantime, Warner Brothers solidified its
position in the industry by going on a spending spree, the likes
of which had never been seen even in the movie business. It
began in September 1928 with the purchase of the Stanley
chain of three hundred theaters and a one-third interest in
First National. By the end of 1930, it controlled all of First
National, had boosted its assets from $5 million to $230
million, and had grown to among the greatest of all movie
companies.

The speed with which the industry accommodated the sound revolution was truly remarkable. Within a mere three years, the victory of the talkies was so nearly complete that a silent picture could not be found anywhere except in small towns and rural areas. With sound, the industry had entered yet another boom period, so great was the public's infatuation with the talkies.

AT&T 's preeminent position did not go unchallenged for long. Undaunted by the long-term exclusive contracts tying up the major studios, the Radio Corporation of America, AT&T's archrival, simply created a full-blown film company to exploit its Photophone sound system. The new Radio-Keith-Orpheum Corporation, founded in October 1928 as a holding company, merged Joseph P. Kennedy's Film Booking Office, the Keith-Albee-Orpheum circuit of vaudeville houses, and Photophone into a vertically integrated giant containing three hundred theaters, four studios, and $80 million of working capital. RCA thereupon charged AT&T with unlawful restraint of trade. After an out-of-court agreement was reached in 1935, the two companies cross-licensed their sound patents to restore amicable relations. By 1943, RCA was supplying about 60 percent of all sound equipment.

The advent of the talkies was thus directly responsible for the emergence of two additional major companies. It also required fresh capital to finance the purchase of sound equipment, the construction of soundproof studios, the hiring of new talent, and experimentation in the new medium. Production costs rose accordingly to an average of $375,000 in 1930, as against from $40,000 to $80,000 a decade earlier. The changeover to sound cost the industry an estimated $500 million. The majors, which by then had established alliances with leading Wall Street banks and investment houses, had no difficulty making the transition, but the smaller entities in business were not so fortunate. Many independent producers and exhibitors simply closed their doors or sold out to the big theater chains. By 1930, the transformation of the industry into a virtual oligopoly had been completed.

6

JEANNE THOMAS ALLEN

The Decay of the Motion Picture Patents Company

The Motion Picture Patents Company was formed in 1908 to resolve the keen conflicts among the competing members of the American film industry. In 1915, a federal court declared the MPPC in violation of the Sherman and Clayton acts and attributed a number of other motives to the Company: the control of all motion picture production through interlocking agreements, the elimination of competition on the distribution level, and price-fixing of raw film and motion pictures. In its defense, the MPPC claimed that it brought stability and improved efficiency to the market; the competition claimed, and the courts finally ruled, that the MPPC acted to monopolize the industry.

The MPPC dissolved less than ten years after its inception, but the patterns of monopolistic control it established have recurred in the decades since.[1] Indeed, the MPPC's operations illuminate important facts and issues about the nature of the American film industry. Consequently, the events leading to the formation of the MPPC, its business and legal arrangements, the results of these arrangements, and possible reasons for its eventual demise warrant close examination.

The growth of the motion picture business was stymied almost from the

This chapter is an expanded version of an article by the author originally appearing in *Cinema Journal* 10 (Spring 1971): 34-40.

1. See two particular cases of monopoly control exerted in the film industry: Pauline Kael's record of the difficulties RKO experienced in distributing *Citizen Kane* ("Raising Kane," in *The Citizen Kane Book* [New York, 1971]) and Herbert Biberman's account, in *Salt of the Earth* (Boston, 1965), of the Hollywood industry's attempts to prevent the production of *Salt of the Earth*.

start by incessant strife over patent claims. The patent war, as it was called, was declared by Edison in 1897, when he brought suit against Charles H. Webster,[2] continued until 1908, and involved hundreds of legal disputes. Edison patented his camera on August 24, 1891, but it was not until 1896 that he filed for a patent on his film. When he received his letters patent the following year, he took action to capture the market. Edison's lawyers claimed that all manufacturers of motion picture equipment and all film producers were operating in violation of the patents he secured on his Kinetoscope.

Edison's main assaults were aimed at his strongest competitor, the American Mutoscope and Biograph Company. In the ensuing court battles, the courts sustained Edison's camera patent, but not his film's. At the same time, Biograph's camera, which was carefully designed to be noninfringing, was allowed. Since the courts declared neither side the winner, producers began to align themselves as licensees with one or the other hostile camp. This was done as a form of self-protection, but any company was still vulnerable to attack from the other side.

Structure and Operation of the Patents Company

A number of factors supported a peace settlement in 1908. One was that prolonged litigation proved costly to plaintiff and defendant alike. The most important, though, was that the industry had an enormous potential for expansion which could be realized only under stable conditions.

As a result, Edison and Biograph declared a truce to form the Motion Picture Patents Company on September 9, 1908.[3] The MPPC was a patent

---

2. Terry Ramsaye, *A Million and One Nights* (New York, 1926), p. 379.

3. Ralph Cassady, Jr., "Monopoly in Motion Picture Production and Distribution: 1908-1915," *Southern California Law Review* 32 (Summer 1959): 328. Unless otherwise noted, the information on the structure and operation of the MPPC and the General Film Corporation in this article comes from Cassady. Cassady's principal source is the transcript of the legal record of the case of the United States vs. the Motion Picture Patents Company in the District Court of the United States for the Eastern District of Pennsylvania. This record is available at the Princeton University Library in microfilm and the Law Library at the University of California at Los Angeles.

My only reservations about Dr. Cassady's research concern a rhetorical bias toward the beneficial contribution of the MPPC (e.g., Cassady, p. 356: *"There is no question* that the rental service of independent exchanges was deficient. . . . *It is reasonable to assume* that the establishment of a model exchange might well have resulted in improved conditions"). Cassady's use of documentation supplied by the defense (the MPPC) and only light use of the prosecution's data are not argued or justified. Cassady acknowledges that the MPPC was a combination that violated the law, but defends its contribution to the industry's serviceability. This is an important issue and deserves to be as carefully supported as the activities of the MPPC itself. More thorough research into the conditions of the industry prior to the MPPC, not just what the officers of the MPPC said in their own defense, is needed. Notwithstanding this suggestion, this is the best source currently available on the MPPC's activities and organization.

pool organized to hold the sixteen key patents owned by four companies—Edison Manufacturing Company, American Mutoscope and Biograph Company, Vitagraph Company of America, and Armat Moving Picture Company—and to issue licenses for the right to use the inventions or equipment. Ten firms, including the above, were brought in as licensees, but only Edison and Biograph held stock.

Edison and Biograph gained from this arrangement not only because they ceased the costly legal wrangling, but also because they became the

Biograph Studio on East 14th Street, New York

beneficiaries of an elaborate royalty scheme. Although Edison enjoyed a near-hegemony in the market at the time, his company could not have met by itself the rising demand for films from the growing number of nickelodeons. Yet through the MPPC, he could rule the industry.

The MPPC assessed three types of royalties to generate revenue: "machine royalties," "exhibitor royalties," and "film royalties." In return for licenses granting certain companies the right to manufacture projectors, the MPPC exacted a five-dollar royalty per machine. To use these machines, exhibitors were charged two dollars a week. Licensed producers of motion pictures paid at the rate of a half-cent per foot of film produced.

Royalties were distributed at the end of the year in the following manner: Edison received an amount equal to "net film royalties" and Biograph two-thirds of the remainder. The balance was distributed in these proportions: Edison, one-half; Biograph, one-third; and Armat, one-sixth. Vitagraph, the fourth company in the pool, was paid from the top, one dollar for each projecting machine sold.

In order to control business, the MPPC became involved in all segments of the industry: (1) the production of raw film; (2) the manufacture of motion pictures; (3) the manufacture of projecting equipment; (4) film distribution; and (5) exhibition. Through a series of specially designed licensing agreements, each was brought under the MPPC's sphere of influence.

(1) In exchange for mutually supportive monopoly privileges, the MPPC agreed to deal exclusively with the Eastman Kodak Company, the principal domestic producer of raw film stock. Consequently, the Patents Company received a buying monopoly and Eastman a selling monopoly.[4] Eastman was not charged a royalty, but acted on behalf of the company to collect film royalties from licensed producers.

(2) Motion picture manufacture was regulated by the granting of licenses to Edison and Biograph and their former allies—Essanay, Kalem, Lubin, Pathé Frères, Selig Polyscope Company, Vitagraph, and two importers, Kleine Optical Company and Gaston Méliès. The companies were permitted to use only Eastman film stock and could produce any number of pictures, but the importers were restricted as to the footage they could release. The MPPC, not the producers, set the prices that exchanges would be charged for films. The scale ranged from nine to thirteen cents per foot for new releases. In this way, licensees operated in a protected market. No new manufacturer could be granted a license, moreover, unless a majority of MPPC members agreed.

(3) By holding all the crucial patents on projectors, the MPPC held direct control over equipment manufacture and sales. Each projector sold

4. Floyd L. Vaughan, *Economics of Our Patent System* (New York, 1926), p. 107.

for a fixed price—$150 in 1909—$5 of which went to the MPPC as a royalty.

(4) By controlling all aspects of motion picture and equipment manufacture, the MPPC could lay down its conditions to distributors. A licensed distributor had to deal with MPPC members exclusively. Films were leased to him at flat rates; however, in dealing with exhibitors, he could charge whatever price the market would bear. Exchanges were required to "purchase" a minimum of $2,500 worth of films per month. They were not charged royalties but acted as agents for the MPPC by collecting from exhibitors the two-dollar-a-week royalty on projectors. The Patents Company granted licenses to 116 exchanges; the 30 or 40 others were driven out of business.[5] Those that remained under the MPPC aegis led precarious existences. The MPPC held arbitrary power to cancel the distributor's license without cause upon fourteen days' notice.[6]

(5) Since box-office revenues were the major source of industry revenue, the MPPC royalty scheme was aimed primarily at the theater. In return for the right to use licensed projectors (on which the two-dollar royalty was levied each week) the exhibitor had to agree to show only licensed motion pictures. If he violated the contract by exhibiting outlaw pictures, by refusing to pay royalties, or by subleasing prints to other theaters, he could be fined or sued, or have his license revoked.

Through these interlocking agreements, the Motion Picture Patents Company standardized the functions of each segment of the industry and protected its members from outside competition. Exhibitors could not distribute or manufacture films nor could manufacturers engage in distribution or exhibition. There was no duplication of effort, each arm of the business was protected, and product was guaranteed easy access to the market. For those within the MPPC, the long-sought-after stabilization had occurred, but, as the government would later charge, by restraining trade outside the company.

MPPC licensees were free to operate pretty much as they pleased. Producers made their own decisions regarding the number and length of pictures to be produced and sold. Distributors could operate in any market area and charge exhibitors any price they could get for their film service. Exhibitors could purchase whatever program of films they desired from licensed exchanges and set their own admission prices.

The most important activities of the MPPC itself were regulatory in nature: its tasks were to collect royalties, to see that licensees abided by their contracts, and to prevent infringement of patent rights. An integral part of its enforcement policy was obtaining information on the behavior

5. Ibid., p. 55.
6. Ibid.

of its licensees, especially theaters, and punishing recalcitrants. Exchanges were required to keep the company up to date on theater addresses, the names of owners, play dates, and so forth, although it was difficult at times to get exhibitors and exchangemen alike to volunteer business information. For additional information, according to some historical accounts, the MPPC employed an espionage unit to gather evidence for infringement suits.[7]

In any event, it was crucial to the MPPC's regulatory function to monitor the operations of its licensees and maintain a fairly intricate chain of communication. If, for example, the company revoked the license of an exchange, it would notify (1) the exchange itself; (2) the manufacturers supplying the exchange; (3) exhibitors doing business with it; (4) the exchangemen who were to take on the former's customers; and (5) any distributor who needed reminding of the consequences of troublesome behavior.

From the standpoint of the four original patent owners, the most important MPPC function was the collection of royalties. Film royalties, as mentioned earlier, were collected by Eastman Kodak from the licensed manufacturers, and with relative ease.[8] Nor were machine royalties difficult to collect because of the small number of licensed manufacturers. It was the two-dollar weekly exhibitor royalty that proved a problem since the thousands of theaters were widely scattered and many exhibitors bitterly opposed the levy.[9] Rental exchanges, which acted as the collecting agencies, may have sometimes paid the fees themselves to keep from losing customers as a result of license cancellations. Regardless of the difficulties, total royalties collected amounted to $800,000 in each of the years 1910 and 1911, and nearly $1 million in each of the years 1912 and 1913. Edison and Biograph, the stockholders of the company, were the main recipients of the receipts.

Formation of the General Film Company

On April 18, 1910, the General Film Company was organized by the licensed manufacturers as a distribution company for their product. According to the government, the objective was to achieve greater monopolistic control of the business; according to the company, it was to

7. Ramsaye, *A Million and One Nights,* p. 533; Cassady, "Monopoly," p. 347, note 119; Fred J. Balshofer and Arthur C. Miller, *One Reel a Week* (Berkeley and Los Angeles, 1967), pp. 34, 36, 50, 62-64.

8. Cassady does not know how royalties were collected from the importers, if in fact there was machinery for doing so ("Monopoly," p. 349, note 132).

9. Benjamin B. Hampton, *A History of the Movies* (New York, 1931), p. 71.

Kalem Studio, Hollywood

provide better service to exhibitors and the public. The government pressed the former motive in its suit against the MPPC, maintaining that by purchasing a certain number of key exchanges, all others could be driven out of business and distribution profits would consequently accrue to the MPPC. Officials of the Patents Company asserted that exhibitors' complaints of unsatisfactory service forced it to come up with a better operation. Whatever the motive, the vertical integration of production and distribution gave the ten licensed manufacturers a command of another branch of the industry.

General Film was capitalized at $2 million, later reduced to $1 million. The ten members of the Patents Company purchased equal amounts of the stock, which was to yield a continuous 12 percent annual dividend.[10] With this financial base General Film set out to acquire exchanges. There were sixty-nine licensed exchanges at that time. Beginning with the purchase of two from MPPC member George Kleine, General Film acquired eleven in one month, twenty-three within three months, and by January 1, 1912, a

10. William I. Greenwald, "The Motion Picture Industry: An Economic Study of the History and Practices of a Business" (Ph.D. diss., New York University, 1950), p. 23.

total of fifty-eight exchanges. After ten others were canceled, there remained only William Fox's Greater New York Film Rental Company. Except for the New York market, there was but a single source of licensed film available to all the exhibitors in the United States.

MPPC's agreement with General Film was basically the same as those with former licensed exchanges, with one significant exception—General Film had to pay royalties on a footage basis in return for its exclusive contract.

To regularize the market, General Film introduced new selling practices which outlived the era of the Patents Company and influenced the future organization of the industry. To this time, a regularized pricing system of film rentals did not exist; exchanges merely bartered with individual theaters. [11] General Film, however, changed this. First of all, it fixed the price for positive prints from licensed manufacturers at ten cents per foot. This price was based on average costs and wage scales; it was fixed and producers had to stay within it. Second, General Film classified theaters according to location and hence potential drawing power, with the result that it could charge the biggest and best situated houses higher rentals for motion pictures. Rentals were then standardized according to the class in which the theater belonged—ranging from $100 or $125 for the most important houses to $15 for the marginal ones. [12]

Dissolution of the Monopoly

As previously mentioned, the only film exchange free of General Film's control in 1912 was William Fox's Greater New York Film Rental Company. Fox had at one time been an MPPC licensee, but when he refused to sell his exchange to the newly formed General Film, the license was canceled. Not only that, General Film threatened to cut off the supply of films to his chain of theaters as well. As a result, Fox began to produce pictures on his own and retaliated by instituting a suit against the MPPC under the provisions of the Sherman Antitrust Act.

The government in its original complaint against the MPPC charged the combination with unlawful conspiracy in restraint of trade. The case went to trial in the District Court of the United States for the Eastern District of Pennsylvania on January 15, 1913. In its decision, handed down on October 1, 1915, the court ruled that the MPPC combination was illegal. A patent holder could seek protection of the law against infringement, said the court, but could not impose unreasonable restraints on commerce and

11. Hampton, *A History of the Movies,* p. 70.
12. Ibid., p. 71.

Essanay Studio, Chicago. Courtesy Bruce Torrence Historical Collection,
c/o First Federal of Hollywood

monopolize an industry under the guise of defending himself against
encroachment. The court ruled that the MPPC had gone "far beyond
what was necessary to protect the use of the patents or the [government-
granted] monopoly which went with them, and that the end and result . . .
was the restraint of trade condemned by law."[13] Although not spelled out
specifically by the court, the MPPC violations of the Sherman Act
included the following:

1. the attempted control of all industry activities through the use of
interlocking agreements;

2. the attempted exclusion of new competitors (in certain phases of
the industry at least) by vesting the power of granting entrance to those
already in the industry;

3. the attempted elimination of independent distributors and their
replacement with the "Trust"-affiliated General Film Company exchanges;

4. the fixing of prices for raw film (sold to manufacturers) and for
motion pictures (leased to exchanges); and

13. Quoted in Cassady, "Monopoly," p. 387.

5. the employment of various types of harassing tactics designed to impede the activities of would-be independents in all branches of the industry.[14]

The court therefore ruled that the petitioner, William Fox, was entitled to relief. Filing this decree in January 1916, the court enjoined the defendants and their officers from continuing the unlawful combination. An appeal of the decision was subsequently dismissed in 1918 and the MPPC was declared legally dead.

What Caused the MPPC's Decline?

The ineffectiveness of the MPPC is generally thought, however, to have resulted long before 1918. Lewis Jacobs suggests that the trust had actually become wholly ineffectual by 1914.[15] Other historians seem to agree that the actual court decision was merely the stone on the tomb.[16] Jacobs believes that when Fox's lawsuit entered the courts in 1913, disintegration within the Patents Company was rapid. Similarly, Michael Conant claims that the success of the government's antitrust action encouraged independents and contributed to the decline of the MPPC from 1915 on.[17] Perhaps the federal suit placed the MPPC in disrepute publicly and therefore encouraged the independents to compete. But to measure the extent of this influence would necessitate analyzing how the suit was reported in the mass media, whether there was any consensus of attitude toward it, what comments the independents made publicly in reaction to it, and what activity on the part of the independents could be attributed to the influence of legal action. Ralph Cassady suggests that court action influenced the independents by way of precedent or warning against pursuing monopoly tactics.[18] At this point of the discussion, the argument for the decay of the Patents Company from the influence of litigation against the MPPC appears to be more of an assertion derived from inference.

The second explanation for the collapse of the Motion Picture Patents Company is closely bound up with the characterization of that company attributed by the majority of film historians and commentators. The

14. Ibid.
15. Lewis Jacobs, *The Rise of the American Film* (New York, 1968), p. 84.
16. Gertrude Jobes, *Motion Picture Empire* (Hamden, Conn., 1966), p. 109; Michael Conant, *Antitrust in the Motion Picture Industry* (Berkeley and Los Angeles, 1960), p. 21; Cassady, "Monopoly," p. 388.
17. Conant, *Antitrust,* p. 21.
18. Cassady, "Monopoly," p. 390.

image that is commonly presented of the Patents Company resembles a Populist scenario of the conflict between a big Eastern business of "robber baron" proportions and the struggling, innovative, and independent businesses fleeing to the West Coast. *One Reel a Week* describes the "cloak and dagger" techniques of Patents Company detectives like Al McCoy who persisted in reporting and harassing activities of the independents.[19] Jacobs and Hampton both claim that the conflict erupted in open violence amounting to guerrilla warfare.[20] Kenneth Macgowan discusses the repressive measures used by the Patents Company—court injunctions, infiltration of hired obstructors, sheriffs, seizing cameras—and the fight of the independents to overcome their harassment.[21]

No doubt there is factual basis for such a picture. But there is also the possibility that the extremity of this description of two polarized camps in the film industry between 1908 and 1918 is oversimplified. Did the Patents Company fail for the reason that all repressive monopolies tend to fail in a free enterprise system: because its dogmatic policies failed to keep up with the pace set by free competition?

A closer examination of both primary and secondary source material suggests that the conflict between the film companies was not merely a titanic struggle between Thomas Edison and William Fox but a much more complex situation. The independents are credited with the innovation of longer feature films and moving to Hollywood, California.[22] To the Patents Company is attributed the burden of inflexibility as a result of its size and the use of lawsuits to protect exclusive rights.[23] In the course of the ten years between 1908 and 1918 these distinctions blur in actuality, some of them from the start.

The growth of Hollywood is frequently estimated as a consequence of the attempt of the independents to remove themselves from the Edison influence and control, and thus Hollywood is seen as a product of the MPPC/independent dichotomy. While Los Angeles may have been conveniently remote from New York, the independents were not the only ones

19. Balshofer and Miller, *One Reel a Week*, pp. 34, 36, 50, 62-64.
20. Jacobs, *Rise of the American Film*, p. 84; Hampton, *A History of the Movies*, pp. 73, 76.
21. Kenneth Macgowan, *Behind the Screen: The History and Techniques of the Motion Picture* (New York, 1965), p. 137.
22. Maurice Bardèche and Robert Brasillach, *The History of Motion Pictures* (New York, 1938), pp. 61-62; Conant, *Antitrust*, p. 21; Jacobs, *Rise of the American Film*, p. 85; Jobes, *Motion Picture Empire*, p. 110.
23. Bardèche and Brasillach, *History of Motion Pictures*, p. 64; Hampton, *A History of the Movies*, p. 73; Jobes, *Motion Picture Empire*, pp. 121-28; Macgowan, *Behind the Screen*, p. 139. Part of this consensus is due to the fact that Bardèche bases his section on Hampton—Bardèche and Brasillach, p. 59n.

Robert Henderson-Bland and Alice Hollister in *From the
Manger to the Cross* (Kalem, 1911)

who "discovered" California. In January 1908, Selig (an MPPC member)
made the first big California feature, *The Count of Monte Cristo,* and in
1910, D. W. Griffith went to California for filming while he was still with
Biograph (likewise a member of MPPC).

One of Macgowan's arguments for the Patents Company's failure is
what he calls the "by-products of monopoly": inefficiency and resistance
to change.[24] The MPPC, he reports, dogmatically insisted on one reel and
later two. Yet a member of the MPPC (Kalem) brought the first feature
to a Trust screen in 1913 with *From the Manger to the Cross.* Essanay's
George K. Spoor was supporting five-reel films in November 1916.[25] In
October of that year, *Moving Picture World* reported Edison using five-
reel features.[26] If his hesitancy to use films of more than one reel is
construed as an explanation for why Biograph and Edison folded in 1917,

24. Macgowan, *Behind the Screen,* p. 139.
25. *Moving Picture World,* November 18, 1916, p. 1030.
26. *Moving Picture World,* October 21, 1916, p. 408.

then why do Mutual, Triangle, and Thanhouser meet a similar fate in 1918 with such feature men as Griffith, Ince, and Sennett on their staffs?

The feature film argument for the collapse of the Trust seems even more confusing in regard to the introduction of the Italian *Quo Vadis* into American theaters. If this film "single-handedly rang the death knell for the Trust"[27] in April 1913, why then did George Kleine import it from Europe and rent the Astor in New York for its debut showing? As a member of the Trust, Kleine must have supported the idea of the longer feature film; this of course contradicts the assertion that the MPPC and GFC resisted films longer than two reels.[28]

The return of Selig to the Patents Company suggests more flexibility on the part of the Company than is usually assumed. Selig had gone to Los Angeles in 1906 presumably to escape Edison lawyers and to make adventure films for which he hired Indians, cowboys, and a collection of wild animals.[29] But Selig later signed a peace with Edison and joined the Patents Company with the understanding that he was free to develop films of this genre.[30]

The picture of the MPPC's bigness and the independent companies' smallness is supported by the fact that in 1915 the MPPC became VLSE (Vitagraph, Lubin, Selig, Essanay) and in 1916 KESE (Kleine, Edison, Selig, Essanay). Yet the period between 1912 and 1919 witnesses the rise of big independent corporations like Universal, Triangle, and World. In November 1916, Famous Players-Lasky Corporation combined with Morosco Photo Play Company and Pallas Pictures; then, in December, it acquired a controlling interest in Paramount.[31] Finally, in August 1921, antitrust action was taken against Lasky. It was accused of dominating the industry by means of block-booking contracts and theater control. Apparently the MPPC's example had not been sufficient to caution the independents, as Cassady suggests.[32] Monopoly was certainly not sought only by the MPPC in the American film's early history.

Lawsuits were not the particular province of the MPPC either. Trade journals of the period indicate that such suits were commonplace among

27. Bardèche and Brasillach, *History of Motion Pictures,* p. 66.

28. Lewis Jacobs gives the feature film credit for being the fatal blow to the patents trust. Introduced from abroad, it was supposedly first adopted as a regular device by an independent. The film which proved that the feature film would dominate the future was *Quo Vadis,* nine reels in length. Jacobs never mentions that a patents member imported and showed it first (*Rise of the American Film,* pp. 90-92).

29. Bardèche and Brasillach, *History of Motion Pictures,* p. 65.

30. Ibid.

31. *Moving Picture World,* November 11, 1916, p. 704; December 23, 1916, p. 1778.

32. Cassady, "Monopoly," p. 390.

independents. In October 1916, Selznick threatened Mastbaum with a suit based upon the Sherman law, and Fox threatened Brenon the same month. In December 1916, several film exchanges and companies, including a former MPPC member, Méliès, brought a lawsuit against the MPPC to recover triple damages aggregating over $18 million.[33] Pathé, after disassociating itself from the MPPC, defended the concept of film exchange associations on the grounds that "persons have a right to associate for the purpose of advancing their own interests by discriminating against other persons, if such discrimination is based upon legal grounds."[34] Pathé seemed to find the MPPC's rationale useful even after leaving the Trust.

Another factor working against a clear-cut distinction between the Patents Company and the independents is the fluidity of employees and staff not only among the independents and among the members of the Patents Company but actually between the two. The swapping and pooling of staff prevents the polarized view of the two camps from having complete validity.

Several film historians believe that one of the results of the competition between independents and the MPPC was the rise of the star system.[35] As a function of intense rivalry, leading actors and actresses became a focal device in luring audiences from one company's productions to another's. The cast was not the only object of trading between companies; directors and sales personnel were similarly involved. For example, in October 1916, two former Pathé men joined the World Film forces, one of whom had been with Pathé for the preceding ten years. A key distributor for World Film that month resigned and was immediately picked up by Selznick Enterprises, Inc. Both *Moving Picture World* and *Variety* are filled with articles in the late teens with brief statements of staff changes and juggling.

Changes in status of staff occurred within the Patents Company itself. In October 1916, a lead article in *Variety* reported that Vitagraph bought out the Lubin interest in VLSE so that Lubin was barred from making other new films under his own name.[36] Why did Lubin sell out? What did he do then? Does such a change suggest a conflict within the Company itself?

Certainly the degree to which Patents Company staff left to form

33. *Moving Picture World,* December 2, 1916, p. 1302.
34. *Moving Picture World,* October 28, 1916, p. 526.
35. Jacobs, *Rise of the American Film,* pp. 86-89; Ramsaye, *A Million and One Nights,* p. 523. Hampton, on the other hand, claims that the most significant factor in the growth of the star system was the demand for celebrities by the American public (*A History of the Movies,* p. 89).
36. *Variety,* October 6, 1916, p. 21.

independent companies or to be employed by independents indicates that they were not content with their status in the Trust. The brain drain away from the MPPC contributed to the fluid picture of the film industry's swapping and pooling of employees. However, the degree to which the trend is evident among the independents, too, indicates changing positions may have been due to reasons other than the repressive policies of the MPPC as a film trust. This brings us to the third explanation for the MPPC's dissolution.

Whether or not they left for more freedom to experiment or for a higher-paying position, members of the Patents Company themselves appear to have contributed to the breakdown of the MPPC's effectiveness. As early as 1909, Bison acquired Charles Inslee from Biograph as their dramatic expert. Actophone later hired Henry Ferrini as cameraman from Edison's studios. The new Actophone director had been trained in the Edison studio by Edwin S. Porter. Pathé left the Patents Company and joined the independents in 1910, as did Biograph's Griffith in 1913. He had just completed *Judith of Bethulia,* which was not a financial success "because the Trust's system of distribution was so poorly organized."[37] Griffith's cameraman, Billy Bitzer, had originally been with Biograph also. Tom Cochrane, member of the advertising agency which placed Laemmle in business, hired William Ranous of Vitagraph as first director of the concern, Independent Motion Picture Company. The independent movement soon gained Edison's director and producer of *The Great Train Robbery,* Edwin S. Porter, in the formation of the Defender company (1909).

Besides directors and cameramen, actors were also lured away by independent companies. Two of them, Gilbert M. Anderson and Mary Pickford, eventually set up their own independent companies. Essanay had sent Anderson ("Bronco Billy") to San Francisco to investigate sites away from Edison lawyers in the East. He chose Niles Canyon, near Oakland, as his base and began making weekly pictures. In 1910, the American Film Manufacturing Company set up shop in Chicago after luring the majority of actors, technicians, and executives away from Essanay.

The suggestion that members of the Patents Company not only left for the independents but cooperated with the latter while remaining within the Company is offered by Terry Ramsaye himself.[38] Ramsaye claims that Lubin, one of the original members of the MPPC, rented a Philadelphia studio that he had outgrown to the head of Actophone. Dintenfass then was promised protection from the Edison lawyers in the Patents Com-

37. Bardèche and Brasillach, *History of Motion Pictures,* p. 65.
38. Ramsaye, *A Million and One Nights,* p. 494.

pany's own studios. Lubin supposedly made no report of this to the
Patents Company, and Ramsaye offers as explanation that, having been
considerably pursued by Edison agents in the days before the Patents
Company peace, Lubin sympathized with Dintenfass.

In November 1916, *Moving Picture World* reported that Thomas Ince,
who had been a director for ten years, left Vitagraph to form a large
company which he would head himself. He was going to use the Bay Shore
Studios secured from Vitagraph. Ince stated that he was motivated by a
desire to carry out ideas "that are not in line with Vitagraph's policy," but
that he was leaving with "mutual expressions of good will."[39]

The Ince case brings up several questions about the tendency for
directors and actors to leave the Patents Company to set up companies of
their own. Where did they find the capital for these ventures? Why would
potential rivals be on such good terms as were Vitagraph and the new Ince
company? Why would Vitagraph rent studios to Ince? Might they have
retained a controlling interest in his company financially? If so, would this
suggest a more widespread pattern of Patent Company investment in non-
Trust film enterprises?

In order to discover whether or not members of the Patents Company
engaged in non-Trust enterprises, thus contributing to the breakdown of
the MPPC's power from within its own ranks, one would have to analyze
the financial records of the new independent companies when they incorporated. Was the Lubin/Vitagraph cooperation with the independents
remunerated? Was their example followed by other members of the
MPPC? How extensive is this record of cooperation between independents and the Patents Company? Although histories and trade journals suggest it, the accounts and business records of the new companies
alone could prove it—and it is possible that very basic agreements never
appeared in the books at all.

The traditional reasons given for the breakdown of the Patents Company do not seem to be conclusive when the complex picture of the film
industry in the years between 1908 and 1918 is closely examined. The
distance between the MPPC and the independents was not as wide as
frequently drawn, and the characteristics which distinguish the two camps
not as polarized. Fluidity and, in some cases, cooperation between the
independents and the Patents Company point to a more complex explanation for the eventual failure of the MPPC than the triumph of free enterprise over monopoly. The onslaughts of the independents and the federal
government were important, but the dissolution of the Patents Company
may have been almost as much the doing of the members themselves.

39. *Moving Picture World,* November 11, 1916, p. 876.

7

TINO BALIO

Stars in Business: The Founding of United Artists

On January 15, 1919, five of the biggest names in motion pictures staged a revolt. Mary Pickford, Charles Chaplin, Douglas Fairbanks, D. W. Griffith, and William S. Hart issued their "Declaration of Independence" against the corporate establishment announcing their intention to form a distribution company to be owned and operated exclusively by stars for the benefit of the great motion picture public.

The declaration, which resulted in pyrotechnics unusual even for an industry that existed more or less on fireworks, read as follows:

A new combination of motion picture stars and producers was formed yesterday, and we, the undersigned, in furtherance of the artistic welfare of the moving picture industry, believing we can better serve the great and growing industry of picture productions, have decided to unite our work into one association, and at the finish of existing contracts, which are now rapidly drawing to a close, to release our combined productions through our own organization. This new organization, to embrace the very best actors and producers in the motion picture business, is headed by the following well-known stars: Mary Pickford, Douglas Fairbanks, William S. Hart, Charlie Chaplin and D. W. Griffith productions, all of whom have proved their ability to make productions of value both artistically and financially.

Adapted from *United Artists: The Company Built by the Stars* (Madison, Wis., 1976), chaps. 1-3.

135

We believe this is necessary to protect the exhibitor and the industry itself, thus enabling the exhibitor to book only pictures that he wishes to play and not force upon him (when he is booking films to please his audience) other program films which he does not desire, believing that as servants of the people we can thus best serve the people. We also think that this step is positively and absolutely necessary to protect the great motion picture public from threatening combinations and trusts that would force upon them mediocre productions and machine-made entertainment.[1]

Hollywood was too cynical to take the revolt seriously. "Film magnates and a number of lesser stellarites in celluloid," said *Variety,* saw Adolph Zukor behind the whole affair in just another attempt to weaken First National.[2] Others prophesied that the all-star combination would soon be riven by jealousies and never get off the ground. And then there came Richard Rowland's famous wisecrack, "So the lunatics have taken charge of the asylum." A more accurate assessment, however, comes from Arthur Mayer, who remarks, "The founders of United Artists displayed the same brand of lunacy as Rockefeller, Morgan, and du Pont."[3]

The Founders

Mary Pickford

Mary Pickford's movie career began in 1909, when D. W. Griffith hired her for $5 a day at Biograph. Although only sixteen, she was a trouper with three years' experience on the stage and a position in David Belasco's eminent theatrical company. Her special appeal was soon evident on the screen. Long before her name appeared in movies, audiences began to identify her as "the girl with the curls" or as "Little Mary," the character name most often used in her films. So with a foresight that would characterize her entire career, she went to the Biograph executives to suggest that they capitalize on her drawing power by releasing her name to the public and by building her up in the press. The studio bosses refused.

But Carl Laemmle, a scurrying independent producer, had a hunch that Little Mary could be made into a star. An offer of $175 a week lured her to his Independent Motion Picture Company in December 1910, and the name Mary Pickford was revealed to the movie public. Production standards at IMP were too low for Miss Pickford's tastes, however, so she left the company within a year. After an even briefer stint with Majestic, she returned to Biograph in 1912. Finding that their stodgy mentality still

1. *Moving Picture World,* February 1, 1919, p. 619.
2. *Variety,* January 31, 1919, p. 58.
3. Arthur Mayer, "The Origins of United Artists," *Films in Review* 10 (1959): 390.

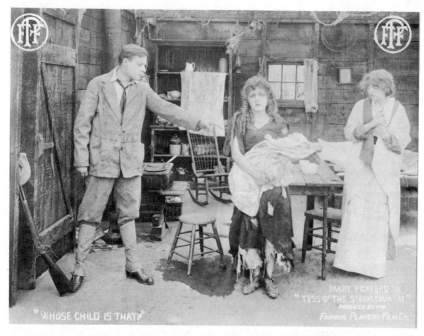

Mary Pickford in *Tess of the Storm Country* (Famous Players, 1914)

prevailed, Miss Pickford resumed her stage career with Belasco in 1913. She was performing in the Broadway production of *A Good Little Devil* when she caught the attention of Adolph Zukor, who soon convinced her to join his Famous Players.

Mary quickly became Zukor's most effective box-office attraction, and her starting salary of $20,000 a year was raised to $1,000 a week. With *Tess of the Storm Country* in 1914, Mary Pickford became a household word.

Her meteoric fame and salary caused trade practices of the industry to be revamped. Famous Players had been releasing through Paramount, a distribution company that supplied theaters with two or three features a week. Theater owners contracted for the entire Paramount program, which included the Pickford pictures, in a block-booking arrangement. Although this practice was standard in the industry, it changed when Mary's mother heard that salesmen were saying, "As long as we have Mary on the program we can wrap everything around her neck"—that is, exhibitors would buy the entire Paramount output to get the Pickfords. If her daughter's neck was that strong, she reasoned, Mary was entitled to more money.

Zukor passed the problem to Paramount's president, W. W. Hodkinson. Mrs. Pickford's demands would have to be met, he decided, and Mary's weekly salary was raised to $2,000. The money would not come from the Paramount coffers, however, but from the exhibitors. Hodkinson proposed selling the Pickford pictures as a "series," and charging more for them than for the regular Paramount program. This apparently slight departure from the program system eventually broadened into a completely new method of distribution. "It made possible the high salaries that were to come to actors, the increase in admittance prices to the great theaters that were to be built, and the enthusiastic endorsement of both by the public."[4]

Hodkinson's distribution plan proved so successful that in the following year, 1916, Charlotte Pickford suggested that her daughter's salary could be boosted still further. Her logic could not be denied. To accomplish this, Mrs. Pickford proposed that Mary become an independent producer (until then she had been a contract player). Thus, in partnership with Adolph Zukor, the Mary Pickford Corporation was formed. Zukor became the president, and Mrs. Pickford, representing Mary's 50 percent interest, became treasurer with the authority of approving all expenditures. In addition to receiving half of the profits on her pictures, Mary was to earn $10,000 a week, to be paid every Monday of the year. The number of pictures she would make each year was reduced from ten to a minimum of six to enable her to improve their quality. A separate distribution company, called Artcraft, was formed to handle the Pickford features, which thereafter were to be sold individually rather than in a series. On June 24, 1916, Mary Pickford became the first star to be a producer of her own pictures and to win a considerable degree of control over her work.

The Artcraft pictures that followed marked some of the greatest achievements in Miss Pickford's career. Among these were *The Pride of the Clan* and *The Poor Little Rich Girl,* both directed by Maurice Tourneur; two Cecil B. DeMille films, *A Romance of the Redwoods* and *The Little American;* and *Rebecca of Sunnybrook Farm, A Little Princess,* and *Stella Maris,* by one of her best directors, Marshall Neilan.

Despite her popular success and enormous salary, Miss Pickford was dissatisfied. She wanted complete autonomy over her work, including script approval. Moreover, Paramount's salesmen, she discovered, were forcing exhibitors to rent other pictures in order to get hers. Knowing that Miss Pickford's contract expired in 1918, First National made an unprecedented bid for her services.

Here was the offer: First National would pay her $675,000 for three negatives plus 50 percent of the profits. To Mrs. Pickford, for her good

4. Benjamin B. Hampton, *A History of the Movies* (New York, 1931), p. 148.

offices, $50,000. Equally important, Mary would have complete autonomy over her productions, from the selection of the script to the final cut of the release print. First National would top Artcraft's distribution, she was told, so that her net revenue would be $1 million, perhaps even $2 million a year. This type of competition was too much even for Adolph Zukor, who regretfully bid Mary Pickford farewell.

Charlie Chaplin

Charlie Chaplin had caught the eye of Adam Kessel, a partner to Mack Sennett in the Keystone company, while touring America with Fred Karno's English pantomime company in 1913. Kessel signed him up to work in Mack Sennett's Keystone comedies at a starting salary of $150 a week, three times what he had been making as an acrobat, pantomimist, and clown in Karno's program, "A Night in a Music Hall."

In a single year's time at Keystone, Chaplin made thirty-five pictures. Popular acclaim was immediate. "Nothing like it had ever been seen before," says Edward Wagenknecht. "Chaplin swept first America then the world. This was not anything that had been expected or planned for by the motion picture industry or by Chaplin himself; both indeed were greatly surprised by it."[5]

Sennett tried to keep his star in quarantine at the studio, but, as the story goes, an agent from Essanay got to Chaplin by hiring out as a cowboy extra. Yes, Chaplin would switch—for $1,250, nearly ten times his Keystone salary, and the right to direct his pictures. "Comedians could be very serious when talking about money," as Hampton puts it.[6] Essanay promoted the pictures vigorously and the Chaplin craze intensified. After only two years in movies, he had become the top drawing-card in the business. Essanay earned well over $1 million on the Chaplin series.

Chaplin went over to Mutual on February 26, 1916. With his new salary of $670,000—$10,000 a week plus a bonus of $150,000—he had once again multiplied his earnings of the previous year by ten. Not bad for a young man of twenty-six who just three years earlier had embarked on a career in vaudeville. The twelve pictures Chaplin made for Mutual, all two-reelers, were masterpieces. Among them were *The Floorwalker, The Count,* and *Easy Street.* Along with increasing fame came visits from such world-famous figures as Paderewski, Leopold Godowsky, Nellie Melba, and Harry Lauder. Even the intellectuals took notice and began to write appreciations of Chaplin's art.

5. Edward Wagenknecht, *The Movies in the Age of Innocence* (Norman, Okla., 1962), p. 190.

6. Hampton, *A History of the Movies,* p. 155.

Charlie Chaplin in *Behind the Screen* (Mutual, 1916)

Mutual wanted Chaplin to make a second series of twelve pictures and offered him $1 million to stay on. This money was to be straight salary; Mutual would bear all production costs. Chaplin, however, rejected the proposition and instead signed with First National. Money was not the major consideration in this decision. The First National contract paid Chaplin $1 million plus a $15,000 bonus for the act of signing. It called for the delivery of eight pictures within eighteen months. Chaplin was to pay his own production costs from the $125,000 advanced for each negative. Since First National agreed to share the profits equally, Chaplin stood to make more money from this deal than from Mutual's. The clincher, though, was that it provided Chaplin the opportunity for going independent. As a spokesman for First National said:

There are no conditions in that contract which permit us to interfere in the least with him as a producer. He is an independent manufacturer, owning and operating his own producing company and the studios in which it works. He can take any length of time he feels is essential to quality in his releases. He is free to choose his own stories. He is not harassed by telegrams and long-distance telephone calls, urging haste in the completion of a picture to make a certain release date. He is entirely independent of any one or any other concern of any character. His contract with us provides for distribution of his output and that, to Mr. Chaplin, is First National's only functional part in his activities.[7]

Douglas Fairbanks

Frank Case, proprietor of the Algonquin Hotel, told the story that when Harry Aitken offered Douglas Fairbanks a chance to join his Triangle film company, Doug balked. Case noted that the $104,000 offer "was not hay," to which Doug replied, "I know, but the movies!" As a matinee idol with some fifteen years' experience, Fairbanks shared his fellow actors' disparagement of the theater's "bastard child." But Doug, like many in his profession, put his artistic principles aside and succumbed to the irresistible attraction of quick money.

Aitken's Triangle company, formed in 1915, became the industry's most spectacular scheme to capitalize on the talents of the stage. The star system was then in vogue, and Aitken and his partners conceived the plan to capture the brightest theater talents and to translate their greatest plays for the screen. Triangle had three master directors, D. W. Griffith, Thomas Ince, and Mack Sennett. In addition to appealing to the upper classes, Aitken's scheme attracted Wall Street financiers, whose money he needed to engage the cream of theater, vaudeville, and musical comedy. In all, he hired nearly sixty players, among them Sir Herbert Beerbohm Tree, Mary Anderson de Navarro, Weber and Fields, De Wolf Hopper, Billie Burke, and Dustin Farnum.

Although Doug Fairbanks was one of the less-celebrated stars, Aitken chose Fairbanks's *The Lamb* to open the first Triangle program at the Knickerbocker in New York on September 23, 1915. This theater was taken over by Aitken to be the metropolitan home of his company, and its pictures were presented there at the standard Broadway price of two dollars. Doug's debut was well received, at least by *Variety*, which said, "After viewing 'The Lamb,' it is no wonder the Triangle people signed up Fairbanks for a period of three years at any salary within reason. . . . He registers on the screen as well as any regular film actor that has ever appeared in pictures and more strongly than most of them."[8] After the picture was released, Aitken doubled his $2,000 weekly salary.

Part of *The Lamb*'s appeal lay in Doug's acrobatics and stunts; he let a rattlesnake crawl over him, tackled a mountain lion, and jujitsued a bunch of Yaqui Indians. Griffith, however, was not impressed and suggested that Doug's acting style was better suited to Sennett's comedies.

7. *Variety*, November 1, 1918, p. 42.
8. *Variety*, October 1, 1915, p. 18.

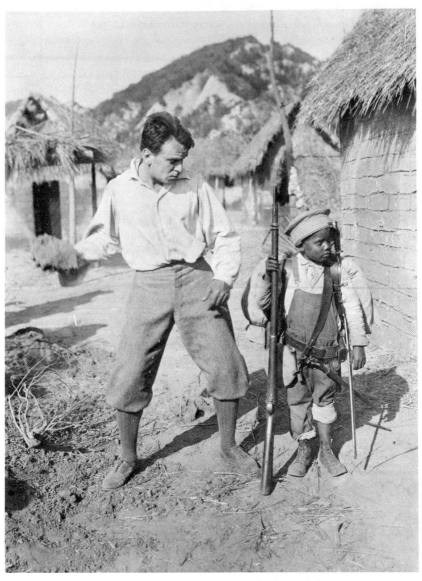

Douglas Fairbanks in *The Lamb* (Triangle, 1915)

With that, Griffith shunted Fairbanks to the care of Frank Woods, who "acted as a sort of cowcatcher to Griffith productions, sweeping accumulated embarrassments away from the path of the Master."[9]

As coordinator of productions, Woods guessed that the rambunctious Doug would probably have much in common with two others on the Triangle payroll, director John Emerson and scenarist Anita Loos. It was this precocious girl, still in her teens, who had the insight to realize that acrobatics were an extension of Doug's effervescent personality; if they continued to be written into his scenarios, he would develop into an immensely entertaining screen character. She was correct, for after *His Picture in the Papers,* Fairbanks's third Triangle picture, the public accepted him as a new kind of popular idol.

Fairbanks made thirteen pictures for Triangle. By the time his contract expired, Aitken was paying him the princely sum of $10,000 a week. With the exception of Doug, Aitken's high-priced stars were inglorious failures. He learned too late what Zukor had discovered at the outset of his Famous Players venture, that most actors trained for the stage could not communicate on the silent screen. Audiences stayed away from their pictures, and exhibitors refused to pay the high rentals Aitken had to ask to meet his astronomical payroll.

Sensing that Triangle was on the verge of collapse, Zukor moved to pluck its prize box-office attraction. He would help set up Doug as an independent producer and distribute his pictures under the Artcraft banner, just as he had done for Mary. No longer having qualms over making movies, Doug accepted. The Douglas Fairbanks Picture Corporation was formed at the end of 1916.

To perfect the formula developed at Triangle, Doug hired Emerson and Loos. They collaborated with him on four of the five pictures he made in 1917; in 1918 he made seven more pictures, all satires on contemporary mores. As Richard Griffith describes his output, "He spoofed Couéism, the new and growing octopus of publicity, psychoanalysis, social snobbery, pacifism, and practically anything else that came along to snatch the momentary interest of the American people."[10] By the time United Artists was formed, Douglas Fairbanks was idolized as "the ideal twentieth century American . . . a mentor, a model for growing boys, a homespun philosopher of the generation after Will Rogers."[11] He was also a millionaire.

---

9. Alistair Cooke, *Douglas Fairbanks: The Making of a Screen Character* (New York, 1940), p. 14.

10. Richard Griffith, *The Movie Stars* (Garden City, N.Y., 1970), p. 145.

11. Cooke, *Fairbanks,* pp. 20, 21.

D. W. Griffith

D. W. Griffith had the singular distinction of being the only director whose name above the title had greater drawing power than any actor in this star-crazed era. When his *The Birth of a Nation* was released in 1915, "the most important single film ever made was thus given to the public." Says Iris Barry in her appreciative essay for The Museum of Modern Art:

> The response was overwhelming: people had not realized they could be so moved by what, after all, is only a succession of photographs passed across the screen. All depends, they found, upon what is the order and manner of that passing. *The Birth of a Nation,* which had cost about $100,000 to make, grossed $18,000,000 in the next few years. Even more important, it established the motion picture once and for all as the most popular and persuasive of entertainments and compelled the acceptance of the film as art.[12]

Griffith had presented himself to Biograph as a scenario writer and actor in 1908 only because he was a thespian "at liberty." His new employment, which paid $5 a day, would be temporary, he hoped, until something, anything, became available for him in the theater. Griffith was soon asked to try his hand at directing. Biograph was in a precarious condition and needed more and better product to strengthen its competitive position. On the basis of his initial effort, *The Adventures of Dollie,* Griffith was given other movies to direct, and on August 17, 1908, he received a contract. His salary was $50 a week plus a commission of not less than $50 based on the footage he turned out. In his first year, Griffith directed 130 pictures; in his second, 100; and in his third, another 95. Biograph now owed its financial strength to Griffith's output, but his salary was still a ridiculously low $75 a week. Although royalties brought Griffith's income to about $3,000 a month, he was still essentially an employee.

For his fourth contract, Griffith insisted on receiving Biograph stock. The shrewd Jeremiah Kennedy refused and also turned down Griffith's request for 10 percent of the company's profits. By the end of 1912, Griffith had made 423 films. He complained about the commission arrangement; nonetheless, as long as he could control his artistic destiny, he remained with the ungrateful Biograph.

But Biograph would not grant him that freedom. Griffith wanted to make longer films, even features, rather than the one-reelers that were Biograph's staple. Why tamper with success, he was told; one-reelers were earning handsome profits at the box office. Griffith replied that the length

12. Iris Barry, *D. W. Griffith: American Film Master* (New York, 1965), p. 20.

of the film should be determined by the requirements of the story rather than by arbitrary restrictions. Kennedy gave in only to the extent that if Griffith felt an urge to go over the one-reel limit, he would have to secure Kennedy's special permission.

For the first time, according to Robert Henderson, Griffith saw his directorial prerogatives threatened. "The freedom that he enjoyed at Biograph, the absolute control over his acting company, over the selection of stories to film, and the entire creation of his films, had led him to regard the Biograph executives as merely salesmen and paymasters. This assertion of administrative control was both frustrating and frightening to him."[13]

Griffith broke with Biograph in September 1913, to join Harry Aitken's Reliance-Majestic Company, which distributed through Mutual. Here, too, Griffith made program pictures, but Aitken gave him the independence of film making, including budgeting, that Biograph had denied him. Moreover, Griffith was given the opportunity of making two independent films a year. One of these was *The Birth of a Nation.* When Mutual's board of directors became increasingly distressed over the mounting costs of the picture, however, Aitken and Griffith ended up producing and distributing it on their own. Even so, after the profits from *Birth* were spread among its many investors, Griffith's cut was not as great as one might expect—about $1 million.

The sensational box-office returns of *Birth* did not vindicate Aitken in the eyes of Mutual's board, of which he was president. In a fit of jealousy, his associates ousted him from their ranks. Undaunted and riding high on the success of *Birth,* Aitken formed Triangle Film Corporation, taking with him Mutual's principal assets in the persons of Ince, Sennett, and Griffith,

Griffith soon became totally preoccupied with his most ambitious directorial project—the making of *Intolerance.* As each day this project grew in scope and expense, it began to tax even Aitken's ability as a money raiser. The result was that Griffith assumed control of the picture by forming his own companies to finance and distribute it. Griffith became the largest investor by pouring into the venture his profits from *The Birth of a Nation;* the fifty others who helped put up the $2 million for the production costs included Aitken and his brother, Roy, Lillian Gish, and Mae Marsh. *Intolerance,* as we know, became a *succès d'estime;* Griffith's prestige was enhanced, but his production venture was bankrupted.

Griffith switched to Zukor's Artcraft in 1917. Although the fate of

13. Robert Henderson, *D. W. Griffith: His Life and Work* (New York, 1972), p. 120.

D. W. Griffith's *Intolerance* (Wark Producing Corporation, 1916)

Intolerance at the box office was yet to be determined, Griffith foresaw
Triangle's downfall. His objective now was to own and control his own
studios so that he could make his films without interference. Joining
Artcraft was but a first step on the road to independence.

W. S. Hart

W. S. Hart, although in on the early planning stages of United Artists,
decided that discretion was the better part of valor, and remained with
Famous Players-Lasky rather than take the risks of going independent.
Zukor helped him to reach this decision by offering him $200,000 per
picture to stay put.

The Confrontation

By 1919 an adjustment of industry conditions was clearly imminent.
Richard A. Rowland, president of Metro Pictures, proclaimed that
"motion pictures must cease to be a game and become a business." He
wanted to supplant the star system. Metro, he said, would thenceforth

decline from "competitive bidding for billion-dollar stars" and devote its energies to making big pictures based on "play value and excellence of production."[14]

Other moguls felt the same way. Production costs were rising rapidly. Negatives that before World War I cost $10,000 to $30,000 were now requiring expenditures of $50,000 to $100,000 and more. It was not just the salaries of the stars that were cutting into profits. Audiences had come to prefer feature-length pictures to the one- and two-reelers and wanted stories having more than rudimentary plots. More money was needed for plays, novels, and scenarios, for better sets and more expensive costumes. Nevertheless, the consensus in Hollywood, concurred in by supporting actors, was that too much of the gross was going to the star.

Rumors, conjectures, and guesswork about mergers filled the air: mergers that aimed to control the industry; mergers that spelled the death of the star system; mergers that eliminated the small fish of filmdom. At a convention of the First National Exhibitors Circuit in the Alexandria Hotel in Los Angeles in January 1919, A. H. Giebler of *Moving Picture World* surveyed the scene and said:

Did Dave Griffith eat a little snack of lunch with Sam Goldwyn, a merger was seen in the offing. Did J. D. Williams stop Adolph Zukor in the lobby and say, "Dolph, this certainly beats New York for climate," the nucleus for a new combination was born.

Did Winnie Sheehan shake hands with Hiram Abrams and ask him politely for news from Broadway, the name of William Fox was written large on the dope sheets. . . .

Did those two mysterious strangers from the East, Hiram Abrams and Benny Schulberg, parade their slow and solemn way along the length of the lobby, eyes were rolled in their direction and bated voices asked: "What have those two wise birds got up their sleeves?" . . ."The First National will control all the stars." "The First National is going to form a combination with Famous Players, Artcraft, Goldwyn, Metro, Fox, and after that they'll tell the stars just where to get off in the matter of salary."

"Doug has signed up with First National." "Doug has done no such of a thing." "Charlie's going to Europe. . . . Mary will renew her contract with First National." "Mary will not." "Mary may, but Charlie won't." "See me in the morning, and I'll give you the whole story." "Don't quote me, but here's the right dope. . . ."

Thus it went on all day long, from getting up time until hay time—everywhere— all over the big hotel, upstairs and down, in parlor, bedroom and bath, lobby, grill, tearoom, candy shop and barber shop, until voices grew husky and imaginations were worn to a frazzle.[15]

14. *MPW*, January 4, 1919, p. 53.
15. *MPW*, February 1, 1919, pp. 607-8.

The stars had reason to believe that something was afoot. Chaplin had gone before First National's board during the convention to request an increase in his production budget and had been turned down. He, Chaplin, who was earning millions for First National! He conferred with Mary Pickford and Douglas Fairbanks and found that although their contracts, with First National and Famous Players-Lasky, respectively, were about to run out, they were not receiving the customary offers from the big companies. They hired a private detective, who uncovered plans for a $40 million merger of all the producing companies, which would tie up every important exhibitor in the country in a five-year contract. The stars felt they had no choice but to form a company of their own.

The fears of the artists that a merger was brewing to deprive them of their bargaining power in the industry were subsequently borne out when the Federal Trade Commission in 1927 completed its investigation of Famous Players-Lasky for alleged infringement of antitrust laws. In one of its findings, the FTC stated that Adolph Zukor, in 1919, "endeavored to form a combination with First National by which the latter would produce no films, exhibit no films other than those produced by Famous Players-Lasky Corporation, and finally become subsidiary to, or merge with, Famous Players-Lasky Corporation."[16] The merger did not go through, as it turned out, but that did not stop Zukor. After failing to lure First National's officers to his company, he continued to struggle for control of the industry by attempting to acquire First National theater franchises. And this battle he won.

Even without this threat, the founding of United Artists was inevitable. A distribution company to market and exploit their pictures fully was but the next step for these artists in achieving autonomy over their work. Pickford, Chaplin, Fairbanks, and Griffith each started out as employees under contract. With star status came the right to form independent production units, which meant more artistic control and a share of the producer's profits. By becoming their own employers, they would now receive all the profits from their pictures. To be sure, they would have to provide their own financing, but a well-managed distribution company would certainly minimize risks.

Forming the Company

The artists wanted William Gibbs McAdoo to head their company. His credentials included being head of the Federal Railroad Board during the war, Secretary of the Treasury before that, and son-in-law of President Wilson. Pickford, Fairbanks, and Chaplin had come to know McAdoo

16. *In re* Famous Players-Lasky Corp., 11 F.T.C. 187 (1927).

well during the Third Liberty Loan campaign when the three toured the country selling millions of dollars' worth of bonds to support the war effort.

McAdoo declined the offer, but suggested that if Oscar Price, his former assistant on the Railroad Board, were named instead, he would gladly serve as counsel for the company. This satisfied everyone; McAdoo, in the words of an editorial in *Moving Picture World,* would bring "prestige second to that of no other business man in the country. His association marks another step in the progress of the business side of the screen, and it goes without saying his voice will have large influence in many quarters where large influence sometimes is very necessary."[17] For a while, anyway, the skeptics would be silenced.

United Artists was formed on February 5, 1919, as a distribution company to promote, exploit, and market motion pictures. First and foremost, it was to provide the service of securing for its producers the highest revenues possible for their films.

This was a cooperative venture in every respect. To finance the company's operations—opening exchanges, hiring salesmen, and the like—each of the founders agreed to purchase $100,000 of preferred stock. In return for equal units of common stock, each agreed to deliver a minimum of nine pictures to the company. Griffith was required to direct his, and the others were to play the leading roles in theirs. McAdoo was issued a unit of stock in consideration of his becoming general counsel.

The common stock had cumulative voting power, enabling each of the stockholders to elect his own representative to the board of directors. Thus control of the management and policies of the company actually rested with the stockholders and not the directors. To prevent the company from slipping out of the hands of the owners, the company was given prior right to repurchase the common stock in the event that a stockholder wanted to sell his interest in UA to an outside party. To ensure complete equality among the parties, the stockholders were prevented from forming partnerships with each other. And to further stimulate the cooperative spirit of the venture and as a gesture of mutual trust, the owners decided to adopt an unwritten law stating that no proposal, policy, or decision could be effected without unanimous consent.

A key feature of the distribution contracts stipulated that each picture was to be sold and promoted individually. Block booking was out. In no way could one United Artists release be used to influence the sale of another UA picture. Merit alone would determine a picture's success or failure. The distribution fee was set at 20 percent of the gross in the United States and 30 percent elsewhere. If in the future the company gave

17. *MPW,* February 15, 1919, p. 899.

one owner better terms, a "most favored nation" clause guaranteed similar adjustments in the other contracts. These fees were well below what Famous Players-Lasky and First National had been charging because United Artists was conceived of as a service organization rather than an investment that would return dividends. Profits would accrue to the owners as a result of the company's securing the best possible rentals for their pictures. With this in mind, the owners reserved the right to approve through their representatives in the home office all contracts with exhibitors.

On April 17, 1919, UA's certificate of incorporation was filed with the secretary of state of Delaware. The board of directors consisted of Albert Banzhaf, Nathan Burkan, Dennis O'Brien, Mrs. Charlotte Pickford, and Oscar Price, who represented the interests of Griffith, Chaplin, Fairbanks, Mary Pickford, and McAdoo, respectively. Price was named president; O'Brien, vice president; George B. Clifton, secretary and treasurer; and Hiram Abrams, the former president of Paramount, general manager.

UA's Contribution to the Industry

During the early years of UA's existence, its owners delivered some of the finest pictures of their careers. The première UA release was Douglas Fairbanks's *His Majesty, the American,* which was released on September 1, 1919. Fairbanks went on to produce such spectacular hits as *The Mark of Zorro* (1920), *The Three Musketeers* (1921), *Robin Hood* (1923), and *The Thief of Bagdad* (1924). Miss Pickford's best-remembered pictures were *Pollyanna* (1920), *Little Lord Fauntleroy* (1921), *Tess of the Storm Country* (1922), and *Rosita* (1923). Griffith delivered *Broken Blossoms* (1919), *Way Down East* (1921), and *Orphans of the Storm* (1922), among others. Chaplin came through with the influential *A Woman of Paris* (1923) and his acknowledged masterpiece, *The Gold Rush* (1925).

Despite this record of excellence, which earned for the company the reputation as the Tiffany of the industry, UA by 1924 was in a precarious postion. The battle for the theaters was in full force. More and more of the country's most important houses were falling into the hands of a few giant concerns. These companies gave preference to their own product with the result that UA found it increasingly difficult to secure suitable exhibition outlets for its pictures. UA, moreover, faced a product crisis. It did not have the resources to finance motion pictures and could not lure other stars to go the route of independent production. An early demise for the company seemed imminent until Joseph M. Schenck was brought in as a partner and named chairman of the board.

Schenck had under contract his wife, Norma Talmadge; his sister-in-law, Constance Talmadge; and his brother-in-law, Buster Keaton. He also possessed the business acumen to stabilize the operations of the company. To solve the problem of acquiring the necessary pictures to sustain UA's operations, he formed the Art Cinema Corporation to finance and produce pictures for UA distribution. This company was owned by Schenck and his associates and was not a UA subsidiary. Art Cinema took over the Hollywood studio belonging to Pickford and Fairbanks, who were now husband and wife, named it the United Artists Studio, and went into production, delivering to UA over fifty pictures. Among them were *The Son of the Sheik* (1926), starring Rudolph Valentino; *The Beloved Rogue* (1927), starring John Barrymore; *Evangeline* (1929), starring Dolores Del Rio; and *DuBarry, Woman of Passion* (1930), starring Norma Talmadge. In addition, Schenck personally produced three Buster Keaton masterpieces, *The General* (1927), *College* (1927), and *Steamboat Bill, Jr.* (1928). To further ease the product crisis, Schenck brought in as UA partners Gloria Swanson in 1925, and Samuel Goldwyn in 1927.

To secure suitable exhibition outlets for UA's product, Schenck formed the United Artists Theatre Circuit in June 1926. This was a publicly held company, also separate from United Artists, whose purpose was to construct or acquire first-run theaters in the major metropolitan areas. This move forced the important theater chains to recognize UA as a forceful competitor with the result that these companies accommodated UA's pictures. The United Artists Theatre Circuit is still in existence today operating a nationwide chain of theaters.

Schenck wanted to bring the UA Studio, the independent production units, and the Theatre Circuit under one corporate umbrella, but his UA partners, Chaplin in particular, vetoed the idea. The thinking was that if UA became a fully integrated company involved in production, distribution, and exhibition, it would no longer foster independent production, but would adopt the mass-production techniques of the major studios. UA prided itself on the fact that independently produced pictures were handcrafted to reflect the specialized talents of their creators, as indeed they were, not always with success but at least with an imprint of individuality that set them apart from the majority of pictures produced under the studio system.

Schenck's reorganization made its impact in 1928. UA began the year with a $1 million deficit and ended it with a $1.6 million surplus. Its worldwide gross that year came to $20.5 million, $10 million more than the 1925 figure, when Schenck joined the company. Net profit for 1929 came to $1.3 million. By 1932, UA had retired all of its preferred stock and accumulated a surplus of $2.5 million.

Despite the unsettling effects of the Depression, the motion picture industry by 1932 had stabilized. It had undergone a series of upheavals brought about by the battle for the theaters, the merger movement, and the sound revolution. The next sixteen years would be an era of oligopoly. Schenck's reorganization had created a niche in which United Artists could function successfully.

8

CARL LAEMMLE

The Business of Motion Pictures

There is probably no business in the world with as many curious angles as ours. The things we do and the things we don't do when we ought to do them would fill volumes. As someone put it: "Our business is full of loose ends, but not chaotic."

One day a small theater owner came to me and complained that our posters were not sensational enough. He pointed to one which was hanging on the wall. It was a work of art. At least I thought so. It was an effort to elevate the tone of advertising.

"It has no kick to it," he said. "It is too pretty. There is not enough action in it."

I was peeved. So I waxed sarcastic. In the most biting tones I could command I said, "Oh, I suppose you'd like to have me throw a bucket of blood across this thing to make it more attractive and gory."

His eyes brightened with enthusiasm and admiration and he said, "That's it—that's it! That's just what we need. That will bring the people in."

Just as the motion picture is a development and, occasionally, an improvement of the legitimate drama, so is the motion-picture poster an offshoot of the theatrical poster. Theatrical posters had attained considerable development before the birth of the silent drama, yet the vigor

Saturday Evening Post 200 (August 27, 1927): 10-11+, and (September 3, 1927): 18-19+.

Carl Laemmle and his players. From the left, Priscilla Dean, Harry Carey, Laemmle, Eddy
Lyons, Virginia Faire, Frank Mayo, and Yvette Mitchell

and youth of the budding industry instilled into lithographic paper a new
vitality and a greater scope for imaginative and artistic ability.

The Early Poster

The dimensions of the ordinary one-sheet are forty-two inches long by
twenty-eight inches wide. Posters are graded in one-, three-, six-, and
twenty-four-sheet sizes. In the parlance of the trade a three-, six-, and
twenty-four-sheet are respectively three, six, and twenty-four times the
size of a one-sheet. These posters, or lithographs, invented to catch the

public eye, are only printed in single sheets. No lithographic plant can boast of presses large enough to print anything bigger than a one-sheet poster, consequently the artist's sketches for poster use are divided equally into units measuring twenty-eight inches by forty-two inches. They are then assembled into one poster, depending upon the specifications whether three, six, or twenty-four sheets are required. The larger the poster the greater is the chance of compelling the passerby's attention. In the showman's code posters are often referred to as "paper."

A supply of stock posters representing stock scenes, such as encounters, thrilling rescues, love scenes, and the like, which were found in almost every picture, was kept on hand by the lithographers.

The first motion-picture posters, carrying only the title of the production and the name of the company, were printed in one, two, or three colors, and ranged in size from a one-, to a three-, or occasionally a six-sheet poster. The name of the company on the poster would be altered as many times as the picture changed hands on its round from one state's rights organization to another. This condition continued until the larger companies systematized the business, at least as far as distributors' titles were concerned.

The smaller picture concerns bought stock posters, stripping in a new title. "Stripping in" takes its name from a strip of paper with the imprint of the local theater name and the play date of the picture. This is pasted across the poster either at the extreme top or bottom and is to inform the reader where and when he may see the poster's action visualized on the screen. However, if a picture company filmed a stage play, this addition was not necessary, posters already having been printed for the original stage vehicle.

The early motion-picture posters had stock borders, made up to represent elaborate ornamental frames. These were succeeded by pictorial paper in which a scene still was enlarged to requisite poster size. That the scenes selected were of the most blood-and-thunder variety goes without saying, as there were few restrictions until about 1910-11. Certain subjects, however, had always been taboo, such as scenes showing men shooting one another, stabbing, and too scantily clad female figures. The last-named prohibition was not necessitated by offending motion-picture posters, but dated back to the regulating of paper for burlesque shows.

Although the coloring, situations, and action of the early movie posters were very lurid, some of the early efforts were better than present-day examples, because the artist had a freer rein. He would simply see the film run off once and then picture in his mind's eye some of the melodramatic or farcical situations and proceed to make his illustrations. There were no highly specialized sales executives, no office or censor hindrances in his path, whereas today almost everyone in the organization must pass upon his sketches before they are ready for the lithograph plant. . . .

At the time of my entry into the motion-picture industry the demand for posters was very low and frequently limited to 125 or 150. Naturally, little effort was spent in making small quantities artistic, and it was not until we determined to back up *From the Bottom of the Sea* with an unprecedented number of one-, three-, and six-sheets, that the quality of independent motion-picture posters improved.

In the Circus Manner

It was this picture that gave birth to the six-sheet size; a poster size even now peculiar to this industry. I had noticed in my own, as well as in other theaters, that the maximum flash possible on the boards outside the nickelodeons was a three-sheet. Wishing to double this display, I arranged to have a six-sheet printed, which enabled exhibitors to utilize two boards, placed side by side. The idea proved equally feasible on billboard stands, as these, being four sheets high, made it possible for the exhibitor to stick on a one-sheet date strip.

Although theaters and particularly circuses have often used twenty-eight-, thirty-two-, and even thirty-six-sheet sizes, the motion picture has seldom if ever exceeded the twenty-four-sheet size. One of the first instances of a motion-picture poster following the style of circus paper was our display for the film of the Paul Rainey big-game hunt. These chromos were done in the best Barnum and Bailey manner, and crowded more wild beasts onto a one-sheet than are to be found at a half-dozen water holes.

One of the first examples of a sixteen-sheet used for a picture was its inclusion in the then-comprehensive array of posters made for *Traffic in Souls.* That paper then, as now, possessed patron-pulling power is shown by the fact that there were almost nightly riots at the Weber & Fields Music Hall, where the film was being shown.

Following the first pictorial posters, which were crude chromos quickly made from stills, an era of better and more dignified billboard advertising began. Many prominent, able, and high-salaried artists were engaged, including such well-known designers as Willy Pogany, Charles B. Falls, Arthur Cobey, Arthur Triedler, George Illian, Lou Fancher, Edward Penfield, and George Peters. Their designs were mostly done in the flat German technique, examples of the school established by the Beggarstaff Brothers, two English artists who were pioneers in the use of the pure poster styles.

The laws that govern the show business were recognized hundreds of years before the moving picture was invented, and the advent of the screen has not altered them in the slightest degree. They are as direct as a straight line, and will not change so long as human nature does not undergo a radical transformation.

For the Holiday Mood

Men and women attend places of entertainment in a holiday mood, and are not entertained by that which they do not comprehend. If a considerable portion of the spectators at a moving picture fail to grasp the author's intent until the photoplay is half over and do not sympathize with the disposition he makes of his characters, they are not going to like the picture or speak a good word for it to their friends—a method of ballyhooing that has the advantages of being unrivaled and without cost.

Now, ballyhooing, or, more properly, exploitation, is necessary and, like press-agenting, must be held in check, lest more evil than good result. The circus method of exploitation has suited many photoplays. The circus itself has been pursuing a flamboyant style of advertising since its birth and it still registers at the box office. For years the biggest attraction with the P. T. Barnum show was Phineas himself, and it was his habit to deliver a ballyhoo from the ring that put all his three-sheet posters to the blush. There is a subtle connection between exploitation and the holiday mood in which people are receptive to all forms of entertainment. It is, of course, necessary to adapt the style of exploitation to the nature of the article being advertised, and highbrow methods must be used only with highbrow attractions.

But it is all part of the game. The eye is caught by the array of high-sounding adjectives. One follows the crowd inside the tent, admires the grace, skill, and daring of the performance, and goes again next year.

The Ballyhoo Man

That brings in the exploitation department, which is charged with the responsibility of rendering aid to the exhibitor. It is upon the shoulders of this department that the burden rests of planning the ballyhoo campaign for the theater owner—providing, of course, the latter is scheduled to play the picture.

When a story is in the making the exploitation director procures the synopsis and forthwith prepares a campaign in his own mind that shall go hand in hand with the finished product. He selects the outstanding features of the picture, the name of the star, the star's previous successes, the director's name, the supporting cast, and the theme of the photoplay on which to work for the prospective booker of the film.

In some original manner, he must devise, create, and invent plans, schemes, or stunts which will link with the particular photoplay in question, and they must be sufficiently comprehensive to facilitate the showing in the theater. For be it understood, when an exhibitor fails to herald his attraction to the public, there is always a danger of being greeted by slender audiences—a contingency that is up to the exploiter to avoid as far as possible. This may be accomplished through the medium of newspapers, lobbies, theater fronts, window displays, printed matter, special showings, and the like.

In my time I have noted the following ideas which have been staged by exhibitors cooperating with newspapers: free passes, colorful illustrations, poster contest, model making, to bob or not to bob, similarity contest, tabloid special, ad and lobby contest, treasure hunt, most popular girl, stage recollections, physical contest, special issue, red and green extras, drawing contest, photo identification, window questions, title writing, war heroes, fashion clinic, telegram stunt, popular mothers, timely slogan, most-words contest, street photos, scrambled movie star, fashion designing.

As for the lobbies, I have seen them changed into every conceivable shape, such as a college, desert, South Sea isle, circus, and Western

Jackie Coogan similarity contest

atmosphere, miniature stage, prize ring, and jungle scene. I have seen them house war relics, revolving fans, electric anvils, aeroplanes, burglar tools, handcuffs, fashions, and so on. The following were also utilized for theater fronts: photographic reproductions, masks, lithographs, sidewalk trenches, banners, and electric flashers. Street stunts have included floats, gypsy girls, masked motorists, stationary balloons, horsemen, painted barrels, sheiks, a caged bear, and an auto parade.

The following tried and proved tie-ups have been made upon countless occasions: better-films committee, book tie-up, cartoon strip, shoe-fitting contest, libraries, star identification, typist stunt, flower matinée, merchants' association, key stunt, prize from star, ukulele contest, and so on.

Press Agents' Stunts

Windows in the vicinity of a movie theater have at one time or other displayed money bags, books, a ship model, photos of stars, snow settings, animated signs, old costumes, make-up demonstration, gown display, and the like.

As for other novelties, such as special showings and prologues, they have been repeated as often as the tides, bearing in mind that in no instance could the picture's title, play dates, and name of theater be omitted.

Under the guise of exploitation some of the weirdest hoaxes have been perpetrated on the public, which only served to alienate newspaper editors. It appears that every newcomer who manages to ease himself into an exploitation department carries with him a rather vague idea that his duties consist solely of grabbing off some extra space in the newspapers without having his employer pay. . . . He can concoct some of the strangest, most nonsensical and pointless pranks that the human mind can conceive. Not infrequently his plans bring the desired results, insofar as they find their way into print.

I have yet to learn of a single instance wherein any of these free space seekers have ever contributed a single exploitation campaign that spelled success for their employers. Take, for example, *Tarzan of the Apes,* filmed by a large company. Before this picture was scheduled to open on Broadway the management negotiated for the services of one of the highest-salaried press agents in captivity. A glance at the title and synopsis of the story was enough for this ingenious chap. Immediately his brain commenced functioning, and a procedure was decided upon. He went down to Coney Island, rented a lion, and ordered the animal to be boxed and forwarded to a certain hotel in New York. Next he arranged for one of his aides to register at the hotel as T. R. Zann and leave word with the clerk that his piano was on its way and must be sent up immediately to his quarters.

A Carnivorous Piano

Accordingly, the piano was duly received and sent up to the aide's quarters. Thus far no suspicion of any kind was aroused, but when T. R. Zann ordered ten pounds of sirloin steak sent up to him daily, the room clerk became suspicious, and, during the absence of the guest, dispatched the house detective to the former's suite to make a silent investigation. One glance revealed a lion in the partially opened piano box, and made the house detective beat a hasty retreat.

When the mysterious T. R. Zann returned he was told to leave the hotel with his lion. All of his protestations that his lion was as playful as any lap dog proved of no avail. But before he caged his pet he disappeared into a telephone booth, rang up the City News Association, and told them to hasten up immediately to the hotel, where a Mr. Zann was being ejected from the hotel for maintaining a lion in his suite.

A reporter was not slow in making his appearance, and verified the information from the hotel officials, who even led him to T. R. Zann's room, where he witnessed with his own eyes the chief bone of contention— the king of beasts caged in the piano crate.

Here was a rare spectacle, indeed, to catch the eyes of metropolitan newspaper readers—something apart from the accustomed daily happenings in a workaday world. No city editor, having the proof from his reporter, could let this story escape, and as a result the newspapers the following morning greeted New Yorkers with

MAN AND LION EJECTED FROM HOTEL

T. R. ZANN CLAIMS LION IS PET

and went on to treat of T. R. Zann's difficulties in a humorous vein. The very captions enticed readers to finish the narrative of Zann and his lion. Somewhere in the distance was the man who engineered this hoax, chuckling to himself and presenting, I suppose, marked copies of the dailies to his employer and receiving congratulations for having put across a clever idea at the expense of the newspapers and the public. Let us carry the ingenious press agent's idea out to its logical conclusion and see whether the effort and expense warranted the outlay of all this energy.

Tarzan of the Apes opened on Broadway, aided by an extra-large advertising expenditure which went for billboards and newspaper advertising, yet it failed to bring the people in droves. At the expiration of a week *Tarzan of the Apes* folded its tents and stole silently out of the theater.

As to our own organization, we plead guilty of having been a participant in one of these artless stunts. As president of the organization, it is the fashion for me to shoulder the blame, although I personally was not involved. . . .

I think beyond a doubt that "exploitation" has become the most abused word in the show business today. Its precise meaning in movie jargon has yet to be determined. The film companies valiantly contend that it is one of the means of selling the merits of a picture to the public in order voluntarily to assist the exhibitor in getting bigger returns to the box office.

Some exhibitors, on the other hand, claim that it is a means used by producers to exploit a picture with the sole purpose in mind of making the attraction appear so big that the film company can boost the rental price to the exhibitors. However, no matter what are the various views and definitions, exploitation, as I take it, is merely advertising the picture to the public in an unusual and convincing manner.

Every large producer maintains a staff of experienced exploitation men stationed in all sections of the country. Any exhibitor is free to call upon these men for cooperation, assistance, and advice when preparing a campaign to advertise a photoplay. He is at liberty to call in any exploitation representative from the company whose picture he has agreed to present to his patrons. There is never any charge for this service, as all cost is borne by the producer.

The Campaign Book

When you buy a radio, vacuum cleaner, or other mechanical device, you receive from the company which has made the product instructions and suggestions as to how to get the best use out of it. These suggestions have been evolved by men supposed to be specialists in their line, after a careful study of the radio or vacuum cleaner. Of course, you are free to disregard their suggestions completely and operate the machine just as you please. The likelihood is that you will not operate it as efficiently as if you had followed out the instructions offered you by the manufacturer.

It seems to me that that is analogous to the exhibitor who rents a picture and receives from the producer a campaign book which offers suggestions as to how best to present the picture, as well as advertising accessories, such as sample newspaper advertisements, posters, heralds, slides, scene stills, and other material for use in a campaign.

There is a different campaign book for each picture. Each book is usually divided into four sections devoted to advertising, publicity, exploitation, and accessories.

Specialists in newspaper artwork, copy writing, and layout, poster artists, and exploitation men are instructed to develop, each in his particular sphere, the concrete idea which has been selected as the most effective selling point of that particular picture. Each department con-

A dressed-up theater front

tributes a section to the campaign book and in due course a copy is furnished gratis to every exhibitor who has contracted to play the picture. Usually an illustration with a catch line conforming to it becomes the focal point of the newspaper ads, rotogravures, and so on, which the exhibitor selects as aids to the exhibition of the picture.

The publicity department's contribution to the campaign book is a synopsis of the theme, the cast, advance stories in connection with the picture, and the intimate, chatty type of copy so eagerly relished by the screen fans. These stories are prepared for the exhibitor and save him the writing of his own publicity material. All he need do is cut any story from the campaign book he sees fit, fill in the name of his theater together with the play date in the space provided, and send it along to his local editor, timed with the exhibition date of his attraction.

Expert Advice Free for the Taking

The exploitation department's offering to the book is an entire section devoted to ballyhoos, window and lobby displays, newspaper campaigns, special stunts, and prologues, together with full instructions as to procedure. The prospective patron is therefore sold through an association of ideas which link up all the advertising mediums.

In fairness to many exhibitors, I must state that I have seen some of them who have disregarded the campaign book entirely and used their own ideas of exploitation, advertising, and publicity to good advantage.

On the completion of a picture, and following its viewing by the New York office, the three departments of advertising, publicity, and exploitation combined first on the preparation of the press book or campaign book. This constitutes a complete and encyclopedic guide to the local theater owner in selling the picture to his public. In effect, it places in the employ of the smallest theater owner in the country the services of the best possible advertising, publicity, and exploitation brains that we can secure.

There are publicity stories of all possible usable sizes and on every angle of appeal to which the picture lends itself, which the manager may take to his local newspaper after filling in the name of his theater. There are suggested advertisements from one-inch single column up to page sizes on the more important pictures, that are ready for use with the insertion of his theater's name. The exploitation department supplies a variety of ideas aimed at providing something that the village theater can utilize, as well as ideas for the biggest city theater.

The theater owner may secure matrices or cuts for the illustrations to be used for publicity stories or advertisements at the branch office of the firm from which he secured the picture. In addition, the press book also lists and shows such aids prepared for his use as lithographs, colored photographs for his lobby, cards for use in store windows, and the colored throwaway circulars that we call heralds. These advertising accessories are provided for the theater owner at a price calculated to cover the actual cost plus the expense of handling.

The Time to Strike

Simultaneously with the preparation of the press book the advertising department has had to unlimber its forces on the task of positive advertising selling. There are a half-dozen or so trade publications reaching the motion-picture theater owner, and these are used in proportion to their circulation efficiency. The amount expended will run from an average of $1500 on what might be termed the ordinary run of pictures, to $5000 and away beyond in exceptional cases. Figures and averages are dangerous in discussing motion-picture advertising, because we must strike while the iron is hot. If a picture strikes the public fancy we must heavy-pressure it to get every possible dollar of return.

With the showing of the picture in the first big cities the exploitation department gets into action. Obviously, of course, its work is the selling of the picture to the public in these cities.

But secondarily, and importantly, its task is to show the theater managers throughout the country by actual demonstration that the public will respond to the picture, and also the methods to use in getting that response.

As to the means used by an exploitation man, I can best answer by telling you the sky is the limit. If he can induce the mayor of the city to attend the first performance and consequently secure newspaper space, that is good exploitation. If he can prevail on the police department to hold a parade to the front door of his theater because the picture's hero is a policeman, that is exploitation. If he arranges a special performance for the schoolteachers of the city because the subject is taken from literature, that is exploitation. He uses advertising and publicity, and then as much else as he can think of or get.

. . . I may be asked how long is the advertising life of a picture. Here again I must recall that we strike while the iron is hot and add—we keep on striking as long as it is hot. Three months may be termed the period of high life for an average picture in the sense of advertising it; six months' activity is worthwhile on many. But when you get a *Covered Wagon* or a *Hunchback of Notre Dame,* you can keep right on in the belief that you won't stop until everybody in the country has seen it. Then you'll hide it only for a year or two until they get anxious to see it again.

A word about reaching the public with motion-picture advertising—direct-to-the-consumer advertising, it would be termed by other manufacturers.

We have seen that the publicity department is at work early and late, reaching the public through the means of news. We have seen that the theater man is supplied with advertisements for his use in reaching the public. And we have seen the peculiar ways of the exploitation man.

What about the manufacturer's paid advertising direct to the public? First, the matter of daily newspapers. Of course, during the year all the leading producers spend considerable money with daily newspapers in connection with their own showings of pictures in the bigger cities. But when it comes to the question of daily newspaper advertising as used in other fields to aid the dealers, we have been blocked by marketing conditions. The motion picture is not a product that will be on the dealer's shelves available to the customer at any time he may choose to buy, nor is it a product sold to the dealer for a stated standard price.

Our first problem, therefore, is timing the advertisements so that this local advertising is of value to a great number of our theater owners.

Obviously, to be of value to the biggest customer, the leading theater, it must be placed simultaneously or previous to his showing of the picture. But that means it will have appeared weeks, perhaps even months, before the picture will reach the great bulk of our customers. That isn't good advertising.

Direct Appeals to the Patrons

Suppose we time the ad only with consideration for the biggest customer. Here we have a theater man who prefers to do his own advertising, who does considerable of it. We have a product not sold at a standard price. It is only natural that this customer would consider the amount of money spent by us in advertising is directly taken from him in the rental price he is paying. At any rate, he would prefer to have us take the amount off his rental and allow him to spend his own money in his own way on advertising.

When you leave the question of daily newspaper advertising by picture producers in this unsatisfactory state and come to the matter of direct-to-the-patron advertising by national magazines, you will receive as many opinions probably as there are picture men to interview.

We have first, of course, the problem again of timing our ads with the availability of the product to the reader. Obviously we are not able to do the hammer-and-tongs direct sort of advertising that would sell the reader into a feverish desire to rush around the corner to view a certain picture. When he got there the theater might be showing an entirely different picture.

The alternative is the sort of advertising that lays stress on the institutional, while creating a general interest in the product. This means long-haul advertising—advertising that, once started, must be kept up consistently in season and out of season. You cannot sell an institution by sporadic outbursts.

A word about truth in motion-picture advertising and publicity. In the matter of advertising it did not take long to learn that the truth pays. You won't find the truth actually violated in motion-picture advertising to the dealer or to the public. And at the same time you may not agree with an ad after you have seen the picture. This is because we deal in an intangible product, with an appeal as varied as the number of persons you may find in an audience. The picture advertised as one of the greatest heart dramas ever made may not appeal to your heart at all. But at the same time there will be many in the audience who would go further than the advertising writer, and proclaim it the greatest.

Where is the picture-advertising man to find the lines of demarcation between truth and exaggeration and opinion. He can take only the point of greatest appeal about a picture as it strikes him and do his best to sell all readers he feels will be affected by that type of appeal.

There was a time when our skirts were probably not so clean in the matter of truthful publicity. As an inheritance from the theatrical days, we had the conception of a publicity man as one who stole newspaper space by hook or crook, and the more clever if by crook. Here I want to pay a word of tribute to the work of Mr. Will Hays in this regard. The industry has long since cleaned house; there is no room for the faking type of press agent, creating news out of whole cloth and laughing at editors who fall for his dreams.

A Frame for the Picture

Now, in conclusion, a word about hokum. That's a perfectly good word, admitted to good standing in some of the best dictionaries. Do you know what it is? Well, one dictionary describes it as "a word, act, business, or property used by an actor to win an audience." The aim of every advertisement, whether of pictures or anything else, is to win an audience. So it is legitimate to use hokum in advertising, because to win an audience for pictures you've got to reach its heart, and hokum is nothing in the world but heart interest. The fire engine dashing down the street is good hokum for the people who love that sort of thrill. On the other hand, the classics are good hokum for the so-called highbrow. We pick out the feature of a picture which we think will interest the greatest number of people. Then we hammer away at it and keep hammering until it has been driven home to film followers.

Among the many articles which have been published dealing with the manifold advantages to the exhibitors of advertising their pictures fully, insofar as their lobbies are concerned, one great illustration has been overlooked. It is the effect of the simultaneous showing of two motion pictures with leading stars of equal merit.

We can imagine, for example, two houses in competition, each showing a picture which features a player who, in popular favor, ranks on the same level with the other. There is no need to mention any star in particular, so many can be paired off in their relative drawing powers.

One of the exhibitors decides to stand pat. He will let his posters, stills, or maybe a plain banner, announce the name of the star and allow the drawing power of the actor or actress to do the rest. The other exhibitor, believing in the old maxim of striking while the iron is hot, is not content to stand pat. With a strong hand he plays it for all he is worth. He reasons with himself somewhat in this fashion: "My competitor has a star of equal drawing power to mine. How can I get the inside track and keep it?" And then he naturally thinks of an added attraction for his picture. How can

Attracting attention with a billboard

this be done? First and last, by good publicity. The public mind is influenced by its first impressions; almost entirely so in the case of a motion picture, because the decision is taken before the leaven of a second impression has any time to begin work.

Two Vandykes are on a wall. One is in a frame of perfect setting, with the light so arranged that the marvelous coloring is displayed to the full at the first sight. The other is neglected. The frame is a makeshift one and the true value of the proper light is ignored. Which one gets the first attention and the first word of praise? The second and longer impression may entirely reverse the critic's decision. The neglected one may really be the finer one. But there is no second impression so far as a motion picture is concerned. First impressions do the trick.

The Original Ideas

The exhibitor who knows his business will have a magnetic lobby display that gets the man on the street before his competitor; that stops him surely and quickly and does not let him pass on to the other house.

The reader may attach very little importance to these comments of mine which describe the functions of our publicity, advertising, and exploitation departments as well as the significance of accessories and lobbies to theater proprietors. To be candid, I believe I haven't stressed the importance of these factors too strongly. Each in its own way has spelled success for countless photoplays, and we expended, for example, something like $1,399,416 during 1926 to maintain advertising, publicity, and exploitation departments.

Perhaps here and there we have offended good taste; it may be that our methods have not appealed to some discriminating persons; perchance we transgressed the heights of propriety. But our experiences and problems create just such conditions, and in order to prosper, strategy becomes part of the game of motion pictures. If our seraph superior ever hales us before the bar on Judgment Day, my only plea will be: "Be charitable to the erring."

The Movies as Big Business

In the attention given to the film as art, it is not easy to view the motion picture business through the eyes of those who saw it as nothing more than a business opportunity—a chance to invest with the promise of high returns. And yet, this is exactly what the next selection does. It is a prospectus prepared by the investment house of Halsey, Stuart & Co., and its purpose was solely to attract investors to the securities of the leading motion picture firms. In this light, the movies were placed on the same level with the oil or steel industries. Yet, even the art of the film was influenced by investment houses, banks, and lawyers—for artists often lived or died on the success or failure of these institutions—and no one can come to a full understanding of the history of film without understanding how the business was financed.

The Halsey, Stuart & Co. prospectus provides a good indication of the structure of the industry at the apex of the silent era. When this document was published the industry had stabilized, and even the most conservative banks—National City, Manufacturers Trust Company, the Irving Trust Company, and the National Bank of Commerce—had established commercial banking relations with the soundly managed movie concerns.

The well-known investment banks, observing the burgeoning movie industry, vied to handle new security issues of the major companies. The great expansion of the industry during the 1920s was facilitated by the underwriting of stocks and bonds by Wall Street and LaSalle Street financiers and their purchase by the public. Among the investment banks most prominently involved in the movie business were J. & W. Seligman and Co.; Bankers Trust Company; Kuhn, Loeb & Company; Goldman, Sachs & Co.; Hayden, Stone & Company; and Dillon Read & Company.

169

The Halsey, Stuart prospectus describes those characteristics of the movie business most admired by financiers—characteristics that encouraged the massive infusion of capital into the industry during the 1920s. It tells much about the economic climate of the country, also, reflecting the optimism of those bull-market days when only endless expansion of enterprise was seen on the horizon.

The prospectus is an interesting document in many respects, sometimes amusing and at other times annoying. It links the growth of the industry not to the creative efforts of Edwin S. Porter, D. W. Griffith, Charlie Chaplin, and the artists who won the hearts of the public, but to industrialists like Thomas Edison and George Eastman. The prospectus praises not the film's value as a medium of human expression, but the industry's vertically integrated structure, assembly-line production techniques, efficient worldwide distribution system, air-conditioned movie palaces, and conservative accounting practices. In its enthusiasm, the prospectus inflates attendance figures, ignores the nefarious ways of some of the industry leaders in capturing control of the business, and glosses over the implications of America's domination of the world's screens. But similar criticisms could be made of prospectuses describing other industries. Here, the movies are seen as a business, pure and simple. And since financing played an inexorable role in the growth and direction of the industry, it must be understood.

9

HALSEY, STUART & CO.

The Motion Picture Industry as a Basis for Bond Financing

Motion pictures, meeting at popular prices the universal demand for recreation and amusement, have quickly become an essential part of modern living. People everywhere look to them for their relaxation, their entertainment, and increasingly for their general information and education. Without doubt the "Movies" are today one of the best known of all things American, both in this country and abroad. And yet the great Motion Picture Industry back of the movies—now a major ranking industry in the United States—has until very recently been comparatively unknown in its investment aspects.

It is time that the American people, who know and appreciate their "Movies" so well, should, as investors, become better acquainted with the Motion Picture Industry, its tremendous proportions, its financial structure, its prospects. And as the investor goes backstage, literally "behind the screens," to examine this vibrant new industry which makes possible his favorite form of recreation and education, he will not only find an industry of much larger dimensions than he anticipated, but one which is much more efficient, much better integrated, and more thoroughly seasoned than he could have imagined.

The motion picture industry has grown to its present rank among the great industries of the United States in a brief period of thirty years. But more surprising than even that rapid growth is the fact that in little more

Prospectus, May 27, 1927.

than one generation it has developed into a well-knit, efficiently organized industry.

Any critical appraisal of the motion picture business today will bring out the fact that it is an industry already quite thoroughly "in line" with the best methods of industrial organization and technique. While it is a relatively new industry, it is nevertheless a mature industry. And while it is still growing tremendously, its present development is being achieved along lines closely paralleling the expansion of our great veteran industries.

The integration of manufacturing, wholesaling, and retailing is already well advanced. This condition is not confined, as in some industries, to just one all-dominating corporation, but at least a half-dozen of the leaders in the motion picture field are now established as complete units of operation.

Very effective trade associations have been organized in this industry. It occupies an advanced position regarding public relations. It ranks high in its success in the arbitration of disputes.

The motion picture industry has stabilized itself and won much prestige in recent years through its progressive theater-building program. The big companies have always been strong in earnings, and now their asset situation has been much strengthened. Real estate, in the form of substantial theaters and office properties, bulks large in the typical balance sheet. In fact the motion picture concerns bid fair to become among the most extensive chain owners of business locations in the whole country.

In the production phase of this industry, standardized methods have been established; modern systems of cost control are the rule; conservative policies regarding depreciation are in vogue; film inventory values, based on the cost of producing pictures, are written off rapidly after each release date. And backing up all this is the present program of high-grade research into the economic as well as the mechanical problems of future development.

A Growth Chart of the Industry

If a comprehensive chart could be made to depict the growth of the motion picture industry, all of its graphic lines would start near the zero point about 1896, and rise to points of impressive magnitude by 1926.

The line representing motion picture theaters, for instance, would show approximately 20,000 of these buildings in the country at the present time, while in 1900 there were practically none devoted to pictures exclusively.

Employment figures for this young industry would show that in 1926 more than 350,000 persons found work in its various branches, whereas in 1900 only a few venturesome spirits had dared to think of motion pictures as a sole source of income.

Our chart would show, as well as possible, that the manufacture of motion picture films, which was close to the zero point in 1900, now exceeds 1,250,000,000 feet per year; consumes, incidentally, more silver in their manufacture than is used by the United States Mint; and dominates the film markets of the world.

The invested capital in the motion picture industry was also insignificant in the early years, but by 1926 the investment totaled a billion and a half dollars.

Historical Aspects

The "living picture" had been foretold and its coming cherished since before the Christian era. Early Chinese literature has frequent references to it. In medieval times a most enthusiastic prophet was Italy's great artist, Leonardo da Vinci.

Even the basic principle—"persistence of vision"—upon which the motion picture depends for its effect of continuity, had been known and commented on for centuries. As early as 1824 Peter Roget (better known as the compiler of his famous "Thesaurus") did some precise work in applying this law of human sight.

But many significant discoveries had to be made in widely divergent fields, and many devices were yet to be perfected before the genius of the late nineteenth century could tie them all together and bequeath to the fortunate people of the twentieth century a successful motion picture. Photography had to be perfected by men like Daguerre and Niepce. Engineering difficulties had to be solved by such experimenters as Dr. Plateau of Ghent and Franz von Uchatius of Austria. The electric motor was to be needed; many things in modern chemistry had to be understood. No wonder the people of the world waited long for their motion pictures, and no wonder they received them with great enthusiasm when at last they became a reality.

It is interesting to note what a variety of unrelated purposes inspired progress in the one line of speed photography. A Frenchman named Sellers [Coleman Sellers was American—Ed.], for instance, contributed much through his efforts to get a living picture record of his two small sons performing such commonplace acts as driving nails. On the other hand, Leland Stanford, in America, sponsored a still greater advance because he was willing to spend money without limit to prove, in support of a now-famous bet, that all four feet of a racing horse were completely off the ground at certain phases of its stride.

From Roget to Edison there was no letup in the search for effective devices that would present pictures to the eye in rapid succession. Some worked with parallel revolving discs, others with the hollow cylinder, and still others with crude mechanisms resembling the paddle-wheel. In each case a series of pictures was so placed that when the mechanism revolved they would be seen in quick sequence through prepared slots, or peep-holes. These early impractical motion picture machines were known by the various names Phenakistoscope, Zoetrope, and Kinematoscope.

Edison and Eastman Important Figures

But the practical motion picture had to await Thomas A. Edison's de-velopment of the electric camera in 1888, and the perfection by George Eastman of a flexible film, the same year, which would feed rapidly through both the camera and an exhibition machine. A remarkable coincidence is that neither of these men knew of the work of the other, yet within a few months their contributions had been joined in the production of the first moving picture on modern principles. Still this was only a one-man "peep show" and eight years more were to elapse before a satisfactory projector was developed and an actual screen performance could be shown to an excited audience in the city of New York.

The year 1896, then, is generally regarded as the beginning of the busi-ness of motion pictures. Prior to that the penny arcades with their little "peep shows" had been the only commercial use made of this principle. It is significant that the people had up to that time believed that this would be its final use. Now quickly followed the appearance of "nickelodeons," and the screen production of novelty pictures.

The real business of the motion picture had to await still another mile-stone, however, before it could give promise of becoming a first-rate industry. That was the development of another brand-new idea—the scenario—telling stories in picture form. Like all new ideas, it came slowly. First there were little skits and episodes, but gradually the exhibitors and producers sensed the great fact that it would be narratives, plots, and events which would take with the public in a big way and make the motion picture a commercial success. But all this required another ten years, during which time the movies were used principally to supplement other forms of entertainment. Then, the first "feature" pictures were produced, and the moving picture immediately took its place as a complete entertainment on its own merit.

Organization of the Industry

The motion picture industry resembles in its organization most typical American industries. There are the three phases of production, distribu-tion, and exhibition, which correspond, roughly, to the manufacturing, wholesaling, and retailing activities common elsewhere. Until quite recently these various services were rendered by more or less independent concerns specializing in their respective fields. But economies of production, and the theater demand for an all-year supply of pictures of standard trademark quality have tended to force consolidation in the production end. Exhibitors, too, have found great economy in the maintenance of theater "chains" for the routing of films and large-scale buying. The result is that we now have fully a thousand different theater groups in the United States which represent at least one-half of the seating capacity of the country.

A still further integration of the industry became inevitable as the larger of these chains of theaters felt the need for a dependable supply of high-grade pictures and secured an amalgamation with suitable producing organizations. Similarly, at the other end, leading producers required an assured outlet for their immense producing programs. Hence there has developed in the industry nearly a score of these "complete" producing-distributing-exhibiting organizations, which represent perhaps two-thirds of the motion picture business in the United States, and constitute a well-balanced and seemingly well established state of competitive equilibrium.

Just as the consolidation of the motion picture industry has tended to parallel that in other well-developed industries of the nation, so has its organization into trade associations. In fact, the motion picture industry has been more successful in this line than has almost any other major industry.

Five years ago, as is already well known, the forward-looking motion picture companies got together and organized the Motion Picture Producers and Distributors of America, calling Will H. Hays, former postmaster general of the United States, to be the president of the association. Mr. Hays has proved a genius of the first order and his organization has accomplished great things for the motion picture industry. Its chief activities have been: (a) improvement of public relations, (b) promotion of business comity within the industry, (c) encouragement of better business practice, such as standardized budgets, uniform cost accounting, uniform contracts, and the arbitration of disputes.

The arbitration system between buyer and seller in the motion picture industry has, in fact, become so successful that it is now being studied widely as a model for other lines of enterprise. The public relations work of the Hays association is widely known and very deservedly so. No industry has ever "gone to the people" so effectively. One of the principal aims of its public relations work has been to improve motion picture standards and service to the public.

The Hays regime in motion pictures has been so eminently successful that the member corporations recently underwrote the program for another term of ten years. Motion Picture Producers and Distributors is an entirely voluntary organization. Its membership has grown from nine at the time of organization to twenty-four at the present time, representing 90 percent of the producing end of the industry.

Production

In motion picture production America is not only an outstanding leader in the world today, but dominates the world market as in practically no other line of enterprise. We supply 90 percent of the motion pictures consumed abroad, reaching more than seventy foreign countries. In return, this foreign market contributes as film rentals something like $75 million per annum, estimated by some authorities to be approximately 25 percent of the total income of the production end of the American industry. The importance of this immense foreign market as a stabilizing element can hardly be overestimated, and the prospects for future growth which it entails are entirely beyond present comprehension. The United States is practically the only country at the present time whose market possibilities have even been charted, while competition abroad, as will be pointed out later, is not the fearsome specter which it is in many lines.

Approximately 12 percent of the American motion picture films are produced in New York City and environs; the rest is practically all a product of Southern California, principally of the Hollywood community. The great concentration of film production within that small geographical area is a distinctive feature of this industry. But that concentration constitutes the best assurance of the United States that its present paramount position in world picture production will be maintained indefinitely. The history of other great industries, such as pottery, meat-packing, and steel, has demonstrated how relatively immovable a great production center can be when once the specialized labor, the production equipment, and the marketing habits of the people have become centered in, and directed toward, some one locality.

Hollywood—World Center of the Industry

Hollywood now holds a larger share of the motion picture talent, of producing paraphernalia, and enjoys a more complete dominance in this industry than ever was experienced by Trenton in pottery, Pittsburgh in steel, or Chicago in meat-packing.

It was not mere chance that established the motion picture industry in Southern California. War conditions, it is true, favored American production in the early years, and hence indirectly the Hollywood area. But the actual localization of production there came through a process of pure competitive selection in which the geographical advantages favorable to producers in that region literally forced competing directors and their companies to come to California—and Hollywood.

The advantages of dependable sunshine, permitting outdoor production without delays, and of great variety in scenery at close range (the ocean on one side, the deserts, mountains, and forests in other directions), so that the sequence of almost any picture can be suitably filmed with but little cost for travel—all have militated to establish Hollywood as the center of the motion picture world. Moreover, such natural endowment can never be exhausted by exploitation. Hence the Hollywood advantage is neither imaginary nor ephemeral, and there is no present likelihood of its losing its commanding position, either in America or for the world at large.

There have been rumors as to great postwar competition soon to be expected from Europe, especially out of Germany and France. But the facts do not warrant any precipitate fears along this line. Both of the above countries have produced good films, and their art work is, in some cases, outstanding. But in neither country, nor in any one country for that matter, save Japan, can local producers find a sufficient theater market to make sure that they can recoup on production costs for a heavy schedule of feature pictures. Ambitious manufacturers abroad must therefore look to the American market. Yet the American market is preempted by American pictures, as good as the world affords. While 425 foreign pictures were sent to this country in one recent year, only six were successful in winning a showing in American theaters.

Factory-Studios Are Great Industrial Plants

Motion picture production does not classify with exactness as a manufacturing process, but it combines elements of what is commonly known as manufacturing, with "assembling." Motion pictures are produced by a process of photographing the scenes and sequences needed to build up an effective story. More and more, this takes place within the walls of great studios where, on one huge "lot," are assembled the large variety of buildings and equipment needed in the manufacture of pictures.

In the early days, because everything in this industry was highly experimental, these studios were more or less flimsy and inexpensive. But now production requirements are so constant, so multifarious and extended, that large substantial buildings of brick and stone have been required to take their places. The visitor today to one of these immense studio-factories finds it laid out along paved streets on an extensive campus. The latest western "plant" of this sort to be erected cost $2 million.

The largest buildings on a movie lot are its great enclosed stages—most of them have several—of such large area and height that outdoor condi-

Fox Movietone Studio, Beverly Hills

tions can be simulated in any "corner," and numerous feature pictures be in process simultaneously. Then there are huge electric plants, laboratories of the most modern sort, carpenter shops big enough to accommodate the hundreds of workers, sculpturing and modeling plants on a factory scale, dressing rooms and bungalows to remind one of a residential suburb, general supply warehouses, administration buildings, etc.

Production Standards Are High

The very high standards of artistry now required in motion picture production, and the immense costs involved, tend to place this business in the hands of large-scale companies—producers who can afford expensive machinery, finance million-dollar plants, and carry monthly budgets, as one typical firm does, of as much as $400,000.

The American output of feature pictures is at present about 750 per annum. These will average in length from seven to twelve, thousand-foot reels. Of "short subjects"—comics, newsreels, etc.—there are perhaps two and a half times as many items, but they will average not more than two reels apiece.

The average cost of feature films ranges from $25,000 to $250,000, with the great spectacles which call for historical backgrounds, expensive costuming, and many actors, costing a million or more.

A marked tendency exists among these large companies to run a production schedule of fifty or more strong features per year. This is because they wish to provide as completely as possible for the weekly-release needs of their controlled and client theaters.

The human element plays a large part in picture production, but the following figures on the personnel of a representative organization show that not all the workers are actors, by any means. This particular company gives employment to about 1600 people. Only sixty-two of these are "stars" and featured players, while ninety are writers, eighty-five directors and assistants, fifty-five cameramen. Carpenters, painters, electrical workers, modelers, and wardrobe assistants employed by this firm run into three figures each.

The big problem in motion picture production, as in any type of profitable manufacturing business, is to control costs. This has received much attention in the industry in recent years. A typical "cost analysis" comprehending the expense items of a feature-picture budget will show: labor, 35 percent (made up of actors, 25 percent, directors, cameramen, etc., 10 percent); raw material, 37 percent (including scenarios, 10 percent, raw film, 5 percent, costumes, 3 percent, scenic sets, 19 percent); rent and transportation, 8 percent; and other factory overhead, 20 percent.

The Economics of Star Salaries

So much publicity has been given to the high cost of "stars" that one is surprised to learn, from such figures as the above, that the total actor cost (including the stars) of most films runs under 25 percent. Admittedly it is a big item and has to be watched with the same care as any important cost item in a competitive plant. Delays in picture production must be rigidly guarded against. But time economy is being effected with unusual skill. The production schedule of each picture is minutely blueprinted in advance so that the "shooting" of the various parts may be accomplished with the utmost conservation of salary costs.

Whatever change of emphasis from actor to play which the future may hold, the "stars" are today an economic necessity to the motion picture industry. In the "star" your producer gets not only a "production" value in the making of his picture, but a "trademark" value, and an "insurance" value, which are very real and very potent in guaranteeing the sale of this product to the cash customers at a profit. It has been amply demonstrated that the actual salaries (not the mythical exaggerations) paid to motion picture actors, however famous, are determined by the law of supply and demand in exactly the same way as are the rewards of executives in the business world.

The motion picture "star" of great box-office pulling power must possess a successful combination of (1) personality, (2) acting technique, (3) photographic ability, and (4) that unnameable capacity to grip the public imagination. This combination is rare, and the rewards of its fortunate possessors will doubtless always be among the highest in the business world.

Much of the former uncertainty in picture production has been eliminated. Not only have producers gone into the retail field and thus made sure of a fair "hearing" for their pictures, but the art of production itself has been mastered in a new way. Picture "direction" has become a science, and enough showmanship is now guaranteed for every picture to give it a genuine appeal. Demand has been analyzed and charted so that the "manufacturer" today produces to a relatively known market.

Distribution

The distribution phase of the motion picture industry, though overshadowed by the more spectacular nature of film production on the one side, and theater exhibition on the other, is still a matter of tremendous importance. It is, in fact, of relatively more importance than the comparable jobbing service in other lines of business. Distribution in this industry embraces three important phases: (1) physical deliveries and redeliveries, including the repair, renovation, and replacement of films; (2) the sales work—which is in reality the securing of rental contracts for specific datings; and (3) advertising—directed to theaters through trade papers, and to the public through posters, newspapers, and magazines.

The production phase of a motion picture is not completed when the first negative is finished at Hollywood. From this negative a large number of "positives," or exhibition films, must be made before there can be any distribution. These positives are printed off in various parts of the world, but principally in New York, which is the distributing center of the industry. Probably one hundred positives are made for the average feature film, and these are then consigned with orders to the various exchange cities in the United States and abroad. The film products of a dozen large integrated companies which have both producing and exhibiting facilities are handled through a branch-office arrangement in some thirty or forty "key" cities. About the same number of "state's rights" distributing organizations operate on a national scale, but they usually buy the exclusive territorial rights on films from "independent" producers, and in turn sell exhibition rights to the theaters, either for a flat price or on a percentage basis.

Product Paid For as Delivered

The hard necessity of financing the motion picture industry within itself during its early years tended to force the distribution business to operate on a cash basis. In fact, a great deal of it is, and has always been, on a cash-in-advance basis, with a customary 25 percent down-payment upon the signing of contracts by theaters for the running of prospective pictures. In any case, the films go out to practically all theaters on a C.O.D. basis, with transportation both ways paid by the exhibitors.

Distribution contacts with individual theaters are made through traveling salesmen out of the district offices, while the more important "chains" are sold direct from headquarters. Rental prices are arrived at in two ways. Bargaining prevails within limits, but it is the custom to apportion the expected revenue from a picture to different areas and let that determine the rental charge. The distribution of motion pictures is complicated, but it is also made relatively more important than in most industries, by the fact that there are "first-run" theaters which must be served on schedule ahead of the second-, third-, and fourth-run houses. In fact, the dating and routing of motion picture films requires a very high degree of precise handling. Yet making quick connections and delivering without exception in time for the advertised datings of the films is a standard of performance religiously adhered to in this phase of the industry.

Exhibition

No phase of the motion picture industry has shown a more amazing growth in the last few years than the exhibition end. There are several reasons for this. First, the coming of the era of great pictures made it possible for the first time for the theater manager to charge such admission prices as would permit him to accumulate revenue with which to build suitable "palaces of entertainment." Second, the development of chain theater groups and the integration of the large motion picture companies brought a higher grade of talent to the problems of theater management and construction. Third, and as a sequel to this, the exhibitors launched a very definite policy of catering to the pleasure of the patrons.

The "Show Windows" of the Industry

The success of any motion picture "feature" depends to a very large extent upon its opportunity for showing in certain populous centers, and its reception there. Second only to Broadway's treatment of a picture, the thousands of outlying theater managers are influenced by the acclaim given to new films at their own nearest metropolis. Hence it is now the custom to have a "prerelease" showing at a leading New York theater for every film of great importance, and a "first-run" showing for all feature pictures at strategic de luxe houses over the whole country. These first-run houses are regarded by the production end of the business as their "show windows." This is why producers have given so much attention of late to getting control of representative houses in this class. It is plainly impera- tive that if large production costs are to be compensated for, or profits made, the producers with a heavy schedule of pictures must be able to give them an extensive early showing in these prominent theaters which set the style, so to speak, for the country.

The first-run theaters get their films and are protected in the exclusive showing of them over a specified contract period. Then each picture goes to the second-run theaters according to the terms of their contracts, and so on to the lesser houses, at an ever-decreasing rental charge. American theaters, for the most part, buy their films well in advance of showing.

Foyer of Tebbett's Oriental Theater, Portland, Oregon

Annual Attendance Gain Forcing Expansion

The 20,000 motion picture theaters in the United States at the present time represent approximately two-fifths of the world's total. The number of American theaters has been almost constant in recent years in spite of the fact that the seating capacity of the country has shown a substantial annual increase. The explanation is that the quality and size of motion picture theaters have been improving at a remarkable rate. In ten years the old store-building type of theater has given place almost entirely to commodious houses of distinctive design and elaborate appointments. This tendency originated among the downtown theaters in the great cities, but the vogue of the new de luxe theater has now spread to the smaller cities and towns and into high-grade residential sections everywhere.

The present seating capacity of motion picture theaters for the nation is estimated at 18,000,000, with the weekly attendance registering somewhat above 100,000,000—close to the total population of the United States. More remarkable still is the fact that there is a 15 percent to 20 percent annual gain in motion picture theater attendance. This phenomenally high percentage increase of business in the picture industry has been made possible in the past by the great improvements in the motion pictures

Auditorium of Tebbett's Oriental Theater, Portland, Oregon

themselves, by continued advances in photography and projection technique, by the development of professional movie acting, and by the new
heights of attainment in the art of staging plays for the screen. The
prospect for keeping up this patronage increase in the future is very
bright, with "talking" movies, color pictures, and stereoscopic effects just
beginning to get hold of the imagination of the public.

The Appeal of the De Luxe Theater

Nothing has done more to enlarge the motion picture theater audience
during the present decade than the new type of theater construction. This
will be written down as the era of the advent of big de luxe motion picture
houses. It is certain now that the standard picture theater in America is to
be much more of a real "palace" than prognosticators in the early part of
the century could possibly have guessed. The American public has spoken
a decided preference for luxury in its houses of entertainment. The old
converted store-building theater cannot compete successfully any more,
partly because the new and larger houses can afford to furnish better
music and better talent in their entertainment, and partly because they
bring to their patrons, of whatever status in life, a few hours each day of
something besides entertainment—of genuine luxury in living.

These new attractions of the motion picture theater and its improved
entertainment are not only holding the old type of theater patrons, but
drawing largely from new groups—the music lovers, the church people,
"society"—bringing new throngs to the theaters and creating an irresistible
demand for more seating capacity.

New building activities in the motion picture line have been unprecedented for a number of years. Still the net gain in seating accommodations
is not nearly so great as appears on the surface. This is due to the above-
mentioned transition in the type of theaters. It is estimated that with the
opening of each new "palace" theater (of large seating capacity), from one
to three of the old store type close their doors and revert to former
industrial uses.

Annual Admissions Estimated at $750,000,000

The present investment in motion picture theaters in the United States is
estimated at $1,250,000,000. The current annual building program for
the country runs into impressive figures, but much of this is required for
the replacement of antiquated "movie" houses. Such impressive investment figures for the industry have been possible because of the fact that
the motion picture theaters are dispensing a commodity which the people
of America and of the world regard as a necessity in modern living, and
which they are willing to buy in large quantities, for cash. The present
annual intake of the motion picture box offices in the United States is conservatively estimated at $750,000,000.

Admission charges to the motion picture theaters have gone up markedly along with the increase in the quality of entertainment. Nevertheless they still remain within the reach of the great masses of the people, who have not only shown themselves willing to pay the price of good motion picture entertainment, but to add whatever reasonable surcharge is necessary to provide that luxurious atmosphere so much appreciated in the new picture palaces.

The new theater-building program is practically all of the de luxe type. This is fortunate for the industry. The large theater is a great economy in operation. Many of the operating costs, such as for supervision, advertising, and film rental, may be not materially higher for a 5,000-seat theater than for one with but 1,000 seats. There is a limit to size economy, of course, but when due care is given to seat arrangement and acoustics, this limit is not reached under 4,000 to 6,000 capacity in the average metropolitan area.

The de luxe theater of good location and under able management is a money-maker from the very start. Its opening is an event of importance in the community. Capacity crowds are assured for the first weeks of its operation, and maximum earning power is thus attained at once for this type of investment.

Site Values Appreciate

The danger of obsolescence is a matter of prime concern for fixed capital in almost every line of industry. Yet obsolescence is a small risk in the modern motion picture theater. It is less of a hazard than in most types of manufacturing plants, for instance, where the equipment may go out of date on short notice, with the discovery of new methods. Moreover, the new large movie house is always built with a regular theatrical stage, so it can handle any type of entertainment for which there may be a demand.

From the investor's standpoint the de luxe type of modern motion picture house is almost invariably in a strong position on the score of appreciating realty values. The modern theater is located in populous centers where the increment in real estate values must ordinarily be very substantial. Theater bonds thus have the virtues of other well placed real-estate securities, and in addition, because they are sponsored increasingly by the operators of large chains, and by the great producing-distributing organizations of the industry, they take on industrial prestige as well.

It is conservative to say that few commodities of general consumption have come on the market in recent years which the people have bought with such fervor as they have the product of the modern de luxe motion picture house. That makes the de luxe theater an investment of high order. It makes it, first, a paying investment; and second, because this demand rests upon an insistent human desire for entertainment, and upon a universal need for relaxation in these times of strenuous industrial activity, a permanent investment of real quality.

Looking Ahead in the Industry

The present is reassuring. But what of the future for this great industry which no less an authority than the director of the United States Bureau of the Budget has ranked as fourth in the whole county, while it is still scarcely thirty years of age? What are the prospects for further expansion? And what is the probability that its present popularity and patronage will be maintained?

Every survey of the situation indicates promising conditions ahead. The fundamental human desire for entertainment, the urgent need for recreation and for surcease from the dull routine of factory and office, is most certainly not going to diminish greatly in the near future. Moreover, the motion picture will doubtless increase in its ability to compensate for the drabness of modern industrial life.

The early prospects for adding "depth" to motion pictures—the stereoscopic effect—is a good omen for the industry. This alone will increase the interest and usefulness of nearly all films. Color photography as applied to motion pictures is now a reality and will, of course, be exploited on the screen in a way that will help the box office. In addition, this development promises to expand the usefulness of motion pictures in several directions outside the drama, particularly in education, art, and nature-study.

The "slow movie" has proven to have tremendous value outside the realm of entertainment. It is quite sure to become the most effective means for coaching in physical education and athletics. It will certainly have a wide usefulness in all forms of teaching, both in industry and in formal education.

Importance of the "Talking Movie"

Another pending development, whose importance no one dares even to conjecture, is the talking picture. Two firms have recently perfected the "Vitaphone" and the "Movietone," respectively. The Vitaphone is based upon the principle of synchronizing phonograph records with motion picture projection, while the Movietone depends upon the photography of sound. In this case both the sound record and the visual record are carried on the same film and released by passing through the projector. Each of these processes appears to be basically sound and of large potential signifi-

cance in expanding the service of the films. Their first great usefulness is
the capacity to bring the highest grade singing and orchestral music—now
available as an accompaniment to the films in only the largest centers—
into every theater of the country.

The "talking" movie will revolutionize the importance of newsreels and
the like. It will increase immensely the historical importance of pictures of
notable events. Appealing to both the eye and the ear, it will be able to
teach history, geography, social relations, and practically every phase of
human knowledge in a more effective way than we have known before.

The motion picture has already "introduced" the peoples of the world
to each other. The talking movie will make them acquainted. Perhaps no
other modern invention or industrial development can do so much to build
international good will, and hence for the expansion of international
commerce.

The possibilities of the motion picture in education have long been
realized by forward-looking people, and during the past ten years the
broad foundations for this expansion have been laid. Now, with the added
possibilities in "slow" and talking pictures, we seem about ready to reach
out in the field of education on a large scale.

Great universities like Columbia and Harvard are inaugurating courses
in the use and technique of pictures. Other educational leaders like the
Yale University Press are sponsoring "motion picture textbooks." Several
of the leading dramatic companies are turning out a substantial by-
product of educational films, while two or three large companies have
been organized to specialize exclusively in this line. One of the most significant of all present efforts is that of the Eastman Kodak Company,
which is sponsoring an impressive campaign of investigation and research
into the problems of popular education through motion pictures.

Many state and city school systems are launching ambitious programs.
Ohio, for instance, according to its director of visual education, will
require, after September 1927, that all its first-class high schools be
equipped with picture projectors and material.

Foreign Trade Follows the Film

There are vast uncharted opportunities ahead for the expansion of
motion pictures into industrial, governmental, religious, and health work.
American export manufacturers, as well as foreign competitors, have been
amazed by the tremendous business-building potency of the foreign
showing of American pictures. What the people of the world see their
screen heroes wear, and eat, and use, they want for themselves. They
demand these things at their stores. Business follows the film much more

MGM's "Trackless Train" on world tour in the Netherlands, promoting product

dependably than it follows the flag. Hence the government and industrial leaders are bound to use motion pictures on a vastly larger scale, both for advertising purposes at home, and to carry American goods abroad.

The Red Cross pioneered in the use of motion pictures for health work. Industry has proven their great usefulness in putting over "safety-first" programs and welfare work. Now comes the American College of Surgeons with the announcement that they will explore scientifically the possibilities of the films, both for teaching the healing arts to the students of medicine and for reaching the general public.

No "Saturation Point"

It is impossible now to even think of the "saturation point" for motion pictures. To draw the line on "a picture a day" would be, to say the least, meaningless. With health, education, government, recreation, religion, and entertainment all making their appeals and rendering their services through this medium, it can hardly fail to become as universal an experience as reading from the printed page. It does not seem extravagant to prophesy that the motion picture will come to be regarded as almost as necessary to healthful living as the food which the people eat and the clothes they wear.

The industry behind all this promises to be and will long continue as one of the most serviceable to mankind. In turn it cannot fail to afford a field of unsurpassed opportunity for investment.

A Sound Basis for Financing

The motion picture industry has passed through its experimental period. There has been no perceptible slowing down in its money-making possibilities, but the decade since 1914 (the advent of big feature programs) has seen this industry take giant form, and shape itself along accepted lines of business organization. Production has been systematized during this period until the making of a picture today in one of the great studios is an impressive example of industrial efficiency.

Accounting and other control devices have been worked out to meet situations that were absolutely unique to this industry. The budget system for cost control in film manufacture has proven now to be as dependable a system of forecasting as one finds in many other industries.

The average man may have been led to believe that pictures of even the large companies are produced on a "hit-or-miss" basis; that a certain amount of money is spent in the mere hope that it will come back when the film is released. On the contrary the important and expensive films are sold in advance at the beginning of the year. Many of these pictures are even contracted for before production starts on them, so the company actually knows fairly well what its return is going to be before the filming gets under way. This being the situation, there is constant progress toward cost control, and budgets become increasingly significant. The money plans for a picture not only prescribe its maximum cost allowances, but they reflect a conservative estimate of its minimum net earning capacity.

The need for better inventory methods, balance sheet standards, and for contract forms which would prove equitable in both directions, long constituted serious problems in this industry. But recently these have been ironed out in an effective way.

One noticeably strong feature of motion picture inventory policy is that the entire value of the films which a company owns is written off its books within twenty-four months of their first release. Approximately 80 percent of this is charged off during the first year, regardless of what has been earned or the prospects for contined revenue. When it happens that a film has a long earning life, or proves to have rerun value later on, the entire earnings beyond the first two years, aside from distribution costs, are thus seen to be pure profit. In one recent case a film with a successful record five years ago, which was brought out and rerun to the new generation of theater-goers, netted more than $1,000,000 to its owners. And note that this film had been carried on the books of the company for several years as a nominal asset of but one dollar.

Scientific management and modern research methods have produced striking results also on the exhibition side of the motion picture industry. One illustration is concerned with that natural seasonal handicap—the falling-off of patronage during the hot months of midsummer. To overcome this, the de luxe houses installed refrigeration plants and advertised themselves as "the coolest spots in town." This policy completely reversed the situation in some cities and gives promise of becoming generally successful. Attendance charts for the above places now show an actual bulge in July and August. Moreover, cooling systems have been devised which are financially available to the small houses, down to 300-500 seating capacity, and in many cases are being installed by them.

Strong Banking Position

The bankers of the country have given ample testimony within recent years to their belief in the present soundness of this industry. Whereas formerly the business was compelled to depend almost entirely upon its own resources and financial ingenuity, the leading companies are all able now to obtain both commercial and long-term credits on customary trade terms. Numerous large financial undertakings in the motion picture industry have been consummated by financial houses of high standing. Approximately $200,000,000 in motion picture securities have been financed through Wall and LaSalle streets in the last twenty-four months.

A conspicuous development in financial literature has recently taken place along this line. Stories regarding the business end of motion picture production and distribution are now appearing in leading periodicals with a frequency commonly accorded other industries of leading rank. Both the stocks and bonds of motion picture concerns have been accepted for listing on the New York Stock Exchange, and the trading in these securities at the present time bulks into figures of real magnitude.

The motion picture industry has become the beneficiary in recent years of added confidence from many different directions. Local bankers in all parts of the country have come to see that theater construction on the present large scale and of the present type is not only good for employment but good for land values in any section of the city. Similarly, they have observed that the location of a de luxe theater in almost any type of community tends to draw high-class trade and very definitely improves business conditions there.

Independent moneyed men are turning to the motion picture industry. They have long sensed its great earning possibilities, but now, in addition, they have observed the results of conservative stabilizing policies such as are reflected in an ever-increasing percentage of fixed assets in the balance sheets of all the great motion picture companies. They have been reassured by the expanding and apparently permanent nature of the industry's foreign trade. They have been impressed by the proven earning capacity of modern theater buildings, while the sinking fund provisions that are almost invariably a part of a theater mortgage lend added attractiveness.

Finally, there is a great tribute of public confidence contained in the list of sixty thousand individual shareholders of seven motion picture issues now traded on the New York Stock Exchange, and in the ever-increasing volume of such bonds which are being absorbed by American investors. Manifestly, the great American public, which enjoys so much the phantasy on the screen, has begun to be thoroughly intrigued by the vision of earnings and profits "behind the screen."

The Jazz Singer at the Warners' Theatre

10

J. DOUGLAS GOMERY

The Coming of the Talkies: Invention, Innovation, and Diffusion

The coming of sound provided a dramatic climax to a decade of swift and great economic change within the industry. Following the lead of the innovators—Warner Brothers and the Fox Film Corporation—the major companies moved, virtually en masse, to make the conversion to sound in the spring of 1928. By the autumn of the following year, the dominance of the talkies was virtually complete, with only small towns and rural areas still showing silent pictures. A myriad of technical problems were solved: studios were soundproofed, armies of technicians were hired to service the delicate equipment, and theaters were wired. Scriptwriters were replaced by playwrights skilled in writing dialogue. Actors without stage experience took voice lessons, and those unable to correct foreign accents, faulty diction, or unpleasant voices soon found themselves unemployed. It seems amazing, at least at a casual glance, that during this period not a single major company toppled. On the contrary, the giants enjoyed a surge of profits that served to reinforce their grip on the marketplace.

Sound did not arrive Minerva-like on the screen in the late 1920s but had antecedents reaching back to the infancy of the industry. Its advent can be appreciated by viewing it in terms of the economic theory of technological innovation, which posits that a product or process is intro-duced to increase profits in three systematic phases: invention, innovation,

193

and diffusion. American Telephone and Telegraph Company (AT&T) and the Radio Corporation of America (RCA) played key roles in the initial phase of invention. From 1900 to 1924, they conducted electrical and radio research and developed the first sound systems. The innovation phase (the adapting of an invention for practical use) was dominated by Warner Brothers and Fox, who perfected techniques to produce, distribute, and exhibit sound motion pictures. As for the final phase, diffusion, which occurs when the product or process is adopted for use: initially, the industry hesitated to follow the bold lead of Warner and Fox but, after elaborate planning, made the plunge. The others followed, and because of their enormous economic power, the diffusion process went relatively quickly and smoothly. In each of the three phases, the producers and suppliers of sound equipment carried out their business decisions with a single view toward maximizing long-run profits. This motivation propelled Hollywood as well as film industries worldwide into a new era.

Invention

Attempts to link sound to motion pictures are as old as the industry itself. Most entrepreneurs experimented with mechanical means of accomplishing this union. William Fox—who would later play a key role in the development of the sound-on-film process—once booked a troupe of actors in 1913 to provide a vocal accompaniment for his film version of *Uncle Tom's Cabin*. Mechanical accompaniment followed two lines of development. The first sought to combine the phonograph with the motion picture. Thomas A. Edison instigated the idea as early as 1888 and claimed that his assistant, William Kennedy Laurie Dickson, created the first talkie in 1889 by projecting a motion picture synchronized with a phonograph—in truth a totally unfounded claim.[1] In 1895, however, Edison did introduce his Kinetophone, which was simply a Kinetoscope containing a phonograph. The phonograph was not synchronized with the filmstrip. It merely supplied musical accompaniment which the customer listened to through rubber tubes as he viewed the peep show. Edison's Kinetophone met with public indifference and was withdrawn hastily from the market. Eighteen years later, Edison would bring out a new and improved Kinetophone.

At the same time, other inventors were attempting to link the phonograph with projected motion pictures. One of these was Léon Gaumont,

1. For the complete account of the demystification of Edison's motion picture achievements, see Gordon Hendricks, *The Edison Motion Picture Myth* (Berkeley and Los Angeles, 1961).

who demonstrated his Chronophone before the French Photographic Society in 1902. Gaumont's system linked a projector to two phonographs with a series of electrical cables. A dial adjustment controlled the record speed to keep it in synchronization with the picture. In most situations, two phonographs increased the volume of sound. In attempting to exploit the system, Gaumont used variety acts as subjects for his first pictures, in the belief that they would be most effective in drawing bookings from vaudeville circuits. In 1907 he presented a Chronophone production of Sir Harry Lauder at the London Hippodrome, and the following year he received a license from the Motion Picture Patents Company to market the system in the United States. By that time, his repertoire included opera excerpts, whistling solos, recitations, and even dramatic sketches. Despite Gaumont's bright prospects, his Chronophone failed to find a niche in the marketplace. The reasons for failure were largely economic and technical. The system was relatively expensive to install in theaters, and its performance was only mediocre—crude sound quality, weak amplification, and imperfect synchronization. Gaumont returned to the United States in 1913 for a second try, announcing an improved synchronizing mechanism and a compressed air system of amplification. Exhibitors, however, remembering the Chronophone's unimpressive performance five years earlier, ignored his advertising claims.

Gaumont's was not the only phonograph sound system on the market. There were more than a dozen others introduced between 1909 and 1913, all sharing common technical problems and subsequent failure. The most important of these was the Cameraphone, the invention of E. E. Norton, a former mechanical engineer with the American Gramophone Company. In design, the Cameraphone was nearly identical to Gaumont's apparatus, although in operation the Cameraphone was placed behind a translucent screen so that the sound could come from the direction of the action. Norton employed twenty-two workers in his Bridgeport, Connecticut, factory and actually succeeded in installing his system in a few theaters in larger cities. But Norton was unable to solve many of the same problems that had stymied Gaumont. The Cameraphone was expensive to install, it lacked sufficient amplification to be heard in large halls, the screen produced a dingy gray image, and there were recording and synchronization problems. Despite its early failure, the Cameraphone does find a place in film history, because it was the first American sound system to gain any measure of success during these early days of experimentation.

The Cameraphone was followed by the Cinephone, the Vivaphone, the Synchroscope, and at least ten other phonograph systems between 1909 and 1913. All were failures. In 1913, however, Edison announced the second coming of the Kinetophone. This time, he said, he had actually perfected a talking motion picture, and he gave an impressive demonstration on January 4, 1913, at his West Orange, New Jersey, laboratory. The press discovered that Edison's invention contained three innovations that separated it from its predecessors: a microphone sensitive enough to pick up sounds while a performer was on camera, thus obviating the traditional lip-sync performances for actors; an oversized phonograph with a large mechanical amplifier; and an intricate system of belts and pulleys erected between the projection booth and the stage to regulate the speed of the phonograph.

The demonstration went off without a hitch, enabling Edison to persuade vaudeville magnates John J. Murdock and Martin Beck to install the Kinetophone in four Keith-Orpheum theaters in New York. The commercial première took place on February 13, 1913, at Keith's Colonial. The expectant audience was treated to the synchronized sight and sound of a lecturer who began by praising Edison's wizardry. Adding dramatic evidence to back his glowing tribute, the lecturer then smashed a plate, played the violin, and had his dog bark, all to demonstrate the volume and versatility of the system. A minstrel show, a tenor singing "Silver Threads among the Gold," and a choral finale of "The Star-Spangled Banner" brought the demonstration to a stirring close. The ecstatic audience applauded for fully fifteen minutes.

Edison had paved the way carefully for his Kinetophone. The sterling performance at Keith's Colonial was a crowning success, immediately opening the doors to installation of the new apparatus in other theaters. Unknown to anyone at the time, however, the performance at Keith's was a zenith for the Kinetophone. At later presentations in the Colonial and other theaters, the system performed erratically. At Keith's Union Square, the sound was out of synchronization by as much as ten to twelve seconds. The audience booed the picture off the screen. By 1914, the Kinetophone had established a record so spotty that Murdock and Beck canceled their contract with Edison. That same year, Edison's West Orange factory was destroyed by fire. Although it was quickly rebuilt, Edison chose not to reactivate the Kinetophone operation. The West Orange fire marked the end not only of the Kinetophone but of all early sound-on-disc ventures.

American moviegoers had to wait nine years for another workable sound system to emerge—and when it did, it was based on the principle of sound on film, not on discs. On April 4, 1923, Lee De Forest successfully demonstrated his Phonofilm system to the New York Electrical Society. De Forest described his system modestly: "I have simply photographed the voice onto an ordinary film. It is on the same film with the picture, a narrow strip down one side, so narrow that the picture is not spoiled."[2] In truth, Phonofilm was a highly sophisticated system whose success rested in great measure on the Audion Three-Electrode Amplifier Tube, which De Forest had patented in 1907.

Phonofilm made its public debut on April 15, 1923, at New York's Rivoli theater. The program consisted of three shorts: Fokima performing her swan dance, a string quartet, and another dance number. The musical accompaniment in each was nonsynchronous. De Forest, whose brilliance shone in the laboratory rather than in showmanship or business, could not carry off the première in Edison-like fashion. A *New York Times* reporter expressed only mild interest; others were also as lukewarm. Nevertheless, De Forest maintained unwavering faith in his invention and continued to try to exploit it through his Phonofilm Corporation until 1928.

All the while, he was unable to solve four crucial problems, none of which was technical. First, film industry leaders remained indifferent to the system, principally because of repeated failures of earlier systems. Second, De Forest was never able to put together an effective distribution system for marketing his system. Third, he held a patent pool too small to guarantee patent indemnity. His largest single problem was financing. De Forest was never able to attract enough support to develop large-scale production of sound films. A brilliant individualistic inventor, he was ill-equipped to handle the intricacies of the modern world of finance. Between 1923 and 1925, only thirty-four theaters on the East Coast of the United States, Canada, South America, Great Britain, South Africa, Australia, and Japan showed Phonofilm programs. By 1927, Phonofilm's activities consisted of only a small newsreel unit. By September 1928, when he sold out to a South African exhibition chain, there were only three installations in the United States.

It took American Telephone and Telegraph, the world's largest company, to succeed where others had failed. AT&T's subsidiary, Western Electric, began to experiment with sound recording as early as 1912, not to develop talking motion pictures but to perfect long-distance telephone transmission. Their work, with an interruption for World War I, produced impressive results by 1923. The Western Electric team of engineers, led by Frank Jewett, developed an efficient loudspeaker, a high-quality amplifier, and a smooth-running 33⅓ rpm turntable.

The motivation to apply these inventions to motion pictures came from Western Electric engineer Edward B. Craft. On October 27, 1922, he pre-

2. Quoted in Georgette Carneal, *A Conqueror of Space: An Authorized Biography of the Life and Work of Lee De Forest* (New York, 1930), p. 282.

sented an experimental film, *Audion,* to a Yale University audience. *Audion* was an animated cartoon using a disc system to provide a non-synchronous musical accompaniment. In 1924, Craft supervised the production of *Hawthorne,* a public relations film with synchronized sound about Western Electric's Chicago plant. With these two successful experiments behind them, and with all the legal, technical, and financial resources of a giant corporation, AT&T was ready to market its sound system.

Innovation

Warner Brothers

In 1924, Warner Brothers Pictures, Inc., was a small Hollywood studio. Sam, Harry, Jack, and Albert Warner had come a long way since the nickelodeon days when they crisscrossed Ohio and Pennsylvania exhibiting a used print of *The Great Train Robbery.* Now they had managed to put under contract the great Broadway star John Barrymore, and an even bigger box-office attraction, Rin-Tin-Tin. Despite this potential richness, their future looked constricted, if not actually bleak. They had neither a national distribution system nor access to a steady flow of financing to permit the company to expand. Under these circumstances, thought of

The Warner brothers, Sam, Harry, Jack, and Albert, with Harry Rapf, left

serious competition with the Big Three—Famous Players-Lasky, Loew's, and First National—was impossible.

It took an alliance with a great Wall Street investment house—Goldman, Sachs—to put Warner Brothers into the big leagues, but the experience would be harrowing for all involved. Introduced to Warner Brothers by a friend, Waddill Catchings, the head of Goldman, Sachs's investment division, was impressed with Warner Brothers' strict cost accounting, tight budget control, and managerial talent. He agreed to finance the company only if it would follow the long-term master plan he set up for its growth. Yet Catchings was more than an investment banker; he was also an economic theorist, having authored two treatises on the nation's economic problems. Central to his theory was the necessity for the businessman-entrepreneur to take bold creative action. Only this, coupled with an adequate money supply, could ensure a continued prosperity devoid of economic depressions. Catchings was the most optimistic of all the "New Era" financiers of the 1920s. In taking on the Warner Brothers account, he demonstrated once again his financial acumen.

Harry Warner, president of Warner Brothers, agreed to Catchings's condition and appointed him to the board of directors as chairman of the finance committee. Catchings immediately set up a $3 million revolving credit fund by first approaching New York's National Bank of Commerce, the leading commercial bank in the nation. Although the bank had never loaned money to any motion picture company, not even the mighty Famous Players-Lasky, Catchings was able to persuade National's board chairman, James S. Alexander, that Warner Brothers was a good risk. And, as icing on the cake, Catchings even secured the credit at the going rate. Next he went to the Colony Trust Company of Boston for another share, using the account at the National Bank of Commerce as a powerful tool for leverage, and then to four other banks to complete the underwriting. Catchings had provided Warner Brothers with a permanent and low-cost method of financing future production.

In the meantime, Warner Brothers acquired the Vitagraph Corporation with its nearly fifty exchanges in the United States and throughout the world, two studios, processing lab, and film library. Then, with a $4 million debenture issue, which Catchings floated to provide the company with a stable financial base for expansion, Warner Brothers established a worldwide distribution system. Warner Brothers also acquired ten theaters, established a program of vaudeville presentations, and launched a $500,000 national advertising campaign.

Warner Brothers' final expansionary move set the stage for the coming of sound. At the urging of Sam Warner, who was an electronics enthusiast, the company established radio station KFWB in Hollywood on

March 4, 1925, to promote Warner Brothers' films. The equipment was secured from Western Electric. Soon Sam Warner and Nathan Levinson, Western's Los Angeles representative, became fast friends.

Until then, Western Electric had found no takers for its much-researched sound equipment. The past failures had made a lasting and negative impression on the industry, one shared by Harry Warner and the other movie moguls. The notable exception was Sam Warner. Recalling how Sam had tricked him into attending a talking picture demonstration, Harry concluded: "If [he] had said talking picture, I never would have gone, because [talking pictures]had been made up to that time several times, and each was a failure, and I am positive if [he] said talking picture, I would not [have]gone."[3]

That important demonstration, in May 1925, began with a short subject, a man on the screen who spoke a few words. Harry was not impressed. But a five-piece jazz band fired his imagination. If Warner Brothers could equip theaters with sound to present vaudeville acts as part of their programs, they could compete with the majors. Even the smallest house could exhibit famous vaudeville acts and features with the finest orchestral accompaniments, all at reasonable costs. Harry was thinking not about talking pictures, but about singing and musical films.

Catchings liked Harry's idea and gave the go-ahead to open negotiations with Walter J. Rich, the promoter hired by Western Electric to sell its system to motion picture companies. On June 25, 1925, Warner Brothers signed a letter of agreement with Western Electric calling for a period of joint experimentation. Western Electric was to supply the engineers and sound equipment; Warner Brothers, the cameramen, editors, and the supervisory talent of Sam Warner. The work began in September 1925 at the old Vitagraph studio in Brooklyn. Meanwhile, Warner Brothers continued to expand under Waddill Catchings's careful guidance. Although feature output was reduced, more money was spent on each picture. In the spring of 1926, Warner Brothers opened a second radio station and a new film-processing laboratory and further expanded its foreign operations. As a result of this rapid growth, the firm anticipated the $1 million loss on its annual income statement issued in March 1926.

By December 1925, experiments were going so well that Rich proposed forming a permanent sound motion picture corporation. The contracts were prepared and the parties readied to sign, but negotiations came to a halt as Western Electric underwent a management shuffle. Afterward,

3. *General Talking Pictures Corporation et al.* v. *American Telephone and Telegraph Company et al.*, 18F. Supp. 650 (1937), Record, p. 1108.

Western Electric's new commercial manager, John E. Otterson, represented the company at the negotiation table. Otterson was the former president of the Winchester Repeating Arms Company. Before that, as a graduate of Annapolis, he was a career officer in the Navy for fifteen years. Despite the alliance of his old friend Catchings with Warner Brothers, Otterson was contemptuous of the fledgling company. Since it did not enjoy the status of the Big Three, he demanded complete control over sound operations. Hitherto, Western Electric was content merely to function as a supplier of equipment. Catchings saw this dictatorial stance as typical of a man with a military background unable to adjust to the more flexible world of business and finance. Unfortunately for Warner Brothers, AT&T's corporate muscle backed Otterson's demands.

Only by going over Otterson's head to Western Electric's president, Edgar S. Bloom, was Catchings able to protect Warner Brothers' position and secure a reasonable contract. In April 1926, Warner Brothers, Walter J. Rich, and Western Electric formed the Vitaphone Corporation to develop sound motion pictures further. Warner Brothers and Rich furnished the capital. Western Electric granted Vitaphone an exclusive license to record and reproduce sound movies on its equipment. In return, Vitaphone agreed to purchase for lease a minimum number of sound systems each year and pay a royalty fee of 8 per cent of its gross revenues from sound motion pictures. Vitaphone's total equipment commitment was twenty-four hundred systems during the 1927-31 period.

As *Variety* and the other trade papers announced the formation of the alliance, Vitaphone began its assault on the marketplace. Its first goal was to acquire talent. Vitaphone contracted with the Victor Talking Machine Company for the right to bargain with its popular musical artists. A similar agreement was reached with the Metropolitan Opera Company. Vitaphone dealt directly with vaudeville stars. In a few short months it had the talent to produce the musical short subjects Harry Warner had envisioned. So vigorous was Vitaphone's leap into sound that the firm engaged the services of the New York Philharmonic to record incidental background music for its forthcoming production of *Don Juan*.

In June 1926, Warner Brothers moved the sound studio to the vacant Manhattan Opera House on 34th Street in deference to Otterson, who wanted the operations closer to Western Electric's headquarters. Throughout the summer, Sam Warner and his crew worked feverishly to ready the Vitaphone program for the *Don Juan* opening, while the Warner publicity department carried out a strong effort in the nation's press.

Vitaphone unveiled its marvel on August 6, 1926, at the Warners' Theatre in New York. The first-nighters who packed the house paid up to ten dollars for tickets. The program began with eight "Vitaphone

Preludes." In the first, Will Hays congratulated the Warner brothers and Western Electric for their pioneering efforts. At the end, to create the illusion of the stage, Hays bowed to the audience anticipating the applause. Then conductor Henry Hadley led the New York Philharmonic in the Overture to *Tannhäuser*. He too bowed at the end. The acts that followed consisted primarily of operatic and concert perfomances: tenor Giovanni Martinelli sang an aria from *I Pagliacci*, violinist Mischa Elman played "Humoresque," and soprano Anna Case sang a number supported by the Metropolitan Opera Chorus. Only one prelude broke the serious tone of the evening, and that featured Roy Smeck, a vaudeville comic and musician. Warner Brothers was playing it conservatively.

Don Juan followed after a ten-minute intermission. The musical accompaniment caused no great stir. However, the industry leaders in the audience—Adolph Zukor, William Fox, and Nicholas Schenck among them—were impressed, if not by the evening's performance, then by the potential of the medium that the performance revealed to them. All in all, Vitaphone's reception was warm. That autumn, the *Don Juan* program played Atlantic City, Chicago, and St. Louis, always to packed houses. Still, Otterson remained skeptical and impatient.

Vitaphone presented a second program in October 1926 that was aimed at popular tastes. The main attraction was *The Better 'Ole,* starring Charlie Chaplin's brother, Sydney. The vaudeville shorts featured such "headliners" as George Jessel, Irving Berlin, Elsie Janis, and Al Jolson. These vaudeville acts would have cost $40,000 a week if presented live. The trade press now began to see bright prospects for the invention that could place so much high-priced talent in towns like Akron, Ohio, and Richmond, Virginia. By the time Vitaphone's third program opened in February 1927, Warner had recorded more than fifty acts.

As a result of the growing popularity of Vitaphone presentations, the company succeeded in installing nearly a hundred systems by the end of 1926. Most of these were located in the East. The installation in March 1927 of two systems in the new Roxy theater and the attendant publicity served to spur business even more. Warner Brothers' financial health by now showed signs of improvement. It had invested over $3 million into Vitaphone alone, yet its quarterly losses had declined from about $334,000 in 1925 to less than $110,000 in 1926. It appeared that Catchings's master plan was working.

John Otterson was still not appeased. His goal was to take control of Vitaphone so that Western Electric could deal with Paramount (formerly Famous Players-Lasky), Loew's, and First National directly. To accomplish this he first initiated a harassment campaign by raising prices on Vitaphone equipment fourfold. pressuring for expansion, and demanding a greater share of the revenues. By December 1926, Otterson and Warner Brothers had broken off relations. Next he helped organize a special Western Electric subsidiary called Electrical Research Products, Inc. (ERPI), to conduct the company's nontelephone business—over 90 percent of which concerned motion picture sound equipment. Otterson then stepped in to become ERPI's president and general manager.

Warner Brothers stood by helpless to prevent Otterson from dealing directly with other companies despite the fact that the exploitation function was vested in Vitaphone alone. However, only one firm, the Fox Film Corporation, signed on. The other companies adopted a wait-and-see attitude. In fact, five of the most important companies—Loew's (MGM), Universal, First National, Paramount, and Producers Distributing Corporation—signed an agreement in February 1927 to act together in regard to sound. The Big Five Agreement, as it was called, recognized that there were several sound systems on the market, but also that the inability to interchange this equipment would be a hindrance to the wide distribution of pictures. These companies, therefore, agreed not to adopt any system unless their specially appointed committee certified that it was the best for the industry. As further protection, they agreed not to employ any system unless it was made available to all producers, distributors, and exhibitors on reasonable terms, and that for one year none would adopt sound unless all did. Most important, they wanted to deal with a firm of impeccable financial reputation possessing large manufacturing facilities and technical expertise.

Otterson saw in ERPI's alliance with Vitaphone a major stumbling block in dealing with the industry because most firms would be reluctant to deal with a sound company owned by a competitor. As a result, he sought to break the bond by threatening to declare Vitaphone in default of its contract. Catchings, knowing that this action would destroy his relations with the banks, persuaded Warner Brothers to accede to Otterson's wishes. In April 1927, ERPI paid Vitaphone $1,322,306 to terminate the old agreement. In May, after the two signed the so-called New License Agreement, Vitaphone, like Fox, became merely a licensee of ERPI. Warner Brothers had given up the exclusive franchise to exploit ERPI sound equipment and lost over half its share of the potential fortune in licensing fees.

In breaking with ERPI, Warner Brothers at the same time bought out Rich's 30 percent interest in Vitaphone to make it a wholly owned subsidiary. Vitaphone production work was moved to Hollywood where Warner Brothers had constructed several new sound stages at its studio. While the parent company continued with its production program of silent features, Vitaphone regularly turned out five shorts a week, which became

known in the industry as "canned vaudeville." Bryan Foy, ex-vaudevillian
and silent film director, now worked under Sam Warner to head the newly
created short subjects unit. Warner Brothers also continued to devote
itself to road show specials, and work continued on a new feature to open
the 1927-28 season—*The Jazz Singer.*

At this juncture, Vitaphone's major problem was a dearth of exhibition
outlets for its pictures. By the fall of 1927, ERPI had installed only forty-
four sound systems since the signing of the New License Agreement. ERPI
was holding back on its sales campaign until the three majors made a
decision. Warner Brothers would later charge that ERPI had not used its
best efforts to market the equipment and had defaulted on its contract.
This charge and others were brought to arbitration and, in the 1934 settlement, ERPI was forced to pay Vitaphone $5 million.

The Jazz Singer, starring Al Jolson, opened on October 6, 1927, at the
Warners' Theatre in New York. The picture cost $500,000 to make and
brought Warner's investment in sound to $5 million. *The Jazz Singer* was

Al Jolson and Eugenie Besserer in *The Jazz Singer* (Warner Brothers, 1927)

not an all-talkie, but rather a part-talkie with music and songs by Jolson and two sequences with synchronized dialogue passages. It did excellent business wherever it played. In medium-sized cities such as Charlotte, North Carolina; Columbus, Ohio; Reading, Pennsylvania; Seattle; and Baltimore—where films rarely played longer than a week—it played three to five weeks. It even made return engagements in major first-run theaters. It made a second New York run, playing for two weeks at the Roxy and grossing $200,000, making it one of the top attractions of the season for that theater. In the meantime, Warner Brothers announced production plans for the first all-talking picture and watched its stock skyrocket on the exchange. The innovation strategy developed by Waddill Catchings and Harry Warner was a success. The company was on its way to the top of the American film industry.

The Fox-Case Corporation

Besides Warner Brothers, only the Fox Film Corporation had previously shown any interest in sound. Its head, William Fox, had investigated the Movietone sound-on-film system developed by Theodore W. Case and Earl I. Sponable and found it to be potentially a great improvement over the cumbersome Western Electric disc system. As a result, he and Case joined forces in July 1926 and formed a Fox Film subsidiary called the Fox-Case Corporation to exploit the system commercially. Movietone was imperfect in that it lacked an amplifier, and it was for this reason that Fox-Case approached Otterson. In exchange for the right to use the Western Electric device, Fox-Case cross-licensed its patents and became a licensee of Vitaphone. When Vitaphone broke away, the Fox-Case patents remained with ERPI.

Although Fox-Case began by following Warner's example of making vaudeville shorts with synchronized accompaniments, it soon took a different course—newsreels. Fox achieved his first big success on May 20, 1927, when, less than twenty-four hours after the event, a Movietone newsreel at the Roxy showed Charles Lindbergh's takeoff at Roosevelt Field, Long Island, on his historic trans-Atlantic flight; all the patrons of America's largest theater rose and cheered for ten minutes. Subsequently, Movietone photographed the welcome-home ceremonies for Lindbergh in Washington, D.C., and recorded President Coolidge's speech of introduction and Lindbergh's remarks.

Fox had hit upon a successful formula and began to install the Movietone system in his growing chain of theaters. For the Fall 1927 season he branched out into features by presenting F. W. Murnau's *Sunrise* with a synchronized score plus several shorts and newsreels at his new Times Square theater. In early 1928, Fox began the construction of a new studio in Hollywood. Two if its ten stages would be devoted exclusively to Movietone productions. In May he announced that all of Fox's pictures the following season would contain Movietone accompaniment. Then, with the financial backing of the Chicago investment house Halsey, Stuart & Co., he announced plans to construct a national chain of large deluxe theaters, each seating five thousand and each to be equipped with Movietone. Fox may have gotten a late start, but by moving boldly it caught up quickly with Vitaphone and was soon reaping the profits of a successful investment.

The Big Five

Upon expiration of the Big Five Agreement in February 1928, the major companies decided to make the conversion. Of the several systems on the market, only two received the serious attention of the producers' committee—Western Electric's Movietone, previously described, and RCA's Photophone, a sound-on-film system that was developed between 1918 and 1925 by General Electric and marketed through RCA. The committee's first choice was Photophone, but because RCA's chief David Sarnoff and General Electric wanted to form a holding company with the producers, Photophone was rejected in favor of Movietone. The producers wanted no part of equipment manufacture, preferring to remain exclusively in the entertainment business.

The committee agreement led Paramount, United Artists, Loew's, and First National to sign the Recording License Agreement with ERPI on May 11, 1928. It took six weeks to draft the contracts. Universal, Columbia, and other companies quickly followed. This concerted action and preplanning protected the industry from conversion chaos. It also gave ERPI a virtual stranglehold on the sound market—for the moment. In order to lease the equipment necessary to produce sound pictures, the producers agreed to pay a $500 royalty fee on every negative reel made. Licensees were required to distribute their pictures only to theaters with Western Electric sound systems. Should a licensee want to distribute a picture recorded on another sound system and for which a royalty had been paid, it had to pay a royalty to ERPI nonetheless.

The Rise of RKO

ERPI's preeminent position did not go unchallenged for long. Undaunted by the long-term exclusive contracts tying up the majors, RCA simply created a full-blown film company of its own to exploit its Photophone system. The new Radio-Keith-Orpheum Corporation was the brainchild of David Sarnoff, Joseph P. Kennedy, and John J. Murdock. Founded in October 1928 as a holding company, RKO acquired Joseph P.

Kennedy's Film Booking Office (a small Hollywood studio), the Keith-Albee-Orpheum circuit of vaudeville houses, and Pathé, Inc., another small motion picture firm. These Sarnoff, RCA's vice-president, merged with Photophone to create a vertically integrated giant containing three hundred theaters, a worldwide distribution network, two studios, $80 million of working capital, and a half-dozen subsidiaries.

By no means content merely to wire RKO theaters for Photophone, RCA pressed to compete with ERPI on equal terms for the business of the theaters owned by independents and affiliated circuits. However, the Recording License Agreement, which obligated the majors to distribute only to theaters wired by ERPI, was an insurmountable obstacle. RCA, as a result, prepared to sue AT&T under the terms of the Sherman Act. This threat, plus the pressure ERPI's licensees brought to bear, forced ERPI in December 1928 to open the exhibition market to all sound systems.

Diffusion

The industry's conversion to sound occurred quickly and smoothly, the result of the negotiations and extensive planning of the producers' committee. A huge potential for profits existed, and it was incumbent on the majors to make the switchover as quickly as possible. Paramount released

Rin-Tin-Tin takes to the talkies

its first films with musical accompaniment in August 1928; by September its pictures contained talking sequences; and by January 1929, it released its first all-talking production. By May, one year after signing with ERPI, Paramount produced talkies exclusively and was operating on a level with Warner Brothers and Fox. By the beginning of the 1929 season, MGM, Fox, RKO, Universal, and United Artists had completed the transition as well. Independent producers did not complete the transition unitl 1930. Many of these companies with little capital at their disposal went out of business or were absorbed by the majors.

Elaborate plans had been laid by the industry to facilitate diffusion. In Hollywood, the Academy of Motion Picture Arts and Sciences was designated as a clearinghouse for information relating to production problems. The film boards of trade handled new distribution trade practices. And a special lawyers' committee representing the majors was appointed to handle disputes and contractual matters with equipment manufacturers. For example, when ERPI announced a royalty hike, the committee entered negotiations and procured lower rates instead. Labor presented some difficulties. The American Federation of Musicians tried to prevent the wholesale firing of theatrical musicians; Actors' Equity, now

The sound technician

that professionals from the Broadway stage began to flock West, attempted to establish a union shop in the studios. These difficulties were resolved for the most part within four months, however, and the industry was back on an even keel.

ERPI's task all the while was to keep up with the demand for equipment. It wired the largest and most important theaters first and then, as equipment became available, the subsequent-run houses. Installations were made usually from midnight to five o'clock the next afternoon. By January 1930, ERPI was installing more than nine systems per day. Many smaller theaters, especially in the South and Southwest, could not afford ERPI's prices and signed with RCA, Pacent, De Forest, or one of the many regional sound equipment manufacturers. As of July 1, 1930, fully 22 percent of the theaters still presented silent films, but by 1932 the figure had dropped to 2.6 percent and then to 0.5 percent the following year.

To facilitate the switchover, Western Electric expanded its Hawthorne, Illinois, plant and ERPI established training schools for projectionists in seventeen cities and opened fifty district offices to service and repair equipment. RCA could not match ERPI's maintenance ability and reduced its prices for sound equipment instead to establish a foothold for Photophone.

The Mergers

The public infatuation with sound ushered in another boom period for the industry. Paramount's profits jumped $7 million between 1928 and 1929, Fox's $3.5 million, and Loew's $3 million. Warner Brothers, however, set the record; its profits soared from $2 million to over $14 million. Conditions were ripe for consolidation, and Warner Brothers, with its early start in sound, set the pace. It began by acquiring the Stanley Company, which owned a chain of three hundred theaters along the East Coast and a one-third interest in First National. It then maneuvered to buy out First National's remaining stockholders. In 1925, when Catchings joined the Warner Brothers board of directors, the company's assets were valued at a little over $5 million; in 1930 they totaled $230 million. In five short years, Warner Brothers had become one of the largest and most profitable companies in the American film industry.

Not content merely to establish RKO, David Sarnoff of RCA set out to sever all connections with General Electric and Westinghouse and acquire sound manufacturing facilities of his own. The first step in this direction was the acquisition in March 1929 of Victor Talking Machine Company and its huge plant in Camden, New Jersey. In the process RCA secured Victor's exclusive contracts with many of the biggests stars in the musical world. By December 1929 Sarnoff had reached his goal. RCA was now a powerful entertainment conglomerate with holdings in the broadcasting, vaudeville, phonograph, and motion picture industries.

William Fox had the most grandiose plan of all. In March 1929 he acquired controlling interest in Loew's, Inc., the parent company of MGM. Founder Marcus Loew had died in 1927 and left his widow and sons almost one-third of the company's stock. Nicholas Schenck, the new president, pooled his stock and that belonging to corporate officers with the family's and sold out to Fox at 25 percent above the market price. The new Fox-Loew's merger created the largest motion picture complex in the world. It had assets of more than $200 million and an annual earning potential of $20 million. Fox assumed a substantial short-term debt obligation in the process, but during the bull market of the late twenties he could simply float more stock and bonds to meet his needs.

Adolph Zukor, meanwhile, added more theaters, bringing Paramount's total to almost one thousand in 1929. He also acquired a 49 percent interest in the Columbia Broadcasting System. Then, in the fall of 1929, he proposed a merger with Warner Brothers that would create a motion picture and entertainment complex even larger than the Fox-Loew's combination and RCA combined. Catchings and Harry Warner were agreeable, but the new U.S. attorney general, William D. Mitchell, raised the red flag. If that merger went through, the industry would have been dominated by three firms. As it happened, though, it was to be dominated by five. After the stock market crash, William Fox was unable to meet his short-term debts and had to relinquish ownership of Loew's in 1930. The oligopolistic structure of the industry was now set, formed by Warner Brothers, Paramount, Fox, Loew's, and RKO.

Conclusion

As the innovators of sound, Warner Brothers and Fox added a new dimension to the aesthetics of the motion picture. They made a fortune in the process but did not alter the basic structure of the industry. The more cautious majors had laid elaborate plans to make the switchover and, when sound proved to be more than just a passing fad, they moved decisively to reap the harvest. At the end of the diffusion period, they emerged stronger than ever and lived in harmony for years to come.

Bibliographical Note

This article is based on the author's Ph.D. dissertation, "The Coming of Sound to the American Cinema: The Transformation of an Industry" (University of Wisconsin-Madison, 1975). The research relied heavily on four sets of primary source documents: Congressional reports of investigations of AT&T; records of court cases; the United Artists Collection at the Wisconsin Center for Film and Theater Research, University of Wisconsin-Madison; and trade publications such as *Moving Picture World* and *Variety*.

The most helpful government documents were:

1. U.S. Congress, House, Committee on Patents, *Hearings on H. R. 4523: Pooling of Patents* (74th Congress, 1st Sess., 1935).

2. U.S. Federal Communications Commission. *Telephone Investigation Exhibits* (Pursuant to Public Resolution No. 8, 74th Congress), 1936-37.

3. U.S. Federal Communications Commission. *Report on the Investigation of the Telephone Industry in the United States* (House Document 340, 76th Congress, 1st Sess., 1939).

The most important court cases were:

1. *Electrical Research Products, Inc. v. Vitaphone Corporation,* 171 A. 738 (1934).

2. *General Talking Pictures Corporation, et al. v. American Telephone and Telegraph Company, et al.,* 18F. Supp. 650 (1937).

3. *Koplar (Scharaf et al., Interveners) v. Warner Brothers Pictures, Inc., et al.,* 19F. Supp. 173 (1937).

In addition, the following secondary sources were found to be useful: Laurence Wood's *Patents and Anti-Trust Law* (New York, 1942), pp. 137-42, summarizes the findings of federal investigations and court cases; Frank H. Lovette and Stanley Watkins's "Twenty Years of Talking Movies," *Bell Telephone Magazine* (Summer 1946), pp. 82-100, summarizes AT&T's development of sound technology; Gleason Archer's *Big Business and Radio* (New York, 1939) describes RCA's contributions; Fitzhugh Green's *The Film Finds Its Tongue* (New York, 1929) is a colorful journalistic account of Warner Brothers' venture into sound; William I. Greenwald's "The Impact of Sound upon the Film Industry: A Case Study of Innovation," *Explorations in Entrepreneurial History* 4 (May 15, 1952): 178-92, is still the best short study of the innovation phase; and Benjamin B. Hampton's *A History of the Movies* (New York, 1931) remains the best account of the history of the industry from its beginnings to the introduction of sound.

Part III
A Mature Oligopoly: 1930-1948

Structure of the Industry

By 1930, the motion picture industry had become, in economic terminology, a mature oligopoly. The merger movement had run its course, with the result that five companies dominated the screen in the United States. The largest was Warner Brothers with its one hundred subsidiaries; the wealthiest was Loew's (see ch. 13), the theater chain that owned Metro-Goldwyn-Mayer (ch. 12); and the most complex and far-flung was Paramount. These and two other giants with equally formidable holdings, RKO and Twentieth Century-Fox along with their allied theater enterprises, became known as the Big Five. All were fully integrated: they produced motion pictures, operated worldwide distribution outlets, and owned chains of theaters where their pictures were guaranteed a showing.

With stables of stars, writers, directors, producers, cameramen, and other artists and technicians, each of these companies churned out from forty to sixty pictures a year. Although in total their productions represented at most 50 percent of the industry's annual output, about three-fourths of the class A features, the ones that played in the best theaters and received top billing, were made and distributed by the Big Five (ch. 11). The Big Five's greatest strength, however, was in the exhibition field. Of the twenty-three thousand theaters operating in the United States in 1930, the five majors either owned or controlled only three thousand, but this number represented the best first-run houses in the metropolitan areas and accounted for nearly 70 percent of the nation's box-office receipts.

Operating in a sort of symbiotic relationship with the Big Five were the Little Three: Universal, Columbia, and United Artists. Universal and Columbia had their own studios and distribution facilities and were useful to the majors during the

1930s and 1940s in supplying low-cost pictures to facilitate frequent program changes and double features. United Artists, the smallest of the eight, was unique in that it was solely a distribution company for independent producers. It had no studio, actors under contract, or theaters.

These major companies held monopolistic control of a type that is "frequently hard to trace and appraise, and, though more or less consistently evolved, that varies endlessly in methods of application and degrees of effectiveness," in the words of Robert A. Brady. "One might regard the movie industry as dominated by a semicompulsory cartel," Brady adds "or even a 'community of interests' of the type that typically stops short of the more readily indictable offenses under usual Anti-Trust procedure."[1] By pooling their interests, acting in concert, and establishing a market cartel, the majors succeeded in holding on to their power for eighteen years until 1948, when the Supreme Court and television brought this era of the movies to a close.

Effects of the Depression

Sound staved off the Depression in the motion picture industry for well over a year. But when the novelty of the talkies wore off in 1931, box-office receipts plummeted and Hollywood felt the effects of a disabled economy. Warner Brothers, after realizing profits of $17 million in 1929 and $7 million in 1930, lost nearly $8 million in 1931; Fox suffered a loss of $3 million after a $9 million profit the year before; and RKO's $3 million surplus from 1930 turned into a $5.6 million deficit. Paramount remained in the black that year, but Zukor saw his company's profits fall from $18 million to $6 million, and by 1932 he had a deficit of $21 million. By 1933, Paramount, with its 501 subsidiaries, went into bankruptcy; Fox underwent reorganization; and RKO was thrown into receivership. Warner Brothers, battered by losses of $14 million in 1932 and $6 million in 1933, was fighting to stay afloat. Of the majors, only Loew's had not yet shown a deficit; however, its earnings plunged from $10 million in 1930 to $1.3 million in 1933. As for the minors, Universal had gone into

1. Robert A. Brady, "The Problem of Monopoly," *Annals of the American Academy of Political and Social Science* 254 (November 1947): 125.

receivership; Columbia and United Artists were wounded, but not down.

Admission prices were slashed, audiences shrank—average weekly attendance dropped from an estimated eighty million in 1929 to sixty million in 1932 and 1933—production costs more than doubled because of sound, and revenues from foreign markets dwindled, but these factors in themselves did not cause the collapse. It resulted from the companies' having overextended themselves, first in the ferocious battle of the majors for control of the country's theaters in the 1920s and then in the tremendous capital investment in studios and theater equipment required for the conversion to sound. In short, the Big Five could not meet their fixed-cost obligations, which means, simply, they did not have the cash to pay their mortgage commitments, short-term obligations, and the heavy charges on their funded debts.

Correspondingly, the common stock value of these majors was reduced from a 1930 high of $960 million to $140 million in 1934. Theater after theater went dark. Paramount found it

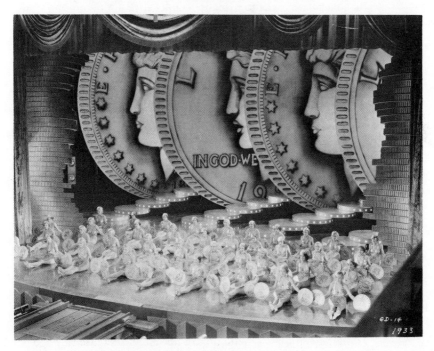

Gold Diggers of '33 (Warner Brothers)

cheaper to close many of its unprofitable smaller houses than
to pay overhead costs. The company also shut down its Long
Island studio and laid off almost five thousand employees who
had been earning between $35 and $50 a week. The number of
unemployed and underpaid extras in Hollywood became a
national scandal. Wages for those lucky enough to find work
dropped from $3 a day to $1.25.

When President Roosevelt declared a nationwide bank
moratorium in March 1933, Hollywood reeled from the shock.
Universal immediately suspended all contracts by invoking the
"national emergency" clause. Fox notified its employees that
salaries would not be paid until bank funds became available,
and studio heads met in emergency conferences to contemplate
the temporary suspension of production activities.

Such was the state of the motion picture industry at the
dawn of the New Deal. In a comprehensive attempt to revive
industry, President Roosevelt drafted the National Industrial
Recovery Act (NIRA), which became law in June 1933 and was
administered by the National Recovery Administration (NRA).
Its general aim was to promote cooperative action among trade
groups. The act assumed that collective action was superior to
cutthroat competition and that members of the business community would be willing to put aside selfish interests for the
good of the nation. It stipulated that industries were to draw
up codes of fair competition enforceable by law. Business could
ignore antitrust laws but, in return, had to make concessions
such as guaranteeing labor the right of collective bargaining
and establishing minimum wages and maximum hours.

Code of Fair Competition for the
Motion Picture Industry

The Code of Fair Competition for the Motion Picture
Industry was signed into law on November 27, 1933. Reflecting
the vertically integrated structure of the industry, it regulated
trade practices among producers, distributors, and exhibitors.
In conformity with NIRA guidelines, the Code banned company
unions, set minimum rates of pay, and allowed labor to
organize and bargain collectively. Working conditions and pay
scales for professional extras improved as a result; studio
craftsmen enjoyed a reduction in hours, an increase in wage
rates, and greater job security. One hundred and forty

different labor unions in the industry approved and signed the Code without controversy.

Hollywood's chief industrial imbalance, however, was not the underpayment of labor but the overpayment of professionals and executives. Louis B. Mayer had quelled public indignation somewhat by taking a temporary cut in pay from $10,000 to $750 a week. Other high-priced executives followed suit, so that during the turbulent months while the Code was being prepared, the production chiefs felt free to blame the financial difficulties of their studios on the star system. They wrote in provisions barring star raiding, curbing the activities of agents, and limiting the high salaries of creative artists. The reaction in Hollywood was frenzied. Actors and writers bombarded Washington with telegrams, held mass meetings, and launched publicity campaigns opposing the control of salaries on any basis other than free competition among producers. As the deadline approached for the signing of the Code, they threatened to strike. Eddie Cantor, representing the newly formed Screen Actors Guild, spent Thanksgiving with President Roosevelt, a meeting that later resulted in the permanent suspension of the obnoxious provisions in the Code.

The bitterness engendered by this fight stimulated the spread of unionization in Hollywood, to the chagrin of the studios. By the time of the NRA, most trades and crafts were organized under the jurisdiction of the International Alliance of Theatrical Stage Employees, affiliated with the American Federation of Labor. The passage of the National Labor Relations Act in 1935 spurred actors and other talent groups to organize as well. The Screen Actors Guild was recognized as the bargaining agent for actors on May 15, 1937, and won important concessions regarding wages, working conditions, and overtime for lower-paid actors and extras. The Screen Writers Guild was certified by the National Labor Relations Board on August 8, 1938, to bargain for writers, and in May 1940 union shops were established. The Screen Writers Guild was made the sole arbiter of screen credits, speculative writing was banned, and minimum wages were established, among other concessions. Soon after, the Screen Directors Guild won recognition. By the outbreak of World War II, practically all studio employees below the rank of executive producer had become unionized.

The integrated companies had more at stake in marketing

practices, and when it came time to draft provisions for the
Code governing these, the majors were victorious. They succeeded in receiving government sanction for the trade practices
that they had spent ten years developing through informal collusion and that enabled them to make the highest possible
profits. In short, the Motion Picture Code legalized the
monopolistic structure of the industry.

The controversial trade practices sanctioned by the Code
may be divided into two classes: the first comprised the
components of the block-booking system, which had been used
by the majors to maximize profits at the expense of the
independent exhibitor; the second included clearance and
zoning, setting of admission prices, and overbuying. These
latter practices had been used either to drive independents out
of business or to keep them in a subordinate position.

By presenting a united front, the majors got what they
wanted. The agency for effecting this was the Motion Picture
Producers and Distributors of America (MPPDA), called the
"Hays Office" after its president, former postmaster general
and chairman of the Republican National Committee Will H.
Hays. It was the dominant trade association for the industry
composed of the Big Five, Little Three, and several lesser
production companies. Created in 1922 primarily to combat
the widespread indignation over scandals in Hollywood and the
threat of censorship, the Hays Office by this time had armed
itself to resist interference of any kind, most particularly from
the courts through antitrust actions.

On May 27, 1935, the Supreme Court in a unanimous
decision invalidated the NIRA on the grounds that Congress
could not enact laws regulating the business practices of firms
in intrastate trade or attempt to delegate its legislative
functions to the President. The immediate effect on the motion
picture industry was slight. It had come through the
Depression virtually intact. Business improved steadily after
1933, and within two years all the companies were once again
earning profits, with Loew's the undisputed leader. By 1935,
Paramount and Fox had undergone reorganization. In 1936,
after selling off its theaters, Universal came out of receivership.
RKO was not stabilized until 1940. Just as important, the
industry's monopolistic trade practices remained in force
without significant alteration. However, the debate over them
continued in the halls of Congress, the Department of Justice,

and the courts, culminating in the antitrust case in 1938, *United States* v. *Paramount Pictures, Inc., et al.* The case reached the Supreme Court ten years later, after thousands of pages of testimony and exhibits, two consent decrees, two lower-court decisions, and appeals. In a landmark decision, the Court held that the Big Five were parties to a combination that had monopoly in exhibition as a goal. One result was that the five integrated companies were directed to divorce their theater holdings from the production-distribution ends of their businesses. The industry thereafter experienced serious upheavals, as will be seen in Part IV.

Double Features

The Depression spawned several new forms of exhibition practices. In an attempt to prop up sagging box-office receipts and to compete with first-run theaters, independent exhibitors

The Trail Blazers in *Death Valley Rangers* (Monogram, 1943)

introduced games with premiums and cash prizes, such as
Screeno, Banko, and Bingo. Although these were
comparatively short-lived, an innovation destined to make a
lasting impact on the industry was the double feature.

Until the 1930s the accepted movie program consisted of one
feature and a number of short subjects. In 1931, double
features, which originated in New England, began to spread to
other areas, as independents experimented with this form of
price cutting to draw more patrons. Although affiliated
theaters at first fought this practice—since they wanted to
protect their privileged position—they eventually followed suit.
In 1931, approximately eighteen hundred theaters, or roughly
one-eighth of the number in operation, adopted twin bills; by
1947, the fraction had risen to nearly two-thirds.

The wide acceptance of double features changed the
character of exhibition, presented many perplexing
distribution problems, and, more importantly, put a heavy
burden upon production facilities. In the long run it did not
affect attendance figures. As more and more theaters in a
given area adopted this practice, business was no better than it
would have been if all the exhibitors had continued to show
only single features. A significant reason was that few
exhibitors could afford to pay the rentals of two quality
pictures on a single bill. An exhibitor typically showed one
strong attraction and one cheap class B picture. And since he
wanted to spend as little as possible for the package, rentals
per play date for both kinds of pictures tended to decrease on
the average. Hollywood, in turn, lowered its production
budgets and geared itself for the most part to quantity rather
than quality.

The Production Code Administration

The development of the industry, in addition to being
affected by the Depression, was strongly influenced by the
pressure of organized religious groups. In an attempt to stymie
outside censorship, MPPDA members had voluntarily agreed
to comply with the rules governing cinematic proprieties
formulated by the Hays Office. They were codified into twelve
commandments and adopted by MPPDA members on March
31, 1930 (ch. 14). The Studio Relations Committee was
established to work with producers throughout all stages of

production, from the writing of a scenario to the final editing
of the picture, to see that the standards of ethics were
maintained.

Up until the Depression, producers were fairly conscientious
in abiding by the Production Code, but when attendance
plummeted in 1932-33, they began to introduce salacious
subject matter into their pictures in an attempt to attract
patrons. Moreover, producers were not sure that the 1930 Code
really represented or reflected what the public wanted. The
Catholic Church cried out in protest, as did Protestant and
Jewish groups. The Catholics were the most militant and
declared war against the industry by forming the Legion of
Decency, which would classify motion pictures according to its
own standards of acceptability. At the height of its crusade,
more than eleven million Church members signed pledges to
boycott offensive pictures.

The Legion of Decency exerted irresistible economic
pressure. Faced with the potential loss of revenue from such a
large group of patrons at a time when the industry was

Our Dancing Daughters (MGM, 1928), an exploitation stunt.
The picture provoked the wrath of local censors.

practically bankrupt, the majors decided to put teeth into the Production Code. On July 1, 1934, Will Hays and the board of directors of the MPPDA concluded action amending and amplifying the Production Code. Joseph I. Breen was placed in charge of the Production Code Administration, the successor to the Studio Relations Committee, and having considerably more clout. His findings were subject to review only on appeal to the company presidents of member companies in New York. Breen's department would continue to scrutinize all scripts and pictures with the knowledge that each release had to have the Hays Office seal of approval before it could be exhibited in theaters affiliated with MPPDA members. Any member violating this rule was subject to a $25,000 fine. Without access to these theaters, of course, no picture with a budget of any consequence could return its investment, let alone earn a profit.

The Catholic Church called off its threatened boycott and, along with other religious groups, decided to give the industry another chance at self-censorship. So pervasive had the Production Code Administration become that in 1937 it reviewed and approved approximately 98 percent of all pictures exhibited in the United States that year.

Although the agitation for reform was ultimately more helpful than harmful to the industry, the Production Code severely restricted the subject matter that American motion pictures could deal with. For the next generation, the industry would produce the "family" film, which addressed itself to the undifferentiated mass audience. Motion pictures might be technically polished and contain the so-called expensive production values, but they would not deal with pressing political or social issues in an honest and truthful fashion.

Effects of World War II

The Foreign Market

As hostilities spread in Europe and the Orient during the thirties, American film companies saw their foreign markets dwindle. Spain was the first casualty of the industry, following the outbreak of the Civil War in 1936. By 1938, Japan had occupied parts of China, Manchukuo, and the Kwantung Peninsula. Nearly half of the Far Eastern market soon came under Japanese control.

In the wake of the German *Anschluss,* the industry retreated from Austria, Czechoslovakia, Norway, and Occupied France. Continental Europe, where the majors had done over a quarter of their worldwide business in 1936, practically vanished as a market by 1941. The only business conducted on the Continent during the war was with neutral Sweden and Switzerland.

Of greater consequence was Great Britain, the principal outlet for American films abroad. Revenues fell off alarmingly after war was declared in September 1939. The Nazis began to bomb London and other English cities, which necessitated the evacuation of more than three million people. Until the threat of air attack subsided, theaters remained closed. By 1940, however, all but about 10 percent of the country's forty-eight hundred movie theaters were open once more, providing escape and relaxation from danger and war-related work. Average weekly attendance in Great Britain increased from nineteen million in 1939 to more than thirty million in 1945, and gross box-office receipts nearly trebled.

Although business in Great Britain did not suffer, U.S. companies could not share in the bonanza because of currency restrictions. Immediately following the declaration of war, Britain reduced the amount of sterling that American distributors could remove from the country; half of their former revenues, or $17.5 million, could be taken out in 1940, and only $12.9 million in 1941.

Currency restrictions such as those imposed by Great Britain were nothing new to American distributors. They had long been subjected to quotas, taxes, contingents, and tariffs of all varieties. The rise of nationalism in Europe was one cause; another was protectionism for national film industries. Although the Americans successfully fought these protective measures in the past—with the help of the U.S. Government, it should be noted—the war severely damaged the foreign film market (ch. 18).

To offset conditions in the war-torn European countries, Hollywood turned to Latin America. There, although the industry had a near-monopoly, the market had never been fully exploited. The Department of State aided Hollywood's cause by creating the Office of the Coordinator of Inter-American Affairs (CIAA) in October 1940. Its objective was to promote the Good Neighbor Policy and to initiate programs that would combat pro-Axis sentiment in South America. CIAA opened

its Motion Picture Division almost immediately, under the
directorship of John Hay Whitney.

Whitney's first goal was to convince the industry to abolish
the stereotyped bloodthirsty Latin-American villain from its
movies and to produce films having Latin-American themes
and locales. His second was to neutralize propaganda flowing
into Argentina, Brazil, and Chile from Axis wire services,
features, newsreels, and documentaries. Whitney created the
Newsreel Section for this purpose, and by 1943 the CIAA had
shipped to South America more than two hundred newsreels
produced in cooperation with Paramount, Pathé, Universal,
Fox, and Hearst's News of the Day. These pictures reached an
audience of more than eighteen million by 1944, according to
CIAA estimates.

Business in Latin America improved steadily during the war,
but not as much as expected. Several factors help explain this:
first, shipping between the two continents operated erratically
and less frequently than before; second, the films on war

Wallace Beery as Pancho Villa in *Viva Villa!* From the MGM release *Viva Villa!* © 1934
Metro-Goldwyn-Mayer Distributing Corporation. Copyright renewed 1961 by Metro-
Goldwyn-Mayer Inc.

subjects, which Hollywood churned out in great numbers at the beginning, had little mass appeal; and third, national film companies, especially in Mexico, stepped up their own production.

The Domestic Market

By the time America entered the war, it was apparent to the industry that it would have to rely on the domestic market. Fortunately, conditions at home created a boom in business. Dollars were plentiful, while commodities were not. Movies were the most readily available entertainment. Although gasoline restrictions hurt attendance in some rural areas, the integrated companies, whose theaters were more favorably situated, flourished. Domestic film rentals for the eight majors jumped from $193 million in 1939 to $332 million in 1946. As *Variety* noted, "Every night was Saturday night" at the movies. B pictures, low-grade pictures, pictures featuring unknown players—all commanded an audience. Weekly attendance by the end of the war reached ninety million, its highest ever.

Air Force (Warner Brothers, 1943)—World War II as depicted by Hollywood

As business improved, pictures ran longer and longer to capacity houses, with a significant result. The eight majors released 388 pictures in 1939, but only 252 in 1946. In other words, studios were receiving more and more dollars for fewer and fewer pictures. Production costs rose during this period, to be sure, but not as fast as profit margins. Paramount's earnings, for example, soared from $10 million in 1941 to an incredible $44 million in 1946.

Favorable market conditions during the war stimulated independent production. Before 1940, there were only a handful of independents, but by 1946, there were more than forty. The drop in output together with the increasing demand for movies had the effect of making independent production a less speculative venture. Another reason for the influx had to do with the Treasury Department: the wartime income tax rates had badly eroded the take-home pay of high-priced talent. By operating his own production company, a producer, director, or star in the top income tax bracket could reduce his effective tax rate from 90 to 60 percent. Moreover, under certain conditions, an interest in a completed picture could be sold as a capital asset, making the profit from such sale subject to a 25 percent capital gains tax.

Since independent production was anathema to the studio system, most independents during the war years distributed their pictures through United Artists. But postwar conditions, most particularly those created by television and the Supreme Court's disposition of the *Paramount* case, forced the majors to welcome them with open arms.

The industry easily overcame two obstacles that potentially threatened revenues. The first related to personnel. At least one-fourth of the male employees of Hollywood, including some of the biggest stars, went into uniform. But the increased demand for movies—all kinds of movies—which enabled the companies to play their releases for longer runs, offset this personnel shortage. The other obstacle was the shortage of raw film stock. When the government reduced basic allotments by 25 percent on January 1, 1943, the industry, having anticipated this move, had already adopted conservation measures and hoarded films. Studios had on their shelves more than one hundred unreleased pictures, enough to get them through until the rationing was lifted.

Hollywood continued much as always during the war.

James Cagney in *Yankee Doodle Dandy* (Warner Brothers, 1942)

During the 1941-42 season, about one out of every four pictures related in some way to the war effort. By 1944, however, Hollywood's product began to show a pronounced trend toward lighter and mellower diversion. Films became escapist once again, with musicals and comedies the staples.

The machinery created by the majors carried them to the crest of prosperity in 1946. Paramount's profits for that year have already been stated. Earnings for the other members of the Big Five were as follows: Twentieth Century-Fox, $22 million; Warner Brothers, $19 million; Loew's, $18 million; and RKO, $12 million. Afterward, the industry underwent a period of retrenchment, reappraisal, and reorganization.

11

MAE D. HUETTIG

The Motion Picture Industry Today

Some Questions to Be Answered

Despite the glamour of Hollywood, the crux of the motion picture industry is the theater. It is in the brick-and-mortar branch of the industry that most of the money is invested and made. Without understanding this fact, devotees of the film are likely to remain forever baffled by some characteristics of an industry which is in turn exciting, perplexing, and irritating. Emphasis on the economic role of the theater is not meant to belittle the film itself. Obviously it is the film which draws people to the theater. Nevertheless, the structure of the motion picture industry (a large inverted pyramid, top-heavy with real estate and theaters, resting on a narrow base of the intangibles which constitute films) has had far-reaching effects on the film itself.

This may seem farfetched. Most writers on the motion picture industry rather studiously avoid its duller aspects, i.e., those dealing with the trade practices, financial policies, intercorporate relationships, etc. But the facts indicate clearly that there is a connection between the form taken by the film and the mechanics of the business, even if the connection is somewhat obscure. It is true, as one student has pointed out, that "the issues involved are not peculiar to the motion picture industry."[1] Despite

Abridged by the editor from *Economic Control of the Motion Picture Industry* (Philadelphia, 1944), pp. 54-95.
  1. Howard T. Lewis, *The Motion Picture Industry* (New York, 1933), p. xiii.

this lack of uniqueness, the problems of organization, intercorporate relationships, and financial policy in the motion picture industry deserve more than passing mention. The attitude of the industry itself toward discussion of these problems has not been completely candid. A great reluctance to disclose factual information with respect to its operations has unfortunately characterized most of the leaders of the industry.

Among the many questions which lack a reliable answer are: How many people attend movies? How often? How large is the industry in terms of invested capital and volume of business? What is the annual income of all theaters? How many theaters are owned by what groups? What type of film is most uniformly successful? What is the relationship between the cost of films and their drawing power? Little is known of the industry's place in the broader pattern of American industry, or its method of solving the specialized problems of commercial entertainment. There are few reliable statistics available (and of these none is compiled by the industry itself) with regard to these questions.

What Is the Economic Importance of the Industry?

There are various ways of measuring the role of an industry in our economy. The indices most commonly used are: (1) volume of business, (2) invested capital, and (3) number of employees. The value of such criteria is limited, since comparison between all types of industries produces results too general to be significant. However, in the case of the motion picture industry, these indices are valuable as a means of delimiting its economic importance and recording some basic information regarding its size. This question assumes importance partly because the industry itself seems to be under some misapprehension with respect to the answer. It may well be true, as Will Hays frequently says, that the motion picture is a great social necessity, an integral part of human life in the whole civilized world, but this value is in no way minimized by an accurate statement as to the industry's economic importance. "Standing well among the first ten (or the first four) industries in this country" [for a similar statement, see ch. 9, for example—Ed.] has so often prefaced the remarks of industry spokesmen as to indicate that the facts are not generally known.

Here, then, let it be noted that insofar as size of industry is measured by dollar volume of business, the motion picture industry is not only not among the first ten, it is not even among the first forty. It is surpassed by such industries, to name only a few, as laundries, hotels, restaurants, loan companies, investment trusts, liquor, tobacco, and musical instruments.

Viewed thus as a part of our national economy, the motion picture industry is not a major bulwark. There are forty-four other industries, out of the total of ninety-four industrial groups enumerated by *Statistics of Income* (Bureau of Internal Revenue), that reported a larger gross income in 1937 than did the combined motion picture producing and exhibition corporations. In terms of employment, the motion picture industry accounts for somewhat fewer than 200,000 persons in all three branches of production, distribution, and exhibition.

When motion picture corporations are compared with those in other branches of the entertainment field, another story is presented. The entire field of commercial amusement, including billiard halls, bowling alleys, dance halls, etc., is dominated by the motion picture industry.[2] Motion picture corporations, constituting 44 percent of the total number of amusement corporations in 1937, accounted for 78 percent of the gross income and 92 percent of the total net income of the group. This should prove what has long been suspected and probably needs little proof: that movies are the favorite form of entertainment for most Americans.

Production versus Exhibition

From the point of view of the moviegoing public, one of the most important questions about the industry is: Who decides what films are made; or, as it is more commonly put, why are films what they are? From the industry's point of view, too, this question of the kind of product released is ultimately its most important single problem. Quality of product is increasingly vital now that the motion picture business is settling down into a semblance of middle age, devoid of the novelty appeal it formerly had.

The answer to the question posed above is in the relationship among the various branches of the industry. By virtue of the division of labor within the business, film distributors and exhibitors are much more closely in touch with the moviegoing public than are the producers, and they trade heavily on their advantageous positions. From their seat in the box office they announce that so-and-so is "poison at the box office," that what the public wants is musicals or blood-and-thunder westerns, that English stars murder business, and that sophisticated farce comedies leave their audiences completely cold.

2. In 1938, amusement corporations constituted roughly 2 percent of the entire number of active corporations filing income tax returns. The gross income of all amusement corporations was slightly over $1 billion, or less than 1 percent of the total gross income ($120 billion) of all corporations filing returns. Net income (less deficit) of amusement corporations was $52 million. Bureau of Internal Revenue, *Statistics of Income*, 1939.

Broadly speaking, and omitting the relatively unimportant independent producers, the relationship among the three branches of the industry may be described in two ways. First, there is the relationship between a major producer and theater operators not affiliated with his company. Secondly, there is the relationship *within* a major company among the various departments of production, distribution, and exhibition. The intracompany relationship is the more important with respect to the kind of films made, since contact within the organization is much closer than contact between the unaffiliated exhibitors and producers. The unaffiliated exhibitors are not generally consulted by producers with respect to the nature of the films to be made. However, they occasionally make their views known through advertisements in the trade press and probably express their opinions quite freely in talking with the sales representatives of the producers. Most of their arguments are ex post facto, however, and affect the future lineup of product negatively, or not at all.

On the other hand, the sales and theater people *within* the integrated

Academy Awards Dinner, 1935—Irving Thalberg, Bette Davis, Frank Capra,
and Victor MacLaglen

companies are extremely important in determining the type of picture to be made, the number of pictures in each cost class, the type of story, etc. It is not intended to give here a detailed account of the manner in which these decisions are reached, but in general the procedure is as follows: The person in charge of distribution announces the number of films wanted for the following season. This figure is presumably based on some estimate of what can be profitably sold, but it is also related to the needs of the company's own theaters for product. The chief executive announces the amount of money available for the total product. The amounts vary among the individual companies from $7 or $8 million for the smaller companies to $28 million for Loew's. The next step is the division and allocation of the total amount to groups of pictures. The names given these classes vary, but the grouping is in accordance with the quality to be aimed at as defined by the amount of money to be spent. That is, there are the "specials" and the more ordinary "program" features. There are "A" pictures and "B" pictures. The latter are designed, more or less frankly, to meet the need for the lesser half of the double-feature program. Once the allocation of production funds is made, the next step is that of determining the budgets for the individual pictures within each group. The amount spent on a given picture is presumably related in some way to the anticipated drawing power of the particular combination of talent and production values planned for the given picture. After the detailed budget is worked out, a tentative release schedule is prepared for the use of the sales force (distribution). From this point on, the problems belong primarily to the production department.

Note what this cursory outline reveals. Company executives, i.e., theater, sales, and production people, determine the following: the number of pictures to be made, the total amount of money to be spent, the distribution of the funds among the various classes of pictures, the budgets of the individual pictures, and the dates when the pictures are to be finished.

It is not meant that all such issues are decided by ukase and handed down from the front office to the production staff. The interdepartmental conference technique is customary, with every department chief valiantly defending his own position. At work are all the usual subterranean factors which determine where power ultimately rests. There are, however, certain objective factors which are present to some degree in each of the five large majors. These tend to give decisive policy-making power regarding the kind of films made to the groups farthest removed from production itself, i.e., the men in distribution and theater management.

The objective factors are found in a prosaic listing of the various sources of income to the five principal companies. In approximate order of importance, they are: (1) theater admissions, (2) film rentals, (3) the sale of film accessories, and (4) dividends from affiliated companies. The relative importance of each source varies for the individual majors, but in almost every instance the chief single source of income is theater admissions. Although there is an inseparable connection between the quality of films and company earnings from film rentals and theaters, the division of functions within the company structure operates to give the preponderance of power to those nearest the principal source of income, i.e., the theaters. Furthermore, the earning power of a given chain of theaters depends not so much upon the quality of films made by its parent company as on the quality of films in general. If successful films are available, the dominant group of affiliated theaters in a given area generally has preferential access to them, regardless of which major produced them. In other words, the successful theater operations of each of the majors depend largely on the return from the theaters. But successful theater operation for a major company is not directly dependent on the quality of its own pictures, although this contributes, of course. By virtue of the regional division of the theater market, there is in effect a pooling of the product; the affiliated theaters in their separate areas have access to the best pictures available. Consequently, competition in the production of pictures has no real parallel in the theater organization. A good picture, i.e., one successful at the box office, redounds to the benefit of each of the theater-owning majors since each shares in the box office. This interdependence seems a unique characteristic of the motion picture business. In other industries, an exceptionally good product is feared and disliked by other producers or sellers of similar goods. But of the small group of dominant movie companies, it is really true that the good of one is the good of all.

The production and exhibition phases of the business behave toward each other like a chronically quarrelsome but firmly married couple and not without reason. The exhibitor group controls the purse strings; it accounts for more than nine-tenths of the invested capital and approximately two-thirds of the industry's income. Nevertheless, it requires films. Consequently, the conflict between the two groups more nearly resembles a family quarrel than is ordinarily true of trade disputes, since the essential interdependence between production and exhibition is recognized by all. To a theater operator there is no substitute for "celluloid." Conversely, the producers of movies have no real alternative to the theaters as outlets for their product. The normal interdependency between supplier and customer is accentuated in the motion picture industry by the combination of functions within the same corporate framework. But difficulty results from the fact that while the selling of entertainment is a commercial process, making films is largely creative and artistic in nature. Moviemakers, like artists in other fields, are generally inclined to experiment with new techniques and are not above wanting to interpret or affect their surroundings. Exhibitors, on the other hand, may not know much about the art of the film, but they know what has been good box office before. Consequently, theirs is the conservative influence; they are

On the set of Samuel Goldwyn's *Dead End*, directed by William Wyler
(United Artists, 1937)

the traditionalists of the trade, exerting their influence in the direction of the safe-and-sound in film making.

Structure of the Industry

As a result of the dominance of the integrated companies, the structure of the motion picture industry cannot be described along simple functional lines of production, distribution, and exhibition. Each of the major companies is a replica of the industry in all its activities. In addition to the five majors, there are approximately six or seven producing-distributing concerns (principally Universal, Columbia, United Artists, Monogram, Republic, and Producers' Releasing Corporation) and a large number of exhibition companies. These, in turn, are divisible into two groups; the individually operated theaters and the chains of four or more theaters.

The Majors

The best single source of information about the major motion picture companies is the Securities and Exchange Commission, with which registration statements and annual reports are filed. These provide considerably more factual data than have ever before been available to outsiders, making it possible to delineate the structure of the companies and their relationship to each other with respect to size, volume of business, their financial policies, profitability, executive remuneration.

Examination of the list of subsidiaries reported by any one of the five large companies indicates that the production of films is merely one of many activities and not necessarily the most important. Warner Brothers Pictures, Inc., for example, lists 108 subsidiaries. They include the following: a film laboratory, Brunswick Radio Corporation, and a radio manufacturing subsidiary, a lithographing concern, a concern that makes theater accessories, ten music publishing houses, real-estate companies, booking agencies, several broadcasting corporations, a company called Warner Brothers Cellulose Products, Inc., theater management companies, recording studios, and a television company—all this in addition to a film-producing unit and numerous theater subsidiaries, controlling approximately 507 theaters.

Loew's, Inc., consists of approximately seventy-three subsidiaries controlled more than 50 percent, plus twenty additional corporations in which effective control was disclaimed. The subsidiaries are primarily theater concerns, but include distribution companies, vaudeville booking agencies, music publishing houses, and several realty concerns. In fact, three of Loew's most important subsidiaries are registered with the S.E.C.

Gate of Hope, Paramount Studio, Hollywood

as real-estate corporations. Control without majority ownership of the stock in many of the theater subsidiaries operates either through written agreements or through acquiescence of the remaining stockholders. In practice, this generally means that the owners of the theater have agreed to share control with Loew's in exchange for a franchise to exhibit Loew's pictures.

Paramount Pictures, Inc., is the most complex of the five, although its activities are apparently less ramified than Warner Brothers'. Whereas it originally bought out entire circuits of theaters, financing most of the purchases with bonds, reorganization in 1935 brought with it many changes in policy and structure. Today, most of its theater enterprises are partnerships; Paramount participates but does not exercise complete control. This is borne out by the fact that only 95 of its 203 subsidiaries are controlled 50 percent or more. Decentralized theater operations have been the approved policy at Paramount since the failure in 1933 of an attempt to manage in detail some 1,600 theaters from New York. It is estimated that at least half of Paramount's theaters are now run by their original owners on a part-ownership and contract basis, and that Paramount's average interest in its theaters is somewhat less than 70 percent.

The smaller producing companies are less complicated in structure and less far-flung in their activities. However, even concerns like Columbia Pictures and Universal Pictures operate twenty-eight and thirty-four subsidiaries, respectively. Most of these are distribution units. Universal Pictures Corporation is itself a subsidiary of Universal Corporation, a holding company which controls almost all its common stock. Both Universal Corporation and Columbia Pictures Corporation are managed by voting trusts.

The diversity of functions demonstrated by the large movie companies is reflected in the executive personnel, that is, the directors and officers of the companies. If the production of movies is but one aspect of the corporate existence, it follows that representation will be given to the other activities in some proportion to their importance. Take Paramount, for instance. Its board of directors includes the following: Harvey D. Gibson, banker, affiliated with the New York Trust Company, Manufacturers' Trust Company, the Textile Banking Company, etc.; A. Conger Goodyear, manufacturer and financier; John D. Hertz, partner in Lehman Brothers, founder of the Yellow Cab Company; Maurice Newton, partner in Hallgarten and Company, investment banker with diverse interests in tobacco, rubber, petroleum, and real estate. The president of Paramount is Barney Balaban, a Chicago theater man; vice-president is Frank Freeman, also originally a theater operator. Chairman of the executive committee is Stanton Griffis, broker and partner in Hemphill, Noyes, Mr.

Adolph Zukor, the company's founder, occupies the somewhat honorific post of chairman of the board of directors.

The structure of the major companies is important because there is a real and direct connection between the way in which they are set up, the kind of people who run them, and the kind of films produced. This is the reason for emphasis on the fact that the capital assets of the dominant companies are so largely land, buildings, and real estate. Where the investment takes this form, it is not surprising that the executive personnel should consist of men skilled primarily in the art of selecting theater sites, managing real estate, and financing operations, rather than of talented producers.

The balance sheets of the five theater-owning majors show that from half to three-quarters of their total assets are "land, buildings, and equipment." On the other hand, for the two producing-distributing companies (Universal and Columbia), this proportion is under 15 percent.

In itself, the fact that the majors' assets are chiefly theaters, i.e., real estate, might have little significance. However, most of the theaters were acquired with the aid of bonds and other forms of long-term debt. The policy of debt financing has been of great importance in the history of the industry. More than 30 percent of the total invested capital in the seven major motion picture companies is borrowed. The case of several individual companies is even more extreme. Nearly half of the total capital of Warner Brothers and Paramount, for example, is borrowed. Thus, it is no accident that the principal corporate officers of four out of the five big majors are bondholders or their representatives. Debt financing has had many important ramifications affecting the stockholders, dividend policies, and internal corporate practices. Most important, however, to the moviegoer, is this fact: The production of films, essentially fluid and experimental as a process, is harnessed to a form of organization which can rarely afford to be either experimental or speculative because of the regularity with which heavy fixed charges must be met.

Originally, the motive behind the acquisition of theaters by producing companies may have been the need for the security represented by assured first-run exhibition for their films. Today, however, the majors derive most of their income from their theaters, and production is less important as a source of revenue than exhibition. In fact, the chief advantage of continued control over production and distribution is that it enables them to maintain their advantageous position as favored theater operators. Thus, the production of films by the major companies is not really an end in itself, on the success or failure of which the company's existence depends; it is an instrument directed toward the accomplishment of a larger end, i.e., domination of the theater market. This does not mean that there is no attempt to make successful films or that film production is itself unprofit-able (although three of the five largest major companies have regularly incurred losses in production); it means simply that the principal concern of the men who run the major companies is their theaters.

The relative importance of production as a source of income to the majors is shown in Table 1. The analysis is incomplete because the amounts obtained in film rentals from foreign markets are not included. However, even adding the 35 percent generally imputed to the foreign market by industry spokesmen does not substantially alter the argument.

TABLE 1

Income from Domestic Film Rentals as Percent of Total Volume of Business
Five Major Motion Picture Companies, 1939

Company	Domestic film rentals	Volume of business	Film rentals as percent of volume of business
Loew's	$ 43,227,000	$112,489,000	38.4
20th Century-Fox[a]	33,150,000	53,752,000	61.0
Warner Bros.	28,917,000	102,083,000	28.3
Paramount	28,227,000	96,183,000	29.3
RKO	18,190,000	51,451,000	35.3
	$151,711,000	$415,958,000	36.4

[a] The case of Twentieth Century-Fox differs somewhat from that of the other majors. During a complicated reorganization in 1933, control of the Fox theaters changed hands, ending up eventually in General Theatres Equipment Corporation. This company, in turn, was controlled by Chase National Bank. Fox, newly merged with Twentieth Century in 1935, possessed a 42 percent stock interest in General Theatres Equipment Corporation. The company's income from theaters takes the form of dividends on the stock interest and is therefore not comparable to the amounts listed as income from theaters for the other majors.

TABLE 2

Gross Film Rentals from Distribution Within the United States
of Ten Motion Picture Companies, 1939

Loew's	$ 43,227,000	21.5
20th Century-Fox	33,150,000	16.5
Warner Bros.	28,917,000	14.4
Paramount	28,227,000	14.0
RKO	18,190,000	9.1
Universal	14,161,000	7.0
United Artists	13,478,000	6.7
Columbia	13,194,000	6.5
Republic	6,160,000	3.1
Monogram	2,532,000	1.2
Total	$201,236,000	100.0

These same figures are of interest for what they reveal of the relative strength of each of the large majors in the realm of production, insofar, at least, as film rentals reflect the demand for a given company's product. Taken in conjunction with the film rentals of the non-theater-owning majors, the distribution of business among the various producing units is as shown in Table 2.

It is quite apparent that there is no direct correlation between the number of theaters owned by a given major and its income from film rentals.[3] Paramount, for example, has more theaters than any of the other majors, but its income from film rentals is substantially lower than that of three other companies with fewer theaters. The difficulty of interpretation here is increased by the fact that individual companies may have varying policies with respect to film rentals charged their affiliated theaters. For instance, in one company it may be desirable for the controlling group to show greater profitability in theater operations than in production; accordingly, low film rentals may be charged up against the theater department. However, there is no way of allowing for factors of this kind. We can only take the figures at their face value, keeping in mind complications arising from metaphysical accounting practices.

If there is no direct correlation between theater ownership and income from film rentals, what is the chief value of the integrated form of organization? If a company owning relatively few theaters can earn more from its films than one with many theaters, why does it bother with theater operation at all?

From the producer's standpoint, theater ownership is valuable for two reasons. Theaters function as a kind of insurance policy, in that (1) they provide first-run exhibition, and (2) they offer a minimum market for films which might otherwise not be well received. This market is difficult to evaluate, but it is unlikely that the affiliated theaters of a given company account for more than 25 percent of its total film rentals. Paramount, for example, the largest theater owner, is said to receive approximately 25 percent of its film rentals from its own theaters. It is reasonable to assume that the other majors, with substantially smaller theater

3. Theater holdings of the major companies are approximately as follows:

Paramount	1,239
20th Century-Fox	517
Warner Bros.	507
RKO	222
Loew's	139
	2,624

holdings, receive an even smaller proportion of their total film rentals from their theaters. Loew's receives approximately 10 percent of its total film rentals from its affiliated theaters. None of the major companies receives a dominant share of its film rentals from its own theaters. They could not, in other words, guarantee great success for films which would otherwise find no market, but they do act as a partial buffer against complete failure.

To summarize: The major motion picture companies engage in a variety of activities. The production of films is one such activity, but not the most important one with respect to the amount of corporate income for which it is directly responsible. This is reflected in the fact that executive personnel of the large majors is chiefly financial and composed of real-estate men rather than experts in the realm of production. Control of the producing companies passed into the hands of the present financial group when they became primarily theater concerns, with the consequent emphasis on problems of financing theater expansion and real-estate operation. Today, approximately two-thirds of the total capital of the majors is invested in theaters. Furthermore, most of their income is derived from theaters. There is, however, no apparent connection between the number of theaters controlled and the profitability of the company's producing activities. The highest-grossing films are produced by the major with the fewest theaters, i.e., Loew's. From the point of view of the producing groups within the majors, the chief advantage of having affiliated theaters is the assurance of a minimum market. From the point of view of the theater departments within the majors, however, the advantage of having production facilities is incalculably great. It gives superiority over competing unaffiliated theaters, whose choice of product is always secondary to that of the dominant major in any given area. Thus the chief advantages of integration are in the domain of exhibition.

What Kind of Theaters Do the Majors Own?

The value of theater ownership is not a function of number only but of location, size, and quality as well.

Average seating capacity of all theaters in the United States is 623. The de luxe metropolitan houses, most of which are affiliated with the major producing companies, have an average seating capacity of 1,445; the theaters owned by independent circuits average 897 seats, as compared with an average of 515 for the independently owned theaters. For the theater group as a whole, ownership of seating capacity is reported to be as follows: Of a total of approximately eleven million seats, affiliated theaters have 22 percent; unaffiliated circuits, 27 percent; independently operated theaters (fewer than four theaters operated by the same individual or group of individuals), 51 percent.

The situation in a specific area is described in figures recently published by the New York Film Board of Trade. The total number of theaters in the

Hell's Angels première at Grauman's Chinese Theater, Hollywood. Courtesy Bruce Torrence Historical Collection, c/o First Federal of Hollywood

Greater New York area in 1940 was 1,208. Of this number, 197 or 16.3 percent were affiliated with the major producers. Their theaters contained 28.4 percent of the total number of seats in the area, averaging nearly 2,000 seats per theater, as compared with an average seating capacity of 1,093 for independent chain theaters and 777 for individually owned theaters. It is relevant to note that the affiliated theaters provide the major producers with nearly 70 percent of their entire film rentals from the New York area. Since film rentals usually represent a percentage of the box-office gross, it is reasonable to conclude that the affiliated theaters probably received a proportionate share of the total theater receipts for the area.

A further point to be made in this connection concerns the location of the theaters owned by the major producing companies. Seating capacity is highly concentrated in the large metropolitan centers; 2.5 million seats out of the total of approximately eleven million were in thirteen cities with population of over 500,000 each.

These thirteen large cities have 2,251 theaters located therein and, while housing almost one-fourth of the total seating capacity in the entire country, represent only 14 percent of the number of theaters. In other words, a very large number of the theaters in the United States are small theaters in small towns.[4]

As a result of this concentration of large theaters in the metropolitan centers, 60 percent of the total film rentals of the major producing companies was derived from the exchange areas containing the thirteen cities with population over 500,000.

The most important aspect of theater ownership, however, arises out of the differentiated nature of the theater structure. Just as various products may be distinguished from each other on the basis of price or quality, so, in the case of theaters, can the distinction be made almost entirely in terms of the "run" that each has. "Run" refers to priority rights in the showing of films for the particular community in which the theater is located. The first, second, and third runs account for all but a small proportion of total theater receipts. First-run theaters receive a share of the business altogether disproportionate to their number as well as to their size, although this latter disparity is less marked.

Most first-run houses are owned by the five major companies. They own or control the operations of 126 out of 163 first-run theaters in the twenty-five largest cities of the country. Only 37 first-run theaters in the entire

4. Motion Picture Producers and Distributors of America (the Hays Office), Annual Report of Theater Service Department, February 1939.

country are independently owned and operated. The number of first-run theaters each controls, through either ownership, management contract, or pooling arrangement with a competing distributor, is distributed as follows:

Company	Number of Controlled First-run Theaters
Paramount	29
Warner Bros.	28
20th Century-Fox	26
Loew's	24
RKO	19
Nonaffiliated	37
Total	163

To summarize: The theaters owned by the major companies are among the largest in the industry, located for the most part in the metropolitan centers, and include 77 percent of the important first-run houses.

Why Are the First-Run Theaters Important?

First-run theaters are important because: (1) they receive the bulk of the business; (2) producers receive a substantial proportion of their total film rentals from first-run showings; (3) control of these important theaters is, in effect, control over access to the screen; (4) last, and probably least important, they provide a testing ground for the pictures by means of which the prices to be charged for individual films may be determined.

The precise importance of the first-run theaters varies from city to city. In general, the larger the city, the less the relative importance of the first-run, and the more important the neighborhood houses. In New York and Philadelphia, for example, the first-run theaters provide between 20 and 30 percent of the total film rentals, whereas in Atlanta and Kansas City they provide well over 50 percent of the total. The importance of the first-run houses appears to depend on the nature of the theater-control situation in each particular city. In Philadelphia, for example, where the first-run theaters account for less than 30 percent of the film rentals, Warner Brothers, the dominant company in that area, owns not only first-run houses but also many subsequent-run houses. It has eight large theaters in Philadelphia and 183 others in Pennsylvania. None of the other majors has a first-run outlet in Philadelphia.

In this situation the relevant question is not how much of the gross comes from first-run theaters, but how much comes from the affiliated theaters. Philadelphia is almost entirely Warner Brothers' territory by virtue of the absorption in 1929 of the Stanley Company, one of the most powerful theater circuits in the country. Over 75 percent of all film rentals from the Philadelphia area is derived from affiliated theaters, which means, in this case, Warner Brothers theaters. In Atlanta, on the other hand, over 80 percent of the total film rentals comes from first-run theaters, of which there are five. Paramount owns four; Loew's, one.

The extent to which the majors absorbed other than first-run theaters in any given area apparently depended upon the nature of local movie-going habits. Movie-goers in large decentralized cities tend increasingly to patronize neighborhood theaters, with a consequent reduction in the relative importance of the first-run movie palace. In such situations, the majors extended their theater ownership to include the subsequent-run houses, the source of most of the patronage. In Atlanta, and most of the smaller cities, however, patronage is concentrated in the de luxe theaters. Unaffiliated theaters are permitted to retain that portion of the total volume of business which remains for the subsequent runs. Nearly three-quarters of the total film rentals paid by Atlanta theaters are derived from affiliated houses.

In New York City, on the other hand, first-run theaters produce not more than 20 percent of the total. Of the total subsequent runs, affiliated theaters produce in the neighborhood of 80 percent. For the city as a whole, affiliated theaters of all runs produce nearly 70 percent of all film rentals. Thirteen percent of the total film rentals paid in the United States are from New York City.

To summarize: It is very likely that in all but the largest cities of the country the first-run theaters provide well over 50 percent of the total revenue, in some areas as much as 80 percent. Where this is the case, the theater holdings of the majors are confined to first-run theaters. In that type of theater situation in which movie attendance is dispersed through neighborhoods, the theater interests of the majors are more extensive, including strategically located subsequent-run houses. In any event, the net effect of theater ownership by the major producing companies (with respect to income from the production of films) is that they are their own best customers. They provide themselves and each other with the bulk of the market for films.

By no means less important than the revenue offered by the first-run theaters is the power which accompanies their ownership. This power rests upon the peculiarities of the market for films and is tantamount to authority to decide what films may reach the public. Originally the first-run theater developed out of the willingness and ability of enterprising theater owners to pay higher rentals for the first showings of better-

quality films. It then had the effect of stimulating competition among producers for access to this important segment of the market. Today, owned
by the major producing companies, first-run screen time is occupied
almost entirely by their own pictures. As a market for independent producers (i.e., those other than the eight major companies) first-run theaters
are virtually closed.

How was it possible for this power to be concentrated in such a small
number of theaters? The answer to this question is partly in the realm of
applied psychology. It involves the deeper question of why people go to the
movies at all and why they go when they do. Inescapable is the fact that at
least one factor in influencing moviegoing is the advance buildup given a
picture, the barrage of publicity and exploitation which accompanies the
release of a new film, the reviews by critics who see the film as it opens its
run, and all the other multifarious activities of publicity agents. Great importance is attached to these activities by the people within the industry.
Consequently, when an inexpensive picture achieves public acclaim
without the preliminary fanfare usually reserved for the more costly
pictures, it is called a "sleeper," a term which indicates that even the
producer of the picture was taken by surprise.

A measure of the industry's faith in advertising is the estimated $110
million annually spent on it. Consequently, exhibitors the country over
receive requests from their patrons: When is the next Super-Colossal
going to show? When is Clark Gable's new picture coming here? They
have heard; they know that the leading man in such-and-such a picture is
actually in love with the star; they read fan magazines and columnists;
they listen to radio programs devoted exclusively to Hollywood gossip—in
a word, they care. Who are the exhibitors to ignore such a wealth of
feeling? At first, the importance of first-run theaters was related to the
public's appreciation of the material superiority of the theater, its greater
comfort and beauty. This in turn gave greater earning power, permitting
payment of higher rentals for the better films. The process whereby their
influence was extended over moviegoers outside their immediate jurisdiction has been described as follows:

The new Palace theatres became liberal advertisers in newspapers and publishers
responded by giving their shows publicity in news columns and reviews. The
newspapers in thirty to fifty metropolitan centers throughout the country—key
cities—circulate in all neighboring cities and towns, and the advertising and
publicity of a first run in a key city create a demand for the picture in the surrounding district. Theatres in Long Island or New Jersey, for example, learned
that a photoplay first shown at the Strand or the Rialto, in New York, would draw
large audiences, while a film with no first run in the metropolis would attract little
attention. Soon exhibitors everywhere in the United States followed the line of

least resistance, giving preference to pictures with the prestige of key-city first runs, ignoring all others or renting them only at very low rates. Within a few years photoplays without first runs were not regarded by theatre-goers as first class, and unless a producer could obtain first runs his chance of making money grew very slim.[5]

As long ago as 1917, representative feature films, if given first-run exhibition, grossed from sixty to one hundred thousand dollars; without adequate first-run exhibition, earnings would drop thirty to forty thousand dollars, amounts which usually failed to cover costs.

The line of least resistance adopted by the exhibitors—that is, their refusal to book pictures other than those which had received big city openings—was somewhat short-sighted, as it later turned out. It had the effect of forcing independent producers out of the field, making much simpler the task of the forces working toward control through integration. Obviously, if most exhibitors book only those pictures which receive first-run showings, then control of the first-run theaters is, in effect, control over all the others. Once the independent producers were denied access to the screen, the process of encirclement was complete: The major producers were also the major exhibitors. It was for them to say whose pictures would be shown.

The final result is clear. The majors show their own films and each other's. If the film of an independent producer gives promise of box-office success, they may take over its distribution, showing it in their own theaters and selling it to nonaffiliated theaters. For this service they charge the producer a price which usually amounts to 35 percent of the total gross. Such, for example, is the arrangement whereby RKO distributed the product of the Walt Disney Studios, the beloved Mickey Mouse and Donald Duck cartoons, as well as the more recent feature-length pictures. Such product is, for all practical purposes, part and parcel of the rest of the merchandise distributed by the major; from the point of view of the nonaffiliated theater owner, it is immaterial that the production was independent. His access to it is subject to exactly the same restrictions as surround all other films released by the major; it does not compete independently with the product of the majors.

The exhibition policy of the first-run theaters is analyzed in the petition of the federal government in its recent antitrust suit against the majors. Data collected by the Department of Justice show that, for the exhibition years 1934 through 1937, not less than 95 percent of all pictures shown in the first-run metropolitan houses of each of the majors consisted of the releases of the eight companies. Over 99 percent of the films exhibited in

5. Benjamin B. Hampton, *A History of the Movies* (New York, 1931), pp. 172-73.

Loew's first-run theaters were released by the majors. "As a result," the petition reads, "the independent producer does not have access to a free, open, and untrammelled first-run market in metropolitan cities in which to dispose of his pictures. Entrance to this market by an independent producer is only at the sufferance of (the defendants herein) who control it."[6] The petition neglects to add an equally important fact, namely, that with the closing of this market to the independent producer, the remainder of the market, the subsequent run is, in effect, also closed.

As a control device, the development of strategic first-run theaters as the showcases of the industry proved remarkably effective. Ownership of these relatively few theaters gave control over access to the market; this enabled other sources of supply to be shut out with a consequently enhanced value for the remaining product. Add to this the fact that ownership of these theaters carries with it the bulk of the theater receipts, and the rationale behind the structure of the motion picture industry becomes clear.

Relationship between the Big Five and the Little Three

It might be asked, why are the three smaller companies (Universal, Columbia, and United Artists) included in the category of the majors? (This usage is accepted by the industry at large and all government agencies dealing with it.) They own no theaters, they account for but fractional shares of the industry investment, they receive proportionately little of the total business. What makes them major companies? There seems to be but one reliable criterion here—they have access to the screens of the first-run theaters owned by the Big Five.

No one studio today turns out enough pictures to provide a year's supply of films for a double-feature program. First-run theaters showing double features on a weekly-change policy use from seventy to one hundred films a year. Subsequent-run theaters, most of which run films no longer than three days and play double features, may use three hundred feature films annually. Since, as has already been indicated, the theaters are the chief source of income for most of the integrated majors, their need for good box-office films is sufficiently great to warrant opening their screens to the product of other producers on occasion. This also explains, in large measure, why Hollywood as a whole rejoices when a successful picture appears, regardless of which studio produced it. A good picture, as almost anyone in Hollywood can tell you, is one that makes good at the box office. The box office, in part at least, belongs to each of the five majors,

6. *United States* v. *Paramount Pictures, Inc. et al.*, Petition, 1938, p. 71.

Michael Curtiz' *The Adventures of Robin Hood* (Warner Brothers, 1938): Melville Cooper, Basil Rathbone, Olivia DeHavilland, Claude Rains, and Errol Flynn

although in varying degrees in different regions. For example, the Philadelphia theater situation is dominated by Warner Brothers. A picture made by Metro (Loew's producing company) when exhibited in the Philadelphia area appears in Warner Brothers theaters. Loew's has little choice in the matter; all the first-run theaters in Philadelphia belong to Warner Brothers. It is therefore to the advantage of Warner Brothers for Loew's to release successful pictures since it means good business for Warner's theaters. Loew's, it should be noted, benefits doubly from a successful picture: first, in the form of box-office receipts of its own theaters, and, secondly, in the form of higher film rentals from other theaters.

No studio in Hollywood today produces more than sixty-five feature films a year. With the exception of United Artists, most of the companies release between forty-five and fifty-five features; hence, the need of the theater-owning majors for the product of other companies. The need is not merely for film, but for films of a special type—for the most part, inexpensive class B pictures to make up the lesser half of the double-feature program. This use of fill-in pictures is quite apparent from the fact that so few of the films of the smaller companies are given first place on the program.

To summarize: The demand for films is greater than the output of any one major company. While giving preference to its own films in all instances, each of the theater-owning majors needs supplementary product from two or more of the other companies. If, by some miracle, double features were to cease, a substantial part of the market for the films of Universal and Columbia would disappear.

Role of the Majors in Production and Distribution

Although the total number of active motion-picture-producing corporations is variously cited as 246 (*Statistics of Income* 1937), 100 (*Standard Statistics*), and 83 (*Biennial Census of Manufacture* 1937), the importance of the eight majors with respect to volume of production is perhaps best indicated by the following analysis. Five of the majors make 100 percent of the newsreels produced; the eight majors released 396, or 85 percent of the total of 452 feature films released in 1939. The 1939-40 *Motion Picture Almanac* lists, under the heading "Motion Picture Production Organizations," the names of seventy-three companies. Of this total, the number actively engaged in producing feature films (including the seventeen independent producers whose pictures are released by the majors) is very small, probably not more than thirty. A check of the names of the independents against a list of all features released in 1939 reveals that only ten of the independent companies named had produced any features whatsoever during this period.

Four of the smaller companies distributed the product of these ten, namely: Republic Pictures, Monogram Pictures, World Pictures, and Victory Pictures. Their combined releases amounted to fifty-six features, of which Republic released twenty-one, Monogram twenty, World Pictures twelve, and Victory Pictures three. These numbers, however, are misleading as a guide to the importance of their productions, since it is very unlikely that any substantial number of these pictures played in the larger city theaters. Almost all the pictures were inexpensive westerns, aimed at a market which holds little interest for the majors.

Virtually the entire market for feature films and newsreels is supplied by the releases of the major companies. The estimate made by officials of the Motion Picture Producers and Distributors of America that the majors account for 80 percent of the value of total film production probably errs in the direction of understatement, since with rare exceptions the amount of money spent by the independents on their productions is fractional compared with the majors.

The theater people, however, maintain firmly that no film which has box-office merit has any difficulty in finding a first-run release, that the eagerness of theater owners for attractive films is so great that it would be impossible for any combination of producers to keep worthy independent product off the market; furthermore, that the theater-owning majors would probably be the first to book any potentially successful films produced independently since they would thereby profit from increased theater receipts. This suggests that there may be reasons, other than market restraints, which account for the predominant role of the majors' product. It also raises the question, what is worthy product?

Right or wrong, it is a fixed belief in Hollywood and throughout the motion picture industry that the quality of a film is generally commensurate with its cost. Theater operators following this line of reasoning tend to value the product of a given company in accordance with the amount spent (this, it might be noted, is an additional factor in any explanation of the premium on extravagance of which Hollywood is so proud). Without, at the moment, examining this assumption too closely, let us look at the figures on production budgets of the several companies.

Loew's spends $28 million annually on its program of feature films; Twentieth Century-Fox, Paramount, and Warner Brothers spend approximately $23 to $25 million. RKO allows $20 million for its feature films. Universal and Columbia, on the other hand, spend $11.6 million and $8.8 million respectively. As it happens, the order in which the companies are named is exactly the order in which they rank in terms of the amounts they receive in film rentals (see Table 2).

The breakdown for Loew's shows that approximately $28 million was spent on forty-one feature pictures. Six of these, or 14.5 percent, cost more than a million dollars each; over half of the total number of films cost more than $500,000 each. None cost as little as $100,000. The average cost per picture was $683,000.

As proof of the importance attached to the cost of films by the industry, witness the advertising of Loew's in the trade press. For example, the release of *Ziegfeld Girl* was announced in a double-page spread as follows:

Take Your Seats, America!

You've got a date with the girls from the Follies! M.G.M. has kept its promise to top "The Great Ziegfeld"!

It took money to do it! It took months of planning, months of dreaming dreams! With No Expense Spared! M.G.M. proudly presents "The Ziegfeld Girl." It is a Pageant of Stars and Song and Spectacle! Ten marquees could not hold its names in lights! James Stewart. Judy Garland. Hedy Lamarr. Lana Turner. And countless other great entertainers and Girls! Girls! Girls! Darlings in diamonds, honey-haired blondes, red-heads, brunettes. M.G.M. combed America for its most famous beauties. Celebrated models, famed faces from the magazine covers. Never such a wealth of feminine loveliness! Spectacular musical numbers one after another! "Minnie from Trinidad," "You Stepped Out of a Dream," and others. More than you'd find in a whole season of Broadway musicals!

Lights! Curtain! Bravo!

Lest it be thought that this advertisement is unrepresentative, here is Republic's announcement to the trade of one of its extraordinary attractions. This is also a double-page spread in several colors. In large letters, the banner is: "Gene Autry's First $500,000 All-Star Production, *Melody Ranch*, 'Exhibitors Everywhere Can Play *This* One with Confidence.'"

It should not be inferred from this that lavish spending is a sure-fire formula for successful film production. If success is measured in terms of the return-per-dollar-invested, the quickies turned out by Universal and Columbia are frequently ten times more profitable than the all-star spectacles of Metro or Fox. In fact, a tabulation of the earnings of a season's output by one of the more extravagant producers reveals that of a total of forty-nine films, fourteen did not return their negative cost. Of the fourteen, eight had cost more than $1 million each.

Thus it appears that the answer to the question, what makes a major producer, runs as follows: The major producers are those whose product has access to the first-run theaters of the country. This access in turn depends partly on the amount of money spent on a production. Only in part, however, since the money is important merely for what it will buy in the way of talent and production values. Thus, having, let us say, $500,000 available for investment in a picture is no guarantee of a first-run release for the finished picture unless talent of recognized standing in the trade can be obtained. For instance, John Hay Whitney is a recurrent investor in film productions. He does not undertake to make films himself; he enters into an arrangement with a producer of great prestige in the Hollywood community, David O. Selznick, whereby he advances the funds for the production of *Gone With the Wind*. His financing, Selznick's production, and a cast of widely publicized talent suffices to secure a release through Loew's, on terms profitable to all concerned. The point is that the money is not more important in this situation than the fact that a producer of Selznick's status is undertaking to make the picture. Almost any of the established actors, directors, etc., are willing and eager to appear in a Selznick production. Money alone might not suffice to obtain big name actors for a picture unless the persons in charge of the production also had the confidence of the talent groups.

The obstacles in the way of securing talent for independently produced pictures are twofold in nature: first, and most obvious, are the contractual commitments of the established players. These contracts do not bind the artists entirely; they generally provide that the company holding the contract has the power to determine the productions in which the person may work. This serves several purposes. In the first place, if the artist is already famous and important, the employing studio regards him or her as a "property," the value of which might easily be impaired by injudicious

David O. Selznick's *Gone With the Wind,* directed by Victor Fleming: Vivien Leigh, Clark Gable, and Olivia DeHavilland. From the MGM release *Gone With the Wind* © 1939 Selznick International Pictures, Inc. Copyright renewed 1967 by Metro-Goldwyn-Mayer Inc.

appearances in unsuccessful movies, or in roles which contradict a carefully nurtured public sentiment about the actor. This factor is quite important in shaping the decisions on lending of players. In the second place, salaries of valuable personnel as fixed by contract are so high, in many instances, that their cost places them beyond the reach of most independent producers.

The contract system provides an additional means of controlling talent. For example, when it is considered desirable to punish an actor, he may simply be lent to an independent producer for a picture generally regarded as certain not to succeed. This is the Hollywood equivalent of Siberia, and undoubtedly an effective means of discipline.

An additional important obstacle in the way of securing established talent for the independently produced pictures is the artists' fear of jeopardizing their status. The fear may center around the questionable success of the picture. If no major release is obtained for the picture, it is destined for the low-grade markets represented chiefly by the cheaper theaters specializing in horse-operas and lurid sex-dramas. Appearance in such pictures is almost certain to decrease the actor's bargaining power with the major producers. Stars firmly established or with promising careers seldom venture into independent productions. For the most part, actors in this class of product are either still unknown or passé.

Such are a few of the factors affecting the availability of talent to the independent makers of films. The recital may not be complete; certainly the majors deny any monopolistic hold on the market for artists. The facts, however, are indisputable, regardless of the interpretation as to cause. During the years between 1933 and 1939 the seven major producers loaned to each other a total of 2,005 actors, directors, writers, and cameramen. To independents, a total of 180 loans was made. Whatever reluctance the companies may have to lending their personnel to independents is, of course, reinforced by the unwillingness of the artists themselves to work at lower rates of pay than their contracts provide. In fact, it is customary, when a major lends another company one of its stars, for the price paid to exceed the regular contract rate by as much as 75 percent. In other words, the borrowing company pays not only the salary of the star during the period of the loan, but also a pure rent to the lending company. This extra charge is justified as a means of compensating the home studio for the idle time of contract players, i.e., the time during which they are paid by the home studio but not used.

It should, perhaps, be repeated here that none of the obstacles described has any reality for those so-called "independent" producers whose pictures are released through the majors. For example, Selznick was able to borrow Clark Gable from Metro for *Gone With the Wind*. A major release is, in itself, sufficient to obtain working capital, production facilities, and personnel. One of the first bankers to take an interest in film production said long ago that he would lend the entire cost of production to a producer who has "a good distributing contract in a good distributing organization."

That the situation had not changed appreciably is evident in the following news item:

Bankers financing film production report a sudden increase in applications for loans from off-the-lot producers [independent producers]. . . . Pressure for loans is stronger than it has been in many years. Financial men say, however, that it is easier to grant a $50,000 loan than $15,000. Virtually all applications for small budget films are being turned down as unjustified by prospective returns. Big loans are more readily granted because pictures in that category are usually intended for a major release which must be set before the banks advance the usual 50 percent of the cost.[7]

7. *Variety,* September 10, 1941.

This, as the moviegoer often has occasion to say, is where we came in. The circle is complete. The independent producer is, by definition, one whose pictures are not distributed by the majors. Without such distribution and access to the first-run theaters, his market is extremely limited. This, in turn, makes both talent and capital shy of appearing in independent productions. Hence, independently made films are rarely considered fit for exhibition in metropolitan theaters where audiences have, by now, developed a modicum of sophistication.

Because the product of the independents is not considered fit for extensive exhibition, the principle market for films belongs to the major companies. If the reasoning seems circuitous, the facts are even more so.

12
FORTUNE

Metro-Goldwyn-Mayer

Metro-Goldwyn-Mayer, largest of 124 subsidiaries owned by Loew's, Inc., is a corporation devoted exclusively to the business and the art of producing moving pictures. Its plant—fifty-three acres, valued at a trifling $2,000,000—is in Culver City, California, on the dusty outskirts of Los Angeles, opposite three gasoline stations and a drugstore. In operation, the plant presents the appearance less of a factory than of demented university with a campus made out of beaverboard and canvas. It contains twenty-two sound stages, a park that can be photographed as anything from a football field to the gardens at Versailles, $2,000,000 worth of antique furniture, a greenhouse consecrated to the raising of ferns, twenty-two projection rooms, a commissary where $6,000-a-week actors can lunch on Long Island oysters for fifty cents, and a Polish immigrant who sometimes makes $500,000 a year and once spent the weekend with the Hoovers at the White House. On MGM's Culver City lot there is room for the practice of 117 professions, but the colored shoeshine boy outside the commissary considers himself an actor because he frequently earns a day's pay in an African mob scene. When he is neither acting nor powdering the brown suede riding boots of an Oklahoma cowboy who has just learned how to play polo, the shoeshine boy is likely to be the chauffeur of one of MGM's sixteen company limousines.

MGM's weekly payroll is roughly $250,000. On it are such celebrities as Marion Davies ($6,000), Norma Shearer, the three Barrymores, who get

From vol. 6 (December 1932), pp. 51-58+.

about $2,500 a week each, Clark Gable, Jean Harlow, Joan Crawford, Buster Keaton, Robert Montgomery, Marie Dressler (whose pictures take in more than any of the others'), Helen Hayes, Jimmy Durante, Conrad Nagel, Ramon Novarro, Wallace Beery, small Jackie Cooper, who makes $1,000 a week, John Gilbert and, until very recently, Greta Garbo. Miss Garbo is likely soon to return from Sweden where she recently retired after amassing a fortune of $1,000,000. If she does return, she will doubtless have a chance to make another million. Actors' salaries are only a small part of MGM's outlay. The biggest and most expensive writing staff in Hollywood costs $40,000 a week. Directors cost $25,000. Executives cost slightly less. Budget for equipment is $100,000 a week. MGM makes about forty pictures in a year, every one a feature picture or a special feature. Average cost of Metro-Goldwyn-Mayer pictures runs slightly under $500,000. This is at least $150,000 more per picture than other companies spend. Thus Metro-Goldwyn-Mayer provides $20,000,000 worth of entertainment a year at cost of production, to see which something like a billion people of all races will pay something more than $100,000,000 at the box office. *Motion Picture Almanac,* studying gross receipts, guesses at a yearly world total movie audience of 9,000,000,000.

For the past five years, Metro-Goldwyn-Mayer has made the best and most successful moving pictures in the U.S. No one in Hollywood would dream of contradicting this flat statement. In *Film Daily's* annual critical consensus of the ten best, MGM scored fourteen times in the last five years (last year *A Free Soul, Min and Bill, The Sin of Madelon Claudet*) as against ten for United Artists and eight for Paramount. In *Motion Picture Almanac's* ranking of the fifteen box-office leaders of 1931, MGM led with five (*Trader Horn, Susan Lenox, Politics, Strangers May Kiss, Reducing*). MGM bids fair to show the same statistical success in 1932. Very few people know why this is true. It may be luck. It may be the list of MGM stars, vastly the most imposing in what moving-picture people describe, significantly, as "the industry." It may be MGM's sixty-two writers and eighteen directors. It may be MGM's technicians, who are more numerous and more highly paid than those of MGM's competitors. It may be Irving Thalberg—Norma Shearer's husband. If no one in Hollywood knows the reason for MGM's producing success, everyone in Hollywood believes the last. Irving Thalberg, a small and fragile young man with a suggestion of anemia, is MGM's vice-president in charge of production. The kinds of pictures MGM makes and the ways it makes them are Irving Thalberg's problems. He is what Hollywood means by MGM.

Mr. Thalberg's earnings of $500,000 a year have come mostly from a unique bonus arrangement explained later. His actual salary is now only

$110,000. But despite recent cuts MGM's costs begin with a battery of "executives" who get as much as railroad presidents. As for "artists," it was at MGM that Pelham Grenville Wodehouse was employed for a period of a year in which he later admitted with the intention of being politely grateful, he had been paid $2,000 a week for doing nothing. It was not, however, Mr. Thalberg who hired Maurice Maeterlinck to stay at a Pasadena castle and write a scenario—which MGM will never use—of which the hero was a bumblebee. It is frequently asserted that as many as ten of MGM's staff of writers may be set to work simultaneously, in groups of two or three, on the same story. There are said to be unproduced stories in MGM's files which cost $1,000,000. Because Mr. Thalberg thinks a superspecial about Soviet Russia would be popular, $200,000 has been given to scenarists who have nonetheless been unable to fabricate one. A picture called *The Bugle Sounds* and another one appropriately entitled *The March of Time* have cost $250,000 or more apiece and have been postponed.

Mr. Thalberg's methods, however, would be infinitely more comical if they were a little less efficacious. It was Mr. Thalberg who decided, to the great advantage of his company, that MGM pictures should have not one star but two, like *Red Dust* or *Faithless,* or a whole galaxy, like *Grand Hotel* or *Rasputin.* It was Mr. Thalberg who caused retakes—the immensely expensive process of remaking pictures when they have theo-retically been completed—to be an integral part of MGM procedure, instead of a last resort for correcting particularly appalling blunders. The $20,000,000 of MGM's money that slips through Mr. Thalberg's thin and nimble fingers usually returns to them, but Mr. Thalberg really has better things to think about than the familiar legerdemain of profit and loss. His brain is the camera which photographs dozens of scripts in a week and decides which of them, if any, shall be turned over to MGM's twenty-seven departments to be made into a moving picture. It is also the recording apparatus which converts the squealing friction of 2,200 erratic underlings into the more than normally coherent chatter of an MGM talkie.

Most of MGM's executive offices are in a white wooden building near the shabby colonial façade that faces the three gasoline stations. Mr. Thalberg's beaverboard sanctum is on the second floor, flanked by a fire escape that leads onto a viaduct to his private projection room (with three desks, two pianos, and twenty-seven velvet armchairs). It is usually not much before ten o'clock when Mr. Thalberg's black Cadillac squeezes through the iron grille gates of the studio and stops under the catwalk to his projection room. By this time there are people all over the lot who want words with him.

He enters—a small, finely-made Jew of about thirty-three, changeable as the chameleon industry in which he labors. He is five and one-half feet tall, and weighs 122 pounds after a good night's sleep. This lightness, in calm moments, is all feline grace and poise. In frantic moments he appears as a pale and flimsy bag of bones held together by concealed bits of string and the furious ambition to make the best movies in the world. He seats himself, in his moderne, beaverboard office, at a massive, shiny desk, in front of a dictograph which looks like a small pipe organ and partially hides a row of medicine bottles. Before him are huge boxes of cigarettes, which he never opens, and plates of apples and dates into which he sometimes dips a transparent hand. Squirming with nervous fervor in the midst of his elaborate apparatus, he speaks with a curiously calm, soft voice as if his words were a sort of poetry. He describes parabolas with one hand and scratches his knee with the other. Rising, he paces his office with stooped shoulders and hands clasped behind him. This reflective promenading he learned from Carl Laemmle, Sr., who discovered Irving Thalberg when, recently released from a Brooklyn high school, he was an office boy in the Broadway shop of Universal Pictures.

There is naturally no chance that Mr. Thalberg's activities will fall into routine. His efforts follow no pattern whatsoever, except that they consist almost exclusively of talk. He deals with actors, whose simple wants of avarice or vanity he finds it easy to appease. He deals with writers, with whom he seldom commits the unpardonable blunder of saying: "I don't like it, but I don't know why." He is ceaselessly aware of Dolores Del Rio's gifted husband, Cedric Gibbons, who designs MGM scenery, and of the tall, twittering hunchback Adrian, who drapes MGM's loveliest bodies. He deals with M. E. Greenwood, the gaunt studio manager, who used to be an Arizona faro dealer and now tells MGM's New York office how much the company has spent every week and how much to place on deposit for MGM's account at the Culver City branch of Bank of America. Through Mr. Greenwood, and sometimes more directly, Irving Thalberg observes the 2,000 of the skilled but unsung: "grips," assistant cameramen, "mixers," cutters, projectionists, carpenters, unit managers, artisans, seamstresses, scene painters. Often he calls a group of these underlings into the projection room to consider pictures with him.

Mr. Thalberg must know how to focus all this talent. Beginning with an Idea. Ideas are the seeds of motion picture production—the most valuable commodity in Hollywood—Ideas for whole films, Ideas for episodes, Ideas for a single scene. At RKO the brilliant, young new chief, David Selznick, spends his days and nights grasping at Ideas. Working for Paramount in New York, George Putnam (spouse of Amelia Earhart) is paid to do nothing except have Ideas. Men get huge salaries for generating and sifting Ideas. Mr. Thalberg gets the hugest. He had the Idea that the sleek Park Avenue romance *Tinfoil* needed a worldly sort of actress who wasn't to be found on MGM's payroll. Presto, came another Idea—he borrowed Tallulah Bankhead from Paramount. Tallulah Bankhead whose eyelids, according to the costumer Adrian, "are so heavy they look like the fat little stomachs of sunburned babies." It was RKO's Selznick's Idea that a great success could be achieved by putting all three Barrymores—Ethel, Lionel, John—in one picture. But Mr. Thalberg had no sooner heard of it than it clicked with him and he promptly snatched Ethel (who preferred MGM anyway) from Selznick's all but completed grasp—with a bid of $2,500 a week. And then he immediately set two scenario writers to achieve another Idea—a script which would allow the Barrymores to agitate their eyebrows and twitch their nostrils without at any time pretending a sexual interest in one another which might offend a priggish public. The result was *Rasputin.* To direct this Russian pageantry it was naturally Mr. Thalberg's Idea to appoint the crafty, understanding Slav, Richard Boleslavsky, late of the Moscow Art Theatre, author of *The Way of a Lancer.* Had the Barrymore script been an adventurous, outdoor affair, Mr. Thalberg would probably have selected W. S. Van Dyke, who directed *Tarzan* and *Trader Horn.* He has a versatile panel of directors to choose from: Howard Hawks, the realist who did *The Criminal Code;* Sidney Franklin, the cosmopolitan of *Private Lives* and *The Guardsman;* Sam Wood, specialist in light comedy, college, and football pictures; Edgar Selwyn, a masterly tearjerker; Clarence Brown, very tactful with veterans like Marie Dressler; Tod Browning, a connoisseur of the vicious, who directs best when the principal characters are deformed, as in *Freaks.*

Ideas permeate the studio structure and the Thalberg day. While Thalberg makes telephone calls, he authorizes Cedric Gibbons to spend $30,000 on a set for *Pig Boats* and orders his scenario chief Sam Marx to assign three new writers to the task of adapting *Reunion in Vienna.* In between conferences, in which he reveals himself as a person of opinions on underdone lovemaking or overdressed heroines, Mr. Thalberg gnaws a red apple and looks at rushes of *Tinfoil,* pronouncing half of them trash. With one eye on a copy of *Variety* he considers his casting director Ben Thau for the position left vacant by the suicide of gentle, masochistic Paul Bern, husband of Jean Harlow, and decides that *Tinfoil* had better be called *Faithless.*

The frantic morning terminates confusedly in Mr. Thalberg's regular lunch with his ten associate producers. These men are shock absorbers for Mr. Thalberg. It is obviously impossible for him to supervise all of MGM's forty pictures a year. Hence the associate producers. They advise and confer with writers during the preparation of scripts. When the script has been approved by Mr. Thalberg, they attempt to coordinate the efforts of writer, director, and cast. Without being able in most cases to act, write, or direct, they are supposed to know more about writing than either the director or the star, more about directing than the star or the writer. Matters of costs, sets, locations, cast, lighting, and the like are referred to them; all disputes, recriminations, and temperamental teapot tempests are for them to settle or assuage, unless they seem insoluble, in which case they are solved by Mr. Thalberg. MGM's associate producers are likely to work on two or three pictures simultaneously. They are the principal cogs through which Irving Thalberg causes MGM's wheels to spin. Each of these gentlemen gets $1,000 a week or more for communicating Mr. Thalberg's spirit. But as a class associate producers are extremely susceptible to nervous breakdowns which, it has been suggested, is due to the consciousness of enjoying great responsibility without sufficient authority and credit.

While the rest of the studio personnel is munching in the noisy commissary, the associate producers sit down to luncheon with Mr. Thalberg in the "Executive Bungalow," a squatty hut with a Cecil B. De Mille dining room. Hunt Stromberg, a "box-office producer" par excellence, is the only one who, by contract, can work without Mr. Thalberg's approval. He handled Joan Crawford's celebrated trilogy *Modern Maidens, Blushing Brides,* and *Dancing Daughters.* Al Lewin is a college graduate and an ex-instructor of English at the University of Wisconsin. Thus set apart from his confrères, he gets such sophisticated jobs as *The Guardsman* and *Private Lives.* Bernie Hyman does animal stories and Bernie Fineman does *genre* pictures and curios like *Mata Hari;* Irish Eddie Mannix, who looks like a bulldog, is a master of action films such as *Hell Divers.* Marie Dressler, the most profitable star on the MGM roster, is intrusted during production to the supervisory discretion of Mr. Thalberg's brother-in-law, Larry Weingarten. The late Paul Bern used to oversee electric sex fables like *Susan Lenox, As You Desire Me, Grand Hotel,* and *Red Dust.* Harry Rapf, called "Mayer's sundial" because of his nose, played sad airs on the national heartstrings with *The Champ* and *The Sin of Madelon Claudet,* and is now having his nervous breakdown. All these associates—the somber, sagacious Jews, the lusty, impetuous Irishman—are professionally just so many extensions of Irving Thalberg's personality. He has much more to say to them than they to him. Only one important instance of impudence or rebuke to Mr. Thalberg has ever occurred at MGM. When he took to bouncing a twenty-dollar gold piece on his glass-top desk during conferences, his confrères cured this painful habit by hoarding similar coins for the same purpose. Chattering at lunch, Mr. Thalberg and his underlings resemble in their gloomy refectory the personnel of an agitated Last Supper, with Mr. Thalberg as a nervous Nazarene, free, however, from the presentiment that any of his disciples will deny or even contradict him.

His afternoon is as formless as his morning. To say that the manifestation of Mr. Thalberg's efforts at MGM consists of conversation is not so much a sidelight on the way movies are made as it is a comment on Irving Thalberg. He doesn't spend time making infinitesimal calculations because he is an artist, and an artist with a blank canvas to fill doesn't begin by marking off squares. He begins with instinct and checks his results with a meticulous sense of values. He is a stickler for results but he cannot be a stickler for plans. Even so with Irving Thalberg. Nowhere is his artistry more evident than in his expenditure of MGM money. "Look," he says, "a successful feature may take in ten million dollars at the box office. An unsuccessful one may take a million. If the difference is fifty or a hundred thousand dollars in production. . . ." There is, so far as Mr. Thalberg is concerned, no more to be said. It is his artistic instinct which tells him when the extra fifty or one hundred thousand will broaden, like the beam of a projection machine, into an enormous profit. His extravagance has so far justified itself, and he by no means goes haywire with the exchequer. When J. B. Priestley thought *The Good Companions* was worth $50,000, Mr. Thalberg offered $25,000 and came away without the book.

When Mr. Thalberg leaves Culver City at dinner time he takes with him a large pigskin portmanteau, made to order for a peculiar purpose: carrying scripts. In Mr. Thalberg's house at Santa Monica, designed for him by art director Cedric Gibbons, there is a soundproof room. This is so that the sad growling of the Pacific, beside which he lives, shall not interrupt Mr. Thalberg's perusal of the contents of his portmanteau. Life *chez* Thalberg has the atmosphere of neither a saloon nor a dance pavilion. Mr. Thalberg drinks only occasionally, a rather silly release when it happens, and dances very little for one who foxtrots so expertly. The chatter of Mr. Thalberg's working day is replaced at night by an electric silence in which, pallid and intent, he performs the trick of dividing his brain into two parts. One part, reading a script, turns it into a moving picture; the other part watches this imaginary picture and, probably because it is so much like the conglomerate brain of 50,000,000 other U.S. cinemaddicts, tells Mr. Thalberg with an astonishing degree of accuracy whether or not the picture is good. And when he doesn't wish to look at these imaginary pictures in his brain, he can look at real ones—in his own drawing room. Shifty and two-faced, like every other property in a beaverboard industry, this is a projection room in disguise, with a screen which pops up out of the floor. Mr. Thalberg's favorite diversion of nights, while the Pacific murmurs below, is to watch Metro-Goldwyn-Mayer talkies flicker above his hearthstone.

The cinema is both an industry and an art but it is also, more importantly, a new industry, a new art. The problems which confront a producer are somewhat like those which might confront a novelist if the secret of the alphabet had been discovered thirty years ago, except that his tools are more complex and more expensive. So far, very few people have grown up with the idea of expressing themselves, or anything else, in the cinema. They drift into what must remain, for them, "the industry" from journalism, the stage, drafting rooms, laboratories, or the camphorated closets of the wholesale fur business. They are animated thereafter by a defending scorn for an endeavor that has appealed, successfully, only to their avarice. There are a few people in Hollywood for whom the cinema carries a different invitation. For someone like Thalberg it is an avocation, a new language, a necessity. If he had ever had time to be profoundly interested in anything else, if he had been subjected to the complications of formal education or, even momentarily, failure, he would be infinitely less competent, because less focused, then he is. Tutored by a sharper master than adversity—success—he is now called a genius more often than anyone else in Hollywood, which means that the word is practically his nickname. He represents a new psychological type of power, which must be distinguished if you would understand the present age: a man of extremely nervous sensibilities who deals with nervous affairs in a nervous environment—and can keep on doing so. If moving pictures did not exist, Irving Thalberg might not be called a genius, but it is amusing to speculate upon what less glittering objectives he would have dissipated his furious creative concentration.

But MGM is neither one man nor a collection of men. It is a corporation. Whenever a motion picture becomes a work of art it is unquestionably due to men. But the moving pictures have been born and bred not of men but of corporations. Corporations have set up the easels, bought the pigments, arranged the views, and hired the potential artists. Until the artists emerge, at least, the corporation is bigger than the sum of its parts. Somehow, although our poets have not yet defined it for us, a corporation lives a life and finds a fate outside the lives and fates of its human constituents.

Metro-Goldwyn-Mayer came into existence in 1924. It is, from one aspect, the climax of an ancient and ludicrous feud. Back in the days when Norma Shearer was a Canadian schoolgirl, the late Marcus Loew owned a lot of movie theaters and Adolph Zukor was associated with him.

Mr. Loew was none too fond of Mr. Zukor, and his disdain manifested itself in highly original ways. In board meetings Mr. Loew would divert himself by snapping match sticks at Mr. Zukor. When the Loew enterprises moved into handsome new offices Mr. Zukor, although he was treasurer, was not permitted a desk of his own and had to examine the expense accounts standing up. Later, when Adolph Zukor became head of the nearest thing to a movie-production trust the industry has ever known—Famous Players-Lasky Corp.—he avenged himself on Mr. Loew by making it next to impossible for the Loew theaters to get Lasky pictures.

Marcus Loew, in short, had to develop his own production unit. In 1920 he acquired Metro Pictures Corp., started in 1915 by Richard Rowland, now a Fox production executive. Metro was making no money when Loew bought it, but shortly produced *The Four Horsemen of the Apocalypse*, in which Rudolph Valentino darted his first historic glances. Early in 1924 Loew's bought Goldwyn Pictures Corp., started in 1916 by the Selwyn brothers and the able pinochler Samuel Goldfish. Later in the year Mr. Nicholas M. Schenck, who was chief executive of Loew's, negotiated for the Louis B. Mayer Pictures Corp. Mr. Mayer did a great deal of talking on behalf of himself and his partners, Irving Thalberg and J. Robert Rubin. He talked so well that when the contract was signed the Mayer partners got not stock nor cash but a percentage of Loew's profits which changes according to how much of Loew's earnings are accounted for by MGM. And Mr. Schenck was satisfied because he got Messrs. Mayer, Thalberg, and Rubin as a unit all duly bound by contracts to work for Loew's (Mr. Thalberg's contract has five years to go).

As it turned out, this was an elegant deal for all concerned. In other words, the present-day Loew's stockholder is a partner of Messrs. Mayer, Thalberg, and Rubin, but these are not the only ones to share in the profits. Loew's reported that in 1931 president Schenck got a bonus of 2½ percent of the profits, or $274,000, and treasurer David Bernstein one of 1½ percent, or $164,000. This was in addition to salaries of $2,500 and $2,000 a week respectively.

Having acquired MGM, Mr. Schenck might have been content to watch it flourish with Loew's. Instead, when William Fox conceived great designs for the Fox Film Corp. and wanted Loew's theaters as well, Mr. Schenck sold his stock, which had a market value of $47,000,000 to Mr. Fox for $55,000,000. Mr. Fox also bought a large block from Marcus Loew's estate (he had died in 1927), getting a controlling total of 45 percent of Loew's stock. But the transaction, fortuitously, had small effect on the fortunes of MGM. For Mr. Fox's subsequent delusions of grandeur took the form of expanding the Fox chain of theaters and leaving the Loew's circuit strictly alone.

In 1930 Fox collapsed and the ruins were left in the hands of the Chase Bank. During the corporate turmoil which followed, the Law took action (under the Clayton Act) which delighted the hearts of Mr. Schenck and his MGM partners. Three eminent gentlemen were appointed as "trustees of the court" to oversee what had been the Fox holdings in Loew's. The trio which now faces Mr. Schenck at his stockholders' meetings, with 45 percent of Loew's in their pockets, are Thomas W. Gregory, onetime attorney general of the U.S., John R. Hazel, onetime federal judge, and the redoubtable Bostonian Thomas Nelson Perkins. Mr. Schenck probably smiles at these "trustees in the public good" as he never smiled at Mr. Fox or the Chase Bank men. For he knows that, rather than true controllers, they are merely the arms of that benign agent (for Mr. Schenck) which put them there and will ultimately remove them—the N.Y. Federal Court. This leaves the partners of MGM in a most gratifying position where they can run the corporation for their own profit.

MGM happens to be the corporation which has gone through the Depression with less corporate trouble than any other in the industry. This is more than a coincidence. It is a symptom of MGM's internal amiability. Which, along with Mr. Thalberg and Greta Garbo, is another reason for MGM's success. Last summer, when Paramount had just reported the largest loss in cinema history, a quarterly deficit of $5,900,000, MGM was on the point of acknowledging that it would have had one but for the salary cut. Although a panic summer and a few pictures slightly below MGM standard were enough to account for the loss, Mr. Schenck and MGM's attorney and vice president, J. Robert Rubin, made one of their biannual visits to the Coast. After conferring with Mr. Thalberg and Mr. Mayer, however, Mr. Schenck and Mr. Rubin came away satisfied to let Mr. Thalberg continue producing as he sees fit, for the time being at least.

With the old régime of fur peddlers, secondhand jewelers, and nickelodeon proprietors who started all the major cinema companies except RKO and Warner, MGM has now only one connecting link. He, Louis B. Mayer, is probably the most dignified personage in Hollywood. Mr. Mayer arrived in the U.S. from Poland before the turn of the century, helped his father with a New England ship-salvaging firm, and reached Hollywood, unlike most of the producers of his era, after owning only one theater (in Haverhill, Massachusetts). What he did own, however, was a profitable production and distribution business. By the time that his five-year-old producing company became part of the Loew's merger, Mr. Mayer had already started to turn over the reins to young Mr. Thalberg, whom he had enticed away from Universal in 1923. Now, at about forty-five, Mr. Mayer is an MGM vice president, but he probably does not spend more than half his time on matters closely pertaining to MGM. Mr. Mayer would like to have the entire industry reflect the Mayer prestige. One of his hobbies is the pretentious Academy of Motion Picture Arts and Sciences, which sets itself up as an arbitrator of Hollywood squabbles and gives annual awards for all kinds of cinematic excellence. It also satisfies Mr. Mayer to think of himself as the first producer who has gone far beyond mere cinema success, though it is not true that he was offered an ambassadorship, even to so modest a democracy as Turkey. Had it been offered, Mr. Mayer would now be in Angora instead of Hollywood.

Mr. Mayer's entrance into politics was made through his acquaintance with a lady who is now chief of his secretariat, Mrs. Ida Coverman. Mrs. Coverman, then (and now) an ardent believer and worker in the cause of Republicanism, persuaded Mr. Mayer to take a financial interest in the gubernatorial election of 1924. The story goes that she introduced Mr. Mayer to Mr. Hoover when the latter was at Palo Alto after his term as secretary of commerce. Mr. Mayer did hard work in the 1928 campaign and he was doing more hard work for Hoover this autumn.

Mr. Mayer's rôle in the extremely public private affairs of MGM is almost identical with his rôle in his private life of public services. He is the diplomat, the man of connections. His affiliations with the White House (he is the only cinemagnate who ever spent a weekend there) give him a roundabout connection with the Hays organization—MGM can feel assured that such narrow-minded whims as overcome the censors will not be practiced unduly on MGM pictures. Whenever a Prince of Siam or a South American ex-President visits Hollywood he is entertained by Mr. Mayer; this produces pompous publicity for MGM. Mr. Mayer's courtesies to U.S. senators and vice admirals make it easier for MGM to borrow a battleship for *Armored Cruiser* or a fleet of Navy planes for *Hell Divers*. And so far as MGM is concerned, the prospect of Mr. Hoover's defeat was not so appalling to Mr. Mayer as it might have been if he had not been so closely associated with William Randolph Hearst.

Not only MGM but the whole of Hollywood owes Mr. Mayer a debt—thus far expressed only in gratitude—for the maintenance of the Hearst connection. The truth is that Marion Davies' pictures cost MGM a great deal more than might seem, superficially, advisable. In rural districts, where there is a tendency to frown upon Miss Davies' lavish domesticity, her dramas do not draw so well as they did at one time. Her $6,000-

a-week salary alone reaches a total in twelve weeks which would bring her productions near the border line of loss. On the other hand, it would obviously be unwise for MGM to economize in the matter of Davies production. Hollywood understands that by obliging Mr. Hearst in the matter of Miss Davies Mr. Mayer is not only insuring Hearst support for his own productions but also preserving the rest of the industry from the indignation which the Hearst press would doubtless extend to the cinema as a whole if Miss Davies were to suffer some indignity.

Even within MGM, in the hours he devotes to studio affairs, Mr. Mayer's efforts fall into much the same category—of personal connections, intrigues, and affiliations. He is a commercial diplomat. Contacts and contracts are his specialty, and the latter are completely in his care at MGM. This is an exceedingly important branch of MGM's activities. In the cinema industry, no one of any consequence is employed without a written agreement of some sort. This is partly because the traditions of the industry are not those of banking, but much more because a company which gets a Jean Harlow wants to keep her and, conversely, Jean Harlow needs to be sure that a quick shift in public taste—or the suicide of her husband—won't stop her paycheck.

For example, Mr. Mayer was very glad to be able to sign John Gilbert on a five-year contract in 1927. A year or two later he was sorry he had done so. Mr. Gilbert, compelled to start making talkies when his own vocal equipment was as squeaky as experimental sound apparatus, was a far less valuable property in 1929.

As might be expected, Mr. Mayer resents the high salaries that go to MGM actors, but he sees little that can be done about it. It would be very pleasing to Mr. Mayer and to all other Hollywood producers if it were possible to prevent actors from demanding and getting all that they are worth at the box office. This is, in a word, impossible, and Mr. Mayer knows why. "If the major producers agreed not to pay a certain star more than, for instance, $800 a week," says Mr. Mayer, "some independent producer would offer him more, if he were worth more. Accordingly, there is no chance for the studios to combine to control actors' salaries. Besides, it would be illegal."

It is obvious that the process of contracts is a highly individual matter of bargain and barter, and beyond the routine of being tactful, diplomatic, and, so far as is legal, sly, Mr. Mayer can have no rules for his procedure. It is his business simply to get the most and give the least. Yet, so far as Mr. Mayer has a policy, his policy of bargain making must parallel Mr. Thalberg's policies of picture making.

There may be disagreements—Mayer, Thalberg, Schenck—but behind the disagreements there is an essential loyalty (a successful corporation does not necessarily inspire loyalty, but it certainly tends to inspire such loyalty as may be based on the human desire to create successfully). And above the disagreements arises a great consistency which is not the policy of Thalberg or Mayer or Schenck but the policy of MGM. The various elements in this policy, which are the reasons for MGM's outstanding success in the last five years, we can now recapitulate:

First, there is that corporate smoothness, that amity among executives which we have mentioned above and which is so understanding that Mr. Mayer has felt free to rebuke Mr. Thalberg's wife for being "yellow" because she balked at working with director Reginald Barker on *Pleasure Bound*. Internally, MGM keeps just about the quietest of Hollywood's many mad households.

Second, there is Mr. Thalberg's heavy but sagacious spending. It is the most outlandish feature on MGM's face, and one of the most effective. There is no sign of its being submitted to economical plastic surgery. Utilizing a one-half square mile of inlaid floor, 2,000 yards of gold cloth, and fifty pounds of beards, the picture *Rasputin* cost $750,000 long before its completion, and director Boleslavsky was so inwreathed in genuine, expensive Russian atmosphere that he was able to forget Lionel Barrymore's profane and scornful mutterings. MGM would seem to have shown conclusively that although vast expenditure is no guarantee of good results, economy is decidedly *not* the secret of profitable movie production. Economy may be of great importance in the relatively constricted economics of the legitimate stage. But in the movies, as Mr. Thalberg observes, differences of hundreds of thousands in expenses are easily justified when they may make differences of millions in the "take."

Third, there is the kind of picture MGM makes with its money. All questions of MGM policy ultimately boil down to the fact that MGM is show business and in show business the show's the thing. MGM pictures vary from *Private Lives* to *Tarzan,* from *Smilin' Through* to *Fu Manchu.* But there is a certain common denominator of goodness which MGM expects and Mr. Thalberg tries to get out of Culver City. It is easier to state what this goodness is *not* than what it *is*. It is not innovation. MGM was the last of the big companies to adopt sound, and its most advanced camera technique has been borrowed from Russia, Germany, and France (of course Mr. Thalberg now sees to it that MGM sounds are as clear as bells and that its cameramen avoid the stodgier angles). It is not superior direction. Probably no MGM director is as gifted as Ernst Lubitsch or Josef von Sternberg, for instance, both of whom work for Paramount. It is not superior writing. MGM has the largest literary staff in Hollywood—its superiority, however, is debatable.

But when we consider acting, we strike a real clue to MGM's preeminence. Here arises a delicate question. Some people feel that movie celebrities really act; others stay convinced that, even in these sophisticated days, movie acting as a whole remains not so much acting as the exuding of personality. Now while there may be some dispute about MGM's acting, no one will deny that the MGM roster exudes more personality than any other in Hollywood. MGM has under contract at least a dozen of those hypnotic ladies who are asked to send their height, weight, bust dimensions, and autograph to dreamy admirers all over the country. And a half-dozen male performers of equally mesmeric power. MGM can claim to have developed many of these, such as Shearer, Garbo, Davies, Harlow, Crawford, Gable, Gilbert (now trying a comeback), Montgomery, Novarro. It is currently developing Virginia Bruce, Dorothy Jordan, Myrna Loy, Karen Morley, Robert Young, Johnny Weissmuller, and others. And MGM does well by those luminaries it acquires with a reputation in advance, such as Wallace Beery, Marie Dressler, the Barrymores, and Jimmy ("Schnozzle") Durante, who among them do more acting of all sorts than the rest of the list combined. Irving Thalberg has lately made much of the fact that he is discarding the old "star" system. It is true that there are a diminishing number of pictures in the old movie tradition—pieces of utter whiffle for the display of some jerkwater matinee idol—and that there are more movies with an intelligent basis today than there were ten years ago. But what Mr. Thalberg substitutes for the "star" system is a galactic arrangement whereby two or more "stars" appear in one film: Davies and Montgomery in *Blondie of the Follies,* Garbo and Gable in *Susan Lenox,* Harlow and Gable in *Red Dust,* Bankhead and Montgomery in *Faithless.* So long as personality per se counts for so much at the nation's box offices, so long will some sort of star system, unit or multiple, persist. And so long as MGM keeps as much personality on tap as it has at present, so long can MGM hope to be well up in the Hollywood van. The day may come when a superb actor like Alfred Lunt will prove a bigger movie drawing card than the "cute" and widely heralded Robert Montgomery—if and when it does, the motion picture industry will make another story.

The glamour of MGM personalities is part of a general finish and glossiness which characterizes MGM pictures and in which they excel. Irving Thalberg subscribes heartily to what the perfume trade might call the law of packaging—that a mediocre scent in a sleek flacon is a better commodity than the perfumes of India in a tin can. MGM pictures are always superlatively well-packaged—both the scenes and personalities which enclose the drama have a high sheen. So high a sheen that it sometimes constitutes their major box-office appeal. MGM's versions of *Grand Hotel* and *Strange Interlude* are cases in point. The consensus of critical opinion held that neither of these pictures had the dramatic value of the stage plays from which they were adapted. But for *Grand Hotel* Mr. Thalberg assembled the Barrymore brothers, Greta Garbo, and Joan Crawford, a quartette no movie addict could resist if they were playing *Charlie's Aunt.* Cedric Gibbons designed a circular staircase which is already more famous than that at Blois and, by way of contrast, Lionel Barrymore emitted the loudest belch in the history of the drama. The highly touted "unspoken thoughts" in *Strange Interlude* weren't very successful because the actors "mugged" the lines so violently, but Norma Shearer was never more subtly gowned, the great Clark Gable audience was delighted to see its hero as a real gentleman rather than a de luxe yegg, and the whole picture gave the hinterlands the idea that sex didn't need to be represented in terms of Marlene Dietrich's garters. Irving Thalberg's willingness to toy with such sophisticated stuff as *Strange Interlude* is encouraged by the fact that a large majority of Loew's and hence MGM's theaters are in urban centers and especially in Greater New York. But in general he is betting on good taste as nationally salable, and if his actors' names are still more important than the themes they delineate, it remains true that Irving Thalberg treats both actors and themes with a fine eye for contour and polish. In this regard, the quality and texture of Miss Shearer's gowns for some drama of the *haut monde* can be compared with the quality and texture of the hippopotamuses that Mr. Thalberg hired for *Tarzan.*

The rule of the cinema industry, which is still too adolescent and eccentric to be subject to any formulas derived from its past, is that no company can long remain preeminent. Shifts in personnel, shifts in audience taste that contradict the taste of executives, overexpansion, vanity, have so far been effective to prevent any Hollywood producing organization from permanently besting its rivals. Hollywood expects the same rule to affect MGM. MGM's rivals would doubtless dearly love to cut MGM's throat; they are effectively restrained by the fact that they would cut off their own noses if they did so. So long as MGM makes the best pictures in the U.S., it is valuable to its competitors by filling their theaters better than they can do it with their own product. This is one of the basic rules of behaviorism in the cinema—which remains, among industries, a loud but somewhat furtive giant and, among arts, a young muse who appears to be a trollop.

Loew's, Inc., home office, 1540 Broadway, New York. Unknown to most movie fans, the unpretentious offices above the State Theater coordinated the operations of a $144 million entertainment empire controlling the glamorous production activities of the MGM Studio, an international distribution organization, and over one hundred theaters resting on some of the choicest real estate in the country.

The Loew's theater chain, though not the largest in the business, was consistently one of the most profitable—the result of Marcus Loew's genius for building in correct places. This rendering of John Eberson's design shows a theater meant to provide a little baroque splendor for Akron, Ohio.

Loew's 150 salesmen gathered each year at a convention to map strategy for peddling the next season's product to the country's 11,000 theaters.

Mayer presiding over ceremonies marking the merger of Louis B. Mayer Pictures and the Metro-Goldwyn Company, April 26, 1924. Pictured on the rostrum is Marcus Loew, founder and president of the parent company.

Construction begins on twenty-two sound-proof stages during the transition to the talkies. MGM expanded its studio operations in Culver City to accommodate fifty productions a year.

Irving Thalberg, MGM vice president in charge of production, with Norma Shearer, John Gilbert, King Vidor, and Eleanor Boardman

MGM celebrities in *Dinner at 8*. Thalberg modified the star system to create a galactic arrangement whereby two or more stars were featured in a picture. The actor roster exuded more personality than any other studio's in Hollywood and boosted MGM's weekly payroll to $250,000.

An early directorial roster. Although the names changed,
block booking kept the number constant.

The prop department contained, among other things, $2 million worth of antique furniture.

The costume shop. Every contributor to motion picture production, from seamstress to director, belonged to one of Hollywood's forty trade unions.

Box lunches for hungry extras. Central Casting Corporation handled the placement of extras. Two-thirds of the 20,000 extras earned less than $500 a year in the thirties.

The annual publicity and advertising budgets amounted to over $5 million.

13
FORTUNE

Loew's, Inc.

Mr. Nicholas M. Schenck, for the last twelve years president of Loew's, Inc., is the author of that optimistic saying, "There is nothing wrong with this industry that good pictures cannot cure." It has been the easier for Mr. Schenck to say that about the movie business because Loew's picture-making unit, Metro-Goldwyn-Mayer, has for at least eight years made far and away the best pictures of any studio in Hollywood. Metro's gross revenue from film rentals has been consistently higher than that of other studios, and as a result Loew's, Inc., has been and still is the most profitable movie company in the world. So vital are Metro pictures to Loew's earnings that whereas Mr. Schenck, the undisputed boss of the whole shebang, received some $220,000 from his profit-sharing contract last year (over and above a salary of $2,500 a week), Mr. Louis B. Mayer, the employee who runs Metro, received $763,000 on his profit-sharing contract, over and above a salary of $3,000 a week. That's what Mr. Schenck and his board of directors are willing to pay for "good pictures."

When *Fortune* looked at Loew's in December 1932 [see ch. 12—Ed.], the whole story was devoted to Mr. Mayer's fabulous studio. Today, however, Mr. Schenck is faced with one or two problems, not then anticipated, which Mr. Mayer may not be able to solve for him singlehandedly. The chief one is the antitrust suit that the Department of Justice brought against Loew's and seven other major units of the movie industry in July 1938. Loew's, like its four biggest competitors, is engaged in selling and

From vol. 20 (August 1939), pp. 25-30+.

exhibiting, as well as in making pictures; and the government, on behalf of the small producers and independent theater owners who feel squeezed by this vertical trustification, seems resolved to break it into halves. The fight is proceeding to trial very, very slowly, but only the vagaries of the law, and not good pictures, will ultimately end it.

Another thing in the back of Mr. Schenck's mind is the fact that Metro pictures, while still possibly the most successful in the world, have recently been failing to make their customary splash in the trade. The absence of splash was loudly heard last fall, when the expensive superspecials *Marie Antoinette* and *The Great Waltz* were presented to an American public that has not even yet shown any inclination to return to Metro their negative costs. Jeanette MacDonald's *Broadway Serenade* and Joan Crawford's *Ice Follies of 1939,* coming along in the spring, helped to confirm the impression that Metro had struck a slump; so did the news that the touted *I Take This Woman* (Spencer Tracy and Hedy Lamarr) has been indefinitely postponed. In a company that had grown used to releasing a *Grand Hotel, Mutiny on the Bounty, Thin Man, Test Pilot, Boys' Town, Captains Courageous,* or their box-office equivalents every month or so, the recent Metro crop of turkeys has not been reassuring. Insofar as this constitutes a problem for Mr. Schenck, he can hardly turn solely to Mr. Mayer, for it might be Mr. Mayer's fault. It is certainly Mr. Mayer's responsibility. But it has not been costing Mr. Schenck any sleep. The fact is that Metro's gross picture rentals, which reflect the average popularity of the studio's entire product of fifty or so pictures a year, are ahead of the 1938 gross to date by some $2,000,000. The number of exhibitors who are buying the product has also been steadily climbing. Hence if Metro is indeed in a serious slump, the only measure thereof is the volatile thermometer of Hollywood gossip. To be sure, Hollywood gossip is itself sometimes a hard business factor, in its effect on people in the industry.

The antitrust problem, though more tangible than the studio problem, has not troubled any Schenck sleep yet either. He believes that Loew's cause is just, and that the government will either drop its suit (which Assistant Attorney General Thurman Arnold denies) or lose it. Some people say that even if the five big chains were to be divorced from the five big studios, the effect might be to stimulate Loew's profits rather than to stop them. It would be a different sort of picture business from the one Mr. Schenck knows, however. A trust is a delicate thing to monkey with, and not even Trustbuster Arnold dares envision the result if he should bust this one. We can best tell what both he and Mr. Schenck are up against by looking at Loew's as a whole, to see how the richest of the movie trusts gets its ephemeral product made, distributed, exhibited, and turned into such surprising quantities of cash.

Although Loew's assets, some $144,000,000, are exceeded by those of Warner Brothers, its profits have for eight years been well ahead of those of any rival. Its gross revenues are also larger. In 1930 and 1937, on grosses of $129,500,000 and $121,800,000 respectively, it earned some $14,500,000. Last year, on a gross of $122,700,000, it earned just under $10,000,000; and even in 1933, the poorest movie year since sound, its profits were $4,000,000. With the somewhat special exception of Warner Brothers, Loew's was the only one of the five integrated "majors" to weather the Depression without bankruptcy, reorganization, or shake-up of any kind.

For a company with such a record, the home offices over the State Theater at Broadway and Forty-fifth Street, New York, are modest to the point of dinginess. Overshadowed by the Paramount Building and by many a flyspecked Times Square hotel, the sixteen-story Loew's building gives no hint of the size of the checks that are signed on its seventh floor. The executives, too, present what is for Broadway an almost conservative front. There are no fluted vests, but they are all well fed and healthy-looking with Florida tans, and are mostly free from that apprehensive quickness of speech and gesture that the uncertainties of show business stamp on so many of its votaries. For Loew's men, show business is not uncertain at all. And a surprising number count their service to Loew's in decades, not in years. Mr. Schenck himself, for example, has not worked for anyone else since 1906, and being a quiet, imperturbable, almost diffident man, he has succeeded in holding the loyalty and affection, as well as the services, of his executives. He still talks with an accent carried all the way from central Russia, which he left when he was nine, but it is unaccompanied by the bombast, the flailing gestures, the arrogance commonly associated with men who have reached large positions in pictures. Mr. Schenck has an uncanny eye for profitable pictures, and a genius for building theaters in the correct places. But he eschews any self-glorification. He plays the ponies for a profit as well as for fun, and keeps a fast speedboat and an unpretentious yacht on Long Island Sound. The speedboat he uses mainly for commuting between Manhattan and his estate next to Walter Chrysler's at Great Neck. The estate is inhabited by Mr. Schenck, Mrs. Schenck (née Pansy Wilcox of Morgantown, West Virginia), and three daughters, who are their father's main interest in life. The Schenck ménage is a gracious place of unobtrusive luxuriousness, resembling an English country house in mood and having only one boisterous detail—a set of tremendous brass cuspidors labeled "Great Expectorations" in the bar.

Among the other veterans in the Loew's building are the secretary, Leopold Friedman (twenty-eight years of service with the company); David

Bernstein (thirty-four years of service), vice-president and treasurer, and "one of the world's greatest financial minds," according to Nicholas Schenck; Charles C. Moskowitz (twenty-six years of service), plump, jowly manager of the metropolitan theaters, who has never married because he thinks a wife would interfere with his work; vice-president J. Robert Rubin (twenty-four years of service), the MGM studio's handsomely dressed eastern ambassador, general counsel, and literary properties man de luxe; Joseph Vogel (twenty-nine years of service), amiable, soft-spoken, philosophic manager of the out-of-town theaters. All told, the reigning executives of Loew's are a conservative group with traditions, and from them the company takes much of its character. No less an arch-Bostonian than Thomas Nelson Perkins has sat on the Loew's board of directors.

It would be an exaggeration to say that these men run Loew's, Inc., as coolly and conservatively as other men might run a bank. You know at once that you are dealing with an excited sort of business from the number of telephones on some of the executive desks, with which they have to play a kind of shell game whenever there is an incoming call. They not only concern themselves with the story buying, selling, and publicity aspects of pictures—subjects all garish enough—but they are in control of such miscellaneous Loew's affiliates as two artists' booking services, a radio station (WHN), three music-publishing companies, and any number of those strange noctivagants known as talent scouts. Still, of the 125-odd subsidiaries of Loew's, Inc., that it is their duty to coordinate, at least a hundred are theaters, which is to say real estate. And by and large the language and psychology of business, not of art or of nonsense, set the tone of the New York office of Loew's, Inc. Conservative business at that. Loew's was the first picture company (1926) able to sell long-term debentures on the New York Stock Exchange, and $15,000,000 worth of Loew's ten-year bonds were sold three years ago (through Dillon, Read) at the lowest rate in the history of the industry, a trifle over 3.5 percent.

Marcus Loew

Some of the reasons for this conservatism stem from the present policies of the officers, but the most important ones are to be found in Loew's history. Twelve years dead, the founder of the company, Marcus Loew, did certain things and avoided doing others that largely account for the organization's prosperity today. Marcus Loew was strictly a theater man. Reared on the streets of the East Side Manhattan ghetto, he sold newspapers when he was eight, entered the fur business, grew an aggressive black mustache, and presently bought his way into a company that Adolph Zukor had started to exploit peep-show motion-picture devices in penny arcades. Zukor's company opened its first show place in Union Square, Manhattan, and made $20,000 the first year, while Marcus Loew headed a subsidiary company developing out-of-town locations. No sooner had the venture been firmly established than the partners started wrangling, and the Automatic Vaudeville Co., as it was called, shortly dissolved. Loew was left with three penny arcades, including one in Cincinnati, and soon turned them into nickelodeons. The films of the period, which ran less than five minutes on the screen, were of deplorable quality, and the business was thoroughly disreputable. David Warfield, who had an investment in his friend Loew's enterprise, refused to let it be known that he had anything to do with the nickelodeons for fear of blighting his name on the stage.(Mr. Warfield, now seventy-two, is still a director of Loew's, Inc.) Loew rented vacant stores and lofts, at first, and furnished them with benches or secondhand chairs to seat the audiences. Later on he acquired regular theaters, and boosted attendance by cashing in on—as well as helping to inspire—the vaudeville craze. "Vaudeville and Pictures" was what the Loew houses offered, and it was ten years or so before the line was changed to "Pictures and Vaudeville."

To Marcus Loew, indeed, goes more than a little of the credit for the cinema's development as an adult medium of entertainment. Realizing early that the screen would never progress beyond the nickelodeon stage unless production improved, his constant demand was for pictures that told stories, pictures that were dignified, pictures that would appeal to a more intelligent public than the peep-show addicts. When he was finally able to secure such pictures—from Zukor himself, among others—he began unloading nickelodeons and purchasing larger, tonier houses judiciously selected with an eye to population shifts and neighborhoods. Sometimes it was necessary to regenerate particular theaters before nice people would start going to them. Loew purchased an old harlot of a burlesque house called the Cosy Corner, in Brooklyn. The police had raided the place so often that it finally closed, and was taken over by the Salvation Army. Loew bought it for a song, fumigated it physically and then morally by putting on a troupe of Italian actors who played only Shakespeare and d'Annunzio. In a few months, as the Royal, it became the loftiest theater in the borough, and Loew was then able to introduce in it high-class vaudeville and pictures, to his future profit.

It was just after the war that the movie industry, dislocated by the zooming of production costs under the competitive influence of the star system, began to assume the vertically integrated shape it has today. First National, a circuit of exhibitors, began it, first by financing producers, and then by building a giant studio in 1922. Adolph Zukor had already merged Paramount (distributing) and Famous Players-Lasky (producing) in 1916; now he began to buy theaters, and by 1927 owned more than a thousand.

Marcus Loew, who by 1919 had more than a hundred theaters, and whose Loew's, Inc., was a $25,000,000 company listed on the New York Stock Exchange, followed the trend. In 1920 he bought an impoverished independent producing and distributing company called Metro (then run by Richard Rowland) and poured $2,000,000 of his theater profits into it. Mr. Loew, soon afterward, acknowledged himself "surprised to learn how many things about picturemaking an exhibitor did not know." But in 1924 he went deeper into production by buying the Goldwyn Pictures Corp., from which the eccentric Sam Goldfish had already retired, and also the independent producing unit run by Louis B. Mayer.

With the Mayer company Loew's also took unto itself a new and subsequently controversial business practice. The chief assets of the Mayer company were the men in it, including Mayer himself, J. Robert Rubin, Irving Thalberg, and others whom Mayer had lured from other studios with the offer of profit-sharing bonuses. After the formation of Metro-Goldwyn-Mayer as a Loew's, Inc. subsidiary, the three among them were entitled (after dividends of $2 per common share) to 20 percent of Loew's net up to a withdrawal of $2,500,000, and 15 percent above that. In 1930 they divided a $2,200,000 melon on the $14,500,000 profits. As comparable payments ensued, certain stockholders began to doubt whether any men in the world were worth that much to any company, and suit was brought in 1938 to revoke the bonus contracts. But it was proved as definitely as anything of the kind can be that Messrs. Mayer, Rubin, and Thalberg had been indispensable, and that Loew's mounting profits depended largely on their efforts. At any rate, Mr. Sidney Kent, president of Twentieth Century-Fox, testified that his company would be glad to have them on his lot if they could be weaned away. The profit sharers—including Messrs. Schenck, Arthur Loew, and Bernstein, who have contracts of their own—were made to repay some $528,000 to the company; but the reason for that was a mere bookkeeping error, as Judge Valente made perfectly clear. Today, with additional contracts made this year, the bonuses of fourteen executives on both coasts average about 20 percent of net, Mr. Louis B. Mayer leading the field with 6.77 percent.

Marcus Loew died in 1927, leaving an estate of more than $10,000,000 and a staff of executives trained for years in his conservative—for the picture industry—methods. During the late twenties, when Paramount, Fox, and Warner Brothers were borrowing money to buy or build as many theaters as they could get, Loew's sat tight with its chain of ten dozen or so high-class houses. "The day of reckoning will come," Mr. Schenck kept saying, resisting the pressure to join his competitors' spree. Indeed it did. When box-office receipts dropped in the Depression, Fox, Paramount, and the others were left holding a bagful of inflated real estate and debt. The greater part of the industry went down in a dismal heap of bankruptcies, lawsuits, shake-ups, and reorganizations, in which control passed largely to Wall Street. Loew's, however, stood like Gibraltar, keeping its theaters and its financial independence as well.

There was a period, to be sure, when Loew's independence was in serious doubt. In 1929 William Fox bought a 45 percent interest in the company, obtained mainly through purchase of stock from the Loew estate, Nicholas Schenck, and other executives. There was some idea of eventual merger, and Fox put a couple of directors on the board. But he never got around to interfering with the Schenck management. Before he had the chance, his own huge chain of theaters was in the most absorbing difficulties, and on top of that the government as an antitrust measure sued to restrain him from voting his Loew's stock. The stock was sequestered and three directors "in the public interest" went on the board. After Fox was dethroned from his own company, his Loew's stock reverted to the Chase Bank and other creditors, and has since been disposed of gradually in the open market. Nobody owns so much as 10 percent of Loew's 1,600,000 shares of common or 137,000 shares of preferred today.

Loew's strength in the Depression—a dividend was paid in every year—was only partly due to Mr. Schenck's caution in the matter of the theaters. There was only one year, 1932, when the profits from the theaters ($5,000,000 that year) exceeded the profits from the studio ($3,000,000). The rest of the time it was just the other way around. For while the theater chain had been keeping itself within handy and profitable limits, Metro-Goldwyn-Mayer had been setting the industry by the ears. Getting off to a good start after 1924 with *He Who Gets Slapped, The Big Parade,* and the Garbo-Gilbert silents, the new sixty-three-acre studio at Culver City rapidly became encrusted with more stars and triumphs than Hollywood had seen in one place since the great Wallace Reid days of the old Paramount lot. And Culver City had something else that Paramount had never had. This was a studio chief whom all Hollywood united in calling a production "genius," the small, pale, nervous youth named Irving Thalberg. To his golden touch with stars and stories Metro's amazing profits were almost universally ascribed. Thalberg, by attempting with a good deal of success to oversee every consequential production on the lot, drove himself to a physical breakdown, and although he took things a little easier thereafter, he died three years later, in September 1936. In examining the Loew's of 1939, it is logical to begin with the rich heritage of Culver City that Thalberg left behind.

Star Factory

"They won't miss him today or tomorrow or six months from now or a year from now," a studio executive remarked at Thalberg's funeral. "But two years from now they'll begin to feel the squeeze." With the release of *Goodbye, Mr. Chips,* MGM parted with the last picture that Irving Thalberg had anything to do with, and his admirers, a group that includes many who never knew him, have been pointing out symptoms of the squeeze for about a year. After his illness there was, of course, a determined effort to fill his shoes. There has been a long parade of would-bes— David Selznick (*David Copperfield, Tale of Two Cities*), Hunt Stromberg (*Maytime, The Thin Man*), and Mervyn LeRoy (*Wizard of Oz*), among others—and the Culver City lot today burgeons with characters who believe themselves to be undiscovered second Thalbergs. Thalberg is almost as pervasive an influence at Culver City today as he was in his lifetime. Recent errors of executive judgment are ridiculed in his name, and compared with the master's performance in similar situations. During his illness, Deanna Durbin and Fred Astaire were tested at Culver City, and turned down. On the subject of Astaire, some hapless underling scrawled on his report card, "Can't act; slightly bald; can dance a little." The Irving Thalberg Building, which harbors the executives, is super-air-conditioned and hermetically sealed. This, the wags allege, is so that the ghost of Thalberg can't get in to see what his successors are doing.

But if MGM no longer has a Thalberg, it still has a weekly studio payroll of $615,000 and a production force of 6,000 people. Among these are the twenty-six MGM stars, which the trade has been told are "more stars than there are in heaven." They are headed by the veterans Crawford, Shearer, William Powell, Garbo, and Gable, and include Loy, Donat, Spencer Tracy, Eddie Cantor, the Marx brothers, Robert Taylor, James Stewart, Rosalind Russell, Jeanette MacDonald, Nelson Eddy, Hedy Lamarr, Mickey Rooney, Wallace Beery, and Lionel Barrymore. There are fifty-odd featured players; eighty writers, among them F. Scott Fitzgerald, Ben Hecht, Anita Loos, and Laurence Stallings; the Class I directors, like Jack Conway, Victor Fleming, W. S. Van Dyke, Robert Z. Leonard, King Vidor, Sam Wood, Frank Borzage, H. S. Bucquet (a graduate of the shorts department and the current white hope of the studio), Norman Taurog, Clarence Brown, and George Cukor. There are the usual host of grips, maids, artists, flacks, and other proletariat, among them such unclassifiables as the man who, during the recent making of *The Wizard of Oz,* stood by the men's room to make sure that none of the many midgets employed in that picture fell into the full-sized commodes. There are also the executives.

Chief of these, of course, is Mr. Louis B. Mayer himself. Now fifty-four, Mr. Mayer is essentially a businessman, although in that capacity he does a good deal of informal acting and is sometimes known as Lionel Barrymore Mayer. In an effort to induce Jeanette MacDonald to unfreeze for her songs in *Maytime,* for example, he called her to his office and sang *Eli*

Eli to her on the spot. He is also a tireless pinochle player and rumba dancer, and the possessor of a tough and energetic physique. A hard-shell Republican, he got a lot of kudos in the old days through his friendship with Hoover, which no doubt helped to reconcile the inner Mayer to sharing so much of the credit for Metro pictures with Thalberg. Perhaps he misses his kudos today. But, being a good businessman, he has not tried to fill Thalberg's shoes himself. His job remains what it was, to oversee the entire studio, to handle the delicate diplomacy of contract negotiations, and to refer the tougher problems to Mr. Schenck, whom he calls "The General" and with whom he talks on the telephone two or three times a day. Mr. Mayer, perhaps the most feared man in Hollywood, is also responsible for the general lines along which Metro pictures are constructed. Unlike the rest of the world, these have not changed since the days when Mr. Mayer was a White House guest.

The chief of these policies is a ringing faith in the star system. Metro has created most of its own stars, and has even recreated a few (William Powell, Wallace Beery) whom other studios had virtually given up. How costly the making of a star can be is illustrated by *I Take This Woman,* already mentioned as having been shelved after considerable production expense. Because Hedy Lamarr is potentially a very valuable property, Metro dropped the money rather than get her off to a bad start. (Of course, the picture may yet be completed and titled, say the wags, *I Retake This Woman.*) But the making of a star, although it calls for a judicious selection of material to begin with, also imposes penalties on the star's casting thereafter. Metro pictures are more often vehicles than stories. Mr. Rubin and his aides are constantly combing the world for creative matter of all kinds, and they pay the best prices for it, but many of their best story buys are twisted out of recognition to fit expensive reputations. Even history can be bent to Metro's purpose, the most conspicuous recent example being Norma Shearer's *Marie Antoinette.*

Naturally there is no issue of taste or social conscience to be raised by this timidity; but there is a question of studio morale. Since the ingredients of a successful picture are nothing but people and ideas, an atmosphere of courage and inventiveness can be just as vital to a studio as a chestful of contracts for stories and stars. Many Hollywood gossips believe that the recent series of Metro fiascos can be traced to a decline in morale. In spite of the slogan on the executive walls—"Don't let Metro's success go to your head"—a good deal of complacence can be sniffed in the Culver City air. Mr. Mayer's executive staff—Eddie Mannix, Sam Katz, Ben Thau, Joe Cohn, and Al Lichtman—is an honest and competent group, but, like Mr. Mayer himself, some of them have been there an awfully long time. The studio manager is sufficiently unpopular to convince Mr. Schenck that he must be a good one, but he happens to be Louis Mayer's brother. Not that Mr. Mayer practices nepotism as extravagantly as some other studio heads, even if—having a nephew and two nieces on the payroll—somewhat more literally. But the gossips agree that a lot of the energy that used to go into good pictures seems to be going somewhere else. Leaving some rushes of his last picture, one of the twenty-three Metro producers yawned. "Really," he was heard to say, as he made for a telephone to see how they were running at Santa Anita, "really, I suppose I've got to find a production I can really interest myself in."

But we are here dealing with intangibles; and there is obviously no good evidence yet that Metro, like Paramount before it, has passed its prime. It should be pointed out that all studios have suffered and survived slumps, including Metro itself. And the tangible evidence of the whole product shows no slump at all. Metro has figured about as heavily in the annual Academy Awards in the last two years as it ever did, and in 1938 it produced four of the "Ten Best Pictures" (*Boys' Town, Marie Antoinette, The Citadel,* and *Love Finds Andy Hardy*) selected by *Film Daily*'s poll vote of critics all over the country. For the coming season about fifty pictures are scheduled on a studio budget of $42,000,000. This, as usual with Metro, is the highest per-picture budget in the industry, and probably the proportion of hits, duds, and break-evens will not change very much. This summer (always a movie low spot) Metro has already released a big hit in *Goodbye, Mr. Chips,* made in its English studio. *Tarzan Finds a Son* also looks like a big grosser, as do the forthcoming *Lady of the Tropics, Wizard of Oz,* and—to be sold by Metro, though made by David O. Selznick—*Gone With the Wind.* Meanwhile the studio is getting from three to five times the negative cost out of its Dr. Kildare and Hardy Family series, which are produced for less than $300,000 apiece and have struck a new note in screen fare by being quiet, homely, pleasant, and increasingly successful.

Bricks and Mortar

The health of the studio is, of course, of prime importance to Mr. Schenck. Of his $122,700,000 gross revenues last year, around $75,000,000 came from film rentals, as did some $7,000,000 of his $10,000,000 profits. But his other assets, if less spectacular, are more reliable. Between Loew's on the West Coast and Loew's on the East there is not only a difference of 3,000 miles, but a gulf in the method of doing business. Of the business that Marcus Loew started, there are now 125 Loew's theaters in the U.S. and Canada, of which seventy-six are in or near New York City and the rest scattered throughout the country. There are another twenty-eight theaters abroad. Of the total, Loew's owns more than half outright, the others being either controlled, leased, or managed. The total depreciated theater investment is about $62,000,000 and the theater profits, which have been remarkably steady, amounted to about $3,000,000 last year.

Approximately half the Loew's U.S. theaters are first-run houses; the rest are subsequent-run with double features, or with double features and Screeno, depending on the location and the strength of the product allotted them. The salaried theater manager, who makes from $75 to $100 a week, is given some initiative in deciding whether some added attraction beyond pictures is needed to satisfy his clientele, but his pictures are all booked for him by Loew's. Even the Screeno question would probably be taken up with Charles Moskowitz (in charge of the theaters in the New York area) or Joe Vogel (who supervises the houses outside of New York). Since the mechanics of theater management are comparatively simple, consisting mainly of seeing that the projection and sound equipment is in good order, that the cooling system works properly, and that the personnel is properly uniformed and properly deferential, the manager's job is one of bookkeeping, of public relations, and, more important, of film "exploitation." In this he is assisted up to a point by the MGM publicity department, headed by Mr. Howard Dietz, the well-known musical-comedy librettist. He also has the guidance of Oscar Doob, who directs theater advertising for Messrs. Moskowitz and Vogel. But he is expected to think up publicity tricks of his own, and to maintain pleasant relations with newspapers and others.

What it means to "exploit" a run-of-the-mill picture can be judged from inspecting an "Exhibitor's Service Sheet," which is sent out to the managers of all theaters, Loew's and others, some time in advance of the film exhibition dates. Take, for example, the service sheet for *Bridal Suite,* a "hilarious romance" with Robert Young, Annabella, Walter Connolly, Billie Burke, and others. This twelve-page booklet contains newspaper stories with headlines like "Love Laughs at Psychiatry in Comedy Attraction," "Too Many Gags Kill The Story, Avers Director," and "Robert Young Says Comedy Role Is Lazy Man's Job. . . ." There is also an assortment of "catchlines"—"Howl Bent For Laugh Heaven, Four Zanies Tangle With Cock-Eyed Love!" is typical. Then two prepared newspaper reviews—"Teaming Annabella and Robert Young, *Bridal Suite* made its romping debut on the screen of the . . . . . Theatre last night." This material is sent out in mat form without charge by the MGM film exchanges, but exhibitors must pay for colored posters and display material like white paper wedding bells to hang in the lobby, arrows saying "THIS WAY TO THE BRIDAL SUITE," and chastely printed mailing cards announcing that "Annabella and Robert Young will be At Home. . . .

You are cordially invited to attend," with the footnote "Regular Admission Prices Will Prevail." In addition to all the foregoing, there are admonitions that exhibitors secure the "cooperation" of hotels and have bellboys page fictitious couples in the lobby and summon them loudly to the "bridal suite." Another exploitation scheme suggested is the construction of "peephole and shadow-box displays" in the theater lobby and adjacent store windows. "There is bound to be a natural curiosity where the title *Bridal Suite* is concerned," the sheet explains. "Nor is it necessary to become suggestive or nearly indecent in order to make box-office capital. . . ."

Of course Mr. Dietz gets out other types of publicity, too, and it is only fair to say that Mr. Doob himself might well chuck out press books of the *Bridal Suite* type, which are designed for small-town exhibitors. Mr. Dietz, for example, confected the much-admired *Pygmalion* advertising campaign, in which the figure of George Bernard Shaw, as being known to a wider public than any of his works, was shrewdly exploited, Mr. Dietz's department is a big business in itself, spending about $2,500,000 a year. So, for that matter, is Mr. Doob's, which spends another $3,000,000 on advertising alone. It is Mr. Dietz's emissaries who instruct exhibitors all over the country in the technique of securing free newspaper space; but Mr. Doob's men think up the local exploitation angles for the Loew houses.

Meanwhile Messrs. Vogel and Moskowitz are constantly prodding the Loew managers, too. As buyers, Messrs. Vogel and Moskowitz actually see every picture that comes out of the eight major studios—some 350 to 400 a year. This ceaseless viewing also helps them decide how to exploit each one. "We shout the good ones and gumshoe the bad ones," says Mr. Moskowitz. It was Mr. Moskowitz who recently got every theater manager in the metropolitan area to a meeting at 12:45 A.M. to discuss ways and means of fighting the competition of the World's Fair. A Brooklyn theater manager struck a novel blow in this fight. When Denys Wortman, dressed as George Washington, was traveling in a stagecoach from Washington to Flushing to help open the Fair, the Brooklyn man, who was playing *Stagecoach* at the time, hitched his own banner-covered stagecoach onto Wortman's equipage, so that the whole parade seemed to be advertising the picture.

To make any generalizations about overhead or earnings of an "average" Loew's theater is impossible on account of the spread that exists between first- and subsequent-run houses, to say nothing of variables such as good and bad pictures, weather conditions, and seasonal fluctuations in attendance. For example, the Penn Theatre in Pittsburgh, operated by Loew's as a partly-owned affiliate, is a first-run house seating 3,300. Rent, taxes, depreciation, interest on bonds, and amortization total $5,500 per week, and operating expenses (including salaries of $1,500) come to $3,600 weekly. The Penn exhibits only the highest quality "A" features, and selects fifty-two pictures a year from the total output of MGM, Warner's, Paramount, and United Artists. Film rentals in houses like the Penn are invariably on a percentage-of-gross basis, with the theater paying over to the distributor a portion of the total receipts taken in during the run of the film. Thus *Sweethearts,* with Nelson Eddy and Jeanette Mac-Donald, grossed $25,000 at the Penn in one week, and the 40 percent rental came to $10,000. But at Loew's Lee Theatre, a subsequent-run house in Richmond, *Sweethearts* grossed $470 over the weekend, with the theater paying a rental of $190. The Lee has 600 seats, costs $740 a week to operate, including cost of films, and usually grosses no more than $950.

Little theaters like the Lee, however vital to their neighborhoods, are far less important to Loew's than its first-run houses, especially those in the big cities. In Rochester, New York, for example, where Metro pictures are sold to twenty-five different theaters, Loew's owns just one first-run house, but that one customarily pays twice as much rental for a film as all the other twenty-four put together. Outside of New York, home of the big Loew neighborhood chain, there are only five Loew theaters that are not first-run. Still, the whole U.S. chain is only 125 houses strong. Other people own first-run houses, too; and a Metro picture, to break even on its domestic sales, must play something like eight thousand theaters. Which brings us to the problem of distribution.

Pig in a Poke

The trouble with the movie business, say statisticians, is that it is over-seated and underproduced. The 16,250 theaters now open in the U.S. can seat about 10,000,000 people at once, whereas average attendance in 1938 was only 80,000,000 a week. The average seat is thus occupied only two or three hours a day. But the first-run houses are nearly full most of the time, which means that the others are proportionately empty. Moreover, so many theaters change bills twice a week or more, and double features at that, that the four hundred features or less turned out by all eight major studios in the course of a year are scarcely enough to keep all the theaters going. In order to assure himself of "product," every exhibitor therefore has to make an annual contract for a steady supply of pictures. The studios, on their part, try to sell only to those exhibitors who will give them the fullest representation in each town. As a result there has grown up a bargaining system that makes the process of getting the pictures into theaters the most confusing part of show business. Over Loew's part in this confusion sits one William Rodgers, who took the job in 1936.

To call on the 11,000 theaters with which Loew's is able and willing to deal, Mr. Rodgers sends out his 150 salesmen early every summer, when the selling season begins. In trying to make annual contracts, the salesmen are under some handicap because, while they talk freely about Culver City's plans, they can guarantee nothing, not even a definite number of pictures. They used to guarantee a certain number of Gables, Crawfords, and perhaps one Marx Brothers, but Loew's found itself with so many unfulfilled contracts that Mr. Rodgers changed that. Now the sale is made on the basis of the previous season's performance, or what Mr. Rodgers calls "the integrity of our company." The salesmen don't have a price list either. What they offer, with wide variations depending on the strategic importance of the account, are four unnamed superspecials on which they want about 40 percent; perhaps ten lesser bombshells at about 35 percent; another ten at around 30 percent; and a residue of twelve or more program pictures—the "B's"—mostly at flat rentals. But the salesman's object is clear: to get the best available house in each neighborhood to contract for as many pictures as possible. If he can, the salesman insists on the exhibitor's taking the whole line; well over half of Metro's contracts are on that basis. Robert Benchley, Pete Smith novelties, and other shorts also figure in the deal. Through a slit in this poke can be seen a tip of the pig's ear. This is the cancellation clause, which permits the exhibitor to cancel up to 10 percent of the pictures after he has read the reviews.

This system, called block booking and blind selling, has of course been roundly attacked. The Neely bill now before the Senate would bar it altogether, and Claude Fuess, the headmaster of Andover, is one of the high-minded people who have written in support of such a measure, presumably from his experience as a picture buyer for the Saturday-night shows in the auditorium. Many an independent exhibitor objects to block booking, too. But the chain exhibitors apparently do not. It would seem more of an evil, perhaps, if the average exhibitor did not need two or three hundred pictures a year anyway, a number that could not represent much intelligent winnowing on his part even under the most favorable circumstances. And indeed the loudest exhibitor complaints are directed not at block booking as such, but at questions of priority rights to good releases, "clearance" (how soon afterward what rival gets what picture), and the percentage brackets to which the various releases are applied.

The blocked deals made by Mr. Rodgers' salesmen are mainly limited to five or six thousand independent theaters. These theaters account for about 40 percent of Metro's gross. There are also the deals made with the large independent chains (10 to 15 percent), and still more vital are those made with the five big chains of the "trusts." These deals Mr. Rodgers himself gets in on. Some 48 percent of the Metro gross comes from Mr. Rodgers' deals with Loew's, Paramount, Warner, RKO, and National Theatres (affiliated with Twentieth Century-Fox). The Loew chain alone, small as it is, accounts for 15 percent of Mr. Rodgers' gross. An interesting fact about the chains, which the government pointed out in its opening petition in the antitrust suit, is that except in metropolitan areas (the downtown de luxe theaters) they tend to complement rather than compete with each other. Loew is concentrated in New York State, Paramount in Canada, New England, and the South, Warner in Pennsylvania and New Jersey, Fox on the West Coast, and so on.

In such a setup, the big studios obviously need each other's chains very badly in order to get national distribution for their pictures. Mr. Rodgers makes the best deal he can with Joe Bernhard, head of the Warner chain, while Warner's sales manager Gradwell Sears is talking to Joe Vogel and Charles Moskowitz. When you add up all these Big Five deals, multiply them by repeated quarrels over preferred showing, clearance, percentages, and the dozen other points raised by each release, you get a very complicated situation indeed. It is so complicated that it is only natural to suppose that the boys would like to sit down together, all at the same table.

Although the government has been bloodhounding the industry for many years, nobody has ever yet found such a table. Nor is there any positive evidence that any sales manager, aggrieved by bad representation in a competitor's town, ever tries to use his own company's theaters as a club—that would be illegal, too. What probably happens is that the bargaining strengths of the various chains all cancel each other. At any rate, the battle for the best showings is settled in the long run by the comparative drawing powers of the different studio products. If the Loew chain were twice as big as it is, the gross revenues of Metro pictures would probably not be any bigger than they are.

The government claims that Mr. Rodgers sells his pictures to the big chains on terms more favorable than he gives to the independent exhibitors. Mr. Rodgers says it is the other way around. The considerations of priority and clearance are so shaded and complex that either claim would probably be impossible to prove. Naturally Mr. Rodgers gives theaters in the Loew chain a certain edge, which helps account for the Loew chain's impressive contribution to the Metro gross; and this may put *some* independent exhibitors at a disadvantage. But Mr. Schenck will challenge you to find a single independent who has been forced out of business by chain competition. And industry figures show that while the number of Big Five chain theaters in operation has been standing still, the number of independent theaters—especially the number affiliated with independent chains—has been increasing. Meanwhile Mr. Rodgers has been doing his bit to stave off the Neely bill and similar symptoms of "indie" agitation by a long-range appeasement program, instituted in 1936. Metro, the hard-dealing company that first broke the Balaban and Katz refusal to make percentage deals in the Chicago area, now advertises itself to the trade as "the Friendly Company," and goes to great lengths to the end that no exhibitor can blame his losses on a Metro deal. Each of Mr. Rodgers' sales or district managers has a fund from which he can rebate on the spot to any exhibitor whose books show an unjust deal; Metro turns back several hundred thousand dollars a year on this account. Mr. Rodgers is also chairman of the industry's code committee, which is busy drawing up new trade practices, including a 20 percent cancellation clause.

The concentration of economic strength in Loew and its rival trusts is probably not very different from that observable in many other industries, and can certainly have happened without collusion. But the government, besides wishing to divorce the chains from the studios, brings the further claim that the big studios are not really competing with each other at all. This complaint takes us back to Hollywood. One of the commonest practices out there is the renting of stars by one studio to another. The lending studio usually charges about 75 percent more than the star's salary, as a contribution to the lender's burden of idle star time. For its part the borrowing studio gets the star it wants for no longer than it wants. An especially frequent borrower from Metro's opulent star stable has been Twentieth Century-Fox, of which Joseph M. Schenck, Nick's massive brother, is chairman of the board. The far-tentacled Mr. Mayer is also related to the Fox studio, through his son-in-law William Goetz. It is undoubtedly easier for Fox to borrow Spencer Tracy than it would be for an independent studio like, say, Republic; but that is not because of the managerial kinship. Both Metro and Spencer Tracy would certainly feel safer with Darryl Zanuck in charge, even if Republic paid in advance. And Mr. Mayer can still gnash his teeth when Darryl Zanuck produces a hit and gloat when he lays an egg—provided, of course, a Metro star isn't in it. At any rate, the practice of star pooling has proved so useful to Hollywood that it is difficult to envision the making of pictures without it.

A similar fogginess, indeed, envelops the vision of any part of the movie business in which the government's suit may be successful. Astronomical budgets, which give Metro pictures their high commercial gloss if nothing else, can be supported only by a nationwide (plus an international) market, and that means that the pictures must be sold to some kind of chains. On the other hand, a strong theater chain that could get nothing but a shoestringer's pictures, however artistic, would soon be financing another Lasky, Zukor, Goldwyn, or other successfully extravagant showman, and start the cycle all over again. The problem is so complicated that Mr. Arnold himself has no suggestions as to how his suit will improve matters, or what shape an ideal picture industry ought to take. But if a cleavage comes, and Mr. Schenck must decide between his theaters and his pictures, the theaters would presumably be sold. Steady earners though they are, they haven't the golden possibilities that Metro still has. It would then become Mr. Schenck's even more urgent duty to keep Metro ahead of the field with "good pictures." Perhaps his aphorism is the answer to this problem after all.

14

FORTUNE

The Hays Office

The story was the not wholly original one about the small-town girl who dreamed of a career in the theater. Her name was Mazie, and she had roughly $50 in cash. After a few chapters in which her career in the local emporium became duller and duller, the author one night placed Mazie on board a bus marked "New York." Almost as soon as the bus arrived, Mazie's dream gave way to disillusionment. First there was the round of producers' offices; nothing. Then there was the round of commercial photographers' offices; nothing. Mazie's $50 dwindled to $1.75 and finally she was reduced to stealing milk from doorsteps. One night, exhausted, she fainted while staring at some paunchy diners in a Park Avenue restaurant. A young man named Ferdinand was passing and carried her into a restaurant. Revived by some caviar canapes, Mazie learned that he was a millionaire and that he wanted to put on a show but couldn't find a leading lady. He stared at Mazie, and Mazie stared at him. Mazie couldn't go back to her boardinghouse because she owed rent, and Ferdinand took her home with him to his apartment. Presently she became his leading lady, and on the opening night of the big show she married him. They lived happily for about six months; then Ferdinand took to drink and became impossible. Mazie left him and went abroad to get a divorce. In Paris she met a maharaja and fell prey to his exotic attentions. She was on the point of sailing to Calcutta with him, when Ferdinand heroically reappeared. The maharaja turned out to be bogus—not even an Indian

From vol. 18 (December 1938), pp. 69-72+.

295

but an Abyssinian and a white slaver, to boot—and Mazie and Ferdinand remarried.

The author of this epic, one Joe Jones, pondered a title for several days. Finally, with a little sigh, he scrawled *The Glorious Madcap* across the top of page 1, and mailed the manuscript to a publisher. It was his first novel, and he was amazed when the publisher accepted it. He was even more amazed when Hollywood started making offers. Colossal Pictures bid $20,000 for the screen rights, and Gigantic $25,000; both offered, in addition, three-month contracts as a staff writer at $1,000 per week. Mr. Jones naturally sold to Gigantic, and took a plane to the Coast.

After a series of conferences with Gigantic's producers, Jones learned that he was expected to make a screen adaptation of *The Glorious Madcap* that would not only suit the requirements of Gigantic's leading pair of screen lovers, Mr. Romeo Romeo and Miss Juliet Julliette, but also the requirements of the Motion Picture Producers and Distributors of America, Inc., which was never called anything but "the Hays Office." It developed that the Hays Office, of which Mr. Jones was only vaguely aware, had a number of serious objections to *The Glorious Madcap,* and the gentlemen at Gigantic were surprisingly docile in accepting them. Indeed, from the moment that Mazie met Ferdinand the story ran into trouble. First there was the matter of Mazie's sleeping in Ferdinand's apartment. The Hays Office insisted that this be toned down because it implied an irregular sex relationship, made this relationship look like "the accepted or common thing," and "presented it attractively," in the language of the Hays Production Code. Worse, after Mazie had run away from him, Ferdinand consoled himself with the wives of some of his friends, and the Hays Office noted sternly that this reflected badly "on the sanctity of the institution of marriage and the home" and would have to be changed. Furthermore, *The Glorious Madcap* harrowed the reader with profuse descriptions of Ferdinand's debauches, and the Hays Office insisted on either eliminating some of the drinking scenes entirely or pointing them up as the cause of his downfall, since the "use of liquor in American life . . . will not be shown," except when it is essential to plot or characterization.

But it was after Mazie reached Paris that the Hays Office criticisms began really to pile up. Mr. Jones had unleashed his imagination on a chapter dealing with Montmartre night life, detailing lewdness and excesses that served as a sort of prelude to the phony maharaja. The juiciest of these scenes were categorically rejected, and next the maharaja himself was marched to the guillotine. The Hays Office tried to spare Mr. Jones's feelings, but the maharaja was so utterly wrong in every way that nothing could be done to save him. First of all because of the discovery of his Ethiopian blood there was a hint of miscegenation in Mazie's dealings with him. Secondly, he was a white slaver, and at times he acted suspiciously like a pansy, not in accordance with the edict that "sex perversion or any inference to it [*sic*] is forbidden." Again, while strangely attracted by him, Mazie at several points in the dialogue referred to the maharaja and people of his race in low terms. This would give offense to Indian and Abyssinian moviegoers because the "history, institutions, prominent people, and citizenry of other nations shall be represented fairly." On these counts the maharaja was in clear violation of the Production Code, on which all the objections of the Hays Office were based.

That about summed up the fundamental errors of *The Glorious Madcap,* and Mr. Jones began constructing a new plot that would get around them. In addition, he had orders—not given as such but amounting to the same thing—to make changes in a number of incidental scenes. In the original story, for example, Mazie and Ferdinand were married at three in the morning by a minister in pajamas who was so sleepy that he got mixed up in the ceremony. A rewrite was necessary on this because it tended to make the minister ridiculous; the wedding was transferred to a cathedral at high noon. But the Hays Office warned that pictures of church ceremonies were generally taboo on English screens and would probably be cut from the print in the British Isles. Ultimately, Mazie and Ferdinand were married by a justice of the peace.

After innumerable conferences and innumerable suggestions from Gigantic people as well as from the Hays Office Jones and several others (for he acquired helpers as time passed) produced the second version of *The Glorious Madcap* and started writing dialogue. Single scenes and even single pages were now being sent to the Hays Office for approval, and shooting began on sequences that were passed. Discussion on the others narrowed down to individual words, minor characters, bits of action, even properties. Jones had Mazie yelling "Fire! Fire!" at one point when she saw a hook and ladder on Park Avenue; the Hays Office cut it out on the ground that it might create panic among theater audiences. The words "hell," "damn," "God," "lousy," "fanny," "dump," "nerts," "wop," "nigger," "slut," "floozy," and the phrases "on the make," "in your hat," "nuts to you" were expunged from the script. The line "I feel better for that drink," spoken insinuatingly by Mazie, went out. A taxi driver was forbidden to give a Bronx cheer for another taxi driver. In a scene in an Italian restaurant Ferdinand was shown coming out of the men's room; the sign "Men's Room" was changed to "Lounge" on grounds of taste. In the same scene the Italian waiter spilled Chianti on the tablecloth and apologized with a flood of language and wild gestures; the language and gestures went out because the Hays Office advised that the Italian government refuses permits to pictures casting Italians as comics. A double bed became twin beds in Ferdinand's apartment because of the squeamishness of British censors. A shot of Ferdinand staring fixedly at a French magazine cover featuring a nude female was cut. The director of *The Glorious Madcap* was careful to have a Hays Office man attend a rehearsal of a floor-show number in a nightclub scene; the Hays man pointed out that the chorus girls' costumes didn't quite cover their navels, and the costumes were changed. He also took the director aside and suggested that the girl who sang a song in this same scene should avoid expressing herself with what in burlesque circles is known as the "grind." When the scene was shot the girl sang the song straight; there was no grind.

Jones's contract expired long before the shooting had progressed very far, and he went back to New York with no idea of what it was all about. He felt that *The Glorious Madcap* had been censored until it was almost unrecognizable, but the censorship had worn kid gloves. He had never been told that he *had* to make a change; always he had been "advised" or "urged" to make it, and some of the time alternate suggestions were presented that definitely improved on the original. Except on one or two small points the Gigantic people agreed with the Hays staff, meekly accepted all revisions, and kept consulting with them. Jones knew, of course, that Gigantic itself was actually a part of the Hays Office, contributing to its support, and he also knew that somewhere on the scene there was a man named Will H. Hays. But while he had visited the offices of the Motion Picture Producers and Distributors of America on Hollywood Boulevard several times he had never caught sight of the head of the Hays organization. Instead, most of his words had been with a chunky Irish-American named Joseph I. Breen, a man who could be as genial as a May breeze one minute and as eruptive as a volcano the next. Mr. Hays has his main office in New York, and visits Hollywood only four times a year, yet he is so important in the motion picture industry that when a question comes up requiring consultation between Hays and, say, a dozen Hollywood lawyers, the lawyers go to Hays in New York before Hays goes to the lawyers.

The Cat's Whiskers

Will H. Hays, postmaster general for a time during the Harding Administration, has an acquaintanceship that would make a respectable showing alongside the acquaintanceship of Postmaster General James A. Farley. One of his warmest admirers and best friends was the late Mr. George Eastman, head of the Eastman Kodak Company, which supplies the motion picture industry with a good part of the 27,000 miles of film that it handles daily.

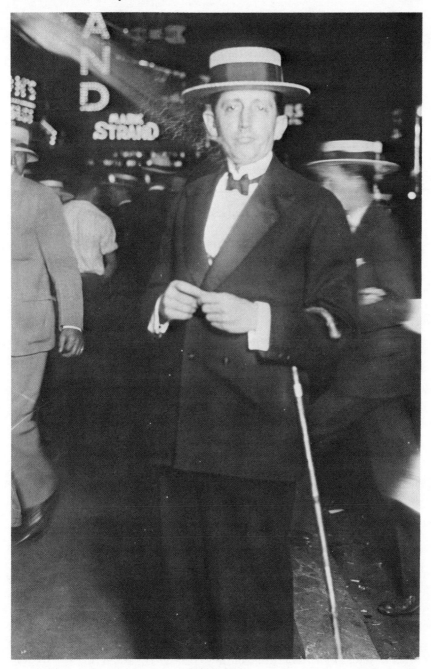

Will H. Hays

Mr. Eastman one day called on Mr. Hays and brought with him a distinguished-looking British gentleman with a "Sir" prefixed to his name. In the course of a rather elaborate introduction Mr. Eastman said: "Hays here is the cat's whiskers of the motion picture industry"—and went on to explain that the industry relies on Hays to guide it through tight places and around dangerous corners the way a cat relies on its whiskers for approximately the same purposes. The U.S. cinema industry represents an investment of about $2 billion and does an estimated annual gross business at the box office of $1 billion. It is an exceedingly fat cat, in other words, and by that token it requires luxuriant and highly sensitive whiskers.

To look at him, Will H. Hays might not impress you a great deal. He is fifty-nine years old, slightly graying, and of no great physical stature. His features lend themselves readily to caricature—at which Mr. Hays himself is the first to laugh. His voice normally is somewhat shrill, but when needed he can command the sauve persuasion of a supersalesman or the frenzied roar of a Billy Sunday. His well-tended hands are synchronized with his words and voice. When the voice is persuading, the hands lie passively folded or point outspread toward the listener. But when Hays shouts, every inch of him becomes part of his voice. He does not merely wave a forefinger; his whole arm describes a haymaker and deposits his fist on the desk with such a thump that it seems nearly to jerk him off the ground.

Will Hays is most likely to become emotional about two subjects. One is the vast responsibility of his position as the cat's whiskers. The other is the vast responsibility of his position as the defender of the eternal verities and American ideals. Especially is he conscious of his responsibility "toward that sacred thing, the mind of a child, toward that clean and virgin thing, that unmarked slate," as he himself has stated. It is a heavy burden, and by and large he has carried it with few missteps. He is despised by some moralists for being too liberal, and by some liberals for being too moral. By the former group he has been accused of "polluting the universe" and of being "the greatest enemy of civilization." But Will Hays has always tried to find the golden mean, and when the criticisms are blended they indicate that he has not failed.

As movie "czar"—the headline writer's word for the president of the MPPDA—Will Hays enjoys a salary of $100,000 per year. His organization can take much of the credit, and Hays himself most of it, for the fact that today, when the press and the radio industry live in real or fancied terror of political control, the motion picture business is freer of such worries than at any other time in the last twenty years. True, the Department of Justice recently announced an antitrust action against a number of major film companies, but this action concerns certain highly technical industry practices and does not involve anything like censorship. Furthermore, while six states still carry ancient censorship legislation on their books and maintain boards of motion-picture review, these laws and groups have lost much of their raison d'être and they rarely cause the industry any trouble. In effect, the Hays organization anticipates their criticisms and recommends changes to the film producers in advance of distribution with the result that of the pictures passed by the MPPDA last year only a negligible few suffered cuts of any kind from the state censors.

The Hays Office membership includes all the major producing companies and most of the lesser studios with the notable exception of Republic and Monogram. They were the source of around 85 percent of all screen time in the U.S. last year, and for each of the pictures released the companies had to obtain the seal of approval of the MPPDA before it could be distributed. In addition, the Hays Office approved 228 new features made by outside nonmember U.S. companies, which pay the same fee as members for this service.

If approved by the Hays Office the submitted picture receives the same seal that is given to member-produced films, and is eligible for showing in all theaters. Most important of these are the so-called "key theaters"—a good part of them owned wholly or partially by the member companies in the MPPDA. These company-owned or affiliated houses represent only about 13 percent of the total, but they have over a quarter of the U.S. seating capacity and they account for nearly 30 percent of the gross box-office receipts estimated at around a billion dollars annually. It is almost axiomatic that no picture of any investment importance can be expected to be profitable unless it has access to these theaters, for because of their mainly urban location and the fact that they are largely first-run they not only command big audiences but are the main sources of the absolutely vital publicity buildup that every picture must have to succeed. Hays Office member companies have agreed that they will not distribute or exhibit in the theaters affiliated with them any picture that has not obtained the MPPDA seal. A member violating this rule is subject to a $25,000 fine, but there have been no impositions of fines in the four years this has been in effect.

Counting member and nonmember films, then, the Hays Office last year reviewed and approved approximately 98 percent of all feature pictures exhibited in the U.S.—663 titles. To each of these pictures it applied certain tests, taboos, and dicta that have evolved from a meeting of public and film-industry minds that has been going on almost continuously for close to seventeen years, with Will Hays serving variously as master of ceremonies, interlocutor, bellwether, and ear trumpet during that period. The film that meets the Hays Office tests is approved and released to a world market of close to a quarter of a billion persons a week. The rejected pictures constitute only 1.4 percent of the total.

In actual practice there are few unexpected decisions at the showing of completed films, for, as was suggested in the illustrative case of *The Glorious Madcap,* the Hays Office closely follows productions from script to preview, thus ironing out as many difficulties as possible before shooting begins. Indeed, the Hays Office is asked more and more frequently to give opinions on story material before the manuscripts are even purchased. But, while it operates beneficently and with the full consent of the governed, the Hays Office does possess a degree of absolute power that makes the motion picture industry a shining example of effective self-regulation.

Postwar Babylon

The reasons for this go back to the early years of the last decade and spring from the peculiarly unedifying nature of the Hollywood film colony and its product at that time. A wide-open flush town where million-dollar profits could be rolled up in a few months on cash investments of a few thousand but where bankers' money cost producers as much as 15 percent, Hollywood had a naturally raffish appearance that had been exploited to the utmost by the press. Hollywood life was one never-ending drunken orgy, according to the papers, and in the public mind the city had become the greatest fleshpot since Babylon.

By itself this reputation was probably more valuable than otherwise, and Hollywood enjoyed it hugely. But there were righteous people in the hinterland who not only resented this heroic licentiousness but saw it mirrored in the movies that they and particularly their children were attending in ever larger numbers. This resentment might have simmered indefinitely, but shortly after the war there was a succession of scandals culminating in the Fatty Arbuckle case that detonated an explosion of public opinion.

It was not just a vague feeling of hostility that confronted the industry after the Arbuckle scandal. It was a fighting-mad attitude that was channeled and exhorted by scores of women's clubs, church organizations, patriotic societies, youth movements, and assorted uplift and reform bodies of every kind. Direct membership in these groups ran to the tens of millions, and their influence extended to perhaps half the population. They expressed themselves with angry letters, picture boycotts, and Carrie Nation demonstrations, but the ultimate aim of all of them was the same—some kind of censorship.

That they could get what they wanted was obvious, and that they were going to get it seemed certain. Faced with this overwhelming threat, the heads of the industry banded together in the autumn of 1921 and tried to work out a defensive stratagem. It occurred to them that they needed an independent public relations counsel, someone outside the industry who had the public's confidence, who could sell the legend of a cleaner Hollywood, who could head off the censorship legislation, who could stop the agitation against movies. Someone, in brief, who knew the American public's likes and dislikes. For few of these industrial heads—Selznick, Zukor, Fox, Loew, and the rest—were equipped to understand the psychology of Kokomo and Dubuque. Today it is claimed that they suddenly realized what a tremendous cultural and psychological force lay in their hands and that they were moved by a genuine desire to turn it to better uses. No doubt this was something of an afterthought, but, whether motivated by spiritual considerations or by a sound instinct for self-preservation, the industry's house-cleaning decision was sincere enough, and its ultimate effect on the cinema would have been the same in either case.

The nominees for Man to Remake the Movies narrowed down to a field of three—Herbert Hoover, Hiram Johnson, and Will H. Hays, an Indiana lawyer-politician who had been chairman of the Republican National Committee in the 1920 campaign, and had passed to his inevitable reward as postmaster general under Harding. The final selection of Hays was largely fortuitous, but it was nonetheless logical. For Hays was eminently respectable. Like his father, he was an Elder in the Presbyterian Church, a teetotaler, a nonsmoker, and a small-town boy who had kept the common touch. More, Hays was an extraordinary publicity man, a man who had friends everywhere, especially among politicians who might be helpful in fighting censorship. He had been a sort of dark-horse presidential possibility at the Republican Convention of 1920, and while another dark horse had run ahead of him, yet it was something to think about. He had, by his own talents and by spending $1,200,000 over his receipts, engineered the Harding landslide, putting a Republican in the White House for the first time in eight years. In the course of the campaign Hays had met Louis Selznick through an old Indiana friend named Charles C. Pettijohn, then a Selznick executive and now general counsel in the MPPDA. Furthermore, Hays had ingratiated himself with the film industry by treating newsreel men with unaccustomed respect during the campaign. All in all, he was a horse less dark in Hollywood than he had been at the Republican Convention.

In December a committee headed by Selznick called on Hays in Washington, explaining the proposition, and offering him a $100,000 annual salary. Hays asked for time to think it over, and it wasn't until 1922 that he decided to accept. He has explained many times since then how he happened to make up his mind. It was the result of a visit to his home town, Sullivan, Indiana, at Christmas. Hays brought a present of some cowboy suits for his six-year-old son, Bill, and Bill's two playmates. He expected the boys to begin playing Wild West, but instead they at once chose parts in the latest Bill Hart movie thriller. "A new vision of the motion pictures came to me," Hays says of that moment. "I saw them not only from the viewpoint of men who had millions of dollars invested in them but from the viewpoint of the fathers and mothers of America who have millions of children invested in them."

So in March Will H. Hays quietly entered the cinema industry with a five-man staff and an office located in New York City far from the "Hollywood atmosphere" but close to the headquarters of the producing companies that were, in turn, close to the money market. Hays then knew less about pictures than the average moviegoer, and he had no concrete program of action. The only sure thing was that he would be paid $100,000 per year for three years.

The Buildup

The articles of incorporation of the Motion Picture Producers and Distributors of America gave Hays no specific power to force anyone to do anything, and in the beginning his only weapons were his own persuasiveness and the terror that gripped the industry and made its separate units, ordinarily hostile, amenable to cooperative action.

The overweening threat when Hays took office was the reformer-inspired censorship legislation that had been introduced in more than half the states in the Union. To meet the threat Hays literally went to the people. Three months after his job started he called together in the old Waldorf Hotel a meeting of representatives of some sixty organizations—groups ranging from the Boy Scouts of America to the D.A.R. and the National Council of Catholic Women. Banking on the belief that these people as well as the general public were fundamentally opposed to political censorship, he pleaded with the delegates to help the movie industry purify itself, and to abandon support of censorship bills until it had a chance to prove its good intentions. The delegates were impressed by this, and presently they formed a Public Relations Committee to act as intermediary between the reform organization and the industry. The committee was expected to study the industry's problems with producers, on the one hand, and to review new pictures and make reports to the organizations on the other. Before long the committee system proved to be cumbersome and inefficient, and the organizations asked Hays to install in his office a representative chosen by them. His salary was paid by the MPPDA, and in 1926 he was transferred to Hollywood and continued his work out there.

Meanwhile, to demonstrate the all-important fact that the U.S. people did not want censorship, Hays decided to make a test case of a fight that was going on in Massachusetts. In 1921 the legislature had passed a censorship bill similar to one previously vetoed by Governor Coolidge, and the exhibitors in the state had gathered enough petitions to force a referendum on the bill in the elections of November 1922. The Hays Office lined up the newspapers of Massachusetts, made "free speech" the great issue of the referendum, and persuaded countless women's clubs to withdraw their original resolutions favoring the bill. The result was a vote of over 550,000 for repeal of the bill to less than 210,000 for its perpetuation, and the majority was the largest ever registered for or against anything in the state up to that time. The majority was so overwhelming, in fact, that politicians who had been championing censorship in other states took alarm, and ultimately all of the censorship measures up for action that fall were either abandoned or defeated.

Out on the West Coast, where Hays first appeared in person a month after taking office, there were no such dramatic triumphs. The immediate necessity was to get a better press for Hollywood. Publisher Harry Chandler of the *Los Angeles Times* started the ball rolling by inviting one hundred newspaper publishers to send first-string reporters to Hollywood at his expense and exposing them to the healthier aspects of the film colony that had been neglected in previous reports. Simultaneously the studios were advised to soft-pedal dollar-mark publicity about stupendous production costs and to cut out references to champagne baths, solid gold plumbing fixtures, $25,000 automobiles, and the rest of the cinema luxuries that plain people associated with immorality. Impressed by the need for caution, studios admonished their stars to start leading the good life or at least to keep their private affairs private, and eventually studio contracts included a new clause, the famous "morality" stipulation that could be used to void agreements with actors and actresses who involved themselves in scandal.

Countless persuasive talks with countless people in countless places were the means used by Hays to achieve these things, and he employed the same means, from necessity, to bring about that improvement in pictures that he had pledged to the public. What he had promised to work for, actually, was good taste; as he expressed it in the early days to one director: "When you make a woman cross her legs in the film maybe you

Little Caesar (Warner Brothers, 1930), starring Edward G. Robinson

Scarface: Shame of the Nation (United Artists, 1932), starring Paul Muni, Ann Dvorak, and George Raft

Rain (United Artists, 1932), starring Joan Crawford and William Gargan

Anna Christie, starring Greta Garbo. From the MGM release *Anna Christie* © 1930 Metro-Goldwyn-Mayer Distributing Corporation. Copyright renewed 1957 by Loew's Incorporated

don't need to see how high she can cross them and stay within the law but how low she can cross them and still be 'interesting'." This was a fairly radical notion and it did not sink in overnight, but before long the formerly critical press was noting that the "motion-picture industry is succeeding marvelously well in its great mission," and asking: "Is it not . . . time to stop heckling the movies about 'cleaning up'?"

How many were won over by Hays's personal adroitness and how many were influenced through fear of the forces of public opinion that he represented, it is of course impossible to tell, but fear certainly played a part. Incidentally, among the first resolutions adopted by the members of the association was a general agreement to cease depicting Mexicans as bandits, a practice going back at least to 1914, when an inspired producer placed Pancho Villa under a $25,000 contract to have him do his fighting by day instead of night so that the battles could be filmed. President Obregón of Mexico in 1922 became so annoyed with the bandit motif that he declared an embargo on all American pictures, and it took the MPPDA agreement plus six weeks' diplomacy by a Hays man to get this lifted.

In 1924 Hays's original $100,000-a-year contract was superseded by a three-year extension at $150,000 per year (cut to $100,000 again in a later contract), and the association was established as a permanent fixture. Little by little it increased its influence and authority while gradually codifying its ideas about cinema proprieties. In 1924 the association established a formula for considering the suitability for screening of current novels and stage plays. Later it concluded an arrangement with the Authors' League of America whereby material unsuitable for screening might be rewritten so as to preserve dramatic values and then be screened under a new title. This agreement accomplished two purposes. It prevented editorial trickery that might occur if a producer bought a notorious play, filmed a completely innocuous revision, and released it under the first title. It also pacified the Authors' League.

In 1927 the association formulated its first comprehensive written list of specific rules—eleven "don'ts" and twenty-six "be carefuls" intended as a guide for producers. In 1930 the "don'ts" and "be carefuls" were recast, following the introduction of sound pictures, into the twelve commandments of the Production Code. Up until the Depression the major units in the industry had been fairly conscientious in following the Hays Office edicts even though they were still backed up by nothing but persuasion. However, when the nation seemed to be going to pot in 1932-33, the ranks broke, and the general moral tone of the cinema declined to its lowest point since 1922. Frightened by the falling-off in film attendance, some producers tried to reverse the trend with liberal applications of sex, this technique reaching its flower in the Mae West pictures that appeared in 1932 and 1933.

For a time, indeed, it looked as if the Production Code and all the other accomplishments of the Hays Office might be wiped out. But anticipating that the new libidinousness of the screen would have serious repercussions, the leaders of the industry met in New York in 1933 and reaffirmed the Code. Scarcely had they done this when the gathering storm of public opinion broke. Protests began to pour in from approximately the same organizations that had been so active before Hays took office, and there was a new and formidable-looking film-reform society of Catholics who called themselves the Legion of Decency. In 1934 the Catholic bishops in America let it be known that while they would not undertake to tell Hollywood what new purification rites were indicated they would review films and instruct their flocks to stay away from the evil ones. It would have been interesting in many ways to have seen whether the hierarchy had the power to do any serious box-office damage in this way, but before the Legion of Decency had been fairly started, the MPPDA members, always sensitive to an organized minority, had put teeth into the Production Code through a resolution to levy $25,000 fines against recalcitrants.

The Codes

The agitation of 1934 was unpleasant while it lasted, but in the long run it helped the industry far more than harming it. For it brought home to producers the desirability of strengthening the machinery of enforcement. And the net effect, says Mr. Hays today, was to advance the cause of better films by at least a decade. The Code is a rather curious document, containing three general clauses to the effect that no picture shall "lower the moral standards of those who see it" or portray other than "correct standards of life" or ridicule natural or human law. Then there are a dozen particular applications of these principles, broken down into: Crimes Against the Law, which prohibits explicit presentation of criminal methods, murder, etc., and outlaws the illegal drug traffic as a theme; Sex, a nine-part definition of decency; Vulgarity; Obscenity; Profanity; Costume, prohibiting nudity and indecent exposure; Dances; Religion; Locations—"The treatment of bedrooms must be governed by good taste. . . ."; National Feelings; Titles, prohibiting "salacious, indecent, or obscene titles"; Repellent Subjects, calling for care in the treatment of hangings, third-degree methods, brutality, surgical operations, the "sale of women," etc.

Similarly an Advertising Code containing the general principles and many of the specific points of the Production Code was presented by the

MPPDA in 1930 and became binding with a penalty in 1935. From the beginning advertising had been one of the chief reasons for public criticism of the film industry, but it had not responded very well to the Hays treatment. While pictures themselves gradually improved, posters, trailers, and other advertising remained about as wild as they had been in the early days. Indeed, the publicity departments appeared to be trying to compensate for the relatively innocuous films by plastering the most lurid exaggerations on billboards. To meet the situation the producers authorized an MPPDA committee to pass on all advertising and provided fines ranging from $1,000 to $5,000 for failure to honor its decisions. Advertising as well as film decisions can be appealed if it is felt that they are unfair, but such action is comparatively rare.

The Departments

Most of the actual work of "servicing" films under the Production Code takes place in the Hollywood office of the Hays organization, with a staff of seven men under the direction of Joseph Ignatius Breen, whose promotion in 1933 to the top of the Studio Relations Committee, now the Production Code Administration, may or may not have been due in part to the fact that he is a Catholic. The Production Code Administration is the most publicly celebrated department of the MPPDA, but it represents only one phase of the organization's work, and possibly not the most important one.

While the Production Code Administration deals exclusively with the studios, the Community Service Department, headed by Carl E. Milliken, a former governor of Maine, deals mainly with the public. Will Hays realized long ago that it was useless to attempt to improve films in accordance with the public clamor unless the public was prepared to show its appreciation for the improved product at the box office. In effect, he told the sixty national film-reform groups that had helped him beat the first censorship crisis that the industry was willing to study and apply their criticisms, but that they in turn must support the industry. The first occasion for putting this formula to work came in 1924, when *Abraham Lincoln,* one of the best of the early post-Hays pictures, opened at a first-run Broadway theater and played to houses of fewer than a hundred persons. Hays attended the opening, saw that it was going to be a colossal flop in New York, but passed the word to his cooperating public groups that *Abraham Lincoln* was worthwhile. When the final accountings were made, *Abraham Lincoln* turned out to be a box-office success. Later on Hays applied the same quick hypodermic to the films *Nanook of the North* and *Grass, A Nation's Battle for Life,* with gratifying effect. It is generally conceded by leaders in the industry that productions like *A Midsummer Night's Dream* (called "The Dream" in the trade) would have been unthinkable even ten years ago, and that Hays's national publicity grapevine, reaching several millions of the "best people" who attend movies infrequently, has been the chief factor in making them possible.

However, the Community Service Department grapevine operates continuously, and is not simply a first-aid measure. Its most specific work is the coordination of the civic, religious, educational, and other organizations. Many of these have New York or Hollywood representatives who attend previews of virtually all pictures and report on them. When requested, these reports are published in the Community Service Department's monthly list of "Selected Motion Pictures" that circulates among club presidents, organization heads, and other public arbiters. These individuals in turn transmit the recommendations in "Selected Motion Pictures" to members of their groups, sometimes through elaborate chain-telephone systems whereby each member calls certain designated friends and urges them to attend such-and-such a picture. It is said that for the opening of *Romeo and Juliet* in Memphis, Tennessee, ten thousand persons were reached over a telephone chain in a day. In addition to this kind of direct action, the six thousand "local-support groups" listed by the department inspire a vast amount of helpful publicity, in the form of radio and newspaper reviews, church sermons and announcements, talks before meetings, and the like. The department also conducts an elaborate and painstaking campaign to promote wider recognition of the educational value of selected films, and in this work it has the cooperation of an advisory committee of educators, including three university presidents. This campaign is aimed chiefly at librarians and teachers, and a particular effort is made to have them draw attention to historical films having a literary or educational interest.

While the Community Service Department carries on certain operations in Hollywood, most of its work is done in and from New York, and this is more or less true of the other departments in the MPPDA. These include the Title Registration Bureau, which keeps an index of the 36,000-odd film titles and arbitrates disputes over title infringements; the Conservation Department, which campaigns to eliminate fire hazards in the handling of film; the Foreign Department; and the Theatre Service Department.

The Foreign Department, headed by Frederick L. Herron, a lifelong friend of Will Hays, has the twofold duty of trying to keep foreign distribution channels open for U.S. films, and of informing Hollywood about the idiosyncrasies of foreign censors. Around 35 percent of both the gross and net income of the industry comes from abroad, mainly from the British Empire, and the Foreign Department has a tremendous responsibility. In dealing with other governments on matters pertaining to quotas, tariffs, and exchange restrictions it necessarily works mostly through the Department of State, and the MPPDA maintains a small Washington office where Major Herron spends half his time. Occasionally, however, members of the organization go abroad to supplement official diplomacy with personal persuasion, and never with greater effect than when Will Hays visited Mussolini two years ago and secured an extremely favorable revision of an extremely unfavorable law.

The Theatre Service Department devotes itself to the study of trade relations, theater operations, and various practices incidental to film distribution and exhibition. At present the antitrust action brought by the Department of Justice against the eight major motion picture companies, twenty-five associated and subsidiary companies, and 132 individuals makes these matters more than usually significant. For years the Hays Office in general and the Theatre Service Department in particular have been urging a compromise of the antagonisms existing between the independent producers and theater owners and the major film distributors. These antagonisms spring from complicated sales and distribution methods with which the Hays Office has nothing to do, but the basic reason is the fact that the major producers are the major distributors and also the major exhibitors, via their interest in 2,300 owned or affiliated theaters in the U.S., many of which are "key theaters." The independent exhibitors claim that the major producers discriminate against them in supplying first-run pictures, while the independent producers contend that their pictures are largely excluded from the "key theaters." Although the government suit against the major producers is concerned with a variety of allegedly unfair trade practices, its principal object seems to be the divorcement of theater ownership from motion picture production. So far the eight defendant companies in the antitrust action—companies that are, of course, members of the MPPDA—have not filed answer to the declaration by the Department of Justice.

So much for the Hays Office departments. The industry invested $845,000 in the MPPDA last year. This sum, contributed by member companies on a sliding scale, included Hay's $100,000 salary and the salaries of the hundred-odd employees of the organization, the overhead of its New York, Hollywood, Washington, Paris, and London offices. The sum is about equivalent to the cost of one good feature picture, and the industry cannot complain that it doesn't get its money's worth. Besides acting as watchdog the Hays Office furnished tangible and intangible benefits accruing from an extensive educational and public-relations mission of national scope, costing altogether around $350,000. It performed valuable services in protecting the industry's foreign markets, spending $100,000 on this phase of its work. It fought some of the industry's battles in courts and before legislatures, and it made studies of certain of the industry's internal problems, these two activities accounting for $48,000. Finally, it spent $46,000 on its administration of the Advertising Code.

Sitting Pretty

It is conceivable that through its antitrust action the government may ultimately force Paramount, MGM, RKO, Warner Brothers, and Twentieth Century-Fox to divorce themselves from their theaters. That would have the effect of somewhat limiting the scope of the Hays Office, but it would have practically no effect on the standing of Will H. Hays. For in approximately seventeen years Hays has progressed from hired figurehead of the motion picture industry to something like its master, and the industry might have to think a good many times before deposing him, even if it wanted to. Hays in the beginning was set up as the industry's gift to the public, and he still says that his success is due largely to the cooperation of the industry's leaders, and their determination to make good on their promises. But he has ended by being the public's fellow traveler within the industry, and it is likely that no other man in the U.S. could quite take his place.

Today Will Hays has largely delegated to his department heads the details of procedure, although once every twenty-four hours he reads reports from each department and every so often he reviews an appeal from a decision by the Advertising Advisory Council or, with the directors of MPPDA, passes on an appealed decision of the Production Code Administration. Today he is primarily concerned with the larger aspects of industry policy both in the U.S. and abroad. He sits behind a large desk in a paneled office in an antique building within earshot of Times Square.

He ordinarily puts in at least a twelve-hour day on the job, starting with the mail and urgent departmental reports when he arrives at the office at eight-thirty. Next he may have a conference with company representatives on a title dispute or some other matter, then call the State Department in regard to a foreign quota problem, meet the emissary of a public organization, conduct a meeting of his own staff, confer with a member-company president, lunch in his office, chat with his son Bill, who is now at Yale Law School, talk over the treatment of aviation in pictures with a representative of the aviation industry, receive a call from a Hollywood producer, make a call to Breen in the Hollywood office, hold another interview with staff members and another conference with a company president, meet with a group of foreign managers of producing companies, go out for an appointment, return to his office to sign mail, dictate, and have further telephone conversations with Hollywood, and, finally, end the day's work by going to a preview of a new picture.

Will Hays is still the cat's whiskers. He is respected by the heads of the industry, and by the vast body of common men and women who fill the movie theaters day after day. Altogether he has done an enviable job of preserving the screen for entertainment, and so far he has without too much agony reconciled honesty of theme and presentation with the multiplying social, economic, and racial prejudices of the world's population. True, he is criticized by the lay intelligentsia and by a faction of Hollywood writers and directors for being an inartistic prude who stifles the cinema's creative impulse. But such criticisms are not directed at Hays, in the final analysis, but at the notion of censorship popularly associated with Hays. Such criticisms are resentful of the fact that motion pictures, an adult form of entertainment, must be mindful of their juvenile audiences. Such criticisms overlook the fact that without Hays motion pictures might be under a far more prudish, stifling, and capricious censorship exercised by politicians. Finally, such criticisms ignore the immense indignation that a touchy public can display, and that Hays has so far soothed and salved. As Joseph Breen lately remarked, apropos of screen villains, "A villain can be only a native-born white American with no college, no fraternity, no political affiliations, no profession, and no job." Probably the "no job" clause in this definition will not last very long, for recently the WPA complained about the movie portrayal of one of its members.

Part IV
Retrenchment, Reappraisal, and Reorganization: 1948—

After the war, things were never the same for the movie industry. Beginning in 1947, the winds of ill fortune blew incessantly for ten years, during which weekly attendance declined by about one half. The decline began even before television. When servicemen returned, the birth rate increased sharply; families with babies tended to listen to the radio at night rather than go to movies. Veterans swarmed into educational institutions, and studies cut into their leisure time. And because the country was at peace, goods and services were diverted to civilian purposes. Houses, automobiles, appliances, and other commodities were purchased in abundance, cutting in on disposable income.

Television began its real commercial expansion in 1948. The number of sets in use soared by more than 1000 percent, from 14,000 in 1947 to 172,000 a year later. In 1949, the number went up to 1 million, in 1950 to 4 million, and in 1954 to 32 million. By the end of the 1950s, nearly 90 percent of the homes in the United States had television sets. Simultaneously, the number of commercial television stations rose from 7 to 517. Television had grown to replace the movies as the dominant leisure-time activity of the American people.

With the precipitous drop in attendance, annual box-office receipts declined from $1.692 billion in 1946 to $1.298 billion in 1956, or about 23 percent. Revenues declined more slowly than attendance, primarily because ticket prices rose by nearly 40 percent, from thirty-four cents to fifty cents on the average. Over 4,000 conventional four-wall theaters closed their doors during this period. The introduction of drive-ins, however, offset that loss. Nonetheless, since it was difficult to convert a movie house to another purpose, these former exhibitors were hard hit by the drop in real estate values.

Over the same period, on the production level, the gross revenues of the ten leading companies fell from $968 million to $717 million, or 26 percent. Combined profits fell more precipitously, from $121 million to $32 million, or 74 percent. As a result, Hollywood underwent a period of retrenchment. Production was severely cut back as studios trimmed budgets. The stock system went by the boards. In an attempt to reduce overhead, actors, writers, producers, and directors were taken off long-term contracts or pared from the payrolls. Actors were particularly affected: in 1947, 742 were under contract; in 1956, only 229. The labor force shrank as well. Employment fell off from the postwar peak of twenty-four thousand in 1946 to around thirteen thousand ten years later.

The Impact of the *Paramount* Case

The divorcement of exhibition from production-distribution took place at the very time that the industry needed structural

"The Ed Sullivan Show"

stability to deal with its falling market. When the Supreme
Court handed down its decision on the *Paramount* case in May
1948, it was heralded as a landmark victory for antitrust
(see ch. 15). The Court voted unanimously to uphold the
general verdict of the district court. Block booking, the fixing
of admission prices, unfair runs and clearances, and
discriminatory pricing and purchasing arrangements favoring
affiliated theater circuits were declared illegal restraints of
trade and their future use by the eight defendants was
prohibited. The Big Five were ordered to terminate all pooling
arrangements and joint interests in theaters belonging to one
another or to other exhibitors. The Supreme Court, however,
rejected the competitive bidding mandate on the grounds that
it would play into the hands of the buyer with "the longest
purse." Concerning the charge of monopoly in exhibition, it
suggested that the district court make a fresh start on the issue
of theater divorcement and divestiture.

RKO and Paramount, apparently tired of the ten-year battle
with the government, began negotiations for consent decrees.
The Department of Justice rejected compromise proposals
calling for the divestiture of selected theaters and insisted on
the complete divorcement of the affiliated circuits from their
production and distribution branches. Both decrees were
approved by the district court in 1949 and contained these
provisions: (1) the prohibition of unfair distribution trade
practices so that each picture would be rented on a separate
basis, theater by theater, without regard for other pictures or
exhibitor affiliation; (2) the splitting of the existing companies
into separate theater and producer-distributor companies with
no interlocking directors or officers; (3) the divestiture of all
theaters operated in pools with other companies, or one or
more theaters in closed towns, that is, where they had no
competitors; and (4) the establishment of voting trusts to
prevent shareholders in the former integrated companies from
exercising common control of both successor companies.

The other three integrated companies—Loew's, Twentieth
Century-Fox, and Warner—refused to go along with these
decrees until the district court and then the Supreme Court left
them with no alternative. Theater divestiture progressed
slowly, until 1957 for the foot-dragging Loew's; nonetheless,
the disintegration of the motion picture monopoly progressed
irreversibly.

As far as Columbia, Universal, and United Artists were concerned, some economists have argued that they should not have been made defendants in the case because they owned no theaters. The Little Three filed for a separate consent decree, not to extricate themselves from the case but merely to modify certain injunctions. The district court, however, subjected the three companies to the same price-fixing and trade-practice prohibitions as it had the majors.

The motion picture industry underwent many revolutionary changes during the postwar period, and, as Michael Conant notes, it may be impossible to separate the impact of the decrees from that of shifts in demand on the part of audiences and the rise of television (ch. 16). He has found, nonetheless, that because producers and former affiliated circuits were forced to deal with each other at arm's length, more competition existed on the exhibition level. The prohibition against block booking enabled the minor distributors, especially the Little Three, to capture a larger share of the market. The independent exhibitor gained more control over his operations, since he was no longer forced to buy a full line of pictures from a producer to get the ones that he wanted.

On the production level, the *Paramount* decision created a boom in independent production. The major companies could no longer usurp the playing time of the first-run theaters, and this, together with the freedom of choice accorded to exhibitors, meant that the independent producer could find an outlet for his pictures. Other factors were at work as well, not the least being the tax laws. With the idle studios and underutilized distribution systems that retrenchment left, the majors vied to provide financing and studio space to independents and to handle their films. These were the same companies that before the war had created the barriers to independent production.

The leader in the independent movement was United Artists, which throughout its history had functioned as a distributor for independent producers. During the period 1953-57, UA released nearly fifty pictures a year. By then most of the companies had emulated the UA pattern, and in 1958, 65 percent of Hollywood's movies were made by independent producers.

Divorcement also affected motion picture content. Since the five majors no longer owned first-run theaters, they could not effectively enforce the strictures of the Production Code Administration. The power of the PCA was further undermined in 1952 when the Supreme Court in a landmark decision read the movies into the First Amendment and "extended to them the same protected status held by newspapers, magazines, and other organs of speech" (ch. 20). As a result, the PCA revised the Code in 1956 to bar obscenity rather than controversial subject matter.

The new freedom of expression accorded to motion pictures, together with divorcement, gave rise to the "art theater." For

Federico Fellini's *La Dolce Vita* (1959): Anita Ekberg

the first time in over a generation, foreign films had equal access to the domestic market. In 1963 alone, over eight hundred were released by about eighty distributors. The art theater circuit during the early sixties consisted of over five hundred houses devoted exclusively to foreign films and an even greater number that played these pictures on an occasional basis. Not all imported films were "art," of course, but many revealed new dimensions of theme and style to American audiences.

Although the *Paramount* decrees restructured the industry, they by no means reduced the importance of the big companies. In 1954, ten companies (the eight defendants plus Republic and Allied Artists) collected nearly all the total domestic film rentals, as did ten companies (not all the same ones) in 1972. The divorced theater circuits divested themselves of their weaker houses in smaller towns while retaining their large first-run theaters. Thus, despite the impact of television, average annual receipts per theater for many of the circuits actually increased. Moreover, their buying power guaranteed their preeminence in the exhibition field. The independent exhibitor, who was supposed to be the beneficiary of the decrees, probably gained the least in relationship to the majors. Those who owned favorably situated theaters or had the capital to acquire drive-ins held their own or even prospered. But the small theater operator found no shelter in the decrees from the vicissitudes of the business brought about by television, shortages of product, and higher rentals.

Responding to Television

As TV began to make inroads into movie audiences, Hollywood's first impulse was to maintain a strictly stand-off attitude toward the new medium. Television was a novelty whose attraction for the public would quickly wane, the hypothesis being, "They'll get tired of it soon enough." The poor-quality TV programing supported this position, since most network programs, produced on shoestring budgets and broadcast live, did not approach the technical polish of the Hollywood product. Moreover, if producers collaborated with the enemy, so to speak, they would damage their best market. Revenues from the distribution of films to theaters were far in excess of what television could pay.

Television, though, had a voracious appetite for programing. It required talent, stories, people, and ideas to put on thousands of separate productions each year. In the early days, films consisting of old westerns and shorts released to TV by minor studios constituted only about one-fifth of network program time. Local stations, possessing neither the facilities nor the financial resources for extensive live broadcasting, had greater needs. Hollywood, as a result, saw the development of an entire subindustry after 1950, consisting of small, independent production companies devoted to turning out series of low-budget telefilms, usually a half-hour in length.

Upon realizing that a sizable portion of the public was not returning to the theaters, the film industry adopted a new adage to replace the debunked hypothesis regarding television. To draw people back to the theaters, Hollywood said, "We'll give them something television can't." The industry decided to differentiate its product and make the most of its natural advantages over its rival. It would exploit widescreens, color, and 3-D.

Cinerama was launched at the Broadway Theater in New York on September 30, 1952. The presentation was *This Is Cinerama,* a color travelogue projected on a huge curved screen, which gave the illusion of third dimension. Cinerama enjoyed long runs, but because the three-projector setup and stereophonic equipment was too costly for most ordinary theaters—around $75,000—only a few houses in large metropolitan areas could afford to make the conversion. Nonetheless, Cinerama proved that "the public . . . was not literally chained to the television tube," in the words of Freeman Lincoln (ch. 17).

After Cinerama's debut, audiences in the 1950s were introduced to 3-D, CinemaScope, VistaVision, and Todd A.O. It should be pointed out that these innovations, like sound and color before them, were developed and perfected by either minor companies or individuals working outside of the mainstream of the industry. This reflects not only the perennial disinterest in research of all kinds on the part of the majors, but also an innate conservatism regarding new ideas and technological improvements. Widescreens and the extravaganzas produced for them gave the industry a shot in the arm but were not the answer to the competition of television.

As a result, another adage had to be adopted: "If you can't whip 'em, join 'em." Collaboration took several forms. One was to produce films directly for the TV market. Columbia pioneered in this new area by forming a subsidiary called Screen Gems, Inc., in 1949 to produce television programs. It was not until 1955, though, that the other companies took the plunge. Warner in that year produced a weekly series for ABC-TV entitled "Warner Brothers Presents," which consisted of hour-long dramatic episodes inspired by several Warner film classics. Other series followed and in 1960 Warner's TV revenue was estimated at $40 million, compared with total revenue of $90 million from all sources in 1959.

By the early 1960s, Hollywood dominated prime-time programs. Nearly three-fourths of its work force owed its employment directly or indirectly to TV film activity. In 1963, there were forty-nine television producing companies operating on the West Coast. Their investment in programing for the 1963-64 season amounted to over $250 million, with production centered mainly in six factory complexes: Universal, Desilu, MGM, Screen Gems, General Service Studios, and CBS's Studio Center.

Another form of collaboration, meanwhile, had been the supplying of old features and shorts to television. Monogram and Republic had released their pictures to the new medium almost immediately. The major companies held out until December 1955, when RKO, deciding to withdraw from motion picture production, sold its film library to a television programing syndicate for $15 million. Two months later Warner Brothers sold its library to Associated Artists Productions for $21 million. Other companies followed suit, and by 1958, an estimated 3,700 features, mostly of pre-1949 vintage, had been sold or leased to TV for an estimated $220 million. The distribution companies that acquired libraries rented pictures to stations or networks for a limited time or for one or two showings. The shorts were especially popular as "fillers" and were gobbled up immediately as a staple diet of local stations.

Television increased the demand for films enormously and, as Hollywood began to release its post-1948 product to the networks, prices rose accordingly. During the early sixties, top-grade features sold for $200,000, as compared with an average sale price of $10,000 per film for the RKO package in

1955—an increase of nearly 2000 percent. The price doubled in 1965 to approximately $400,000. The following year a new high was reached. ABC paid Columbia $2 million for *The Bridge on the River Kwai.* This nine-year-old picture made history; it cut sharply into such popular programs as the Ed Sullivan show and "Bonanza" to reach an audience estimated at between sixty and seventy million people.

Billy Wilder's *Some Like It Hot,* starring Tony Curtis, Jack Lemmon, and Marilyn Monroe (released through United Artists, 1959)

Afterward, competitive bidding on the part of networks became hectic. Prices for big features nudged the $800,000 mark on the average for single or sometimes two showings. CBS wrapped up a deal with MGM for fifty-one old movies and eighteen new ones: purchase price $53 million. ABC purchased a package of thirty-two films from Paramount for $20 million and another seventeen films from Twentieth Century-Fox for a like amount, including $5 million just for *Cleopatra*. Movies became a prime-time staple five nights a week.

Collaboration next took the form of the made-for-TV movie (telefilm). This happened almost immediately after *Kwai*, when NBC signed a deal with Universal to cofinance the production of a series of features to be shown first on television and then in theaters. Later, as Hollywood's feature output continued to decline, the networks would put up the complete financing and commission various television divisions of the major studios or independent companies to fill their programing needs. These were made at a cost considerably lower than a regular feature: around $435,000 for a ninety-minute movie and $700,000 for a two-hour movie. Networks usually acquired the right to broadcast these pictures twice, after which they reverted to the producers, who could sell them to independent stations on a syndication basis and to theaters abroad as features. As of 1974, 130 new telefilms were aired on the major networks during prime time, compared with 118 regular features broadcast for the first time.

The advent of the telefilm sealed the partnership of the movie and broadcasting industries. But other developments helped bring about the coalescence. For example, in 1956, United Paramount Theatres, the largest of the divorced chains, merged with ABC, with permission from the courts to form a motion picture production company called AB-PT Pictures Corporation. Earlier, Paramount Pictures had bought into Du Mont Broadcasting, a radio and TV company and manufacturer of TV equipment, and attempted, unsuccessfully, to create a fourth major television network. In 1959, National Theatres, Inc., the theater chain created after the Twentieth Century-Fox divorcement, acquired National Telefilm Associates, owner of a nationwide TV film distribution system. Lastly, theater circuits and major film producers acquired TV stations. Many industry commentators have observed that these acquisitions and mergers violated the spirit of the *Paramount* decision, if not the letter of the Clayton Act. Nonetheless, the two industries, which started out as rivals, came to support their mutual interests. The vast potential for revenue in the exploitation of pay TV and subscription TV in the future will serve to cement the already strong bond.

Foreign Markets

With the decline of the domestic market, Hollywood's foreign operations took on greater importance. After World War II, the industry set about recapturing lost territories by releasing its tremendous backlog of pictures that had yet to be distributed abroad. The protective barriers established during the 1920s and 1930s had disappeared, and national film industries, with the exception of Great Britain's, had been totally disrupted by the war. Increasing the likelihood that the industry would dominate international business was Washington's regard for American motion pictures as an important propaganda weapon in the Cold War.

Foreign governments, however, pressed just as vigorously to protect their impoverished economies. European nations were heavily in debt and could not afford the luxury of importing films when other commodities essential to their well-being were desperately needed. To stem the dollar outflow, foreign governments passed restrictions reminiscent of those after World War I, but the balance-of-payments problem had added a new twist in the age-old battle with Hollywood: frozen funds. Since exhibitors and audiences alike preferred Hollywood's pictures to the domestic product, governments decided to allow them free entry on the condition that only a portion of their earnings could be taken out. Great Britain was the first country to adopt such a scheme by lifting its 75 percent import duty on pictures in 1948 and stipulating that for the next two years American companies could withdraw only $17 million annually from the country—all other earnings were frozen. France, Italy, and Germany instituted similar measures, with the result that the majors began investing in production abroad by constructing studios, purchasing story rights, and financing pictures. Frozen funds was but one of several factors contributing to the postwar phenomenon of runaway production, the others being the urge to film authentic locales, lower labor costs, and tax advantages. Currency restrictions gradually relaxed with the resumption of more normal international trade. Foreign governments turned to other measures to nurture and protect their domestic film industries, including such forms of financial assistance as prizes, production loans and credits, and subsidies.

The subsidy was found to be the most effective measure and was adopted by most European countries. Although subsidy plans differed in size and operation from country to country, their general purpose was the same—namely, to provide producers with moneys in addition to revenues collected from normal distribution. These moneys were usually generated by increasing ticket prices or entertainment taxes and allocated by a governmental or public agency.

Production subsidies were instituted to aid domestic film makers, but, as Thomas Guback points out, foreign subsidiaries of American companies quickly discovered how to conform to the provisions of the plans so as to become "national" producers of "national" films and gain access to European subsidies (ch. 18). Runaway production was stimulated, and at the same time the international scope of Hollywood's operations was broadened. In 1949, 19 American-interest features were made abroad; in 1969, 183. Guback estimates that "during the five years ending in 1972, about 45 percent of the 1,246 features made by U.S. companies were produced abroad."

Overseas, American film companies dominate the screen just as they do at home. They distribute the biggest box-office attractions and capture the lion's share of the gross. Before the war, about a third of their revenue came from abroad; by the sixties, the proportion rose to over one-half. Thus, Hollywood's quest to capture a greater share of the foreign market to compensate for declining revenues at home was fulfilled. The ramifications of this expansion on the indigenous cultures of foreign nations, especially of the developing countries, are considerable, as Guback's chapter clearly indicates.

The HUAC Hearings

Divorcement, television, and an embattled foreign market made for a beleaguered Hollywood just at the time that it faced

still another assault—this time from the House Committee on
Un-American Activities. HUAC actually made two assaults, by
holding hearings in both 1947 and 1951 on the alleged
Communist infiltration of the motion picture industry.
J. Parnell Thomas, head of the committee in 1947, intended to
prove that card-carrying party members dominated the Screen
Writers Guild, that Communists had succeeded in introducing
subversive propaganda into motion pictures, and that President
Roosevelt had brought improper pressure to bear upon the
industry to produce pro-Soviet films during the war.

The hearings began on October 20, 1947, and lasted two
weeks. The first part was devoted to taking testimony from
friendly witnesses, many of whom were members of the Motion
Picture Alliance for the Preservation of American Ideals.
Founded in 1944, the Alliance was a militant right-wing
organization dedicated to combatting the impression that the
movie industry was made up of "Communists, radicals, and
crack-pots." The parade of friendly witnesses included Jack L.
Warner, Louis B. Mayer, Robert Taylor, Mrs. Lela Rogers
(mother of Ginger), and Adolph Menjou. The second part was

Mission to Moscow (Warner Brothers, 1943), one of the few pro-Russian pictures made
during the war. Walter Huston, Manart Kippen, and Vladimir Sokoloff

devoted to unfriendly witnesses, led by John Howard Lawson, who announced that as a matter of principle they would refuse to answer the committee's question, "Are you now or have you ever been a member of the Communist Party?" Ten were called—they were dubbed the Hollywood Ten[1]—and each invoked the First Amendment. Each was cited for contempt of Congress and subsequently sent to the federal penitentiary.

The 1947 hearings, in the words of Robert K. Carr, revealed "the committee at its worst. In no other committee undertaking were the motivating forces of politics and the personal prejudices of the committee members more apparent; in no other hearing were the over-all strategy and specific procedures more subject to criticism; no other major investigation of the committee ever ended so anti-climactically or produced so little tangible evidence in support of a thesis which the committee set out to prove."[2]

Nonetheless, Hollywood, in typical fashion, panicked. Fifty leading motion picture executives emerged from a two-day secret session at the Waldorf-Astoria on November 24, 1947, to announce that the members of the Hollywood Ten had by their actions "been a disservice to their employers," had "impaired their usefulness to the industry," and were suspended without compensation. More ominously, though, the moguls invited Hollywood's talent guilds to help them eliminate the subversives in their ranks. So began the blacklist, which would hang like a pall over the industry for over ten years.

In 1951, HUAC investigated Hollywood for a second time (ch. 19). These hearings continued sporadically until 1954, during which time ninety prominent industry figures were called to testify. The committee now wanted people to name others they knew as Communists; 324 were cited and blacklisted by the studios. Hollywood had completely capitulated to the Red Scare, its perpetrators, and the right-wing guardians who had mobilized to cleanse the industry of undesirables. It could then add moral enfeeblement to its list of ailments.

1. John Howard Lawson, Dalton Trumbo, Albert Maltz, Alvah Bessie, Samuel Ornitz, Herbert Biberman, Edward Dmytryk, Adrian Scott, Ring Lardner, Jr., and Lester Cole. All of these men were writers, with the exception of Dmytryk, who was a director, and Scott, who was a producer.
2. Robert K. Carr, *The House Committee on Un-American Activities: 1945-1950* (Ithaca, N.Y., 1952), p. 55.

The Industry in the Age of Conglomerates

Today, the motion picture industry is alive and well. Attendance is still well down from its 1946 peak—and has leveled off at around twenty million per week—but box-office revenues have shown a steady increase. In 1974 they totaled $1.675 billion, nearing the 1946 figure of $1.692 billion. Exhibition has stabilized as well. The total number of theaters in the United States today is estimated at approximately 14,700, a drop from the 1948 high of 18,600, but a significant increase from the 1963 low of 12,600. Although the number of drive-ins has decreased by a third, the loss has been more than offset by a new suburban phenomenon—the shopping center theater, which includes multiplex theaters (two or more auditoriums under one roof sharing a common lobby, box office, and concessions counter) and mini-theaters that seat 350 or fewer and have automated projection, as well as conventional four-wall theaters.

Familiar names—Paramount, Warner, United Artists, and Universal—still dominate the business. They once enjoyed oligopoly powers in a vertically integrated industry; now they are constituents of huge multifaceted conglomerates. Universal in 1962 became part of the Music Corporation of America, which at the time was Hollywood's most powerful talent agency. Paramount was acquired in 1966 by Gulf & Western Industries, which held companies in steel, hydraulics, mining, and plastics. United Artists was acquired in 1967 by Transamerica Corporation, a conglomerate in insurance and other financial services. Warner merged in 1969 with Kinney Services, which was active in car rentals, building maintenance, parking lots, and funeral parlors.

Of the former Big Five only Twentieth Century-Fox is still primarily a motion picture producer and distributor; RKO is out of the scene, having suffered a takeover by Howard Hughes, who was more interested in purging the studio of alleged Communists during the McCarthy era than in producing pictures. Hughes sold out his interest to General Teleradio, a subsidiary of General Tire and Rubber Co. in 1955. Two years later the studio was sold to Desi Arnaz and Lucille Ball, who renamed it Desilu Studios, devoted exclusively to producing programs for television. The once mighty MGM now plays a minor role in the movie business.

After Kirk Kerkorian acquired control of the company in 1969, MGM went into the so-called leisure field by constructing a $100 million resort hotel in Las Vegas and laying plans to build a fleet of luxury cruise ships. In the meantime, MGM withdrew from film distribution altogether, auctioned off its vast collection of props, and cut back production to an occasional basis.

Conglomerates were attracted to motion picture companies for several reasons: (1) film stocks were undervalued during the 1960s as a result of erratic earnings records; (2) studios owned strategically located real estate and other valuable assets such as music publishing houses and theaters in foreign countries; and (3) film libraries had the potential of being exploited for cable and pay television as well as for entirely new forms of exhibition by electronic means.

Observers of the industry feared, as the majors became affiliated with conglomerates, that motion pictures would lose their individuality because committees would decide matters of production, or that financiers would become the final arbiters of film content, or that motion picture production might even

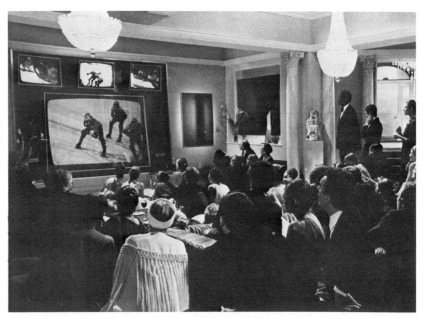

Norman Jewison's futuristic vision of society controlled by multinational conglomerates: *Rollerball* (United Artists, 1975)

be phased out completely if it could not match the profitability of other subsidiaries. So far, these fears have not been realized; on the contrary, conglomerates seem to have exerted a positive influence on the economic stability of their film companies by forcing them to diversify their operations, by providing the financial backing to sustain production programs on a planned basis, and by securing favorable treatment for American films in foreign countries.

The affiliation with conglomerates will explain in large measure why the major companies are still major. David Gordon provides additional evidence (ch. 21), but whether we should "stop worrying and love them," as he suggests, is a matter for the reader to decide.

15

ERNEST BORNEMAN

United States versus Hollywood: The Case Study of an Antitrust Suit

The suit was first filed on July 20, 1938. Thurman Arnold was then in charge of the Department of Justice's Antitrust Division, and his brief, charging the majors with twenty-eight separate offenses, paired the principal objective of theater divorcement with the secondary objective of "abolishing all monopolistic practices in the motion picture industry." He asked for a permanent injunction, the appointment of trustees, and a court order canceling all contracts violating these objectives, while the defendants, on their side, steadily denied the very existence of monopoly. But in March 1939 the distributors, on their own, established a new Trade Practice Code which went some way toward meeting the government's purpose. In August 1939, however, Thurman Arnold ruled the new code illegal. In June 1940 the actual trial began, after thirteen postponements, and ended three days later with an adjournment to permit negotiation between the defendants and the plaintiff. For all practical purposes the case, in this manner, was "settled out of court," for in October of the same year a "consent decree" was published which was, in effect, a compromise, offering minor concessions to the government in exchange for the major concession of leaving theater control in the hands of the "Big Five."

Sight and Sound 19 (February 1951), pp. 418-20+, and (March 1951), pp. 448-50.

The defendants interpreted this temporary consent decree as a permanent approval of their trade practices, and were considerably put out when the government began to negotiate for a new decree. Thurman Arnold had become an appeals judge, and the majors had come to believe that the Justice Department had lost interest in them when, in August 1944, the assistant attorney general, Robert L. Wright, moved for a trial. On October 8, 1945, the trial opened in Foley Square.

For twenty days Robert L. Wright hurled some three hundred documents, secretly and felicitously collected, at the startled galaxy of defendants' counsels. Letters from exhibitors, carbons of contract forms, witnesses' transcriptions, and an FBI investigation of five hundred towns of fewer than 25,000 inhabitants, were included in the plaintiff's prima facie case. Concentrating on "divorcement," the government did not press charges of monopoly, but left them open for a possible appeal to the Supreme Court.

The charges had not changed very greatly during the twenty-five years that had passed since the Federal Trade Commission, in 1921, had filed its first complaint against the predecessors of today's defendants, and the brief filed then might just as well have served Mr. Wright on the day he opened his attack upon the defendants at Foley Square:

On July 22, 1919, the board of directors of Famous Players-Lasky Corporation . . . for the purpose of . . . block-booking, as distinguished from the lease of individual pictures, and for the purpose of intimidating and coercing to lease and exhibit films produced and distributed by Famous Players-Lasky Corporation adopted a . . . policy of building, owning or otherwise controlling theatres, especially . . . first-run theatres in key cities. . . . Therefore it is made difficult for the small and independent producers or distributors of films to enter into or remain in the moving picture industry or market, or to lease individual pictures on merit. . . .

The period to which this 1921 brief referred was known in the industry as "the battle for the theaters," and in many ways it corresponded to that period of England's industrial revolution to which economists now refer as "the enclosure of the commons." The battle was equally fierce. Strong-arm men and purchasing agents sent out by the majors became known among independent exhibitors as the "dynamite gang" and the "wrecking crew." Hundreds of exhibitors who had been in the industry since its infant days were driven out of business by methods which neither side in the battle now cares to remember. In 1920 the few remaining independents began to combine into the first of today's exhibitors' organizations, the Motion Picture Theatre Operators of America. For many a gaudy month the battle seesawed from coast to coast. The exhibitors held their ground as long as they owned it; they lost it when First National, largest of the exhibitors' organizations, was broken by Famous Players-Lasky. They lost it, characteristically, because Zukor bought out the key members of the pool, one after the other, till the whole organization collapsed from the inside. Sam Katz, the head of the Balaban and Katz theater chain in Chicago, who had carried the spearhead of the battle against Famous Players by advocating the transformation of the company into a fully integrated production-distribution-exhibition organization able to compete with Zukor on his own ground, at long last himself joined Famous Players. The battle which had begun as a maneuver for the maximum number of theaters, regardless of location and size, then suddenly began to veer round to a strategy for the acquisition of so-called "first-run" theaters (i.e., theaters large enough and sufficiently well appointed to serve as show cases where new productions could be presented at special prices).

Since the operating costs of large and small theaters do not differ as much as their admission prices, and since the public seemed willing to be grossly overcharged for the right of seeing a new film earlier than their neighbors, the first-run theaters henceforth became the keystones of the majors' theater empire. "Approximately 50 percent of the revenue for a film is derived from first-run showings within six months from the date of the release of the picture," said the Federal Trade Commission in 1921. This rate has not basically altered since.

But the blame for the growing rigidity of the industry did not entirely rest with the majors. The independent exhibitors themselves, with the small businessman's preference for a sure thing, helped to strengthen the majors' monopoly over production by refusing to show pictures made by the independent producers. Since the independent producer, by dint of the majors' distribution monopoly, could not possibly obtain first-run exhibition, he had no chance of obtaining any run at all, and if exhibitors refused to show films which had not had the benefit of first-run exhibition, the whole attempt to produce independently became futile.

In point of fact, this meant that control of the total theater field became vested in the control of a diminutively small number of first-run theaters, and the monopoly vested in the control of the first-run houses allowed the forcing of prices in all other houses, regardless of whether these subsequent-run houses were actually owned by the majors or not.

Control of first-run theaters meant, in effect, control of the screen, and the process of doling out licenses designating this theater as first-run and that as second-, third-, fourth-, or nth-run was the means by which the control over the whole of the motion picture industry was first achieved, and is still maintained. The regional assignment of "runs" became known as "zoning," while the temporal assignment of runs was known as "clearance." These two terms were the hinges upon which the whole argument turned.

During the trial the majors contended that since none of them owned more than a very small fraction of the nation's theaters, they could not be held individually responsible for any monopoly control of the market. Conceding this to be true, the government argued that although none of the defendants owned sufficient theaters to control the market singly, all of them together owned enough first-run theaters to exert a monopoly in conjunction, and that no proof of actual conspiracy had to be provided since, in effect, the very existence of the majors was sufficient to exclude all competition. Collectively, the government claimed, 3,137 theaters, or 70 percent of the nation's first-run market, were controlled by the majors, and 437 of these theaters were being operated under "pooling arrangements"— that is to say, two or more theaters, normally in competition, were being operated as a unit whose policy was controlled by the majors.

Theater pools, operated by renegade independents, had a way of breaking the morale of the exhibitors' united front. Pool operators frequently specified that none of the pool members might acquire other theaters within their area without first offering them for inclusion in the pool. In this way, the pool had a tendency to expand and perpetuate itself, and this expansion was further favored by the pool's willingness to lease any of its theaters to any "independent" exhibitor in return for a share of the profits. Frequently, the mere threat by one of the Big Five, or by one of the big pools, to erect a theater in a given area therefore made it necessary for the independent to buy up the projected theater—and in many cases the terms of purchase made by the distributor or the pool might well contain references to certain concessions which, in effect, might henceforth make the independent exhibitor a part of the distributor's network.

There was no way, short of voluntary surrender to the majors, by which an exhibitor could raise the status of his theater from, say, third- to second-run, or second- to first-run. In October 1938, the NRA, in the draft for a new code embodying a standard license agreement, said: "Only in the motion picture business does the situation exist where individuals of creditable standing, with large investments, are unable to purchase in the open market the products which they desire and need for the conduct of their business." In June 1946, during the trial at Foley Square, a brief submitted, significantly enough, not by the exhibitors but by the Society of Independent Motion Picture Producers, enlarged upon this concept by saying: "In other lines of merchandising, if a store is given an 'exclusive' or a priority on some item, it by no means follows that it also has the same rights to all competitive items produced by other competing manufacturers. (A first-run house is first-run not only for one of the majors, but for all of them.) . . . No other theatre may become first-run by the ordinary competitive technique of paying more for the privilege of a first-run. . . . As in a caste system, a theatre is either born into the aristocracy or not."

If the owner of a second-run house was willing to extend first-run privileges to a picture produced by someone other than one of the majors, he had to be prepared to do without any of the majors' pictures henceforth. In other words, he had to be prepared to go out of business. This, as a matter of fact, could happen for even slighter reasons than cooperation with independent producers or distributors. In December 1939, the firm of South Side Theatres completed a 1,050-seat de luxe house at a cost of $80,000 at Inglewood near Los Angeles. The house was expected to obtain second- or third-run rights and to pay its way with admission prices of 30 or 35 cents, but the distributors were unwilling to grant any but fifth-run rights, which, at an admission price of 15 cents, made it impossible for the owner to make ends meet. So, the house remained closed and store facilities in the same building, which were to be rented to other firms, also remained vacant.

At the trial, when the government recounted cases of this kind to prove that the whole system of assigning "runs" was tantamount to a conspiracy in restraint of trade, the majors replied that the only thing of value which they, as distributors, had to sell was the right to exhibit a picture and that the spatial and temporary exclusiveness of this right was the essence of the thing that was being bargained for. To this, the government replied that it would be perfectly legal for a distributor to sell Theater B a film to be played on a date any given number of days behind Theater A, but that it was illegal for the distributor and Theater A to agree on the number of days before the film would become available to Theater B.

When the "Little Three" companies (those having an integrated production-distribution setup but not active as exhibitors) were trying to dissociate themselves from the "Big Five" during the trial by saying that since they owned no theaters they could not possibly be guilty of conspiracy in the exhibition field, the government replied that they had been guilty of perpetuating the monopoly of the Big Five by favoring the latter's theaters over those operated by independent exhibitors, and that the method used to perpetuate the monopoly had been the offering of more favorable terms of clearance and of smaller blocks of product to the theaters affiliated with the Big Five.

This method of selling product unseen, in advance, and in more or less sizable blocks, had been the exhibitors' second complaint for more than thirty years. At the third session of the Seventy-sixth Congress, during the hearings before the Committee on Interstate Commerce in the House of Representatives, Miss Jeannette Willensky, secretary of the Independent Motion Picture Theatre Owners of Eastern Pennsylvania, explained the exhibitors' view of this process of block booking and blind selling with a degree of blandness never since equaled:

Columbia promises to make a minimum of thirty-two and a maximum of forty . . . the work sheet states that the program will be selected from properties of the company and from additional outstanding stories acquired during the year. First National-Warner Brothers Pictures will make twenty-seven. Only numbers appear on the contracts and work sheets. If you buy from First National, you get numbers 951 to 977. If you buy from Warner Brothers, you get numbers 901 to 927. And the distributor also reserves the right to alter the prices and terms of four pictures, by merely giving a notice to the exhibitor. . . . Fox Pictures will make a maximum of fifty and a minimum of forty. . . . The names of features will be given in the trade journals during the year. . . . R.K.O. will make forty-five pictures, identified only by numbers 601 to 646. No description of the subjects. Universal will make thirty-six pictures, founded on published works. . . .

The designation of play dates by the distributor has always provoked the most bitter opposition among exhibitors. Theater attendance varies from day to day in a fairly regular pattern: Monday, Tuesday, Wednesday, and Thursday each contribute 10 percent of the week's gross; Friday provides 15 percent, Saturday 20 percent, and Sunday 25 percent. If the distributor made a cash deal and specified Monday to Thursday as the days of the week on which the exhibitor was licensed to show the picture, the exhibitor naturally felt bitter. If, on the other hand, the distributor made a percentage deal, and specified Friday to Sunday as play dates, the exhibitor felt rooked for different reasons.

The Department of Justice, in its proposed findings of fact, said on June 22, 1946:

The differentials in admission prices set by a distributor in licensing a particular picture in theatres exhibiting on different runs in the same competitive area are calculated to encourage as many patrons as possible to see the picture in prior-run theatres where they will pay higher prices than on subsequent runs. The reason for this is that if 10,000 people of a city population are ultimately to see the picture—no matter on what run—the gross revenue to be realized from their patronage is increased relatively to the increase in numbers seeing it at higher prices in prior-run theatres. In effect, the distributor, by the fixing of minimum admission prices, attempts to give the prior-run exhibitors as near a monopoly of the patronage as possible.

During the trial the majors held that all these practices, though they might occasionally turn to the disadvantage of an odd exhibitor, were essential to the survival of the industry. To this the government replied that if the faithful application of the Sherman Act would really lead to the ruin of the industry, it would be up to the defendants to petition Congress, as the proper legal body, to grant them the right to maintain a special monopolistic position, but that the Department of Justice was not authorized to alter the Sherman Act so as to keep the defendants in business.

On New Year's Eve, in the midst of tin whistles, paper streamers, and funny hats, the court quietly slipped in its final decree. Most of the press ignored it, and the *Herald Tribune,* one of the few papers to notice it at all, came out with a five-inch boner headlined "Eight Film Companies Cleared of Sherman Law Charges." Six days later, before plaintiff and defendants had found time to study the decision, the whole case threatened to blow up with the compliments of the season. The man who had thrown the fire-cracker into Foley Square was Abram F. Myers, general counsel of two of the independent theater owners' associations, who announced his intention to call upon the House Judiciary Committee with a request to investigate "actions and connections" of one of the judges of the Statutory Court. Alleging that Judge Henry W. Goddard's wife was the owner of a theater leased to two of the defendants, Warner Brothers and Paramount, he asked for investigation of the "lengthy delays in the case agreed to by one of the judges," and the alleged "indulgence" of the same judge toward defense counsel's "delaying tactics."

Immediately the government announced its decision to appeal to the Supreme Court, the defendants announced their intention to take cross-appeals, and the independent theater owners, who probably had more at stake than either of the contending parties but had so far been able only to give gratuitous advice as "friends of the court," now announced their intention to intervene actively by petition to the Supreme Court. Everybody knew, however, that no industrialist had been sent to prison in more than forty-five years for a violation of the antitrust laws, and the degree of un-concern within the industry was most clearly indicated by the almost rock-steady tenor of the majors' stocks. The maximum drop after the announce-ment of the decision was about one-fourth of a point, and the enforcement of the court's judgment was seen as so distant as to leave things pretty much as they were under the consent decree.

As in all previous trials, the government had failed to obtain its main objective—theater divestiture—on which all other measures of relief were ultimately dependent. What it had got was a whole grab bag of odd conces-sions which went just a little beyond the terms of the consent decree but had the strange effect of being more violently attacked by the exhibitors, who were supposed to have been the main beneficiaries, than by the majors, the unwilling benefactors.

Technically, the court held the defendants' claim that they had a legal method of doing business, based on their copyright, to be untrue and the method, as such, to be illegal. The decree, in so many words, declared that the defendants had "unreasonably restrained trade and commerce in the distribution and exhibition of motion pictures and attempted to monopolize such trade and commerce." But in effect, while condemning the method by which the defendants had acquired their theaters, the court allowed them to retain control over them, regardless of whether the process of acquisition had been valid or invalid under the Sherman Act. Moreover, the fact that the court had allowed the defendants a free hand with respect to the theaters they owned, while ordering them to sell films to all other competitors on an auction basis, was immediately attacked not only by the independent exhibitors, but also by those semi-independent theaters and chains of theaters which had in the past reached a working agreement with the majors. Instead of full divorcement of exhibition from distribution and production, the court had thrown out the whole discussion of production monopolies and had offered only limited restrictions upon selected distribution practices. Instead of devising a more effective method of arbitration between distributors and exhibitors, the court had washed its hands of the entire arbitration system. Instead of declaring the whole practice of clearance and zoning invalid, the court had substituted competitive bidding on individual pictures for block booking in groups of five. Instead of making the system of competitive bidding compulsory on a national basis, the court had made it optional by limiting it down to "competitive areas." This was a compromise which pleased no one.

"As far as the relief aspects of the case are concerned, the defendants might as well have written the decision themselves," said the assistant attorney general. The government had defined a monopoly as restriction of trade and had recommended dissolution of the monopoly as "the traditional judicial method used to restore competition in industries dominated by combinations." The court had rejected this definition and had chosen instead to define monopoly as *conspiracy* in restraint of trade. While the government had been concerned with the effect, the court had dealt only with the motive; the result was that the defendants were allowed to maintain control wherever the government had failed to prove that such control had arisen from their "inherent vice," or from their explicit "purpose of creating a monopoly." The court, in fact, went so far as to specify that "ownership by a single defendant of all first-run theatres" was no monopoly if such ownership was the result of the independent exhibitors' "lack of financial ability to build theatres comparable to those of the defendants." This definition knocked hell out of the government's whole argument, for it had been the very lack of this financial ability that had given rise to the complaint of restricted competition. The question of "inherent vice" had never entered the government's case, and was therefore felt to be entirely beside the point.

Following the same line of logic, the court had dismissed the complaint of monopoly against the defendants "based upon their acts as producers." "None of the defendants," the court said bluntly, "has monopolized . . . to restrain trade or commerce in any part of the business of producing motion pictures." In the limited sense in which the court had defined monopoly, this was perfectly true. The government's point, however, was not that the defendants, as producers, had attempted to monopolize the studios, but that their triple function as producers, distributors, and exhibitors had allowed them to prevent independently produced films from obtaining distribution comparable to that of their own. The government had, therefore, petitioned for dissolution of production from distribution, as well as for dissolution of distribution from exhibition. The court, having dismissed the first, had logically to refuse the second.

The independent exhibitors, siding with the government, complained that, although the court appeared to have frozen the defendants' theater holdings, it had in fact allowed them to strengthen their hold upon the theater market. Even the clause calling for the divestment of part-owned theaters was felt to be capable of a second interpretation: if a distributor owned 95 percent or more of a theater he was allowed to maintain control of it, and if he owned less than 95 percent he did not automatically have to divest himself of it either but could, on the contrary, petition the court to acquire the whole of it, by claiming that the acquisition did not "unduly restrain competition." If competition was defined as "financial ability" to build or maintain theaters, and if restraint upon competition was defined as "inherent vice," the distributors might well be expected to succeed in obtaining complete control of the theater market with the approval of the very court which had been called to break that control.

Not only were the independent and semi-independent exhibitors concerned, but the "Little Three," who at the beginning of the trial seemed least concerned with its results, suddenly became extremely disturbed about the provision that permitted the Big Five to retain their theaters, but prohibited the lesser defendants from acquiring or building theaters without court approval.

And even the independent exhibitors who, by the spirit of the decree, were the only ones allowed to acquire new theaters, were dissatisfied because they had been allowed to do so even before this decision. The decision's only result, that they could see, was the sudden inflation in the asking price of theaters available for purchase and of real-estate plots suitable for the erection of new theaters.

As for auctioning each picture individually rather than selling all of them en bloc, the exhibitor's first reaction was fear of rising film rentals. When unlimited block booking had been replaced, under the consent decree, by limited block booking in groups of five, the rentals had gone up so drastically that many of the smaller independents had been driven out of business. Now that the expense of auctioning and trade-showing each picture individually had been made compulsory in competitive areas, the exhibitors, aside from the competitive forcing of prices to be expected, saw themselves faced with the possibility of being continually outbid by the majors' affiliated theaters. Some independent exhibitors foresaw the majors bidding as high as 75 percent per film, even at the risk of taking losses, just to keep control of the theaters in a given area. Other exhibitors who, under the old system, had obtained special privileges due to their long establishment in business, now saw the possibility of their being unable to compete with large theater chains, who were certain to try to buy up all theaters unable to meet the new film rentals.

Even recourse to arbitration was not viewed with too much hope by the independents. Unable to afford legal counsel of the same caliber as the majors, the small exhibitor had learnt, even under the consent decree, to desist from arbitration and be content with whatever the majors cared to offer him, rather than to invite their ill will by entering into legal battles with them.

Nor were the majors themselves entirely happy. Pointing out that the court decision had specifically named only eight companies and their subsidiaries, they asked whether the decision had any bearing at all upon the industry as such: whether it would, if and when it became law, be applicable, for instance, to such smaller distributors as Republic, Monogram, and S.R.O., and whether these companies might not be allowed to beat the majors at their own game by acquiring theaters and developing a system of clearances, franchises, formula deals, and all the other tricks of the trade, while the majors themselves were specifically enjoined from pursuing any and all of these practices.

But the distributors' worst fear, and the main reason for their cross-appeal to the Supreme Court, was the possibility that the decision, if permitted to stand on the government's appeal, would constitute a prima facie case of conspiracy for any independent theater owner who might care to bring private litigation against them. The decree, therefore, did not merely threaten them with a possible loss of income in the distant future, but put them in imminent danger of millions of dollars of damage claims stretching back through the whole period prescribed by the Statutes of Limitation.

Small wonder, then, that the Supreme Court, when it came to rule on the various appeals and cross-appeals, found itself with nothing else to do than to throw out all six key issues of the statutory court's decree—theater divestiture, joint ownership of theaters, franchises, cross-licensing, auction bidding, and arbitration. Most importantly, however, it ruled against the whole principle of defining restraint of trade in terms of *intent* and defined it instead in terms of *effect*.

"It is," said the Court in a ruling specifically addressed to the Griffith Circuit, "not always necessary to find a specific intent to restrain trade or to build a monopoly in order to find that the anti-trust laws have been violated. It is sufficient that a restraint of trade or monopoly results as a consequence of a defendant's conduct or business. . . . So it is that monopoly power, whether lawfully or unlawfully acquired, may itself constitute an evil and stand condemned under Section 2, even though it remains unexercised. . . . We remit to the district court not only that problem but also the fashioning of a decree which will undo as near as may be the wrongs that were done and prevent their recurrence in the future."

This, for the first time in the history of the case, was a decision so clear-cut that two of the defendants did not even bother to wait for the district court to "undo the wrongs that were done" before they decided to compromise and apply for a new consent decree. The other three of the Big Five, however, decided to play for time and launch another series of appeals.

What followed was most instructive. Both groups, of course, now accepted the principle of divestiture, but whereas the three die-hard companies—MGM, Warners, and Twentieth Century-Fox—got little more than an extension till July 1953 to carry out the order of the Court, the two conciliatory companies—RKO and Paramount—succeeded in obtaining a major concession: after splitting themselves in two, the new production-distribution outfit was allowed in due course to reacquire theaters while the new theater-owning company was permitted in due course to produce films again.

This, of course, was a direct violation of the spirit of the Sherman Act and, if it proved anything, it proved once more how easily the purport even of the Supreme Court's decisions could be overruled by the weight of economic pressure; but it had also the farcical result of showing how fast the three diehards could run when they saw a good thing.

Warner Brothers was the first of them to apply for a consent decree of its own. Submitted to the trial court on January 4, 1951, the draft immediately raised a question which was to influence all further divorce argument—the question of who was to run the new companies. Would the three Warner brothers, for instance, be allowed to take charge of the three new production, distribution, and exhibition companies?

The government said "No." Whereupon the three Skouras brothers, who run Twentieth Century-Fox, declared that they would only agree to a consent decree which left them in charge of the three new Twentieth Century companies to be set up.

By then, however, a much more serious problem had crept up which took the whole case back to its economic roots. RKO, which was now ready to implement its consent decree, found itself faced with a demand for immediate repayment of $8,500,000 worth of loans. Why? Because the production-distribution end of RKO had been operating at a loss all through 1950 and had been kept above water only by the profits of the theaters.

A quick look at its books told Warner's creditors that things, though less acute, were hardly satisfactory there either; for whereas the theater-owning wing had earned a fair 62 percent of the company's totals over the last ten years, the production-distribution end had earned a bare 32 percent of the net. Since the consent decree now proposed that all stockholders would receive one half share in each of the new companies in exchange for each share in the old one, the question naturally arose whether the gains of the new theater company would continue to offset the possible losses of the new production-distribution company.

So far for the majors, their creditors, and their stockholders. As for the independent exhibitors, who might have been expected to be pleased now that they had at last obtained what they had asked for, the whole situation had been altered by the advent of television. Rightly, they now feared that the new production-distribution companies, unhampered by any loyalties to their one-time theaters or to any others, would now sell freely to television networks, 16mm users, and other nontheatrical buyers, leaving the theaters with a scarcity of films, an increase in competition, and an inflation of rentals.

From enemies of monopoly, the independents now turned into active monopolists, banding together to exert pressure on distributors not to sell pictures to television networks under threat of losing theater-owning customers. The Justice Department's Antitrust Division, once the theater-owners' best friend, now became their worst enemy when it supported the television networks in their battle against theater pressure. And, to make the paradox complete, the independents now began to clamor for a reunification of the divorced majors so as to give the producer-distributors a new vested interest in theater ownership.

That made just about everyone unhappy. When the Justice Department, the Little Three, the Theater Pools, the Large Independents, the Small Independents, and the Big Five had all had their say, everyone thought that everything had been said that could be said. Then a new voice spoke up. The Internal Revenue Bureau, bland as only tax collectors can be, announced that the winners of treble-damage awards in successful antitrust actions brought by independent exhibitors against major distributors would have to declare their awards as personal profits and pay income tax on them at the top rate of 80 or 90 percent. This meant that if he failed to recover his costs, the exhibitor, after paying his attorney's fees, would probably find himself in the red as a result of seeing justice triumphant.

While the merry haha of the ultimate paradox went echoing down the doric halls of the U.S. Court House, the silent man in the visitors' gallery silently got up and walked out to pay homage. Depositing his two quarters at the box office of his local theater, he became once again the consumer who foots the bill. All through the trial, the defendants contended that all their trade practices had been developed precisely so as to bring the best pictures at the cheapest price to the largest number of consumers, while the plaintiff contended that it had been precisely the public which had been most grievously harmed by the defendants' attempts to force prices and withhold pictures from competitive theaters. Neither plaintiff, nor defendants, nor the court bothered to define what was meant by the "best" pictures. It was notable, however, throughout the trial, that whenever a defendant spoke of a "good" film he was in fact referring to one which had been expensive to produce, or which had grossed well at the box office. In either case, *aesthetic value* or, to use the industry's own vocabulary, *entertainment value* had been identified with an economic category of sorts. If any single incident was required to point up the common failure of all parties concerned in the conflict, it was this failure to see the motion picture as something transcending the terms of economic categories.

For what happened to RKO and Paramount after they had begun to put divorcement measures into effect was far from reassuring. Without certainty of theatrical outlets, their distribution offices now began to exert more pressure than ever on the production staff to turn out "sure things" rather than "prestige items." This meant that whereas in the past there had been occasional scope for experimental films in which the production people could do their best work, divorcement had now removed the margin of certainty which theatrical outlets had once provided. Instead of better films, the public got routine grist from the celluloid mill.

The most salient comment on this situation was made by the *Stanford University Law Review,* which attacked the government's brief, the Supreme Court's ruling, the trial court's decree, and the two consent agreements alike on the simple grounds that a form of divorcement which left production at the mercy of distribution, and distribution at the mercy of vast theater circuits, was worse than no divorce at all.

Urging a separation of production from distribution and a breakup of all chains of theaters, the article termed the present system an "oligopoly" which would continue to monopolize the market by dint of the small number of distributors and their excessive power.

In this connection it is significant that the American Civil Liberties Union filed a motion asking leave to intervene as friend of the court on the ground that "the questions involved . . . are of paramount sociological importance and vitally affect . . . the general public in the attainment of maximum freedom and diversity of expression . . . ," and that this petition was denied by the court on the ground that "the interests of the public are amply represented by the government in this case."

The government's brief admitted that public interest was directly involved, inasmuch as the admission prices of all theaters, whether independent or controlled by the Big Five, were in effect controlled by the trade practices of the Big Five; but the very definition of "public interest" in these terms stood as an indictment of the whole procedure.

16

MICHAEL CONANT

The Impact of the *Paramount* Decrees

The *Paramount* decrees were but one of many causes of the revolutionary changes in the motion picture industry in the postwar period. This study will attempt to isolate the particular effects of the antitrust decrees. To the extent this is impossible, we must estimate what share of any change could have been caused by the decrees, as opposed to that caused by the marked shifts in demand and changes in technology. The first section surveys the divorcement of the five theater circuits from the major producers and the divestiture of individual theaters by the circuits. The remaining five sections analyze the impact of the decrees on independent producers, on the defendants that continued as producers and distributors, on the divorced theater circuits, on independent exhibitors, and on the viewing public.

Progress of Divorcement and Divestiture

The first aspect of disintegration of the nationwide combine was the termination of theater-pooling arrangements in many cities where more than one of the five majors had theaters. This had begun in 1947 following

Abridged by the editor from *Antitrust in the Motion Picture Industry* (Berkeley and Los Angeles, 1960), pp. 107-53.

TABLE 1

Domestic Theaters Controlled before and after Consent Decrees

Company	Theaters controlled 1945 (A)	Date of consent decree (B)	Theaters controlled in year of decree (C)	Successor theater company (D)	Estimated theaters after divestiture (E)	Theaters controlled 1957 (F)
Paramount Pictures, Inc.	1,395	Mar. 3, 1949	1,424	American Broadcasting-Paramount Theaters, Inc.	650	534
Twentieth Century-Fox	636	June 7, 1951	549	National Theatres, Inc.	356	321
Warner Brothers	501	Jan. 4, 1951	436	Stanley Warner Corp.	334	297
Loew's, Inc.	135	Feb. 7, 1952	129	Loew's Theatres, Inc.	112	100
RKO Corporation	109	Nov. 8, 1948	124	RKO Theatres Corp. (re-named List Industries Corp.)	89	82
Joint Ownership	361		—		0	0
Totals	3,137		2,662		1,541	1,334

Sources: *United States* v. *Paramount Pictures*, 334 U.S. 131, Finding of Fact 118; *Moody's Industrials* for years indicated, quoting reports to the Securities and Exchange Commission; *Variety*, June 19, 1957, p. 7; *Wall Street Journal*, December 5, 1957, p. 9.

the district court decree and even before consideration of the case by the Supreme Court. The five majors also agreed to terminate all formula deals and master agreements.

The consent decrees providing for divorcement of theater circuits and divestiture of specific theaters were entered on the dates listed in Table 1. The usual time limit for completion of divorcement and divestiture was two years, but most of the firms asked for additional time to complete their divestitures.

In 1954, Loew's was the last of the five majors to set up an exhibition subsidiary and to transfer all of its domestic theaters to it. Four of the five, RKO, Paramount, Fox, and Warners, had distributed the stock of their new subsidiaries to their shareholders, subject to the special trust requirements. Loew's, with a $30 million debt to divide between the production-distribution firm and the new theater firm, did not complete divorcement until March 1959. The changing relative profitability of the two branches of Loew's impeded negotiations for division of the debt. Disposition of the stock of the divorced circuits, which had been put in trust to prevent control by the previous owners of the production company, also progressed slowly.

In spite of the slow progress of divorcement, the facts seem to support a finding that divorcement has been effective. The production-distribution firms deal at arm's length with their former circuits. This was the conclusion of the Justice Department in 1952.[1] As early as 1951, the Paramount Theatre in New York, after divorcement from Paramount Pictures, began booking outstanding pictures of firms other than Paramount for extended first-run showings. Paramount Pictures executives were angry at

1. U.S. Congress, Senate, Select Committee on Small Business, *Hearings on Motion-Picture Distribution Trade Practices—1953*, 83rd Cong., 1st Sess., 1953, p. 682.

no longer having first rights to the Paramount Theatre screen regardless of the quality of the picture offered. Two legal barriers seemed to operate effectively to bar continued preferential treatment by distributors of their former theaters. First, such preferences would violate the divorcement decrees and could lead to contempt action against both the distributor and the exhibitor circuit. Second, the shares of the four circuits which had completed divorcement were publicly held. The officers and directors of each theater firm had a fiduciary duty to their firm to maximize its profits by booking those films which they honestly thought would accomplish this end. Under this obligation they could not legally give continued preference to their former affiliated distributor regardless of picture quality. To do so would have subjected these officers and directors to a possible shareholders' representative suit in which the corporation might collect from them such profits as were lost through their deliberate mismanagement. Likewise, the officers and directors of the distributor firms had a fiduciary duty to maximize their firms' profits by booking their films into theaters that would earn the most for them. They could no longer legally give preference to formerly affiliated theaters unless they considered them to have the highest potential earning power for a film.

Divestiture of individual theaters by the five major circuits also progressed slowly. Numerous extensions of time to dispose of theaters were granted. By autumn of 1954, two years after the last consent decree had been entered, none of the five circuits had completed its divestitures, and it was not until 1957 that the last divestitures were completed. Declining revenues and the very high cost of remodeling theaters for conversion to other uses impeded their salability. Few people wished to enter the theater business when television was becoming popular and its full impact could not be predicted. Hence the five circuits found it very difficult to sell theaters at what they considered were reasonable prices.

As shown in column E of Table 1, the divorcement decrees were designed to leave the five disaffiliated circuits with approximately one-half the 3,137 theaters they controlled in 1945. By 1957 all five of the circuits had disposed of more theaters than were ordered divested. Declining revenues caused them to close many theaters not specified in the decrees, and similar disposals are still under way. In June 1957, three months after completing its divestitures pursuant to its consent decree, American Broadcasting-Paramount Theaters announced that it had plans to sell another ninety theaters.

Impact on Independent Producers

The antitrust prohibition on all block booking and the divorcement decrees can be regarded as a charter of freedom for the independent producers. There were very few independent producers of first-grade films before World War II. The shortage of personnel caused a drop in output by the majors whereas the wartime boom in attendance lowered the risk of loss on productions. Together these factors made possible the increase of independent producers to forty in 1945. In 1946, the peak income year of the industry, the district court decree prohibiting all block booking went into effect. This ruling made it impossible for the majors to resume their prewar practice of usurping the screen time of independent exhibitors with large numbers of class B pictures tied to their better ones. In 1946 it is estimated that the number of independent producers reached seventy. The *Census of Manufactures* reported one hundred theatrical film-producing companies in 1947.[2] This would include the seven producer-defendants in the *Paramount* case. By 1957 the number of full-time producers operating as independents was estimated at 165.[3] In addition, many independent production firms have been organized solely to make one or two pictures or primarily to make shorter television films; they enter theatrical film production only secondarily and if a special opportunity arises.

During the 1946 boom, the majors were able to fill the screen time of their own first-run theaters with extended runs of their own and each others' first-grade films. With the declining attendance thereafter, extended runs were fewer and shorter, and more pictures were needed. As predicted, the result was a boom in independent production. Divorcement, following the 1948 Supreme Court decision, reinforced the independent trend. Under possible penalty of contempt, the majors were ordered to treat at arm's length even those theaters which had not yet been divorced.

The Production Code Administration, the industry's agency of self-censorship which had been a barrier to the entry of independent producers, found its power of enforcement markedly reduced by the divorcement. The majors had used the PCA to bar the entry of novel pictures of many types. Following divorcement, the control which the major distributors had exercised through ownership of first-run theaters was lost. Pictures such as *The Moon Is Blue, Man With the Golden Arm,* and *I Am a Camera* were successfully produced and distributed although they were denied PCA approval. As a result, in order to preserve at least part of its former powers, the Code was revised in 1956 more nearly to fit its original purported purpose of barring obscenity rather than its monopoly purpose of barring novelty.

The removal by the antitrust decrees of illegal barriers to marketing films gave full effect to the factors motivating independent production. The tax

2. U.S. Bureau of the Census, *Census of Manufactures: 1948,* Vol. II, p. 838.
3. *Motion Picture Herald,* October 5, 1957, p. 11.

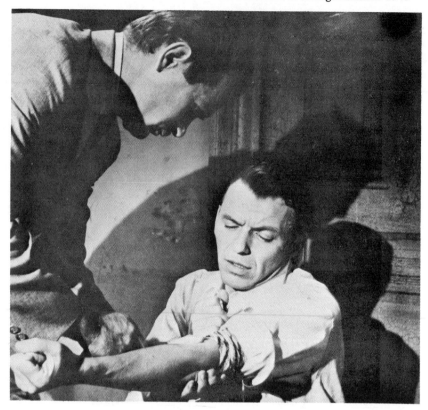

Otto Preminger's *Man With the Golden Arm*, directed by Preminger and starring Frank
Sinatra. Released through United Artists, 1956

savings of independent production were the prime motive for entry. A
producer, director, or film actor in the top personal income tax bracket
could reduce his effective tax rate from 81 percent to 60 percent by
operating his own production company. Under certain conditions, an
interest in a completed picture could be sold as a capital asset, making
profit from such sale subject to a 25 percent capital gains tax. It was not
surprising to find an article in *Variety* headlined, "Look, Ma, I'm a
Corporation."[4] Another reason, perhaps of less importance, for entering
independent production was to secure for the person or group undertaking
a film full and complete freedom of expression, unrestrained by a head

4. *Variety,* March 16, 1955, p. 1.

office. The trite story formulas that had earned money in the 1930s and during the war, which were favored by the New York head offices, were distasteful to those in Hollywood with genuine talent. Many commentators have attributed the improved artistic content of some postwar films to the release of creativity in independent productions. [5]

The effect of the decline in total output of the majors was to create excess capacity in the form of idle studios and underutilized systems of nationwide distribution exchanges. Paradoxically, the very firms that had created the barriers to independent production in the prewar period were by 1950 vying to lease studio space to independent producers and to distribute films for them. By 1951 all of the *Paramount* case defendants except Universal were distributing some independent pictures. The rental charge by a major studio to an independent to make a class A picture varied from $100,000 to $150,000.

Economic facts favored the growth of independent production. Available data indicate that the minimum optimal scale of operations is the production unit organized to produce a single motion picture. Since the production inputs and processes of each picture are unique, the optimum technical unit and the optimum managerial unit both appear to be the production of a single picture. This conclusion is supported by the fact that the major and minor producers organize production for each picture as a semiautonomous unit with a producer in charge. Cost figures for the freer postwar market for motion picture inputs indicate that the flexibility of the independent producer makes for measurably lower costs. [6] Such flexibility is achieved principally by leasing studio space only for the production period of a picture instead of investing in fixed plant and by employing star performers only for individual pictures instead of under long-term contract.

In feature motion picture production, with highly fluctuating supplies of acceptable scenarios and actors, there seem to be substantial diseconomies of large scale. Film company executives characterize this in terms of the problem of reducing studio overhead expense. It must be granted that these costly management structures were created in a period of large monopoly profits. The large firms have not, however, been able to reduce these costs to a level competitive with the leasing costs of independent producers. Consequently, one large firm, Twentieth Century-Fox, has dismantled a major part of its studio and sold the land to a developer. By 1959 two others, RKO and Universal, had sold their entire studios to firms engaged in leasing space to television and feature producers. This is some evidence that studio

5. *Business Week,* November 10, 1951, p. 142.
6. *Variety,* January 5, 1955, p. 10, and April 6, 1955, p. 5.

Hecht-Lancaster's *Marty,* directed by Delbert Mann and starring Ernest Borgnine and Betsy Blair. Released through United Artists, 1955

operation can be more efficiently managed by firms specializing in leasing than ones primarily engaged in feature production.

The cost estimates support the above conclusions. In 1950 the estimated average production (completed negative) costs of films by independent producers were $800,000.[7] Production or negative costs of the major studios were generally higher. Paramount Pictures' costs in 1950 averaged $1,144,000 for 25 pictures produced.[8] For other major studios, with smaller total output, average negative costs were estimated to be as much as $1,800,000.[9] To each of these figures must be added a minimum distribution cost of at least $300,000 per film in order to calculate the minimum rentals required to break even. Distribution cost covers the distributor's fee, print costs, advertisement, and the physical handling of prints.

7. *Business Week,* May 6, 1950, p. 98. Stanley Kramer produced both *Home of the Brave* and *Champion* for total production or negative costs of $938,000. The international prize film of 1954, *Marty,* had negative costs of about $400,000 (*Variety,* April 27, 1955, p. 7).

8. U.S. Congress, Senate, Select Committee on Small Business, *Hearings on Motion-Picture Distribution Trade Practices—1956,* 84th Cong., 2d Sess., 1956, p. 351.

9. *Business Week,* May 6, 1950, p. 98.

These costs on a widely advertised film with expensive color prints might exceed $1,500,000.

It has been asserted that few independents actually are free to decide the film's content and its method of production.[10] Actually, the majority of so-called independents, even since 1950, have had to go to a national distributor for at least part of their equity funds.

For the usual motion picture, 60 percent of the funds can be borrowed from a bank at 6 percent interest in exchange for a first mortgage on the negative. Sometimes second mortgage money of 20 percent is raised by the producer from private sources. Equity funds and completion money usually are supplied by a distributor. Deferment agreements with actors and directors, under which they take a share of the final profits as compensation for their services, are also a source of equity financing.

Leading distributors now favor the rise of the independent producer. Independent production involves less total money commitment by the distributor who underwrites a film than were he to produce it himself. The trend is indicated by the example of Warner Brothers, whose year-end inventories showed advances to independent producers of $1,643,388 in 1946 and $25,093,990 in 1956.[11]

The growing significance of independent producers in the industry is

TABLE 2

Estimated Total Productions Completed Twelve Months Ending
October 1, 1957, Directly and Independently Produced

Distribution company to release production	(1) Produced by distributor	(2) Independently produced	(3 = 1 + 2) Total to be released
Allied Artists	19	22	41
American International	11	3	14
Buena Vista (Disney)	5	2	7
Columbia	18	42	60
Loew's	19	17	36
Paramount	10	9	19
RKO	13	6	19
Republic	7	22	29
Twentieth Century-Fox	17	25	42
United Artists	0	50	50
Universal-International	36	0	36
Warner Brothers	8	21	29
Totals	163	219	382

Source: *Motion Picture Herald,* October 5, 1957, p. 11.

10. *Variety,* September 22, 1954, p. 5.
11. Warner Brothers Pictures, Inc., *Annual Reports,* 1946 and 1956.

further demonstrated by their share of total productions. In 1949, independents produced an estimated 20 percent of the 234 films released by the eight *Paramount* case defendants.[12] Almost half or twenty-one of the independent productions were released by United Artists, which has no production of its own. In the year ending October 1, 1957, as shown in Table 2, 291 productions were completed for release by the eight former *Paramount* defendants. Of these, 170 or 58 percent were produced by independents, fifty were produced for United Artists. The other 120 were produced by independents for the seven former *Paramount* defendants who themselves also produced films, and these 120 constituted 50 percent of their releases. This compares with an estimated 10 to 12 percent released by those seven in 1949. Of all productions completed in the 1957 year for release by the twelve distributors listed in Table 2, 57 percent were produced by independents.

Impact on *Paramount* Defendants: Producers and Distributors

Distribution Structure and Market Shares

The only complete data available indicate that 97 percent of total domestic film rentals in 1954 were collected by the ten distributors with nationwide systems of film exchanges, approximately the same proportion as in 1943-44.[13] These included the eight *Paramount* defendants, Allied Artists Pictures Corporation, and Republic Pictures Corporation. A number of reasons explain why so few new distributors entered following the end of the exhibition combine that had bottlenecked the final market before divorcement. The drop in output by the existing producer-distributors, as compared with that of the prewar period, was not offset by the increase in independent productions. Consequently, the distributors already in the market increased their rivalry to acquire independent pictures for distribution. This factor, in addition to rising distribution costs, tended to reduce, and in some cases wipe out, profits in distribution. Such market conditions were not conducive to the entry of new firms.

The minimum optimal scale of plant for distribution of motion pictures seems to be a nationwide marketing organization with a system of local sales offices. Duplicating the same marketing functions in twenty to thirty major centers can best be planned on a national basis. Scheduling of the movement of prints and coordination of local with national advertising are

12. *Business Week,* May 6, 1950, p. 98.
13. *1956 Hearings,* p. 303, assembled by Price Waterhouse and Co. from data submitted by the distributors; U.S. Bureau of the Census, *Census of Business: 1954,* Selected Services, Motion Pictures, p. 20; Paramount Finding 148 (d).

done best by a national distributor. Comparative cost data and a discussion of the control problem are presented by Professor Lewis.[14] Since a national distributor can fully utilize its plant and sales force only if it markets thirty to forty pictures a year and since the total market will absorb less than four hundred pictures a year at prices covering costs, it is not surprising to find only ten national distributors.

The system of most of the distributors of thirty-two local exchanges carrying out both the selling and physical handling of prints has nevertheless been found inefficient. A 1957 study reported that six companies—Paramount, Fox, Loew's, Warners, Columbia, and Universal—paid $34 million in 1956 or 14 percent of domestic rentals for exchange operations, not including home-office distribution expenses and advertising. The report suggested that the physical handling of prints of all firms should be consolidated. National distributors favored the type of marketing organization adopted by Buena Vista, the Disney subsidiary. This firm employed National Film Service for the physical distribution of prints. Buena Vista was merely a sales organization of eight district offices and fifteen subbranches. Each subbranch had one salesman and an assistant. It was estimated that selling costs were 12 percent of gross rentals, and total costs of distribution to Disney were less than 25 percent of gross rentals, as compared to 30 percent or more in other firms.[15]

Revenues

The ten national film distributors[16] as a group recorded a drop in domestic film rentals of only 9.9 percent from 1947 to 1955. This was in contrast to total theater admission revenues, which dropped 19.3 percent in the same period. The average rental income per feature for the ten firms in 1955 was approximately the same as in 1947. By 1954 most of the leading producer-distributors had adopted a policy of fewer, more expensive films. The 268 features released by the ten distributors in 1955 were 7.6 percent below the 290 released in 1947.

Domestic rental income of the individual firms was not so constant as that of the group. The figures illustrate the great uncertainties of the industry, the unpredictable results of story choice, production technique, and public taste. The available data show a drop in domestic film revenues for RKO Pictures from $41.9 million in 1945 to $18.2 million in 1954, or 56.6 percent. Paramount was able to maintain its domestic rentals above $50 million in most of the postwar years but registered a marked drop to $38 million in 1956. Available figures indicate that Warner Brothers'

14. Howard T. Lewis, *The Motion Picture Industry* (New York, 1933), pp. 12-16.

15. *Variety*, May 4, 1955, p. 3, and October 17, 1956, p. 7.

16. The eight *Paramount* defendants plus Allied Artists Pictures Corporation and Republic Pictures Corporation.

domestic rentals have increased slightly as compared with those of the period 1946 to 1950. Twentieth Century-Fox increased domestic rentals from $54 million in 1945 to $60 million in 1956.

Output

Although rental income data are on a fiscal year basis, they can be compared roughly to the calendar data on films released by the firms. The previous level of releases by the eight largest distributors of more than 350 a year has not been reached since wartime shortages of personnel and film curtailed output in 1943. The five majors, having disposed of their theater circuits and thereby losing their illegal system of interfirm preferential screen access, showed the greatest postwar drop in releases. These five firms released 116 pictures in 1956 as compared with 243 in 1940, a drop of 52 percent. The eight firms as a group showed only a 34 percent drop in total releases from 1940 to 1956 because the increased number of releases by United Artists offset the drop by Columbia and Universal.

The overall drop in output was based upon a combination of factors. In the immediate postwar years, attendance was so high that the majors

TABLE 3
Number of Productions and Average Production (Negative) Costs
of Two Major Firms (1945-1955)

	Paramount Pictures Corp.		Twentieth Century-Fox Film Corp.	
Year	Features produced	Average negative cost per picture (thousands of dollars)	Features produced	Average negative cost per picture (thousands of dollars)
1945	25	$1,065	24	$1,389
1946	23	1,512	24	1,416.8
1947	22	1,307	18	2,328.6
1948	21	1,343	21	1,869.7
1949	20	1,428	24	1,787.7
1950	25	1,144	28	1,634
1951	25	1,485	33	1,370
1952	21	1,337	33	1,298
1953	18	1,605	32	1,422
1954	17	1,949	14[a]	2,286
1955	10[b]	2,195	19[a]	1,989

Sources: Annual Reports of the Firms and U.S. Senate, Select Committee on Small Business, *Motion-Picture Distribution Trade Practices—1956,* p. 351.

[a] Cost data are available only on the CinemaScope productions. In 1954, a total of 22 studio-produced features were released and in 1955, a total of 21 studio-produced features were released.

[b] Excluding *War and Peace,* produced in Italy at a cost of approximately $5 million, and excluding *The Ten Commandments,* produced at a cost of approximately $12.5 million.

exhibited their films on extended runs in their own and each others' first-run theaters. There was no need to increase output to fill screen time in order to deny first-run screen access to the minor distributors. The 1946 prohibition on block booking meant that low-cost class B pictures could no longer be forced on independent theaters, and hence the market for them was sharply curtailed. In 1947, as the public became more particular in its choice of films, the revenue from middle-budget pictures declined most, in some cases as much as 40 percent. Beginning in 1950, declining theater attendance due partly to the increased rivalry of television meant that each picture was allotted shorter screen time by exhibitors. The demand for more pictures was followed by the five majors' increasing releases from 132 in 1949 to 172 in 1951. This was in part an attempt by the majors to spread studio and distribution overhead costs over a larger number of films and thus to lower average total costs. The attempt was a failure.

Costs

In addition to a sharply declining demand, motion picture production was also characterized by increasing costs. This, of course, increased the potential loss on any one picture and consequently increased market uncertainties. Average cost data are collected in Table 3. For major firms such as Paramount and Twentieth Century-Fox, negative or production costs reached an all-time high in 1946 and 1947. In those years both income and taxes were very high. As a result money was spent lavishly and recklessly for production. By 1950, demand and profits had dropped sharply, and cost reduction became essential to prevent net losses. Paramount cut studio overhead from 32 percent of total cost in 1948 to 27 percent in 1950.[17] In 1951, Twentieth Century-Fox reduced 130 top executive salaries from 25 to 50 percent.[18] Loew's did likewise in 1952.[19] Paramount's average negative cost dropped from $1,512,000 in 1946 to $1,144,000 in 1950. Twentieth Century-Fox's average negative cost dropped from $2,328,600 in 1947 to a low of $1,298,000 in 1952. By 1954 more films were being made in color, and new wide-screen production techniques made for increased costs. In 1955 Paramount's average negative cost was $2,195,000, and Twentieth Century-Fox's was $1,989,000. Loew's subsidiary, MGM, reported an average negative cost per picture for eighteen pictures produced in 1956 of $1,926,000.[20]

17. *Variety,* January 4, 1950, p. 23.
18. *Variety,* May 16, 1951, p. 3.
19. Bosley Crowther, *The Lion's Share: The Story of an Entertainment Empire* (New York, 1957), p. 303.
20. *Motion Picture Herald,* April 6, 1957, p. 14.

Rentals of the Minor Distributors

Much of the striking increase in domestic rentals by the three minor defendants must be attributed to the antitrust prohibition on block booking and to the divorcement decrees. Columbia Pictures Corporation's domestic rentals increased 39 percent from 1946 to 1954. United Artists Corporation's domestic rentals in 1957 increased 80 percent as compared with 1945. Universal Pictures Corporation's domestic rentals in 1957 were 38

Stanley Kramer's *High Noon,* directed by Fred Zinnemann and starring Gary Cooper and Grace Kelly. Released through United Artists, 1952

percent above 1945. The antitrust prohibition on all block booking in 1946 gave the three minor distributors equal access with the five majors to nonaffiliated theaters. The decline in total picture output meant that even the affiliated theaters needed more first-grade films than the five majors could supply. These three minor distributors, a large part of whose films were relegated to the bottom half of a double feature program before 1946, found themselves able to bid for screen time in first-run theaters as equals of the five majors. United Artists, always having specialized only in distribution for independent producers, was able to induce many of the new independent producers to distribute through it after it secured open competitive access to the first-run screens of former affiliated theaters. Columbia and Universal, although they continued to make low-cost westerns and class B films with unknown actors, greatly expanded their production of high-grade, first-class films. Following divorcement Columbia was able to market such very successful first-grade films as *From Here to Eternity* and *The Caine Mutiny.* United Artists distributed the profitable films *High Noon, Not as a Stranger, Marty, Alexander the Great,* and *Trapeze;* and Universal had successes with *The Glenn Miller Story* and *Magnificent Obsession.*

Allied Artists Pictures Corporation, formerly named Monogram, and Republic Pictures Corporation were also able to expand production into first-grade, more costly films after the *Paramount* decrees opened the first-run market to them. Allied Artists' domestic rental revenues of $13,854,000 in 1956 were 254 [*sic*] percent of its 1945 rentals of $3,910,000. In 1956 Allied Artists ventured to produce its first picture with more than $1 million negative or production costs. This was *Friendly Persuasion,* with negative costs of about $3 million. Republic Pictures Corporation showed an increase in domestic film rentals in fiscal 1947 of 17.5 percent over 1946, the year block booking ended.[21] This should be compared with the five majors, of whom three showed decreases and two, increases of less than 10 percent in fiscal 1947 as compared with fiscal 1946. Although exact figures on Republic's domestic rentals are unavailable, it is noted that its total revenues increased from $24 million in 1946 to $42 million in 1956, an increase of 75 percent.

Profits

The profits of the five major producer-distributors indicate that they adjusted well to divorcement and the injunctions of the *Paramount* decrees, but that they have suffered from the rivalry of television. Profits,

21. Republic Pictures Corporation, *Annual Report, 1947.* Republic Pictures Corporation discontinued production and distribution of feature pictures in mid-1958.

as measured by the ratio of net income to shareholders' investment, averaged over 10 percent during World War II for all firms except Warner Brothers. They reached a peak in 1946, ranging from 13 percent for Loew's to 29 percent for Paramount. Thereafter, profits declined. However, compared with prewar 1937 through 1941, the years following divorcement show comparable earnings ratios. As the major firms completed divorcement, the costs of litigation and corporate reorganization reduced earnings in the year of divorcement or the preceding year. Nevertheless, three of them, Paramount, Twentieth Century-Fox, and Warner Brothers, showed strong recoveries, earning 12.7, 9.7, and 9.7 percent, respectively, in 1954 on shareholders' investment.

Two minor distributors, Columbia and Universal, both had sharply rising earnings on net worth as their gross revenues increased in 1954 and 1955. Columbia distributed a number of successful independent productions. Universal expanded its own production of higher-grade pictures. In 1955, Columbia's net income reached 13.6 percent of net worth and Universal's, 12.6 percent. United Artists Corporation became a listed corporation in 1957. At the end of its 1957 fiscal year, its ratio of net income to net worth was 21.4 percent.

Income data indicate that in the period before divorcement considerably less than one-half of earnings before taxes were derived from production-distribution and such minor subsidiaries as music publishing which were attached to it. In the case of RKO, the production-distribution branch was a consistent money-loser except for the four boom years of the war and 1951. One reason for these low profits in production-distribution before divorcement was that monopoly power in the industry was concentrated in the five major theater circuits. Their monopsonistic power in

TABLE 4

Total Assets in Production-Distribution and in Theaters
of Five Major Firms in Years of Divorcement

Name of firm	Date divorcement executed	Production-distribution assets	Theater assets
Loew's, Inc. (MGM)	Mar. 12, 1959	$142,873,000	$82,701,000
Paramount Pictures, Inc.	Dec. 31, 1949	108,972,405	84,222,039
RKO Corp.	Dec. 31, 1950	54,259,508	50,086,482
Twentieth Century-Fox Film Corp.	Sept. 27, 1952	108,103,664	59,244,736
Warner Brothers	Feb. 28, 1953	61,506,812	81,178,319

Source: Annual Reports and Prospecti of the firms as submitted to the Securities and Exchange Commission and reported in *Moody's Industrials*.

dealing with the distributors enabled the five circuits to siphon off the largest share of profits in the industry. The total assets invested by the five firms in the production-distribution sector as opposed to exhibition are relevant here. These data are available only for the year of divorcement in each case. As tabulated in Table 4, four of the five firms had greater total investment in production-distribution and minor subsidiaries than in exhibition. Warner Brothers alone had $81 million invested in the theater branch as compared with $61.5 million in production-distribution. Under competitive market conditions, we would expect larger total income by the production-distribution branch than the theater branch in all firms except Warner Brothers. However, there were much greater uncertainties in film production than in exhibition, and particularly in the large circuits which could choose to license only successful films. This would lead us to expect even higher earnings in production, for that branch should have been able to charge large uncertainty premiums for its product. Finally, the copyright of the producer was a government grant of monopoly which should also have enabled him to increase his rentals and earnings. All these factors favoring higher earnings in production-distribution were offset by the contrived monopolies in exhibition.

After divorcement, market power relationships changed. The 1954 and 1955 earning ratios in Paramount, Twentieth Century-Fox, Warner Brothers, Columbia, and Universal tend to support this. In spite of television, these firms which no longer had to face such formidable theater monopolies, earned from 7 to 13 percent on shareholders' investment. The distributors' monopoly power inherent in film copyrights and in the popularity of particular films and actors could be more fully exploited. Many films were licensed at rentals of 70 percent of gross admissions but guaranteed the exhibitor a 10 percent profit after expenses. However, in 1956 and 1957, with the release of pre-1948 pictures to television by all firms except Universal and Paramount, theater attendance took another sharp drop. Distributors' revenues dropped accordingly in many cases and profits also dropped.

Other Factors Increasing Revenues

At least three main factors in addition to the freedom from theater monopolies have increased revenues and earnings in the production-distribution firms. The first of these is the increased significance of the foreign market. Foreign rentals accounted for from 25 to 30 percent of total revenues of the distributors before World War II. Data on seven of the eight *Paramount* defendants (except Loew's whose separated figures are unavailable) show that foreign rentals reached 36 percent of the total in 1946, dropped to 33 percent in 1950, and increased to 42 percent in 1954.[22] Blocked funds also were one factor causing U.S. producers to make pictures in foreign countries. Lower labor costs for production workers also encouraged foreign production. In addition to their foreign rentals, three of the majors received income from foreign theater chains retained after divorcement. The sale or lease of pre-1949 features to television stations has been a large source of income to distributors since 1956. By February 1958, an estimated 3,700 such features had been sold or leased for television for an estimated $220 million.[23]

The final new sources of income were producing pictures specifically for television and leasing studio space to independent producers making films for television. In 1956, it was estimated that about 170 small producers were making half-hour, hour, and ninety-minute films.[24] Their output exceeded the number of feature pictures produced for theatrical distribution. Output of television films of an hour or more in length was expected to exceed two hundred in 1956. By 1957 Warner Brothers, Twentieth Century-Fox, and Loew's, Inc., all had television pictures in production. Paramount was reported to have leased studio space to independent producers. Universal entered the production of television commercials through its subsidiary, United World Films, Inc. In addition to releasing old features, Columbia Pictures' subsidiary, Screen Gems, was reported to be releasing films produced for television.

Impact on Divorced Theater Circuits

Revenue and income data for the five circuits that have been divorced from their former distributing parent indicate that they have been able to adjust to divorcement and the rivalry of television better than most independent theaters. The continued financial success of the divorced circuits can be more logically traced to their ownership of large first-run theaters whose revenues have dropped least and to selective divestiture of those theaters that were showing consistent losses. In most cities where individual theaters were ordered divested, the defendants were allowed to choose which one or ones of a number of theaters they would sell. The defendants retained only the best of their theaters, those whose revenues diminished least since the rise of television. Thus, average annual receipts per theater for National Theatres, Inc., increased from $120,000 in 1950 to $173,000

22. *United States* v. *Twentieth Century-Fox Film Corporation,* 137 F. Supp. 78 (S. D. Calif., 1955), Exhibit AR, and Annual Reports of the film companies.

23. *Motion Picture Herald,* January 19, 1958, p. 13; *Wall Street Journal,* February 10, 1958, p. 3; *Variety,* February 5, 1958, p. 5.

24. *Committee Report based on 1956 Hearings,* p. 37.

in 1956. United Paramount was forced to end its joint ownerships, many of which were in smaller towns or subsequent-run city theaters. As a result, United Paramount's average annual receipts per theater increased from $63,000 in 1949 to $166,000 in 1956. RKO had mainly larger houses in the New York City area. Its average annual receipts per theater increased only from $333,000 in 1949 to $383,000 in 1956. Available figures show that Stanley Warner Theatres' average annual receipts per theater dropped from $183,000 in 1948 to $153,000 in 1953. Loew's has published figures for 1957. They indicate that for 103 theaters, mainly in the New York area (except three in Canada), average annual receipts per theater were $335,000.[25] In retrospect, it would seem that the major theater circuits, by being forced to sell their weaker houses, gained more from their divestitures than they lost.

Following completion of their theater divestitures, the divorced circuits, since 1956, have been allowed to expand in the motion picture field upon special petition to the trial court. Loew's Theatres has purchased a number of drive-in theaters and at least one conventional theater. American Broadcasting-Paramount Theatres petitioned the court for permission to acquire the Mercury Theatre in Chicago. Most of these acquisitions were made without opposition by the Department of Justice, which felt they would not impair competition. Such conclusions are highly debatable, even if there seems to be substantial rivalry in the particular exhibition market of the acquired theater. The buying power of large circuits in dealing with distributors remains a crucial issue in spite of divorcement and some individual divestitures. Does not the bargaining power of the entire circuit (one hundred theaters of Loew's or five hundred of American Broadcasting-Paramount Theatres) stand behind the booking for each of its theaters?

One divorced circuit expanded into motion picture production, and another has petitioned the court for permission to do so. The RKO and Paramount Pictures divorcement decrees did not prohibit production by the divorced circuit. In 1956, American Broadcasting-Paramount Theatres organized AB-PT Pictures Corporation. The firm released four productions in 1957 and engaged Republic Pictures Corporation to distribute its productions. National Theatres, Inc., which was prohibited by its divorcement decree from entering production, petitioned the court for relief from this provision, so that it could produce films. Even before this, Theatre Owners of America, trade association of the larger circuits, had urged the Department of Justice to permit the three circuits prohibited by the decree to enter production. This was all part of an effort to increase the

25. Loew's, Inc., *Annual Report,* 1957.

supply of films. Many exhibitors were willing to contend with the preferential treatment of the circuits' own theaters, if the severe film shortage would be only slightly relieved. Such preferential treatment would exist only in the area where the circuit now operated, whereas before 1946 there was nationwide preference for all five major circuits. There are strong arguments against permitting this reintegration. It may bring additional resources into production, but it is equally possible that existing active production facilities will, instead, be channeled toward a circuit for purposes of serving its preemptive screen rights. Given the continued great size of first-run theater circuits, this could reverse much of what was accomplished by divorcement. Since only a minority of total films receive wide public acceptance and make large profits, it is essential that no local theater monopolies be able to claim even a few of these without having to bid in the market for them.

Impact on Independent Exhibitors

Gains

Independent exhibitors have registered some measurable gains from the divorcement decrees. The end of block booking has given them freedom to license pictures singly and reject poor ones. Many exhibitors, however, found negotiating for each picture individually too time-consuming and preferred to buy films in groups. The breakup of the national combine and the divorcement have together ended the possibility of an exhibitor being forced to sell a one-half interest or possibly his entire theater to the dominant theater circuit in his area. Distributor control of admission prices in film license contracts has been terminated, but the possibility of having one's theater shifted back to a later run is probably a powerful deterrent to aggressive price rivalry by exhibitors. Theaters which previously were assigned to late runs with low admission prices now are free to raise their prices and fully exploit their neighborhood monopoly power.

The continuing jurisdiction of the district court over the trade practices of the defendants, the private treble-damage actions, and threats of such actions have resulted in distributors moving an estimated 20 percent of all theaters to earlier runs and an even greater proportion of shortened clearances.[26] In order to avoid or settle antitrust actions, distributors have attempted in most metropolitan areas to give indoor theaters of comparable size and location an equal opportunity to bargain for films.

In many cities, monopolization of the first two or three runs by an affiliated circuit had been the rule. This traditional pattern of first-run

26. *1956 Hearings,* p. 455.

exhibition in one large, centrally situated (downtown) theater followed by two or three second runs (first neighborhood runs) all in affiliated theaters, was broken down. Many independently owned large, downtown theaters which had previously been relegated to second run became free to bid for exclusive first-run exhibition. Distributors, since circuit bargain-

Mirisch Corporation's *West Side Story*, directed by Robert Wise and Jerome Robbins: George Chakiris. Released through United Artists, 1960

ing ceased to control entire exhibition marketing patterns, have experimented in a few cities with multiple first runs. Successes in such "day and date" first-run booking were reported in New York, Chicago, Pittsburgh, Los Angeles, and Milwaukee.[27]

An even greater number of large neighborhood theaters, which under the prior market regimentation had been relegated to third or later runs, became free to bid for film on first neighborhood run. In Chicago, these runs increased to forty-three following divorcement. Whether so many theaters in early runs increased or decreased total admission grosses on films was indeterminable.

Distributors have resisted movement of some theaters to earlier runs, even though they have raised their admission prices. An optimum pattern of admission and rental price discrimination in most areas still requires one first-run exhibition of a picture and a limited number of second runs. Distributors have refused to allow theaters to move into these early runs where the effect would be to disrupt radically the pattern of rental discrimination. New large neighborhood theaters in at least two areas were denied the opportunity to bid for first-run films by all the leading distributors. In one celebrated case, the eight largest distributors were found to have acted in concert in refusing to allow a large drive-in theater to bid for film on first run. In another case in the same area, five distributors were found to have conspired in assigning a drive-in theater to unreasonably long clearance after first run.[28]

Those independent exhibitors who had foresight enough to recognize the market significance of the rise of the drive-in theater and had access to sufficient capital built drive-ins. The number of active drive-ins rose from 300 at the end of 1946 to 4,500 at the end of 1956, as four-wall theaters declined from 18,719 to 14,509. The 1967 *Census of Business* reported only 12,187 total theaters in the United States, of which 11,478 had payroll. Of these, 8,094 were four-wall theaters and 3,384 were drive-ins.

Because of their size and drawing power, large numbers of drive-ins have been able to bid for the first neighborhood run (second run) access to film, thereby increasing still more the number of theaters moving into that run since the *Paramount* decision. Distributors have resisted attempts by drive-ins to bid for first-run films because conventional neighborhood theaters will refuse to take those films on later runs. However, in at least

27. *Variety,* April 25, 1951, p. 5; May 14, 1952, p. 5; May 11, 1955, p. 25; and January 16, 1957, p. 7; *Motion Picture Herald,* September 28, 1957, p. 11.

28. *Basle Theatres, Inc.* v. *Warner Brothers Pictures Dist. Corp.,* 168 F. Supp. 553 (W. D. Pa., 1959).

one case, this argument was held an inadequate defense to a charge of implied conspiracy.[29]

Losses

A large group of the small theaters in the country, perhaps a majority, have suffered relative losses owing to the combined impact of the antitrust decrees, television, and the advent of the drive-in. One 1956 survey indicated the net results of industry changes on the theaters.[30] It estimated that 5,200 or 27.1 percent of all theaters were operating at a loss; 5,700 theaters or 29.6 percent of the total were operating at the break-even point. With more than half of U.S. theaters unable to earn profits, it was estimated that on a consolidated basis, all U.S. theaters were showing a net loss of $11.8 million.

The antitrust decrees were responsible only to a negligible degree for the demise of more than 4,000 exhibitors and the sharp income drops suffered by many others. Fewer patrons remained for the small theaters because of the greater market saturation on first and second run, as larger independent and circuit theaters moved up to those earlier runs. A freer exhibition market with fewer total runs has meant a more intense rivalry for the admission dollar. Perhaps there were too many theaters for a free market, and the small later-run theaters were being protected under the prior regimented market from the free competition that would have wiped them out. This is speculative and not measurable. It is probable that most of the smaller theaters would have survived the increased industry rivalry had not television and drive-ins appeared.

Divorcement of circuits and the prohibition on block booking have been blamed for the decreased output of films that exhibitors contend is one reason for their losses. The argument is that if the majors were still integrated they would have to produce sufficient films for their own theaters, and compulsory block booking would guarantee them a market in independent theaters. Only under those conditions, argue the smaller later-run exhibitors who used to change the bill three times a week, would there be sufficient films. What these exhibitors fail to realize is that the product shortage exists because television wiped out the demand for class

29. *Milgram* v. *Loew's, Inc.*, 192 F. 2d 579 (C.A. 3, 1951) (2-1 decision), cert. denied, 343 U.S. 929 (1952).

30. In 1948, theaters and drive-ins (allowing 2.5 persons per car) had about 12.5 million seats; in 1954, they had about 10.6 million. Census reports for 1954 showed 13,760 indoor theaters and 3,611 drive-ins, a total of 17,371, as compared to 19,101 estimated by the *Film Daily Year Book.* See U.S. Bureau of the Census, *Census of Business: 1954,* Vol. V, p. 8-12.

B and middle-budget pictures. The theaters that formerly screened some of the second-class films would be in an even worse position if distributors were still allowed to force these films upon them by block booking. Actually, exhibitors prize their present freedom to buy or to reject each picture singly. Even with the reduced supply in the 1954-55 season, Loew's reported that nearly one-half of the nation's exhibitors chose not to license pictures which Loew's classed among its best and most costly.[31]

The reduced supply of pictures has also made for increased prices. Mr. Trueman Rembusch of the Allied States Association of Motion Picture Exhibitors argued that the increase was from 32.5 percent of gross admissions in 1947 to 36 percent in 1955. The distributors argued that the rise was from 26 percent in 1947 to 34 percent in 1953 and a drop to 28 percent in 1955. Exhibitors complain of the 50 to 70 percent of admission grosses as the rental basis for popular pictures.[32] However, a theater which fails to screen pictures which have developed great popular appeal is in danger of losing its regular patrons and suffering permanent damage to its reputation.

Distributors argue that increased rentals are not the cause of failure of small theaters. Y. Frank Freeman, vice-president of Paramount Pictures Corp., stated that Paramount's 7,000 smallest accounts paid an average rental per film of less than $25.[33] Louis Phillips, general counsel of Paramount, stated that 5,500 exhibitors paid Paramount from $12.50 to $50 for a two- or three-day engagement of its best films.[34] These low rentals are a small proportion of a theater's total costs. Hence it is argued that dropping admissions are the prime cause of theater losses, and that in many cases theaters would fail even if films were given to them rental-free.

Competitive bidding for films has tended to increase rentals in some areas. Since the Supreme Court decision in the *Paramount* case rejected bidding as a method of film allocation, distributors institute it only where two exhibitors demand a picture on the same run and the distributor wishes only one theater to screen it on that run. It is estimated that in 1956, competitive bidding was used in from 400 to 750 situations, varying with individual companies, which involve from 1,000 to more than 2,000 theaters. Exhibitors complained that secret, sealed bids stated as flat amounts, a percentage of gross receipts, or a guaranteed minimum against a percentage of gross receipts made bidding unworkable and caused them to bid too high. With secret, noncomparable bids, distributors could award the pictures to whom they chose. To limit such arbitrary

31. *1956 Hearings,* pp. 365-67; see *1953 Hearings,* p. 138.
32. *1953 Hearings,* pp. 25, 59, 171, 178, 362, 452, 488, 491.
33. *1956 Hearings,* p. 355.
34. *1956 Hearings,* p. 434.

power, some effort has been made to require disclosure of bids. On the other side, some distributors reported that they suspected collusion among exhibitors in film bidding.

The final complaint of exhibitors has been that distributors have continued illegal resale price maintenance by indirectly forcing theaters to keep high admission prices. Since price cutting on early runs will upset the pattern necessary for successful price discrimination, distributors have searched for a method of circumventing the injunction against fixing admission prices. They do this not by demanding, but by suggesting appropriate admission prices. In bidding for prereleases and early runs, distributors insist that exhibitors state in their bids the admission prices they will charge. They say that the purpose of this is only to estimate the expected gross on a percentage bid. However, bids are awarded only to theaters which will raise admission prices to the suggested amount. The Antitrust Division apparently found such indirect methods of illegal resale price maintenance excusable.

It would seem that the antitrust decrees have been at most a minor factor in the postwar ills of independent exhibitors. Television and drive-ins have taken a large share of the anticipated theater business. A freer market in the licensing of pictures has enabled larger independent exhibitors in most cases to compete for films on an equal basis with the large circuit theaters. The end of market regimentation in favor of the circuits has undoubtedly enabled many independent exhibitors to survive the declining demand.

Impact on the Public

The ambiguous, unmeasurable injunction against unreasonable clearance and the subsequent private treble-damage actions by independent exhibitors have lessened the degree of temporal price discrimination in motion picture rentals and admissions. At the same time, the rivalry of television and of drive-in theaters has led to the closing of more than 5,000 smaller theaters. These were some of the most conveniently situated neighborhood theaters and most of those with the lowest admissions, the ones that the poorest group in the economy were able to attend. It is quite probable that such lessened price discrimination does not increase society's welfare. As part of these changes, there has been a drop in film output, and first- and second-run admissions have been raised even more than could be attributed to the general inflation. The Bureau of Labor Statistics motion picture admission-price index (1947-1949 = 100) for the year 1958 was 135.7. That for all reading and recreation, of which motion pictures is a part, was only 116.7 in 1958, and the total consumer price index was 123.5.

Are the fewer films, higher admissions, greater inconvenience, and fewer runs in which to see a picture offset by the increased quality of motion pictures? Many of the film critics maintain that there are more pictures of what they consider high quality than were produced in the pre-prosecution period. Much of this change is attributed to the freer entry of independent producers into the market which resulted from the *Paramount* decrees. Since the decreased output and shorter release patterns are only partly caused by the antitrust decrees, it is not possible to draw final conclusions as to whether antitrust actions in the motion picture industry had an overall public benefit. I believe that the opening of the final markets to the independent producers will have a long-run benefit that will offset any increase in current admission prices that could be attributable to the lessened admission-price discrimination resulting from the antitrust decrees.

17

FREEMAN LINCOLN

The Comeback of the Movies

The movie industry, greeting 1955 at the year's world première, watched the January sun come up over Hollywood through a sensational heliotrope smog. Brushing away a stinging tear, the trade was reminded of the dreadful plight it was in only a year or so before, and so was moved to make a New Year's speech. "I'm well again," said the trade solemnly, "and this is a thing, kiddies, that is but *good!*"

This was not the usual, automatic overstatement. Movie people are genuinely excited about the comeback of their business. Aside from a group of exhibitors who feel abused and are singing a high-decibel lament, the rest of the industry, which is always on the crest of the wave or in the trough, appears vastly relieved, happy, and curiously alert.

The reason for the pleased relief is the obvious one that the public, returned from its long, unkind holiday, is again spending its pocket money at the movie houses. The fact that the spending is for particular movies rather than for movies in general suggests that there may be forthcoming a healthy new order of movie things, which in turn may explain the industry's taut, nose-to-the-wind manner.

The key fact is that certain pictures, not just one or two but a respectable number, are making money at the box office in sums beyond even Hollywood's dreams. The all-time monarch of the box office is, of course, MGM's *Gone With the Wind,* which is more of a monument than a picture, and which has grossed something like $35 million in its several

Fortune 51 (February 1955): 127-31+.

371

go-arounds since 1939. Until 1953, nevertheless, any picture that topped $5 million worldwide was a smash hit, and during more than thirty years up to that time all the producers, major and independent, probably did not turn out more than a hundred such hits.

In September 1953, Twentieth Century-Fox released *The Robe,* which has since grossed better than $20 million around the world and is expected to surpass $30 million. If it had stood even briefly unchallenged, *The Robe* would have moved into the niche next to *Gone With the Wind.* Instead, before Twentieth Century-Fox had a chance to shake its own hand, Darryl Zanuck had come up with another mammoth earner, *How to Marry a Millionaire.* So had Paramount (*Shane*), MGM (*Mogambo*), Columbia (*From Here to Eternity*), and most of the others. In the seventeen months since *The Robe* was turned loose, nearly thirty pictures have grossed more than the previously magic $5 million. The present upsurge of the movies is not merely a recovery; it is a major boom.

Off with His Head

The last boom in the picture business was in World War II, when dollars were plentiful while commodities were not, and when the movies offered the best kind of cheap entertainment. Domestic film rentals jumped from less than $300 million in 1942 to over $400 million in 1946. The weekly U.S. attendance in those years went from better than sixty million to an all-time record of more than eighty million.

As business improved during the war years, pictures ran longer and longer to full houses, with a significant result. The industry made 546 pictures in 1942, but only 425 in 1946. In other words, more and more dollars were received by the studios in return for fewer and fewer pictures. To be sure, the cost of making pictures zoomed during this period, but not so fast as the producers' profit margins. These went sky-high.

The ax fell in 1947, and it fell twice. By that time there were plenty of ways to spend money other than at the movies. This in itself might have crippled the victim. What appeared at the time to threaten him mortally, however, was the sale of television sets to people, soon to become hordes, who promptly scuttled into their living rooms and refused to come out.

The movie industry is notorious for its lack of accurate statistics. According to COMPO (Council of Motion Picture Organizations, Inc.), however, movie attendance dropped steadily until the first quarter of 1954 (about a year ago), when it leveled off at 45,900,000 per week. This meant that from the 1946 peak there had been a loss of 36,500,000 weekly admissions. Along with this 45 percent drop in attendance, theater net income slipped from $325 million in 1941 to $46 million in 1953.

There were other troubles. In the lush days the major companies had acquired huge studio facilities, and had long lists of high-priced actors, directors, producers, and writers under long-term contract. In mid-1947 all companies, in accordance with industry practice, had inventories of finished feature films still unreleased. These pictures had been made at high costs and now had to be sold on a crumbling market. Banks, which had never had much love for the movies, were hurt (Bank of America was a heavy loser), and disinclined to extend further credit.

What seemed in 1948 to be the coup de grâce was the successful conclusion of a federal antitrust action aimed at divorcing the U.S. theater chains from their producer-distributor owners. Some of the exhibitors, who had long begged for relief from what they considered the monopolistic practices of the vertical companies, were exultant at the prospect of freedom. Most of the producers, faced with the loss of a sure market, were despondent. (Both parties, as will be seen later, soon sang different tunes.)

Movie people, meanwhile, did the best they could, which, as any practiced second-guesser knows, was not good enough. They cut costs with a big knife, with the result that they made bad pictures. Bad pictures had short runs in the movie houses so that it was necessary to make more and more pictures, which became worse and worse.

The industry began to feel like a man with a loud humming sound in his head. The discomfort was maddening, but there appeared to be no cure other than amputation at the neck. Some of the movie people must have been thinking dark thoughts when, out of an indoor tennis court on Long Island, bounced a thing called Cinerama.

The Big Picture

Cinerama, a motion picture that achieves a three-dimensional effect by the use of three projectors and a broad, curved screen, was introduced in New York in September 1952. It proved to hold such phenomenal public appeal that the original travelogue is still playing to full houses in thirteen U.S. cities.

The moviemakers had their preview of Cinerama when it was in the experimental stage, and concluded at once that the three-projector Cinerama setup would be too costly for ordinary movie theaters. The picture industry, nevertheless, acknowledges a heavy debt to Cinerama, for the public response to it convinced the movies their own cause was not lost. The public, it seemed, was not literally chained to the television tube.

The picture industry shucked its winding sheet, flubbed about with 3-D and large screens. It was Spyros Skouras, president of Twentieth Century-Fox, then in the midst of a desperate stock fight (victorious) for control of his company, who unearthed and purchased CinemaScope, a process invented by a Frenchman named Henri Chrétien. In CinemaScope the lens "compresses" a wide-angle scene onto a narrow strip of film. When this scene is projected through a compensating lens, it is "spread" back to its original shape. In CinemaScope the screen is curved, and is two and a half times as long as it is high. "Stereophonic" sound, in which sound seems to come from the exact point of origin, can be produced by placing horns at either side of and behind the screen.

On CinemaScope, Spyros Skouras bet his company and his shirt. Once Twentieth Century-Fox had acquired the rights, it moved fast. It showed the new system to exhibitors and rival producers, and made it available to both. Speaking for Twentieth Century-Fox itself, Skouras and Darryl Zanuck stated in the spring of 1953 that all their company product would be in CinemaScope. (Theater owners would not invest heavily in Cinema-Scope equipment unless they knew the company was in for keeps.) They announced that the first of the new pictures would be *The Robe, How to Marry a Millionaire,* and *Twelve Mile Reef.*

On September 16, 1953, on a memorable day in the movie trade, *The Robe,* in CinemaScope, opened at the Roxy in New York City. It played at this theater for a crowded, exciting week. Then a hundred other *Robes* opened in a hundred other cities. *The Robe* did an unheard-of business, and the Twentieth Century-Fox picture that quickly followed, *How to Marry a Millionaire,* passed the mystic smash-hit mark of $5 million by a cool $2,500,000.

But not even Twentieth Century-Fox would say that CinemaScope alone was responsible for the public change of heart.[1] Television had seemingly reached what movie people lovingly call "saturation." They explain with polite venom that the novelty of the new entertainment medium had worn off, and that the sets had been paid for so there was money available for the movies. They remark that man is gregarious and likes to get together with his kind. Mother is tired after a week of cooking and housework and wants to get out of the house. The folks can't punish their children any longer by denying them television; the kids just don't care. Nor could anybody blame the little varmints for not wanting to ruin their eyes looking at a midget screen, showing bad vaudeville in black and white and 1932 westerns interrupted every few minutes with unbelievably bad commercials.

Music at the Box Office

Anyhow, by 1953 the people were ready to go back to the movies and the Cinerama-CinemaScope combination was attractive bait. Nevertheless,

1. CinemaScope already has its rivals: Paramount's VistaVision and Todd A.O. (see pp. 383-86).

the customers were proving choosy. Rather than go downtown and pay to see a second-rate movie, they would stay at home and see it for nothing, on television. A good movie was something else again. *The Robe* was only one of the pictures people went to in droves. *Gentlemen Prefer Blondes, Mogambo, House of Wax* (3-D), *Hans Christian Andersen, Peter Pan, How to Marry a Millionaire,* and *Shane,* released in 1953, had a total domestic gross of about $44 million. In the same year Columbia put out what it thought was merely an average-good effort in black and white, a war picture called *From Here to Eternity.* The trade is still talking about the $12,500,000 that *Eternity* brought in. The best guess at the total U.S. industry gross is $550 million for 1953.

Last year was even bigger, with more smash hits than can be mentioned. Columbia had *Caine Mutiny* and *On the Waterfront.* The latter was black-and-white, conventional-screen, and with a cost of only $875,000. While it lacked all the presumed ingredients of sure success, it grossed $7 million to $8 million. Paramount put out *Rear Window,* starring smart, personable Jimmy Stewart. It cost $1 million and grossed $6 million. Although the critics were unanimous in their nasty words about Paramount's first VistaVision picture, released last October, *White Christmas* in its first seven weeks brought in about $6 million.

Some other 1954 bonanzas: *Seven Brides for Seven Brothers* (MGM); *Three Coins in the Fountain, The Egyptian, Désirée, There's No Business Like Show Business* (Twentieth Century-Fox); *The Glenn Miller Story* (Universal); *Sabrina* (Paramount); *The Barefoot Contessa, Apache* (United Artists); *Dial M for Murder, Dragnet, A Star Is Born* (Warner). A rough guess at total worldwide gross of these twelve pictures would be $100 million. A rough guess at total worldwide industry gross would be $600 million. Since about 45 percent comes from abroad, the U.S. gross was about $350 million. Both world and U.S. grosses for 1954 were somewhat lower than those for 1946, but a lot better than for any year since.

As a result of the performances of the big pictures, grosses of the leading companies have jumped. To give two examples: three tremendous box-office pictures sent Columbia's gross from $60 million to $80 million during 1954; United Artists' gross went up from $18 million in 1951 to $43 million in 1954. Few of the pictures released have been in the red. Profits have been high. Twentieth Century-Fox, for instance, had a 1954 before-tax profit of $16 million, which rivaled that of boom 1946.

This major boom, however, should be observed with certain reservations. The recent big-profit pictures, for instance, were made at low cost and released on a boom market. On the other hand, the pictures that have just been made and are still unreleased were made at relatively high cost, so that unless movie attendance takes a really big jump this year, the profits could all but vanish.

Since the movies have gone boom, bust, boom in something like eight years, now may be the time to lay in an extra Mercedes-Benz against next year's bust. More to the point, however, is the fact that in the course of this latest get-rich period the movie industry has changed in a number of ways. Some of the alterations may be lasting.

New Boom, New World

The original Big Five of the movie world, MGM, Paramount, RKO, Twentieth Century-Fox, and Warner Brothers,[2] still loom large on the Hollywood scene, but with one exception their character has shifted. Only MGM still operates on the stock-company system, with its own big stable of stars, producers, directors, writers, and technical people, all under long-term contract. Dore Schary and his men say that there are no plans to deviate from this old system, but they will make no guarantees.

At the other studios the stock company was banished from the scene after World War II, by the simple means of not renewing contracts when they expired. Many of the failures to renew were by mutual consent. In the panic days the studios were anxious to get out from under murderous overheads. The big stars, on the other hand, decided that working for salary was a poor thing. They had to work too hard, often on pictures they did not like, for the little they were able to keep after taxes on their huge weekly paychecks. Why not quit, and make one or two pictures a year under some sort of arrangement that provided a capital gain?

The breakup has not worked out to the complete satisfaction of either the studios or the actors. Now that the good days are back and there are fat sums to be made from a successful picture, the studios recall greedily the time when it was possible to tap a contract star on the shoulder and tell her to go to work. Now the competition for her is hot, and she won't sign up unless she likes studio, producer, director, story, etc., and unless she gets a participation in any profits the picture makes. It is easy enough to see why the major producers would welcome a return of the stock company.

Actors and directors have fared fairly well under their own auspices. The actors, for instance, have what may be the best benefit of all: freedom. They can work or not, for and with whom they choose. By participating in profits, they have their income spread over a number of years. Their

2. Now that these companies no longer own theaters, the historic term "Big Five" is not accurate. For example, Columbia Pictures, which never owned theaters, is now larger than Warner Brothers, which did. Nevertheless, the term sticks.

security looks good just now, even if the movies aren't employing as many people as they used to. Important movie stars may never work for television, but it is nice to know it is there. On the other hand, actors may not have done quite so well financially as they hoped, because it has been hard to convince the Bureau of Internal Revenue that a return for personal service, however disguised, is a capital gain.

Nowadays it is hard to tell a studio by the actors it harbors. Danny Kaye, for example, has a handsome dressing room on the Paramount lot, although he is not under contract to that studio. He happens to like Y. Frank Freeman, the studio head, Don Hartman, the executive producer, and he also likes the participation arrangement that he and his writer-directors, Norman Panama and Melvin Frank (*Knock on Wood*), have with Paramount. Today he is making his third Paramount picture, *The Court Jester,* in VistaVision, but tomorrow he may be gone.

Built-in Irresponsibility

Ironically, the five big companies that lost their theaters as a result of the antitrust action appear to have been virtually unhurt by the severance. Even more ironically, the exhibitors who struggled for legal relief are now saying that this may be the only case in history in which the relief granted the complainant has worked exclusively in favor of the defendant. Delivered of the "ruinous" obligation to buy an entire program of pictures (block booking), the theater man suddenly discovered that he had lost his inventory. Then he complained that he not only was unable to forecast what picture he would be showing next April; in order to have one to show at all, he had to enter into "ruinous" competitive bidding for a commodity that, he was convinced, was produced in minimum quantities so a higher film rental could be squeezed out of him.

The two trade associations of exhibitors, Allied States and Theatre Owners of America, Inc., are close to hysteria over what they believe to be a new conspiracy by the producers. Allied States has issued a Declaration of Emergency, and has threatened to call in the federals again, this time to regulate film distribution and to set fair prices. Alfred Starr, Nashville theater-chain owner and spokesman of the small, independent theater owners, thinks that government intervention should be a last resort. His organization has a scheme to raise money for financing pictures to fill the shortage. He is vehement in his disapproval of the practices and the ethics of the producer-distributors.

Starr says that the figures speak for themselves: 405 pictures in 1948, 354 in 1953, and less than 300 in 1954. He believes this throttling of production has forced the exhibitor to pay exorbitant percentages and film rentals, and to run pictures overlong.[3] He points out that the steep, steady decline in movie attendance did not come to an end until about a year ago, and argues that the improvement since could not, by itself, possibly account for the huge rise in producer profits. He is convinced that those profits are the result of the squeeze put on exhibitors. He believes further that the producers try to "force" people to look at high-budget "quality" pictures when often what they want and like is *Francis, the Talking Mule,* and *Ma and Pa Kettle.* He thinks that movies are a mass-market business and should be supplied with an adequate number of low-rental, cheaply produced, little pictures.

In Starr's view, the movies may be the only industry with a built-in irresponsibility—it looks to him as if the wholesaler sits up nights figuring ways to drive the retailer out of business.

Big Is It

If the producers are sane, they must want to keep the exhibitors in business. There appears to be little realism in the notion that in reducing the output of pictures, the producers are conspiring. During the war, when the producers owned their own theaters, they followed exactly the present pattern of reducing output as business improved. Moreover, a genuine shortage is not apt to last long in American business if there is a way of filling it profitably.

Nevertheless, Mr. Starr is correct in saying that too few pictures are being made today to meet the need. Leonard Goldenson, president of American Broadcasting-Paramount Theatres, Inc., thinks not only that there are too few little pictures, but that the business could use twenty-five more big pictures. He believes they will soon be supplied.

Producers do not deny that exhibitors are paying much higher percentages of the box office than before for film rentals; they acknowledge cordially that producing companies are not above taking advantage of a sellers' market. They point out, moreover, that big pictures are expensive, and they account for their big profits as follows: Even though the improvement came late in the year, attendance in 1954 *was* up, and there was a slight rise in ticket prices, net after admission taxes (which were materially reduced last year). Since almost all current films are rented on a percentage of the box office, these factors have helped profits. The big help, as the producers readily admit, has been the very thing that the exhibitors

3. Some 4,000 of the 18,000-odd U.S. movie houses have closed in recent years, but these have been replaced by approximately an equal number of the new drive-in theaters that from 1952 through 1954 accounted for almost half of the summer movie attendance.

complain about, the reduced number of more expensive, more carefully made pictures.

One example will make the point. In 1953 and 1954 Twentieth Century-Fox Pictures had about the same volume of film rentals, $106 million. In 1953 the company amortized $48 million of feature-picture negative costs. In 1954, because of fewer pictures, the amortization was only $35 million. More specifically, in 1953 Twentieth had a before-tax profit of $8 million on thirty-two pictures, while in 1954 it had a $16 million profit on thirteen pictures. It is small wonder that the producers like a few big pictures rather than a lot of little ones.

Y. Frank Freeman, Paramount vice-president and Hollywood studio head, says that big pictures are more profitable than little ones for a big studio, because the break-even point is relatively lower. The rule of thumb is that to break even a picture has to earn double its investment, but a little picture probably won't pay out even if it earns 30 percent more than double the investment. In the case of a $700,000 picture with a gross of $1,600,000, the distribution cost will be $480,000; prints, $250,000; advertising and publicity, $260,000. These, added to the $700,000 negative cost, amount to $1,690,000, representing a $90,000 loss.

Now, Freeman goes on, take a $3 million picture with a $6 million gross. Negative cost of $3 million, plus $1,800,000 for distribution, $300,000 for prints, $400,000 for advertising and publicity, comes to $5,500,000, which means a $500,000 profit. For a big studio with $30 million to invest in a year's production, says Freeman, it makes more sense to turn out twenty-five pictures at $1,200,000 each, than, say, forty little pictures that have a high break-even point.

The beauty of the big picture nowadays is, of course, that there seems to be no limit to what the box-office returns may be. But while the industry's effort to do things that TV cannot has led it to produce spectacles like Cecil B. De Mille's latest *Ten Commandments,* now being filmed, and while these have been immensely successful, nobody has yet discovered what makes a picture click at the box office.

Mostly, however, the way to gross big money is to spend it, and those who hunger for a $30 million gross should be ready to lay out $10 million. But, as Freeman points out, $10 million is a lot of risk, and usually the risker will include in his package all the built-in insurance he can find. This includes one or more stars (e.g., Gary Cooper, Susan Hayward) so well known that they would guarantee box-office pull, regardless of the story. The story might be a best-seller (e.g., *Not as a Stranger*) with its own following. The locale might have a special attraction (*Three Coins in the Fountain*). The subject matter of the story is of ever-increasing importance. Nowadays it is not enough to satisfy the tastes and prejudices

of the U.S. audience. In 1954 nearly half the industry's total gross came
from foreign countries, with countries other than England contributing a
steadily increasing percentage. A film featuring life in a U.S. sorority
would sell no tickets in Nice.

The big picture, for all its risks, and in spite of the fact that nobody
knows its exact ingredients, is what everybody in the movie industry is
shooting for just now. It is the mammoth jackpot.

The Good Little Picture

It is evident that the B or C picture with a low budget, undistinguished
cast, poor story, and shoddy direction is on the way out, because the
public refuses to pay to see it. On the other hand, there is a real movie
need, which the independent distributor is not at all reluctant to explain,
for the small, low-budget picture that is not shoddy.

This need is threefold. The little picture is almost a necessity to the
exhibitor in a small town where most of the available audience has seen a
picture after a three-day run. The little westerns and other simple action
pictures are important in the many areas where the people genuinely
prefer them to extravaganzas or to "highbrow" problem films. They are in
heavy demand by the hundreds of exhibitors whose audiences insist on a
long evening's entertainment, and so must have a "second feature."

Just now there is an acute shortage of good little pictures, but Leonard
Goldenson of Paramount Theatres is sure that since there is a demand,
there'll be a supply. The supply, Goldenson thinks, will probably come
from ambitious youngsters who are now in television and are anxious to
get into the senior circuit. Either that, or the need will be met by one of the
five alert companies that even now are supplying not only most of the
industry's little pictures but also most of its new-generation tone. These
companies, all of which had big and profitable years in 1954, are: Allied
Artists, Columbia, Republic, United Artists, and Universal.

The Hungry Look

None of these companies is actually young, none of them is hungry, but
they have the appearance of being both. They demonstrate a willingness to
depart from tradition by experimenting with an unusual story told in an
unusual way (e.g., *On the Waterfront*). They have the air of being ready to
make an honest buck, and never mind the grand manner. Theirs is the
land of the independents, where the director is often the actor, and
everybody tries to save a dollar because it is his own dollar.

All five of these companies are fine organizations, but United Artists and Universal will serve to suggest what the next-generation Hollywood may be.

United Artists is essentially a worldwide film-distributing company run by two New Yorkers, Robert S. Benjamin, chairman, and Arthur B. Krim, president. These men, both lawyers, took over this old firm (founded in 1919 by Douglas Fairbanks, Mary Pickford, Charlie Chaplin, and D. W. Griffith) in 1951 when it was almost bankrupt. As refurbished, United Artists is a highly successful organization whose function is to give every sort of service to independent, "package" motion-picture-making deals except advice on how to make the film. Owning no Hollywood studios and paying no stable of stars, United has such a low overhead that it can and does make the good, small picture cheaply enough to earn a nice profit. It can make the bigger pictures inexpensively, too. Benjamin and Krim estimate that their film *The Moon Is Blue,* which in the U.S. alone grossed more than $4 million, would have cost a major company twice as much as the $300,000 it cost United Artists.

If a writer, or a director, or a writer-director comes to United Artists with a proposition for a picture, United Artists will carefully appraise all the elements of the package: the story, producer, director, and cast. If it approves, it will work out the various participation deals involved, and then arrange financing. (Three years ago United Artists had to scratch to raise money, but its record has been so good that today financing is easy.) After this, Benjamin and Krim will help the producer with the mechanics of a picture—leasing studio space, arranging transportation overseas, drawing contracts, etc.

A Picture Is a Business

The producer has absolute autonomy in making the film, with United looking at rushes only if specifically invited. The publicity and distribution of the finished product is, of course, the company specialty.

Benjamin and Krim, who in handling forty projects in 1954 ran directly against the trend of making as few pictures as possible, would like to hit the jackpot, naturally, with a really "big" picture, but they are unwilling to gamble wildly. They are growing from year to year, and feel that they are contributing to the good of the industry. At United, each picture is tailor-made, and since the cost may be well in excess of $1 million, each picture is a considerable business of its own. Krim and Benjamin look forward to the day when half of the four hundred pictures that may then be turned out by Hollywood are independent packages, produced by two hundred individuals with as many fresh, individual viewpoints. Then the movies will be rid of much of the uninspired monotony of major-studio mass production.

Universal Pictures is quite different from United Artists in many ways, but in many of its attitudes it is similar. One of the oldest picture companies producing under the original name, and owner of one of Hollywood's most extensive lots (370 acres), Universal is now the property of Decca Records, and the personal concern of Milton R. Rackmil, who bought it for Decca.

Helpful, Not Lethal

To Rackmil, a big bull-like man of tremendous energy, his new picture deal is just a repetition of what happened to him when he was with Brunswick Records in 1934. Radio became important at that time and everybody in the record business was sure the end had come. Who would buy records when they could turn a switch and get music for nothing?

Convinced that radio would be not only harmless but helpful to the record business, Rackmil helped start Decca Records and made a killing. When television came along and everybody in the movie business was sure of ruin, Rackmil was unable to resist an opportunity to buy Universal Pictures. Again he was convinced that the new entertainment method could live side by side with the old one, and be helpful rather than lethal, and again he has had a windfall.

In 1953, when the industry was cutting down on product, Universal stepped up the number of pictures, and it still has no intention of cutting down on production. Originally a maker of the small picture, Rackmil intends to keep right on making the small picture, but he will add big pictures to the schedule. Whereas most of the big companies are getting rid of their stables of actors, Universal for six years has been building one made up of youngsters. (Three of Universal's popular young contract actors are Tony Curtis, Jeff Chandler, and Rock Hudson.)

Rackmil's strongest insistence is that the movies are a business just like any other. "All the talk about us being dependent on that mysterious thing called creativeness, or creative talent, is a lot of junk. Every business depends on creative talent, and if we use what we've got here along with order and efficiency nothing can stop us."

Rackmil is perfectly honest when he says that he never thought of television as a threat to the movies, but his brother executives in pictures felt differently. Their present scorn of television is the best evidence of their fear of it. They are delighted that today's intellectual snob no longer says he never goes to movies, but says instead that he never turns on his television. It is nice that the pictures have a younger brother to scorn, even if they hate his tripe.

Appendix: The Big Screen

CinemaScope, the popular Twentieth Century-Fox system of showing movies on a huge, curved screen, was preceded as an audience-baiting novelty, in the early 1950s, by Cinerama and feature pictures in three dimensions. Lately CinemaScope has been challenged by Paramount's VistaVision, a system first used in the box-office hit *White Christmas,* released last October, and by Todd A.O., another new system that the public will first see sometime this year in a mammoth production of *Oklahoma!* One of these big-screen systems may eventually prevail over the others, but there is no present indication that this will be so, or, if so, which one it will be.

Cinerama, the system that touched off the present movie boom, is still the wonder of them all. From the beginning Cinerama had the seemingly fatal disability of being far too expensive for the ordinary movie house. The first Cinerama film, essentially no more than a travelogue, has been shown in only thirteen U.S. movie houses since its release in 1952. Still, the audience reaction has been so strong that the film has so far grossed better than $20 million.

Feature films taken in actual 3-D (Cinerama professes no more than the illusion of 3-D) kicked up considerable excitement in 1953, and sold countless thousands of the necessary audience eyeglasses, but for some reason 3-D failed to take a solid hold. It could be, as movie people say, that the public simply refused to submit to

Arch Oboler's *Bwana Devil,* starring Barbara Britton and Robert Stack (United Artists, 1953)—the first feature made in 3 Dimension Natural Vision

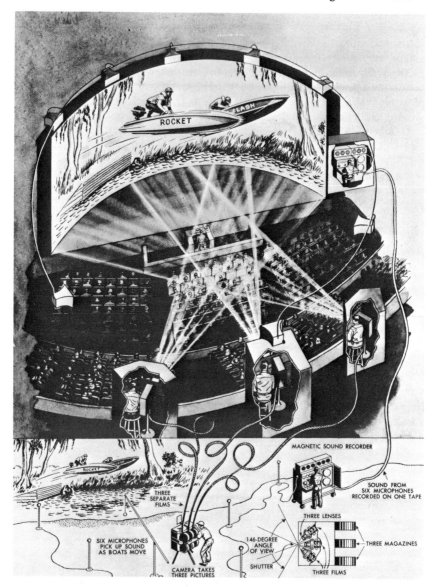

Schematic drawing of the Cinerama process from photography on location to projection in the theater

the inconvenience of donning spectacles. It could be, also, that 3-D was killed by the bad pictures for which it was used.

With VistaVision, Paramount seeks to take advantage of one weakness of CinemaScope, i.e., that the latter requires a theater owner to invest in expensive equipment. Paramount boasts that even if a theater has only an ordinary screen

Window display of *White Christmas* in VistaVision

and ordinary projection lens, the VistaVision film will still be of superior quality; if it is shown on a big screen, through a special projection lens, the picture quality will be superb.

In VistaVision, Paramount runs the negative horizontally rather than vertically through the camera, the picture frames having almost three times the area of the ordinary 35-mm frame. This big frame, with its great amount of photographic information, is reduced for printing and projection to the ordinary 35-mm size in the ordinary projector. On the big screen, a VistaVision picture is in sharp focus from immediate foreground to distant horizon. *White Christmas, Three Ring Circus,* and *Strategic Air Command* were the first three pictures filmed in Vista-Vision. Paramount's president, Barney Balaban, thinks the huge box-office success of *White Christmas* is in no small part due to the appeal of the new system. Paramount will make all its future pictures in VistaVision, and has offered it free to all other producers.

The release of the Todd A.O. film version of the famous musical comedy *Oklahoma!* (costing something like $6 million) may be an important event in the movie world. Todd A.O. (named for showman Michael Todd and the American Optical Co., and devised by American Optical's Dr. Brian O'Brien) requires only one camera and one projector, in contrast to Cinerama's three of each. But it approximates the Cinerama effect so closely that the trade has called it "seamless Cinerama." Like Cinerama, Todd A.O. professes only the "illusion" of three dimensions, but also like Cinerama it promises that its audiences will have a tremendous sense of participation (e.g., they will ride "with" the pilot in his plane). Also like Cinerama, in the opinion of movie people, Todd A.O. will be limited for a time to "road-show" appearances in a few theaters.

Poster of Michael Todd's *Around the World in 80 Days*, shot in Todd A. O.
(United Artists, 1956)

18

THOMAS H. GUBACK

Hollywood's International Market

When the Supreme Court ruled in 1915 that "the exhibition of motion pictures is a business pure and simple, originated and conducted for profit," that was considered sufficient reason to refuse films protection as speech under the First Amendment. Today it certainly is obvious, as it should have been then, that film is not just an ordinary business, but one vested with social consequences because of its communicative powers. As such, film is a mixture of business and art.

It is the commercial aspect of film, however, that establishes the priorities governing production decisions and is responsible for putting on the screen the shadows that captivate and mesmerize us. By being made in such an environment, motion pictures naturally support dominant thought patterns and are especially noncritical of the economic system that nurtures them.

A unique attribute of a motion picture is that virtually its entire cost is incurred in making the first copy. Duplicates require little additional investment, and wide distribution hastens the flow of revenue to producers

This article was abridged by the editor from a longer manuscript prepared especially for this collection. For more discussion on the subject of the film industry's worldwide operations, see the following publications by Thomas Guback: *The International Film Industry* (Bloomington, Ind., 1969); "American Interests in the British Film Industry," *Quarterly Review of Economics and Business* 7 (Summer 1967): 7-21; "Film and Cultural Pluralism," *Journal of Aesthetic Education* 5 (April 1971): 35-51; "Film as International Business," *Journal of Communication* 24 (Winter 1974): 90-101; and "Cultural Identity and Film in the European Economic Community," *Cinema Journal* 14 (Fall 1974): 2-17.

who are obliged to repay loans from banks and financiers. Because exported prints deprive the home market of nothing, while offering the producer a larger base on which to recoup his investment, it is not surprising that film has become a staple commodity in international trade.

Foreign markets are essential because a nation with productive capacities beyond its own needs is compelled to dispose of its excess wares abroad. Hollywood, however, exports films not primarily because it has product surpluses but because high production costs have made it difficult to recoup investments from the home market alone. The exploitation of foreign markets by the American film industry requires attention, for it demonstrates that film, in addition to being a commercial enterprise, is also a conveyor of values and myths.

Forging International Distribution Chains after World War I

World War I was a dramatic turning point for the United States because it changed our status from a debtor to a creditor nation. Between 1915 and 1920, the leading European nations became debtors to the United States, whereas at the beginning of the century over $3 billion of American securities had been held in Europe. The war redirected the international flow of capital, as surpluses in Europe were shot away at the fronts and American capital in the form of war loans and goods was sent abroad.

The motion picture was one product to benefit from these conditions. European film industries had either been disrupted or forced out of business, creating a vacuum into which American pictures flowed, often at alarming rates. In 1913, the last prewar year, some thirty-two million feet of motion pictures were exported from America; a decade later, the amount had more than quadrupled, and by 1925 it stood at 235 million feet. During these dozen years American film exports increased fivefold to Europe and tenfold to the remainder of the world, as the industry developed markets in the Far East, Latin America, and in a few parts of Africa.

It was possible for American films to achieve this dominance because they usually were amortized in the home market, which had about half the world's theaters, and thus could be rented abroad cheaply. Such a policy, of course, was a blow to foreign producers who suddenly found their own home markets glutted by American pictures. A result of the war, therefore, was that American distributors were able to gain control of the foreign field without competition. And by the time capital was once more available for production abroad, American films had obtained almost complete control of world markets.

Baby Doll at the London Pavilion

The exports to Europe, however, were of special significance because they generated about 65 percent of overseas revenue. By 1925, a third of all foreign revenue came from the United Kingdom alone, where American films captured 95 percent of the market. In the same period, 77 percent of the features shown in France came from the United States, as did about 66 percent in Italy. America's entry was achieved often at the expense of foreign producers, by dumping, underselling, and block booking. The quality of European film making was not a factor; on the contrary, Hollywood thought so well of foreign films that it brought directors and stars to America, and freely borrowed European production techniques.

Selling overseas extended American distribution chains around the globe, from which they have never retreated. Sidney Kent, general manager of Paramount Famous-Lasky Corporation, could boast in 1927 that a "foreign negative is shipped to London and then to other countries and averages a hundred and forty-two prints, distributed among a hundred and fifteen foreign exchanges serving seventy-three countries," and that "titles are translated from English into thirty-six languages." In fifty-five countries, Paramount did enough business to warrant having its own offices and staff. Even at that time, it was evident that film was a very special kind of merchandise. As Kent explained:

Motion pictures are silent propaganda, even though not made with that thought in mind at all. . . . Imagine the effect on people . . . who constantly see flashed on the screen American modes of living, American modes of dressing, and American modes of travel. . . . American automobiles are making terrific inroads on foreign makes of cars [because] the greatest agency for selling American automobiles abroad is the American motion picture. Its influence is working insidiously all the time and even though all this is done without any conscious intent, the effect is that of a direct sales agency.[1]

Kent recognized fifty years ago what has since become a commonplace: "The American motion picture bears a great and direct relation to the American trade balance abroad." He meant trade in goods, but he could have included ideas.

In evolving a foreign investment policy in the 1920s, the government encouraged expansion of markets for American goods (and capital). A former U.S. trade commissioner in Europe was able to write that it "is the business of the United States Goverment" to put its information-gathering services overseas at the disposal of American businessmen because "success in foreign trade is based on a full knowledge of the needs and

1. Sidney R. Kent, "Distributing the Product," *The Story of the Films,* ed. Joseph P. Kennedy (Chicago and New York, 1927), p. 206.

conditions in the foreign market." "We have . . . representatives abroad who look after our economic welfare as the diplomats look after our political welfare."[2] As an exportable commodity, therefore, the motion picture was aided along with other goods, and the pattern of assistance continues to the present day. Film also presents propaganda for the system it represents, and government, in turn, has helped the industry remove foreign barriers protecting national film industries from Hollywood's incursions. Thus, on the eve of sound, American films dominated the world market. It was not just that trade seemed to follow the film, but that film was (and is) trade. Bankers, at this time, finally recognized the financial vision of one of their number, A. H. Giannini, and began investing heavily in the film industry, thereby adding Wall Street's power to Hollywood's.

Especially irritating to foreign film makers was their inability to achieve reciprocity in the American market, or for that matter even to penetrate it. In 1913, the United States imported some sixteen million feet of motion pictures, but by 1925 the amount had fallen to about seven million feet. Foreign producers were "denied access . . . for the sufficient reason that this market can now [1926] be profitably reached only through one or more of a group of not more than ten national American distributors . . . each of which is busily engaged in marketing its own brand of pictures through its own sales or rental organizations, and through the theatres owned, controlled, or operated by one or more of this group."[3] In effect, the United States became virtually a closed market, with vertical integration and horizontal cooperation assuring that theaters would exhibit products of the major Hollywood companies first, and those of independents second. The small number of foreign films played mostly in metropolitan centers, where a handful of theaters catered to ethnic audiences. Until the early 1950s, foreign films remained unknown quantities to most Americans. Their seeming lack of box-office appeal "proved" that it was the homemade variety that was "in demand."

Sound solidified the position of American films overseas. By adding to costs, sound made film production for small markets increasingly precarious. As films had to be amortized somewhere, producers who had access to large domestic markets obviously had an edge. As Forsyth Hardy has explained:

When films were silent and the Scandinavian producers could sell their films—as they did—all over the world, their achievement was remarkable in that they were

2. Harry T. Collings, "United States Government Aid to Foreign Trade," *Annals of the American Academy of Political and Social Science* 127 (September 1926): 134, 135.

3. William Marston Seabury, *The Public and the Motion Picture Industry* (New York, 1926), p. 195.

competing successfully with stronger units in larger countries. When sound reached the cinema . . . the mere survival of [their] film-making became remarkable.[4]

Resistance to Hollywood's Exports

In the mid- and late 1920s many foreign countries began to be concerned about the influx of American films. There were two major reasons for their concern. First, on the business side, American pictures preempted exhibition time and rendered locally made films greater financial risks. Consequently, few were produced. The development of talent suffered as well, for there was less certainty that one could profitably pursue a career in film alone. Efforts to produce films on low budgets sometimes led to a reduction in technical standards and artistic excellence, giving such pictures even less chance to succeed either at home or elsewhere in competition with Hollywood's slickly finished exports. There also was concern about the money drawn by American films from foreign countries, amounts that some believed ought to remain at home as long as no reciprocal income was derived from America. Germany, for example, hoped that restrictions on U.S. pictures would give its own pictures a greater chance for exhibition.

Second, on the cultural side, film was considered a great medium of information and persuasion, which not only selectively presented certain traits and ideals but also glamorized them, even if unintentionally. Hollywood's output pointed up American stories and myths, American products and values. In 1926 it was already being charged (by no less than a former general counsel of the Motion Picture Board of Trade in the United States) that "American producers are now actively 'Americanizing' England, her dominions and colonies, and all of Europe."[5] Indeed, the British Empire was being superseded by the American Empire. More than forty years later one could write of the consequences and say that "gunboat diplomacy is now an item in the antiquities showcase but communications diplomacy is a very thriving business."[6]

Germany was the first major market to take action against American pictures. In 1925 it introduced a contingent act governing film imports. Distributors were issued a permit to release a foreign film each time they financed and distributed a German one. The United Kingdom, France, and Italy quickly followed Germany's example. In France, a limit was placed on the number of film imports, whereas in the United Kingdom

---

4. Forsyth Hardy, *Scandinavian Film* (London, 1952), p. ix.

5. Seabury, *The Public and the Motion Picture Industry,* p. 198.

6. Herbert I. Schiller, *Mass Communications and American Empire* (New York, 1969), p. 110.

and in Italy quotas on exhibition required that a certain percentage of screen time annually be devoted to locally made films. The Italian law set it at a conservative 10 percent; the British quota, in the Films Act of 1927, was progressive, beginning at 5 percent and rising to 20 percent in ten years' time. But constant production difficulties led, in Britain, to the making of cheap "quota quickies," preying upon the exhibitors' demands for any national picture to comply with the letter of the law. The Films Act of 1938 attempted to legislate these pictures out of existence by establishing a minimum cost test, while resetting the quota at 12.5 percent, with provisions to raise it to 25 percent by 1947.

In any event, the great wave of American film exportation that started after World War I produced retaliatory import quotas, distributor quotas, and screen quotas, designed either to control the number of such pictures on the market or to reserve a portion of screen time, however small, for domestic film makers. The objective was not merely to protect or stimulate domestic production, but also to prevent a medium of local artistic and cultural expression from being forced out of existence by the commercial strength of America's film industry. The sentiments of foreigners were convincingly summed up in a question once raised by a British governmental official. "Should we be content," he asked, "if we depended upon foreign literature or upon a foreign Press in this country?"[7]

Government-Industry Alliance

These menaces to American commercial interests prompted Hollywood to enlist the aid of the American government, an alliance that has continued to the present. In the late 1920s, the State Department interceded on the industry's behalf in France, Spain, Italy, Germany, Austria, Hungary, and Czechoslovakia (all of which were considering new or revised restrictions aimed at American pictures) by stressing that the building of foreign markets had involved large investments, and that these could be jeopardized by arbitrary measures restricting the distribution of American films. The State Department alleged, in defending Hollywood's trade policy, that foreign restrictions "introduce an element of commercial uncertainty and industrial instability to which American motion picture producers and distributors find it difficult or impossible to adjust themselves." In other words, the State Department along with American companies did not appreciate foreigners trying to protect themselves in their own markets. The tribulations of foreign producers were conveni-

7. Quoted in Political and Economic Planning, *The British Film Industry* (London, 1952), p. 43.

ently overlooked with the argument that was to become standard whenever American film interests were threatened: "This government has adopted no restrictive regulations similar in any way to those enforced in certain foreign countries."[8] The statement created the impression that America was a free market, which it was not because the structure and policy of the industry in the United States quite effectively, without help from Washington, kept the home market for its own films.

Functioning as a sort of watchdog over the international affairs of the industry was the Foreign Department of the Motion Picture Producers and Distributors of America (MPPDA). It maintained contact overseas with the offices of member companies, with foreign government personnel responsible for cinema matters, and with officials of the Department of State and the Department of Commerce. The twofold duty of the department was to try to keep foreign distribution channels open for U.S. films and to inform Hollywood about censorship policies. A great deal was at stake, because until the beginning of World War II, American companies were deriving about a third of their revenue from abroad.

The Foreign Market after World War II

Film industries everywhere naturally felt the effects of World War II. By 1944, Hollywood's foreign market had been reduced to the British Empire, Latin America, and some neutral countries of little economic importance. Companies made every effort to maintain and enlarge their position in the United Kingdom, the most important foreign market, especially when the exhibitors' quota had to be abandoned in 1942 for five years. The war caused a drastic cutback in production in Britain and continental Europe. Afterward, though, opportunities for foreign film makers did not improve. Film making equipment had been damaged or destroyed, and production capital became scarce as war-torn nations rebuilt their economies. Moreover, protective measures developed during the 1920s and 1930s were stripped away, leaving many countries cinematically defenseless. This factor was crucial because, with many markets closed to Hollywood during the war, a tremendous backlog of unplayed films had built up and were ready to be released abroad. In short, the war actually enhanced the status of the American film industry at the expense of others. Ground that foreign industries might have recovered was inevitably—sometimes irretrievably—lost.

The importance that the American film industry attached to its foreign markets became even more urgent after the war. In 1945, the MPPDA changed its name to the Motion Picture Association of America (MPPA),

8. Quoted in Howard T. Lewis, *The Motion Picture Industry* (New York, 1933), p. 406.

and the former Foreign Department took on new life as the Motion Picture Export Association. The MPEA was organized as a legal cartel under provisions of the Webb-Pomerene Export Trade Act of 1918. This legislation was one of the earliest government efforts to stimulate exporting by small and medium-sized firms at a time when few companies were concerned with foreign markets. The act permitted domestic competitors to cooperate in foreign trade by forming export associations that might otherwise have been held illegal under the Sherman Antitrust Act of 1890 and the Clayton Antitrust Act of 1914. This exemption allowed companies supposedly in competition in the American market to combine, to fix prices, and to allocate customers in foreign markets.

The act permitted the MPEA to act as the sole export sales agent for its members, to set prices and terms of trade for films, and to make arrangements for their distribution abroad. In bringing together the majors and allowing them to act in concert through a single organization, the MPEA presented a "united front" to the nations of the world, and by legal internal collusion prevented possible ruinous competition among American film companies overseas. The MPEA facilitated the international activities of its members by expanding markets and keeping them open, expediting transfers of income to the United States, reducing restrictions on American films through direct negotiations and "other appropriate means," distributing information about market conditions to members, and negotiating film import agreements and rental terms. The MPEA maintains a headquarters in the United States as well as an extensive network abroad. As Jack Valenti, MPEA/MPAA president (and former White House aide to Lyndon Johnson), has remarked: "To my knowledge, the motion picture is the only U.S. enterprise that negotiates on its own with foreign governments."[9] It is not surprising that the MPEA is called "the little State Department."

Even before the war's end, plans were being made to recapture overseas markets for American media. As Allied troops liberated Europe, American motion pictures followed in their path, with exhibition arranged by the Bureau of Psychological Warfare. The Office of War Information was handling the distribution of U.S. films in France, Belgium, the Netherlands, and Italy, until American companies could reopen their offices. The propaganda value of such pictures was clearly recognized because, as a Department of Commerce representative explained, "Only the movies which put America's best foot forward will be sent abroad."[10] The Cold

9. Jack Valenti, "The 'Foreign Service' of the Motion Picture Association of America," *Journal of the Producers Guild of America* 10 (March 1968): 22.

10. *Motion Picture Letter* [issued by the Public Information Committee of the Motion Picture Industry] 3 (September 1944) and 4 (February 1945).

War reinforced this stance. By assuming the role of world policeman, the United States instituted vigorous measures to prevent many countries dissatisfied with capitalism from drifting toward the Left. For example, the Marshall Plan provided funds to bolster West European economies and to stimulate production and reconstruction. The exportation of American media materials was deemed essential to the government's effort because they favorably depicted the American system.

The length to which the United States was willing to go to protect its interests was revealed early in 1975. Previously unpublished State Department documents indicated that in 1948 President Truman was so concerned about a possible Communist election victory in Italy that he approved a top-secret recommendation that the United States "make full use of its political, economic, and, if necessary, military power" to prevent it.[11] Part of the American policy, aimed against popular election processes, involved combatting left-wing appeals in Italy with U.S. information programs. Obviously, American films had their role to play. The government vigorously assisted in their global distribution for political reasons, while the industry seconded that view because it was congruent with its economic aims. In 1950, Eric Johnston, MPEA/MPAA president, was able to write: "Many times I have talked with President Truman about the influence of American films abroad, and he has said he regards American films as 'ambassadors of good will.'"[12]

Thus the MPEA launched its postwar distribution campaign with the blessing and indeed the support of the government. The backlog of unplayed pictures, said Johnston, "flooded in, even more than the countries could absorb."[13] The results were described in a UNESCO report:

The large number of cheap American films available . . . apart from adding to the dollar deficit, is only one of the factors prejudicing the development of national film production industries. These industries, unable to recover their outlay on the films which they produce, are stunted in growth and become unable to meet the demands of the national market. The exhibitors, therefore, are driven to depend for their existence upon foreign, largely American, films.[14]

However, European nations, in debt and with little or no dollar reserves, could not afford the luxury of importing American films when essential commodities were needed. These countries, therefore, had to develop

11. *New York Times,* February 12, 1975, p. 9.

12. Eric Johnston, "Messengers from a Free Country," Motion Picture Association of America. The article also was published in *Saturday Review of Literature* 33 (March 4, 1950): 9-12.

13. U.S. Congress, Senate, Committee on Foreign Relations, *Hearings, Overseas Information Programs of the United States* (83d Congress, 1st Sess., 1953), Pt. 2, p. 272.

14. The Film Centre, *The Film Industry in Six European Countries* (Paris, 1950), p. 21.

measures to protect themselves and their film industries not only from American pictures but also from the substantial drain on hard currency that their exhibition entailed. This latter currency problem posed a new complicating factor: balance of payments. To stem the dollar outflow, foreign governments passed measures much as they had after World War I, but in addition they instituted currency restrictions freezing earnings generated by American companies. Hollywood preferred to settle for repatriation of a share and leave the remainder rather than refuse to export films and quit the markets altogether.

As a result, the MPEA, with State Department help, concluded a number of film trade treaties with foreign countries. One, the 1948 Anglo-American Film Agreement, allowed U.S. companies to withdraw annually only $17 million of their earnings (leaving more than $40 million each year to accumulate in blocked accounts), in exchange for access to the British market unhindered by import quotas. However, the pact permitted American companies to spend their frozen earnings in Britain to produce films, acquire story rights, and buy real estate and studios.

Similar terms appeared in the 1948 Franco-American Film Agreement, which allowed U.S. firms to withdraw up to $3.6 million annually in earnings, leaving about $10 million blocked each year. These frozen funds could be spent for joint production of films with French companies, construction of new studios, acquisition of distribution and story rights, and so on. The agreement also permitted 121 American films annually to enter France, although all the rest of the world's producing countries had to scramble for and divide among themselves a total of only sixty-five import permits. This obvious inequity reflected the mighty bargaining position of the MPEA and the State Department, as well as the effect of Marshall Plan aid upon the affairs of many countries.

The 1948 pact, as advantageous as it was, replaced a May 1946 agreement which placed no limit on the importation of U.S. films and provided no obstacles to the dumping of old pictures. Known as the Blum-Byrnes agreement, and bitterly remembered even today by some French cinephiles, it demonstrated the "fine cooperation" between the State Department and the film industry, according to Eric Johnston. He believed as well at the time that the "best possible course is to continue the present policy of the State Department . . . which is based wholly on the traditional American belief in freedom of expression and communication."[15] The effect of the Blum-Byrnes agreement on the French industry was so grave that committees for the Defense of the French Film were organized to draw public attention to it. Obviously the motive of the agreement was to make France

15. *Motion Picture Letter* 6 (February 1947).

a "free market" for the dumping of U.S. pictures, as Italy turned out to be when it received an average of over 570 American films annually in the first four postwar years.

Because the balance-of-payments problem affected other media as well, it was seen by our government as an obstacle to the broad dissemination of the American point of view by private means. To overcome this obstacle, the Informational Media Guaranty Program was established in 1948 as part of the Economic Cooperation Administration. The program guaranteed that our government would convert certain foreign currencies into dollars at attractive rates, provided the information materials earning the moneys reflected appropriate elements of American life. This was a decided advantage to Hollywood companies, for it allowed them to distribute and exhibit their films in difficult currency areas with complete assurance that some of the resulting revenue would become available in dollars. American films then went forward into the world with the rank of ambassador. From the inception of the IMG Program until mid-1966, American motion picture companies received close to $16 million under the currency conversion provision.

Changes in the Domestic Market after 1950

A number of forces intersecting in the early 1950s made a significant impact on the industry and its markets. Theater attendance declined drastically, first as suburban living, new forms of leisure, and an abundance of consumer goods altered the moviegoing habit, and then by the spread of television, which provided not only its own "free" entertainment but also old Hollywood films. Simultaneously, the industry underwent an upheaval brought about by the *Paramount* decision in 1948: the majors were forced to divorce their exhibition branches from their production-distribution companies; the affiliated theater chains had to divest themselves of some houses; and new procedures for marketing films were instituted. Thereafter, Hollywood production-distribution firms sought to maximize their own profits, rather than the profits of their exhibition subsidiaries, as they had done formerly. And since they were no longer obligated to turn out enough films to fill the playing time of company-owned theaters, production was cut back. Exhibitors, who were used to double-features and frequent program changes under the old block-booking system, now complained of product shortages.

This realignment of relations between the majors and the exhibitors allowed foreign films to penetrate the American market, and their broader distribution was linked with the rise of "art house" circuits. Not all imported films were "art," but many offered a striking alternative to Hollywood's slick products by revealing slices of life and dramatic ele-

Michael Cacoyannis' *Electra:* Irene Pappas and Aleka Catselli.
A Lopert Pictures Release, 1962

ments that American films, following the strictures of the Production Code, had failed to develop. Imported films, moreover, were often made more on an artisan and less on a factory basis, and consequently seemed to present more personalized statements than the sanitized and anonymous Hollywood product. Italian neorealist films, the French *nouvelle vague,* and pictures such as Dreyer's *Ordet* in the mid-1950s revealed new dimensions of the cinema to American audiences, after which Hollywood's fare seemed anemic and inconsequential in comparison. Not a few foreign films were able to capitalize on sexual content and frankness, which the Production Code rendered taboo and which television could not deliver into living rooms. Responding to the obvious commercial appeal of sex, some Hollywood majors circumvented the Code by organizing special distribution subsidiaries to bring such pictures into the American market for exploitation. Meanwhile, faced with a product shortage and declining attendance, exhibitors were told in 1954 by an executive of United Paramount Theatres that "it might be wise for [them] to consider ways and means of popularizing the foreign film" and "to establish an audience where there has been none before."[16]

16. *Variety,* September 29, 1954, pp. 3, 18.

Runaway Production

Ultimately, it was the American companies that imported films from abroad. The first attempts to acquire moneys in blocked accounts abroad entailed such ingenious schemes as buying wood pulp, whisky, furniture, and other commodities and selling them elsewhere for dollars. Producers also invested in ship construction and in a variety of other noncinema fields, all with the assistance of the MPEA diplomatic corps. Soon, though, frozen funds were invested in film making. Initially this often meant shooting American films on location overseas, which became known as "runaway production." (Other American industries, in the 1960s and 1970s, were to follow this pattern by moving their production facilities abroad.) In addition to providing authentic locales, foreign shooting provided the opportunity to hire workers whose salary scales were lower than Hollywood's. The impact on American film trade unions was so severe that the House Committee on Education and Labor finally was persuaded to hold hearings on the matter in 1961 and 1962.

By this time, however, runaway production had matured. Films were no longer merely shot abroad instead of on Hollywood's lots; rather, American investment was being channeled into pictures that met every legal requirement for being declared "British," "French," "Italian," or another nationality. The inducement for this existed in a range of production subsidization schemes that were inaugurated in Western Europe in the postwar years. Essentially, these programs recognized the economic vulnerability of private enterprise film production and sought to protect it by stimulants, one of which provided film makers with an increment of revenue above what they obtained by commercial means from the box office. This attempt to close the gap between production costs and ticket revenues was just another in a series of reformist schemes on the part of European governments to keep their film industries viable as commercial undertakings. In reality these programs served limited purposes and only managed to postpone for a couple of decades the coming to grips with the commercial aspect that dominates film making in capitalist market-oriented economies.

Production subsidies quite openly were instituted to aid *domestic* film makers in European countries at a time when capital was short and American pictures dominated the screens. Subsidization laws, to ensure that aid would go to those who needed it, incorporated definitions of "national" producer and "national" film. However, incredible as it may seem, these laws did nothing to prevent foreign subsidiaries of American companies from conforming to the decrees so as to become "national" producers of "national" films. As a result, they had access to European

subsidies and participated in programs designed to encourage European
film making. Understandably, some European producers were bitter over
this latest intrusion. John Davis, president of the British Film Producers
Association, put the matter quite bluntly twenty years ago:

[It] is obvious that the [subsidization] scheme would not have been put forward by
the Government or accepted by the industry on the ground that the levy
recoverable from the box office takings was required to support films made in this
country by American subsidiaries.[17]

It was in the United Kingdom that the American companies concentrated
their production efforts, although they also were active in Italy, France,
and other countries.

It is impossible to determine the precise amounts paid as subsidies to
foreign subsidiaries of American companies. However, it has been estimated that for every dollar-equivalent of subsidy paid in France to U.S.
firms, two are paid in Italy and probably four in the United Kingdom.
Moreover, probably little more than 10 percent of subsidy payments went
to British production companies in the mid-1960s. In some cases of coproduction, American producers have been able to receive subsidies from
three countries for a single film, covering as much as 80 percent of its cost.
It is not surprising, then, that through the 1960s, American films financed
abroad rose from an estimated 35 percent to 60 percent of the total output
of U.S. producers. American interests reportedly produced 183 features
abroad in 1969 at an estimated cost of $234.7 million, while 142 were
made domestically for about $228.3 million. During the five years ending
in 1972, about 45 percent of the 1,246 features made by U.S. companies
were produced abroad, a decline prompted by rising salaries overseas and
devaluation of the dollar.

Data released by the Italian industry reveal that in the decade up to
1967, American companies had spent a yearly average of about $35
million to acquire and to finance Italian features, and to make their own
films in Italy. In the United Kingdom, figures for the decade up to and
including 1971 show that of 489 British first- or co-feature films exhibited
in the two main theater circuits, about two-thirds were financed wholly or
partially by American interests. In fact, U.S. firms were involved financially in almost five times more British films than was the British government's chosen banking instrument, the National Film Finance Corporation.

American investment in European films is now so complex that it is
becoming increasingly difficult to identify precisely the sources of finance

17. British Film Producers Association, *Fourteenth Annual Report 1955-1956*, p. 7.

and the stage of production at which such money is injected. For example, pickup deals allow an American distributor to retard its investment until the picture is completed and approved. Should the transaction, then, be considered production financing or a distribution deal? Likewise, when an American company guarantees a foreign bank loan for a European producer, the question arises as to just where the ultimate seat of authority is and who has final control. About the only thing of which one can be certain is that commerce rules.

American Distributors Remain Dominant

The increased American investment in European films after the early 1950s necessitated bringing them into the U.S. market for exploitation, which meant a departure from the old policy of the major American distributors. British, French, and Italian interests tried to establish their own distribution chains in America, but American distributors were able to maintain a monopoly position in the domestic market, while simultaneously fortifying their worldwide distribution networks. As before, foreign films could profitably enter the U.S. market only by means of American companies, demonstrating that the situation had not changed in half a century. Data show that of those pictures earning $1 million or more in the U.S.-Canadian market during 1973, 65 percent of the rentals were earned by five distributors: Twentieth Century-Fox, Warner Brothers, United Artists, Universal, and Paramount. Another 29 percent or so were earned by five other companies: National General, Columbia, Buena Vista (Disney), MGM, and Cinerama Releasing Corporation.

TABLE 1
Distribution Gross of U.S. Major Companies
($000,000)

Year	Foreign	Domestic	Value in actual dollars	Value in 1963 dollars
1963	$293.0	$239.4	$532.4	$532.4
1964	319.9	263.2	583.1	575.5
1965	343.5	287.2	630.7	611.8
1966	361.5	319.5	680.9	642.1
1967	357.8	355.9	713.7	654.4
1968	339.0	372.3	711.3	626.0
1969	348.4	317.4	665.8	556.0
1970	360.4	381.3	741.7	584.4
1971	347.5	336.7	684.2	517.2
1972	388.8	426.4	815.2	596.7
1973	415.5	390.5	806.0	555.3

Source: *Variety,* May 15, 1974, p. 34.

Overseas, American distribution companies are just as potent. During 1972 in Italy, they released twenty-four Italian features that were among the biggest box-office attractions in the country, prompting charges anew that the nation's film industry had been colonized by U.S. interests. During 1972 in France, seven companies handling mainly American films received 42 percent (about $42 million) of all payments to distributors from exhibitors. The remainder of the distributors' gross was divided among 114 French companies. In the United Kingdom during 1970, seven American distributors were estimated to have received about 84 percent (more than $40 million) of all film rentals. Typically they handle, in addition to their own American and non-British pictures, about 40 percent of the British films on the market, a share that has increased substantially over the last quarter-century, due to the corresponding rise of American investment in British pictures.

Revenues from Abroad

Probably no other major American business is so heavily dependent upon export trade as is the film industry. In the 1950s about 40 percent of the industry's theatrical revenue came from abroad; by the early 1960s, about 53 percent did. Not only is exportation of U.S. films essential to their producers, but, as we have seen, such pictures also are believed to create good will for America and its political-economic system. Furthermore, in view of recent U.S. trade deficits, it is claimed that American film earnings abroad make positive contributions to our balance of payments. The MPEA has estimated that the U.S. film industry remitted $342 million from abroad in 1972.

Data on foreign earnings of American companies and films, although far from being precise, do provide measures of their activity. Table 1 presents estimates of the total distribution gross received by eight member companies of the MPEA: Allied Artists, Columbia, MGM, Paramount, Twentieth Century-Fox, United Artists, Universal, and Warner Brothers. In terms of specific countries, the United Kingdom, which had been the best foreign market for American distributors until 1970, slipped to second place in 1971, and to fourth in 1973. Italy finally captured first position, while Canada moved from sixth in 1963 to second a decade later. West Germany and France rounded out the top five in 1973. Although variations such as those do occur, the rule holds that the top five markets overseas contribute between 40 and 45 percent of foreign revenues, and the top ten account for 65 percent. Foreign business is worth around $400 million annually, and it has grown in actual dollars. But, as *Variety* asserted: "Putting the world data together, the net gain in world film

Maria Schneider in *Last Tango in Paris,* directed by Bernardo Bertolucci. A coproduction of PEA Produzioni Europee Associate S.A.S.-Rome and Les Productions Artistes Associates S.A.-Paris. Released through United Artists, 1972

revenues [for the American majors] over an 11-year period was, in 1963 constant dollars, less than $23,000,000 or about 4 percent and this was due to tiny expansion in the United States."[18]

Overseas the proliferation of television, motor cars, and weekend houses and the decline in the number of theaters have left their impact on earnings of American distributors, especially in Western Europe. Even with increased rental terms, the foreign market can hardly be called a growth area, and if expansion is to come at all, it must be in those regions where the theatergoing habit is in its infancy. Of course, these are also the regions in which television is being introduced, and although TV-set saturation is still low, the development of a movie audience will have to compete with video's attraction.

The Response of Developing Nations

A stagnation in established foreign markets was recognized in the early 1950s by Eric Johnston. He felt that some markets were yielding just about

18. *Variety,* May 15, 1974, p. 34.

as much as they could, and that companies should not exhaust themselves trying to extract revenue from them when the effort could be better applied to virgin regions. In this way, the African continent became important for its economic potential, as it has been for its political position.

The achieving of political independence by many African peoples in the 1960s did not automatically ensure their autonomy, for they were confronted with neocolonialism from Europe and with political and economic intervention from the United States. In some cases, independence meant a restructuring in form, but not in substance, of film-marketing patterns that had existed during colonial rule, and the outcome was that film distribution continued to be dominated by foreign powers who paid scant attention to Africa's cultural identities.

The U.S. industry's first systematic effort to develop the African market took form after MPEA representatives toured the area in 1960. In April of the following year, the American Motion Picture Export Company (Africa) was established and began distributing films of seven Hollywood firms in the English-speaking countries of Ghana, Gambia, Sierra Leone, Nigeria, and Liberia. In September 1969, the West Africa Film Export Company (which later changed its name to Afram Films, Inc.) was created to distribute films of its seven members in fifteen French-speaking countries with a population of about sixty million.

After more than a decade of independence for many African countries, hardly any have been able to develop a national cinema policy. In fact, cinematic relations *among* these nations barely exist, and it is still true that African film makers have to visit international festivals in order to see the works of their colleagues. As a result, American and European interests have imposed a de facto policy of their own. It is a decidedly commercial policy, with little concern for African peoples and their identities. The Senegalese film maker, Mahama Traore, has observed:

Distribution of films in Senegal does not reflect the needs of the people because what we receive are the latest commercial films from France, Italy, and America. It's really an imperialist and colonialist assault—those films are vehicles of violence, sex, and a culture that is alien to us, a culture into which we are not integrated and into which we in fact refuse to be integrated, because we want to remain ourselves.[19]

The Response of Industrialized Nations

Although cinematic problems seem to take their most acute form in developing nations, those in many industrialized countries are just as serious. The age-old resistance to U.S. intrusion takes current form along

19. "'Cinema in Africa Must Be a School'—An Interview with Mahama Traore," *Cinéaste* 6 (1973): 33.

a wide variety of fronts, sometimes expressing itself as a rejection of private ownership altogether, sometimes merely as national or regional fervor seeking local commercial opportunities or independence.

In Europe, the Western European Economic Community has been seen by some as the core around which a European film policy could be built. The program might embrace not only financial measures to strengthen film industries of member states, but also a systematic way of coming to terms with American companies, films, and investments. This could entail the establishment of a European distribution firm to compete with American interests in Europe, and later in other areas as well. However, the only concrete result of the EEC so far has consisted of four directives on film calling for liberalization of trade and distribution among members. There has been no indication at all that EEC authorities are concerned about the large role played by the United States in members' film industries, nor has there been much attention directed to the cinema beyond some elemental commercial aspects. Missing has been a realization that a *European* film industry could not be built upon American investment and distribution.

Elsewhere in Europe, more direct steps were taken to challenge the American position. Among them was the establishment in the early 1970s of the International Federation of Independent Film Producers as an alternative to the International Federation of Film Producers Associations. The latter has been felt by many to be a spokesman for MPEA interests. In the United Kingdom, the Association of Cinematography, Television, and Allied Technicians called in 1973 for social ownership and worker control of the film industry, and urged nationalization without compensation of key interests, including all subsidiaries of American picture companies. In North America, the Council of Canadian Film Makers has recently urged nationalization of the theater holdings of Famous Players, Ltd. (owned 51 percent by Gulf & Western Industries), which operates more than a quarter of all the houses in Canada, and the inauguration of exhibition quotas for Canadian films.

Signs such as these occur regularly, suggesting that in both developing and industrialized nations there is a constant search to express, and sometimes establish through the cinema and other art forms, a national cultural identity. The purpose is not to compete in the making of films for international audiences, but to use the cinema to present or clarify the problems, lives, and aspirations of peoples.

Short-run economic benefits, however, mitigate these aspirations. American films overseas keep theaters open and contribute tax revenue. U.S. investment has also helped to stimulate film making in a few countries, but on its own terms, as is evident in Great Britain whose film

Ken Russell's *Women in Love:* Alan Bates and Oliver Reed. Produced in Great Britain and released through United Artists, 1970

industry is essentially an appendage of Hollywood. We can only speculate about what kinds of pictures a *British* industry would make, if one could be created, turning back half a century of American domination. Jobs have been created and studios kept active with American money, but the slightest cutback can precipitate unemployment crises with the reminder that industries lose their autonomy when they become subservient to foreign corporations who have only their own interests at heart.

Nonetheless, foreign governments, indecisive about progressive solutions, have been reluctant to discourage American investment. Their inaction leaves the cinema in limbo, caught between old revisionist policies that keep the film industries barely alive, and American power that implicitly chokes them. This dilemma feeds upon a myopic belief that the unhindered and free flow of communication is automatically beneficial to exporter and importer alike, and that any attempt to protect domestic cultural and social interests is a blow to international understanding. Of course, unrestricted communication can be destructive to indigenous cultures and can thwart people's chances to develop their own manners of expression.

Multinationals and Conglomerates

The American film industry's international stature must be placed in context and seen as part of the proliferation of multinational corporations and as part of the astonishing growth of U.S. private investment abroad, amounting to $107 billion by 1973, up from less than $12 billion in 1950. In this way, the film industry stands as just another segment of American business that has stretched its operations around the globe, seeking more and more places to market its goods, to return its investments, or to supply it with human and natural resources.

Several major film companies are now subsidiaries of huge conglomerates, meaning that theatrical film production and distribution have become small segments of parent firms engaged in a diversity of enterprises. Paramount Pictures, for example, was acquired by Gulf & Western Industries in 1966, not because it was thriving (actually Paramount was at the bottom of the barrel), but because it appeared to have substantial hidden wealth in its large, undervalued film library. Today, Paramount is part of the Leisure Time Group of G&W, which contributed less than 11 percent of its parent's total operating revenues in fiscal 1974. Revenues of theatrical films ($103 million) accounted for about 3.5 percent of G&W's total, and just a bit more than the $78 million the parent received from theater operations. In 1967, United Artists became a subsidiary of Transamerica Corporation, which was involved in car rentals, data processing, insurance, and various financial services. During 1973, UA's theatrical film rentals of $163.8 million represented less than 8 percent of Transamerica's total revenues. Universal's parent, MCA, received about 21 percent of its 1973 revenue from theatrical films' earnings of $87.5 million.

Companies such as Walt Disney Productions, Columbia Pictures, and Twentieth Century-Fox, which have not been acquired by conglomerates, have diversified into other fields. In 1974, Disney's film rentals brought in $90 million of its total revenue of $430 million; Columbia's generated $11 million of its $257 million total; and Fox's $160 million out of $282 million.

As theatrical film earnings during the last quarter-century diminished in size relative to other corporate pursuits, production has become geographically decentralized with, perhaps, up to half of our pictures being made abroad. Distribution, on the other hand, has become more centralized. In 1970, MCA (Universal) and Paramount formed Cinema International Corporation (a Dutch company) to distribute theatrical films of both firms outside North America. In 1973, MGM withdrew from distribution completely and signed ten-year agreements with CIC and United

Artists to handle its theatrical and television film library. As a report from the Security Pacific National Bank explained, "Hollywood has evolved into the international headquarters of the film industry. Financial and distribution functions are and will remain centered in the area."[20]

American film companies have forged a new empire rivaling those of former days based on spices and minerals, an empire in constant evolution, stretching around the world, and worth billions of dollars. Its impact on human minds can hardly be calculated. However, it is not only the qualitative aspects of film that should command our attention, enticing as they may be. The industry's shape today and tomorrow, as well as the images it produces, are the results of economic, political, and historical forces, unfolding and working themselves out.

20. "The Motion Picture Industry in California—a Special Report," *Journal of the Producers Guild of America* 16 (March 1974): 8.

19

JOHN COGLEY

The Mass Hearings

Hollywood reacted to news of the impending investigation in 1951 with something like panic. A *Life* reporter wired her editor at the time that the movie people put her in mind of "a group of marooned sailors on a flat desert island watching the approach of a tidal wave." The industry was not sure it could take another investigation, which would inevitably bring on more "revelations" and bad publicity and might mean picket lines around the nation's movie houses. To add to this anxiety, business was spectacularly bad. In 1946 domestic film rental stood at a dizzy $400 million; weekly movie attendance climbed to an all-time record of 80 million. But by 1951 television was a going thing and movie attendance was in the lower depths of a decline that finally, about February 1953, leveled off at 46 million.

In the lush days of World War II movie companies had expanded enormously, buying up vast studio facilities and adding to their rosters of high-priced talent. All the major studios had stockpiled costly films. Things looked black indeed. Although the slump lasted for seven years, its most severe effects were felt in the period between Congressional probes. These were years marked by big layoffs and frequent theater closings. The movie companies were finding it difficult to get bank credit and dreaded the consequences of political controversy. What banker in his right mind would put up the money for a picture that might be picketed because one of its stars had the habit of signing petitions? Trouble had piled up on trouble

From *Report on Blacklisting, I: The Movies* (New York, 1956), pp. 92-117.

for the moviemakers. When the government won an antitrust action and theater chains were separated from their distributor-producer owners, the industry—as *Fortune* magazine put it—"began to feel like a man with a loud humming sound in his head." (See ch. 17—Ed.)

In March 1951, just before the hearings began, *Variety* reported that in New York, Joyce O'Hara, acting president of the Motion Picture Association, had met with studio advertising and publicity heads and announced that movie people who did not firmly deny communistic ties would find it "difficult" to get work in the studios after the hearings closed. The Association had no intention of repeating the mistakes that had made Hollywood look foolish in 1947.

The House Committee on Un-American Activities was different too. In December 1949, J. Parnell Thomas was convicted of payroll padding and was later reunited with members of the Hollywood Ten in prison. If the film industry managed to salvage any consolation from that, it was short-lived. For this time the Committee returned to the subject of Communism-in-Hollywood under new auspices (Georgia's John S. Wood had succeeded Thomas as chairman) and vastly changed circumstances.

In 1947 the wartime friendship between the U.S. and Russia was still a fresh memory. By 1951 U.S. soldiers were at war in Korea with the forces of two Communist powers, and the Cold War with Russia was at its height. With the Hiss-Chambers, Klaus Fuchs, and Judith Coplon cases behind it, the nation was becoming ever more security-conscious and, in the opinion of many, was afflicted with a bad case of political jitters. A senator named McCarthy was becoming a front-page fixture. And, above all, the House Committee itself had a spanking new policy implemented by the Committee's new research director, an ex-FBI man named Raphael I. Nixon. Nixon, comparing the 1947 with the later hearings not long ago, commended Parnell Thomas's work but said it was unfortunate that in 1947 the Committee had focused its attack on movie content, "the weakest argument."

Parnell Thomas's pursuit of Communist propaganda in films, admittedly had led the Committee up a blind alley.[1] In Nixon's opinion, the 1947 Committee could have centered a more pertinent and fruitful enquiry on the "prestige, position, and money" the Communist Party picked up in Hollywood. And that is what the Committee went looking for in 1951.

1. At the close of the 1947 hearings, J. Parnell Thomas announced that "at the present time the committee has a special staff making an extensive study of Communist propaganda in various motion pictures." The study was abandoned. Thomas also announced that at the next hearing the Committee would have "a number of witnesses who will deal with propaganda in the films and techniques employed." These witnesses never materialized.

Hollywood was chosen for a "broad base investigation," Nixon explained to a reporter, because of the volume of cooperation the Committee got there. But a critical Democratic congressman whose district borders on the movie capital once suggested another reason. "The yearning for publicity on the part of some members of the Committee," he said, "could only be satisfied by the famous names a movie hearing would produce."

"Crusade for Freedom"—Louis B. Mayer presiding at a Korean War rally on the steps of MGM's Irving Thalberg Building. Sitting behind the podium is production chief Dore Schary

Nixon recognizes that such charges were made against the Committee but argues that it was the newspapers rather than the Committee itself which put the emphasis on big names. "We couldn't overlook our responsibilities just because prominent people were involved."

By 1951, a number of prominent persons were begging the Committee for a chance to testify and the Committee had to disappoint some of them. There were, first of all, the ex-Communists, who by now looked upon the hearings as the only public forum open to them. If they wanted to prove to the world that they had broken with the Party, they had to testify. And until they did prove this, they were unemployable in the studios. The Committee welcomed them. But another class—persons who had never belonged to the Communist Party but suffered from unfavorable rumors— were also eager to go on record as anti-Communist. Many wanted to be heard but, according to Nixon, Edward G. Robinson, Jose Ferrer, and the late John Garfield were the only three called where the Committee had no proof of Party membership, past or present. Robinson requested a hearing. Garfield and Ferrer were subpoenaed because they had been "the subject of considerable interest on the part of private organizations."

At first the Committee wanted Garfield and Ferrer to testify in private session. "But," Nixon said, "we were catching it all over—from George Sokolsky, Victor Riesel, and even from Ed Sullivan. No one came right

John Garfield and members of the Committee for the First Amendment in
Washington to monitor HUAC's 1947 hearings

out in print and said so, but there were intimations of payoffs. Mr. Moulder [congressman from Missouri] was subjected to criticism for stating that he thought Garfield was all right." Nixon also recalls that at the time some inexperienced anti-Communist groups were given to making loose, unsubstantiated charges, and the Committee drew fire for not acting on the "leads" these groups provided. From the other extremity, the Committee was attacked for "establishing blacklists."

Whether or not the Committee was interested in "establishing blacklists," it is now beyond question that many who testified (or who refused to testify) found themselves "unemployable" after they appeared as uncooperative witnesses before the Committee. During the scattered movie hearings of 1951, ninety Hollywood figures, almost all well-established in their careers, appeared on the witness stand. They took a variety of positions. Ferrer and Garfield swore that they had never been Party members; their names did not appear in the Committee's long lists of unfriendly witnesses published later. Thirty others like novelist Budd Schulberg and Sterling Hayden, said they had been Party members and named people they knew as Communists. Their names appeared in the Committee's 1952 Annual Report as "individuals who, through the knowledge gained through their own past membership in the Communist Party, have been of invaluable assistance to the Committee and the American people in supplying facts relating to Communist efforts and success in infiltrating the motion-picture industry."

One of these witnesses, screenwriter Martin Berkeley, named 162 persons he swore he knew as members of the Communist Party. His list included Dorothy Parker, who had spent some time in Hollywood as a screenwriter, Donald Ogden Stewart, Dashiell Hammett, Lillian Hellman, Edward Chodorov, writer-producer, and Michael Gordon, now a Broadway producer. Berkeley had originally been named before the Committee by Richard Collins. Berkeley later testified that after he learned Collins mentioned him, he sent a "very silly" telegram to the Committee. "I charged Mr. Collins with perjury and said I'd never been a member of the Communist Party, which was not true. I was not at that time a member and have not been for many years. [Berkeley left the Party in 1943.] Why I sent the telegram—I did it in a moment of panic and was a damn fool." But before Berkeley realized his "foolishness" and admitted there was truth to Collins's charge, several friends had begun to organize a defense fund for him. This campaign was under way when Berkeley sheepishly admitted that Collins had told the truth.[2]

2. In later years Berkeley was cited by Columnist George Sokolsky as a prime example of an anti-Communist who suffered unemployment for cooperating with the Committee. Many in Hollywood, however, believe that by his erratic behavior Berkeley had made himself unpopular and it was this rather than his anticommunism per se which caused his difficulties.

Berkeley joined the Motion Picture Alliance for the Preservation of American Ideals after his sensational testimony and became a leading figure in the organization. An MPA spokesman said not long ago that the group relied more on Martin Berkeley than on any of its other members to identify Communists and "Communist sympathizers" in the movie industry.

During the hearings that followed the 1951 sessions, other cooperative witnesses who provided names for the House Committee included actor Lee J. Cobb, director Elia Kazan, and playwright Clifford Odets.

A list of 324 names was made available to the public by the House Committee in its 1952 and '53 Annual Reports. Names of those cited as Communists by cooperative witnesses were listed alphabetically. Everyone cited was blacklisted in the studios. But methods varied from studio to studio and from person to person, perhaps to avoid the "illegal conspiracy" which Paul V. McNutt warned against in 1947.

If the named people were under contract when they were identified or called to testify, their contracts were cancelled, bought up, or simply not renewed. If they were free-lance workers, usually their agents told them they could no longer find work for them, and they stopped receiving "calls." Most were urged by their agents or studio executives to "clear" themselves of the charges made against them, either by testifying fully before the Committee or putting themselves in the hands of Roy Brewer or Martin Gang.

Larry Parks was the first Hollywood witness who decided to admit he had been a Communist. Parks was under the impression that it would be possible for him to testify without being required to name others he had known as Communists. While he was on the stand, Committee Counsel Frank Tavenner read off a list of names and asked the actor to tell what he knew about them. Parks hesitated. Then Congressman Charles Potter of Michigan and Committee Chairman Wood took turns with Tavenner in explaining to Parks why he had to involve others.

Congressman Wood told Parks, ". . . I for one am rather curious to understand just what the reasons are in your mind for declining to answer the question." Potter added, "Now, I assume you share the belief that we share that an active member of the Communist Party believes in principles that we don't believe in, in overthrowing our Government by force and violence. Now, you say you would readily give information concerning a man you have knowledge has committed murder. Wouldn't you also give information to the proper authorities of a man you knew or a woman you knew or believed to be working to overthrow our Government by force and violence?" The actor pointed out that it was not yet illegal to be a Communist, but Potter answered: "So when we are drafting men to fight Communist aggression, you feel that it is not your duty as an American citizen to give the committee the benefit of what knowledge you might have. . . ." Parks replied: "Well, yes; I wanted to do that. I think that there is a difference, Congressman, in my opinion. There is a difference between people who would harm our country and people who in my opinion are like myself, who, as I feel, did nothing wrong at the time. . . ."

Congressman Francis E. Walter of Pennsylvania (later chairman of the Committee) came to the actor's rescue: "How can it be material to the purpose of this inquiry," he asked, "to have the names of people when we already know them? Aren't we actually, by insisting that this man testify as to names, overlooking the fact that we want to know what the organization did, what it hoped to accomplish, how it actually had or attempted to influence the thinking of the American people through the arts? So why is it so essential that we know the names of all the people when we have a witness who may make a contribution to what we are trying to learn?"

Tavenner answered Walter: "Although there is information relating to some of these individuals as to whom I had expected to interrogate this witness, some of them have evaded service of process, so that we cannot bring them here. That is one point. Another is that this committee ought to be entitled to receive proof of information which it has in its files as a result of its previous investigation relating to a matter of this kind. There would be no way to really investigate Communist infiltration into labor without asking who are Communists in labor. And the same thing is true here in Hollywood. Those are the reasons I think it is material."

Larry Parks made a last desperate plea: "Don't present me with the choice of either being in contempt of this committee and going to jail or forcing me to really crawl through the mud to be an informer, for what purpose? I don't think this is a choice at all. I don't think this is really sportsmanlike. I don't think this is American justice. . . . I think it will impair the usefulness of this committee to a great extent, because it will make it almost impossible for a person to come to you, as I have done, and open himself to you and tell you the truth. So I beg of you not to force me to do this."

Tavenner's reply is often cited as proof that the Committee was "compiling a blacklist."[3]

3. In its 1953 Annual Report, the Committee noted that, as a result of its work, and the greater "cooperation" received from the motion picture industry, "it can be stated on considerable authority that perhaps no major industry in the world today employs fewer members of the Communist Party than does the motion picture industry." It went on then to acknowledge that ". . . particularly those individuals who have been identified under oath before the committee as one-time members of the Communist Party and who, in turn, invoked the fifth amendment in refusing to testify, have charged that the committee is compiling a 'black list.'

"The absurdity of this charge is obvious when it is considered that these individuals, of their own accord and volition, joined the Communist conspiracy, and that it is on their own

"Mr. Parks," he said, "there was a statement you made this morning in the course of your testimony which interested me a great deal. This is what you said: 'This is a great industry. . . . It has a very important job to do, to entertain people; in certain respects to call attention to certain evils, but mainly to entertain.' Now, do you believe that persons who are in a position to call attention to certain evils ought to be persons who are dedicated to the principles of democracy as we understand them in this country? . . . What is your opinion as to whether or not members of the Communist Party should be in positions of power and influence in the various unions which control the writing of scripts, the actors, and various other things which we have mentioned during the course of this hearing? . . ." Parks answered by agreeing with Tavenner that such people should not be "in any position of power" in the industry. Tavenner went further: "Or to influence the course which [the industry] takes?" Parks agreed again. "Then," Tavenner said, "we will ask your cooperation before this hearing is over in helping us to ascertain those who are or have been members of the Communist Party, *for that particular purpose* which we have mentioned" (emphasis added). Larry Parks, in executive testimony, later offered the Committee the names it sought.

Reticence similar to Parks's was expressed by playwright Lillian Hellman. After she received her subpoena, she wrote to the Committee:

Dear Mr. Wood:

As you know, I am under subpoena to appear before your committee on May 21, 1952.

I am most willing to answer all questions about myself. I have nothing to hide from your committee and there is nothing in my life of which I am ashamed. I have been advised by counsel that under the fifth amendment I have a constitutional privilege to decline to answer any questions about my political opinions, activities, and associations, on the grounds of self-incrimination. I do not wish to claim this privilege. I am ready and willing to testify before the representatives of our Government as to my own opinions and my own actions, regardless of any risks or consequences to myself.

But I am advised by counsel that if I answer the committee's questions about myself, I must also answer questions about other people and that if I refuse to do so, I can be cited for contempt. My counsel tells me that if I answer questions about myself, I will have waived my rights under the fifth amendment and could be forced legally to answer questions about others. This is very difficult for a layman to understand: But there is one principle that I do understand: I am not willing, now or in the future, to bring bad trouble to people who, in my past

---

personal determination that they have refused to affirm or deny sworn testimony placing them in the Communist Party."

The Committee seemed to be describing how and why a "black list" was compiled, rather than how "absurd" it was to say that such a list did result from its hearings.

association with them, were completely innocent of any talk or any action that was disloyal or subversive. I do not like subversion or disloyalty in any form and if I had ever seen any I would have considered it my duty to have reported it to the proper authorities. But to hurt innocent people whom I knew many years ago in order to save myself is, to me, inhuman and indecent, and dishonorable. I cannot and will not cut my conscience to fit this year's fashions, even though I long ago came to the conclusion that I was not a political person and could have no comfortable place in any political group.

I was raised in an old-fashioned American tradition and there were certain homely things that were taught me: To try to tell the truth, not to bear false witness, not to harm my neighbor, to be loyal to my country, and so on. In general, I respected these ideals of Christian honor and did as well with them as I knew how. It is my belief that you will agree with these simple rules of human decency and will not expect me to violate the good American tradition from which they spring. I would, therefore, like to come before you and speak of myself.

I am prepared to waive the privilege against self-incrimination and to tell you everything you wish to know about my views or actions if your committee will agree to refrain from asking me to name other people. If the committee is unwilling to give me this assurance, I will be forced to plead the privilege of the fifth amendment at the hearing.

In his reply, the chairman advised Miss Hellman that "the Committee cannot permit witnesses to set forth the terms under which they will testify."

In her testimony later, Miss Hellman invoked the Fifth Amendment.

In 1951 and 1952, the Committee issued subpoenas in batches of fifteen or twenty to actors, writers, story editors, screen analysts, producers, and directors. The economic pressure to become a cooperative witness was not only implicit in the spreading blacklist, it was underscored by the apparent collaboration between studio executives and House investigators. Subpoenas were delivered in dressing rooms and in the legal offices of studios, though home addresses were known to the investigators who served the subpoenas. Many at first did not admit that they had received subpoenas. Later, as the numbers grew, the subpoenaed grouped together, raised money for lawyers' fees, and formed classes for legal consultation. A sense of shock was experienced by many when they were subpoenaed. One person described it this way:

Even though you know what takes place in that committee, you are so accustomed to respecting government in all its forms that your fear is enormous. Intellectually, you understand what's happening, but you can't control the fear. An insidious form of self-guilt sets in. You accept the views of the committee in spite of yourself. It's quite bewildering. Afterwards, you find yourself guarded and evasive whatever you do, wherever you go.

By the time the 1951-52 hearings were well under way, the Smith Act had been held valid by the Supreme Court.[4] Some of those subpoenaed in the spring of 1951 did not know whether they would be jailed or not. They knew that if they failed to cooperate with the Committee there was absolute certainty that they would be blacklisted. The only real question, then, was what defense they might use to avoid imprisonment. The Ten had been jailed after depending fruitlessly on the First Amendment, and no other defense from a contempt charge for declining to answer questions before a congressional committee had been definitely established. The Fifth Amendment, with its clause protecting a witness against self-incrimination, appeared to many to be their only safe course.

This, however, carried with it a serious disadvantage. In 1950, the Supreme Court had decided in *Rogers* v. *U.S.* that a witness could not refuse to answer a question about the Party under the Fifth Amendment, once he had admitted Party membership. Since the Committee made it clear during the Larry Parks hearing that after a man had admitted Party membership he was expected to name others he had known as Communists, witnesses who would not name others but wanted to stay out of jail had the choice of either denying Party membership and running the risk of perjury indictments, or of refusing to answer the question at all.[5]

This meant that they also had to remain silent about accusations of dis-

4. Smith Act (Alien Registration Act of 1940) provides the following:

Sec. 2. (a) It shall be unlawful for any person—
1. to knowingly or willfully advocate, abet, advise, or teach the duty, necessity, desirability, or propriety of overthrowing or destroying any government in the United States by force or violence, . . .
2. with the intent to cause the overthrow or destruction of any government in the United States, to print, publish, edit, issue, circulate, sell, distribute, or publicly display any written or printed matter advocating, advising, or teaching the duty, necessity, desirability, or propriety of overthrowing or destroying any government in the United States by force or violence;
3. to organize or help to organize any society, group, or assembly of persons who teach, advocate, or encourage the overthrow or destruction of any government in the United States by force or violence; or to be or become a member of, or affiliate with, any such society, group, or assembly of persons, knowing the purposes thereof.
Sec. 3. It shall be unlawful for any person to attempt to commit, or to conspire to commit, any of the acts prohibited by the provision of this title.

All prosecutions under the Act have been on the basis of Section Three (conspiracy to advocate). After the release of the first group convicted under the Smith Act during the Foley Square trial, the government announced its intention to charge them with Section Two, part 3.

5. It is beyond the competence and legal knowledge of the author of this report to venture an opinion on whether they were justified, according to this reasoning, to resort to the Fifth Amendment.

loyalty, espionage, and conspiracy which they were anxious to deny. Two witnesses named as one-time members of the Party, for example, insist they can prove they were serving overseas in the Armed Services when, according to the testimony of the House Committee hearings, they were supposed to be attending Communist Party meetings in Hollywood.

To prepare witnesses and to keep them from answering questions that might cause them to lose their immunity privilege under the Fifth Amendment, teams of lawyers rehearsed their Hollywood clients by simulating the examinations they would be put to on the witness stand. Variations of the Fifth Amendment position were developed. For instance, Carl Foreman, who was the writer and associate producer of *High Noon,* invoked what later became known as the "diminished Fifth." He denied that he was a Party member at the time he was testifying but would not answer the question as to whether he had been a Party member at some previous date. Another variation was employed by producer Robert Rossen (*All the King's Men, Body and Soul, The Brave Bulls*). The first time he testified, Rossen invoked what came to be known as the "augmented Fifth." He said that he was not a member of the Communist Party, that he was "not sympathetic with it or its aims," but declined to say whether he had ever been a Party member in the past. Eventually, though, those who invoked variations on the Fifth Amendment position found themselves as thoroughly unemployable in Hollywood as those who simply "took the Fifth," as the position came to be described.

Tension gradually increased in Hollywood. Once it was clear that the hearings were not to be stopped before the Committee had unearthed every available witness who could provide it with names, pressure to give cooperative testimony was exerted on all sides. Families were divided. Some of the "unfriendly" witnesses moved to new neighborhoods to avoid the ostracism they felt certain they would meet once their testimony was publicized.

Among the prominent Hollywood figures subpoenaed by the Committee was Sidney Buchman, a Columbia producer. Buchman had been an executive assistant to Harry Cohn, in charge of production at Columbia. He wrote the screenplays for *Mr. Smith Goes to Washington* and *Here Comes Mr. Jordan,* produced *The Jolson Story,* and wrote and produced *Jolson Sings Again.* As a Columbia executive Buchman had worked on films featuring many of Hollywood's top stars. When he testified before the Committee on September 25, 1951, he took a position many unfriendly witnesses say they too might have taken had they believed the penalties would be as light as those later inflicted on Buchman.

Buchman testified that he had been a Communist but refused to name anyone he had known in the Party. He did exactly the thing which, according to precedent, should have meant a contempt citation. Observers were puzzled, until it was noted that Congressman Donald Jackson, California Republican, had left the hearing room in the course of Buchman's testimony but before the producer had refused to answer questions. This left the Committee without a quorum and, consequently, unable to issue a contempt citation against Buchman for his refusal to give full testimony. Buchman's lawyer noted the lack of a quorum at the conclusion of the testimony.

Public curiosity about Buchman's good fortune was expressed in various sections of the press. The Committee served Buchman with another subpoena, but this time he did not appear at the appointed time and was cited for contempt of Congress. On March 17, 1952, Buchman was indicted on two counts of contempt—for having failed to appear on January 25 and again on January 28. One count was later thrown out because Buchman had been cited twice on the basis of a single summons.

On March 25 District Judge T. Blake Kennedy in Washington, D.C., fixed the bond at $1,000 after the movie producer had been arraigned and pleaded not guilty. On May 9 a motion to dismiss the indictment was filed, argued, and denied. Ten months later, jurors were sworn and the trial started March 9, 1953. On March 10 a judgment of acquittal was entered on the first count. On March 12 the jury delivered a verdict of guilty. The jury was polled and Buchman was permitted to remain on bond pending sentence. On March 16, 1953, Judge Kennedy sentenced Buchman to pay a fine of $150. The court suspended imposition of a prison sentence, and the defendant was placed on probation for a period of one year.

Edward Bennett Williams, Buchman's lawyer, says that Congressman Jackson left the hearing room at the fortuitous time because he had to drive Senator Potter of Michigan, a guest in his home, to the airport. Williams claims that the reason Buchman got off with such a light sentence was that the jury had been deadlocked, so the judge delivered what is known as an Allen charge: the judge was required to inform the minority in the jury to remember that the majority was acting according to its best lights and then to turn to the majority and repeat the same admonition in favor of the minority. However, says Williams, Judge Kennedy, for some unaccountable reason, became confused and delivered both charges to the minority members of the jury. After the judge realized this, he felt constrained to prevent any further complications in the case and decided to let Buchman off with a light sentence.

Buchman no longer works in the motion picture industry and is engaged in other business in New York City.

The first witness from Hollywood to invoke the Fifth Amendment was an actor named Howard Da Silva, who is as well known on Broadway as in Hollywood. Da Silva had appeared in the original cast of *Oklahoma!*, in

Waiting for Lefty, Golden Boy, A Doll's House, and *Abe Lincoln in Illinois.* For years he had moved back and forth between the Hollywood studios and the New York stage. In 1939 he went to Hollywood for the film version of *Abe Lincoln in Illinois.* From then until March 1951, when he appeared before the House Committee, he played in about forty films, working at all the major studios and serving under contracts for periods at Warner Brothers and Paramount. He appeared in *The Lost Weekend, The Great Gatsby,* and *Keeper of the Flame,* among others. His income showed a continuous increase from 1939 to 1951.

During his 1947 testimony, Robert Taylor said he did not know whether Da Silva was a Communist but that he "always has something to say at the wrong time" at meetings of the Screen Actors Guild. After that, Da Silva had trouble. Between 1947 and 1951, he changed agents four times in an attempt to improve his lot. Again and again, his agents reported that film executives said, "We can't hire him—he's too hot." Da Silva managed to make some films after 1947 and even completed a costarring role after he was subpoenaed. But on March 21, 1951, he appeared before the House Committee and said, "I object to being called to testify against myself in this hearing. I object because the First and Fifth Amendment and all of the Bill of Rights protect me from any inquisitorial procedure and I may not be compelled to cooperate with this Committee in producing evidence designed to incriminate me and to drive me from my profession as an actor."

After that Da Silva found no more work in Hollywood. He returned to New York and found roles in a few radio shows, but he was removed from this medium, too, almost immediately. His agent told him that the William Morris agency, which packaged a show he had been on, had received six letters from American Legion posts objecting to Da Silva's appearance.

Da Silva tried to return to Broadway, but again he ran into serious trouble. Two potential "angels" raised objections when he read for roles and once a producer told him point-blank: "We can't use you because the theater will be picketed. It is a case of blacklist but I can't help it."

Witnesses who invoked the Fifth Amendment were banished from the studios in a variety of ways. Most studio executives, remembering Paul V. McNutt's warning about the illegality of an industry-wide "conspiracy," took pains to conceal the reasons for firings. Howard Hughes, then chief at RKO, furnished an exception. Paul Jarrico, a screenwriter, was working at the Hughes studio at the time he invoked the Fifth Amendment before the House Committee on April 13, 1951. Jarrico recently described his subsequent experiences in Hollywood this way:

In my case the evidence that I was blacklisted was simple and unmistakable. On March 23, 1951, I was subpoenaed to appear before the House Committee on Un-American Activities. The serving of the subpoena was publicized by the Los Angeles press, most of the newspapers quoting me accurately as saying I was not certain yet what my position before the Committee would be, but "if I have to choose between crawling in the mud with Larry Parks or going to jail like my courageous friends of the Hollywood Ten, I shall certainly choose the latter."

I was fired from my employment as a screenwriter at RKO that very day, forbidden to come onto the studio lot even to pick up my personal belongings. I appeared before the Committee on April 13, 1951, and was a most unfriendly witness. I not only exercised my privilege under the Fifth Amendment, I assailed the Committee for trying to subvert the American Constitution.

I was subsequently informed by my agents, the Jaffe agency, that there were no further possibilities of my employment in the motion-picture industry, and on June 20, 1951, at their request, I released them from the obligation of representing me. Though I had worked as a screenwriter more or less steadily for almost fourteen years prior to the date on which I was subpoenaed, I have not been employed by any Hollywood studio since.

In the spring of 1952, I became involved in a highly publicized legal controversy with Howard Hughes. As head of RKO, he had arbitrarily removed my name from a film called *The Las Vegas Story*, which had been my last writing assignment at RKO. I had been awarded a screen credit on this film by the Screen Writers Guild, which, under its collective-bargaining agreement, had exclusive authority to determine writing credits.

Hughes sued me for declaratory relief, asserting that I had violated the morals clause by my stand before the Committee. I filed a cross-complaint, asking for damages. The Screen Writers Guild sued Hughes independently for breaching the collective security agreement. Hughes won, both as against the Guild and me. Successive appeals of the Guild were defeated and the Guild finally accepted a compromise in which it gave up its hard-won authority to determine credits solely on the basis of literary contribution. My appeals were also denied.

In the course of these suits and in the public statements surrounding them, Hughes made it very clear that he maintained and intended to maintain a political blacklist. *The New York Times* reported on April 7, 1952, that RKO "will operate on a curtailed production basis for an indefinite period . . . in a drastic move for time to strengthen a political 'screening' program to prevent employment of persons suspected of being Communists or having Communist sympathies." The *Times* quoted Hughes further as asserting that "every one" of eleven stories, selected as the best for filming out of 150 read by the studio over a period of six months, had to be discarded because "information concerning one or more persons involved in the past writing of the script or original story showed that those writers were suspected of Communist ideas or sympathies." Added Hughes: "All studios have at their disposal information concerning the people who have been connected with one or more of the well-known Communist front organizations."

Jose Ferrer

Larry Parks

Lee J. Cobb

Elia Kazan

At a meeting of the Motion Picture Alliance on May 15, 1952, according to the *Los Angeles Daily News*, Roy Brewer declared that not one of the witnesses who "hid behind the Fifth Amendment" in the previous year and a half of hearings had subsequently been offered employment in the film industry. Later, it became apparent in Hollywood that workers who were named as Communists but had neither been called to testify nor come forth to answer the charges made against them, were also blacklisted. Brewer confirmed this, too, in another public statement. In answer to a charge in *Frontier* magazine that he was "straw boss of the purge," Brewer replied that the only blacklist he knew of was the list "established by the House Committee on Un-American Activities containing names of persons who have not repudiated that [Communist] association by comparable testimony."

Though 324 people had been named between 1951 and 1954, when Hollywood's "mass hearings" ended, they were not all motion picture workers. Some had left town years before they were named, others were wives of studio employees, others were trade-union or Communist Party functionaries who had never held jobs in the industry. But, when these people are eliminated from the list of those named, 212 remain who were active motion picture workers, many of whom had never made their living in any other industry. These 212 do not work in the industry today, though there is a small sub-rosa effort on the part of a few producers to buy the services of some of them (at cut-rate prices!) and present their work to the public under some other name.

The blacklisting proceeded through 1951, 1952, and 1953. Those dropped by the studios were not limited to persons who could influence film content, or who would receive screen credit for their work. The industry had accepted the Committee's new emphasis on "prestige, position, and money."

For example, there is the case of composer Sol Kaplan, who had scored more than thirty pictures in Hollywood between 1940 and 1953. Kaplan received a subpoena while he was working on a Twentieth Century-Fox sound stage. He had never been publicly identified as a Communist. John Garfield, who denied before the Committee that he had ever been a Communist, said in the course of his testimony that Kaplan was a friend of his. Though Kaplan had been under contract to Twentieth Century-Fox for one year, he was fired when this happened. Later he was reinstated on a week-to-week "probation" basis after he protested that many top studio executives (including the man who was firing him) were also friends of Garfield. Kaplan was subpoenaed in April 1953. Shortly before he was scheduled to testify, a Fox business executive in charge of the music department told him that his job, despite economy firings, was safe. During his testimony, on April 8, 1953, Kaplan challenged the Committee to produce his accusers and invoked almost the entire Bill of Rights when he refused to cooperate.

After the hearing, he returned to work at Twentieth Century-Fox. The musician says that his colleagues looked surprised when they saw him in the studio. Nothing happened the first day, but on the second he was told to call one of Fox's top producers. The producer, who was a friend of Kaplan, told him that Darryl Zanuck, production chief of the studio, did not want to fire him. Congressman Clyde Doyle, Democratic member of the Committee, the producer said, did not believe that Kaplan was a Communist. If Kaplan would appear privately before Doyle—which could be "arranged"—he might be able to keep his job at Fox. The producer added that "no one would even know you spoke to Doyle." Kaplan said that he would not consider taking such a position because he did not believe in "deals" where important principles were concerned. Fifteen minutes later he received a telephone call from the same executive who had assured him that his job would be safe in case of economy firings. A new order had made Kaplan's dismissal necessary, the executive told him. When Kaplan pressed him, the studio executive finally admitted that the musician was being fired for political reasons.

If the unfriendly witnesses before the Committee suffered social ostracism and loss of employment, the cooperative witnesses also paid a price. Not only Communists but many non-Communists looked upon them as "informers" (or, as they were described in the official Communist press, as "stool pigeons"). Everyone in the movie colony had seen the British officer contemptuously push the money across the table with his swagger stick in John Ford's classic *The Informer*. Everyone remembered how Victor McLaglen, as the Irish Judas, had picked it up. Also, many Hollywood liberals were bitter about the uses to which, in earlier days, the Communists had diverted their innocent good will to Party causes. Now, when they saw some of these same people playing the "informer" role, they found even more reason to turn on them. The remaining Communists did all they could to encourage the feeling.

For those who supplied the Committee with the names it wanted, social life became extremely difficult. Richard Collins, for instance, remembers going to a Screen Writers Guild meeting after he testified where only a half-dozen persons were willing to speak to him. Meta Reis Rosenberg recalls being denounced as a "stool pigeon" by someone who shouted from the balcony of a La Cienega Boulevard art gallery. Many of the "friendly" witnesses tell stories of how they were insulted and avoided. The wife of one witness says that the only people who offered any sympathy or financial help during this period were members of the Motion Picture Alliance for the Preservation of American Ideals. "When we needed friends as we never needed them before, Ward Bond telephoned and asked how we were doing," she recalls gratefully. Rebuffed as they were by liberal Hollywood, a number of the cooperative witnesses completed the full circuit from the Communist Party to the right-wing Motion Picture Alliance for the Preservation of American Ideals, where they were welcomed.

Social ostracism was not the only price paid by the ex-Communists who gave the Committee "names" during the mass hearings. Some, especially the earliest witnesses, found they were on an informal "blacklist." Only after influential figures in the MPA, powerful individuals like Roy Brewer, and members of the House Committee began to exert pressure on the studios, were the cooperative witnesses reemployed. In the beginning the studio heads were not sure that ex-Communists would find any more favor with the patriotic pressure groups than unfriendly witnesses.

But as the parade of ex-Communists to the witness stand lengthened, it became less difficult for them to find work, though in some circles it was felt that people who played the "informer" were beyond the pale. Even today there are some in the industry who, though they have no sympathy with Communism, feel so strongly about this that they are extremely reluctant to hire any ex-Communists and are adamant about not hiring specific ones.

Martin Gang, according to the blacklisted screenwriter who called on him, spoke of the danger of nationwide picketing by private organizations. That same month, October 1951, movie picketing began in Los Angeles by a group called the Wage Earners Committee. The Wage Earners Committee, according to its executive director, "had the humblest sort of origin." "In typical American fashion," a waiter, a telephone switchman, a small restaurant owner, and a retired salesman formed the organization. The committee—which was later found by the National Labor Relations Board to have accepted financial assistance from an employer who "intended to establish and set up Wage Earners as an instrumentality to offset legitimate collective bargaining"—immediately declared its belief in the "inalienable rights of the individual, as opposed to regimentation, communization, or dictatorship in any form." Politically, it was opposed to "every candidate controlled by the Labor Boss" and pledged itself to give its support to "the honest candidates the Labor Boss is attempting to purge."

The Wage Earners began their attack by picketing a film written by one of those named as a Communist before the House Committee. They carried signs which read: "This picture written by a Communist. Do not patronize." Later the group focused its attack on the film version of *Death of a Salesman*. It picketed a theater where the picture was showing and handed out circulars attacking Arthur Miller, author of the play, Fredric March, the star, and the producer, Stanley Kramer. Picketing of other films followed.

Then the full force of the Wage Earners was turned against Dore Schary, production chief at MGM. Pickets carried signs reading: "Communists are killing Americans in Korea. Fellow travelers support Communists. Yellow travelers support fellow travelers. Don't be a yellow traveler." Another sign read: "Please do not patronize. This is an MGM picture. Dore Schary 'Boss' of MGM. See House Un-American Activities Report. . . . See Calif. Tenney Committee Reports. . . ." Page numbers were listed.

Meanwhile, a publication of the group, the *National Wage Earner,* listed ninety-two films "which employ commies and fellow travelers and contain subversive subject matter designed to defame America throughout the world." The executive director of the committee, R. A. McConnon, announced, in a mimeographed letter demanding retraction of statements published about his organization in *Daily Variety,* that the Wage Earners were dedicated to providing "revelations of the identities and operations" of "subversive propagandists" in the motion picture industry. The group would stop picketing, he declared, "if the Industry would make an honest, and resultantly effective, policing of the medium. And this must include the immediate cessation of all pictures in which Americans are pictured as being intolerant and prejudiced against any so-called minority groups." Representatives of the Wage Earners offered to consult with the studios about the content of motion pictures and the loyalty of artists considered for employment.

In the circulars distributed by members of the Wage Earners Committee, producer Kramer was characterized as being "notorious for his red-slanted, red-starred films." The "true facts" about Kramer, the WEC held, were that he "taught at the Los Angeles Communist training school in 1947" and had employed a certain number of performers with "Communist-front" records. (Kramer's "teaching" actually consisted of a single guest lecture given at the People's Educational Center, where he spoke on a technical aspect of motion-picturemaking.) The Wage Earners belabored Fredric March with charges that had been made against him by the New York *Counterattack*—but ignored the fact that the actor later received a retraction and reached an out-of-court settlement with that publication.

Among the page references in the Tenney Committee reports cited against Dore Schary was a reprint of an article from the *Hollywood Reporter* describing the meeting of the Screen Writers Guild at which Schary announced the Waldorf policy. At the meeting, the trade paper reported, one of the Hollywood Ten had called Schary a "thief." The other references were to Schary's participation in several organizations designated by Senator Tenney as "Communist-dominated." There was no indication in any of the references cited that the film executive was personally "subversive" or "disloyal." The case against him, whatever there was of it, was based solely on "association."

Schary and Kramer both filed suit against the Wage Earners Committee, on grounds of libel and, in Schary's case, of willful interference with contractual relations. Picketing by the Wage Earners was then stopped by court order.

In Washington, D.C., members of the Catholic War Veterans picketed Judy Holliday's *Born Yesterday.* Later, in New York, the Catholic veterans picketed her second picture, *The Marrying Kind,* and distributed leaflets describing her as "the darling of the *Daily Worker.*" Miss Holliday, along with Garson Kanin, author of *Born Yesterday,* was listed in *Red Channels.* Her studio, Columbia Pictures, was alarmed by the picketing incidents. She had won an Academy Award for her first starring role and promised to be an extremely valuable and lucrative "property."

Columbia Vice-President B. B. Kahane told a reporter not long ago that after the picketing started, he questioned the star and was completely satisfied that her loyalty was beyond challenge. Columbia was satisfied, but that was not enough to call off the picket lines. The film company enlisted the services of Ken Bierly, a former editor of *Counterattack* turned public-relations consultant. Bierly's first job for Columbia was to "clear up the confusion about Judy Holliday." Soon after Bierly took over, the picket lines disappeared. Later, he told Merle Miller, author of *The Judges and the Judged:* "You might put it that I had something to do with getting the facts, the true facts to the right people."

It was not only a question of getting the "true facts" to the "right" people but also of getting them to a large number of Americans who had been led to believe that Judy Holliday was a suspicious if not subversive person. A public-relations campaign was necessary if Columbia was to realize its investment in the star. Miss Holliday's future was turned over to a group of skilled publicists. Gradually the rumors about her were silenced.

On March 26, 1952, Judy Holliday went to Washington, D.C., the *Born Yesterday* locale, and testified before the Senate Internal Security subcommittee. She admitted that she had been "duped" into supporting Communist-front organizations but convinced the subcommittee she had

Judy Holliday in the Broadway production of *Born Yesterday,* 1946

always been anti-Communist. Senator Watkins asked her: "You watch it now; do you not?" Miss Holliday in accents reminiscent of Billie Dawn replied: "Ho, *do* I watch it now!"

Other veterans' groups threatened to take an active interest in Hollywood's employment practices. A California unit of Amvets asked studio heads to define their position regarding the hiring of persons suspected of disloyalty. But no further action was reported after a number of persons in the same organization denounced the move as a publicity scheme.

In November 1951, a Hollywood post of the American Legion sponsored a resolution to provide for the picketing of theaters showing pictures which carried the name or credit of "unfriendly" witnesses. The resolution was not adopted. Later, the same post sponsored resolutions before local and regional organizations of the Legion to establish a committee of the California Department which would act as liaison with representatives of the film industry. The committee would be organized "for the purpose of conferring concerning any person now employed or contracted with, by such studio, who is a Communist, or whose acts, ideas, or ideals are inimical to the welfare of the United States, and, in the event a result deemed satisfactory to the committee is not obtained, to take such other and further steps or action as the committee may deem fit and proper, including lawful demonstrations at such times and places as it may deem necessary to carry into effect the purposes of this resolution." But these resolutions also failed to pass.

With all this adverse activity and with the threat of more to come, the Hollywood producers were feeling harassed and put upon. Their brave resolutions after the Waldorf Conference that the industry would not be "swayed by hysteria or intimidation from any sources" seemed less persuasive by the hour. The "mass hearings" of 1951 put Hollywood on the defensive, and the producers were feeling pressures from all sides.

20

RICHARD S. RANDALL

Censorship: From *The Miracle* to *Deep Throat*

On May 26, 1952, the Supreme Court of the United States announced its decision in the case officially known as *Burstyn* v. *Wilson* and declared that motion pictures are "a significant medium for the communication of ideas," their importance not lessened by the fact that they are designed "to entertain as well as inform."[1] In reaching this conclusion, the Court, in effect, read the movies into the First Amendment to the Constitution and extended to them the same protected status held by newspapers, magazines, and other organs of speech. The case, which had involved refusal by the New York State Board of Censors to issue an exhibition permit to Roberto Rossellini's forty-minute award-winning film, *The Miracle,* was the first case of movie censorship the Court had considered in thirty-seven years. Together with an economic crisis in the medium, it helped to precipitate a revolution in the content of films that has probably not yet run its course.[2]

Before the *Miracle* case, a myriad of state and local boards of censors, invested with simple statutory authority to deny permits to films found offensive, had near life-and-death power over cinematic exhibition in their

1. *Burstyn* v. *Wilson,* 343 U.S. 495, 501-2 (1952).
2. For background on censorship before the *Miracle* case and after it through the mid-1960s, as well as detailed examination of governmental censor boards during the latter period, see Richard Randall, *Censorship of the Movies: The Social and Political Control of a Mass Medium* (Madison, Wis., 1968).

432

communities. In its only previous consideration of movie censorship, *Mutual Film Corp.* v. *Ohio,* in 1915, the Supreme Court had found movies were "business, pure and simple . . . not to be regarded as part of the press of the country or as organs of public opinion."[3] As a simple commercial product rather than a constitutionally protected medium of speech, they could be regulated through prior censorship and be stopped before reaching their consumers in much the same way dangerous drugs or hazardous chemicals might; indeed, they were often compared to exactly those items of commerce.

Movies had also become subject to regulation by the industry itself through the Production Code Administration—the "Hays Office," as it was known in its early days. Run by the Motion Picture Producers and Distributors of America (now the Motion Picture Association of America), the organization of a handful of large companies known as the "majors," the agency imposed restraint on the content of films at the production stage. The industry had reluctantly embraced this arrangement in the early 1930s when it faced not only increased possibility of federal censorship and further proliferation of state and local censor boards, but also mounting pressure from many religious groups. Formation of a Roman Catholic reviewing and rating body, the Legion of Decency, and the threat of parish boycott of films constituted, in fact, the chief "gun behind the door." This triad of controls—industry self-regulation, organized religious pressure, and governmental censor boards—effected a censorial stability that lasted nearly a generation. The industry discovered it could live quite easily with these burdens because of the extraordinary profits from the "family" film, the chief product of a censored medium addressing itself to an almost undifferentiated mass audience in the 1930s and 1940s.

In the fifties, new constitutional freedoms and the rapid growth of television upset this equilibrium. The *Miracle* decision did not outlaw governmental censor boards per se, but it did provide a constitutional basis for challenging their rulings and those of the Federal Bureau of Customs in the case of imported films. Specifically, it held that a film could not be denied exhibition merely because it was found to be "sacrilegious." In one line of cases that followed, various other statutory censorial criteria, such as "harmful," "immoral," and "indecent," used freely by censors, were held unconstitutional. By a process of elimination, these decisions made it clear that obscenity would be the only permissible criterion for governmental prior restraint of movies. In a second and even more striking series of cases in the 1950s and early 1960s, many of them involving other media,

3. *Mutual Film Corp.* v. *Ohio,* 236 U.S. 230, 244 (1915).

Anna Magnani in Roberto Rossellini's *The Miracle* (1948)

the Court narrowed the concept of obscenity itself as a proscribable category.

While these new legal freedoms provided film makers with opportunities to explore themes, visual representation, and dialogue that had been off-limits for the family film, economic factors provided the necessity for doing so. With its enormous growth after World War II, television challenged and then in a short time completely usurped the older medium as the prime supplier of American family entertainment. While the number of sets in American homes was increasing fourfold in the fifties, movie admissions fell by 50 percent. For American production companies the crisis was made worse by the growing competition from inexpensively made foreign films, many of which were far more daring and imaginative in their content than the American product. In the fifties, American films were, in effect, acquiring the blessings of a new freedom at the same time that they were losing much of both their audience and their solvency.

These developments alone would have been enough to weaken the industry's own self-regulatory apparatus, but the authority of the Production Code had also been undercut as a result of an antitrust decree in 1948 requiring production companies to divest themselves of interest in theaters. Previously, five majors had controlled 70 percent of the first-run theaters in major cities and about 45 percent of all film rentals in the country. With such concentration, they possessed tremendous economic leverage on all other elements in the industry. In unhinging their power and forcing decentralization upon the industry, the decree indirectly cut the power of their creature, the Production Code.

The Censorship Interest

With the movies forced to find a new role among the media of entertainment and particularly to be something television was not, a radical change in the content of films was inevitable. No less so was the fact that this change and the freedom that made it possible would come under attack from those who would find the new content threatening or believed it harmful. Two questions are appropriate here. What kind of depiction or cinematic representation has been found objectionable? And why? The first is the more easily answered. Over the years, more censorial attention has been given to the portrayal of sexuality and sexual immorality than to depiction of any other realm of everyday life. Almost every governmental censor board has been empowered to censor obscenity, and, in the pre-*Miracle* period, many were authorized to ban or cut films their members thought to be indecent or immoral as well. Likewise, the industry's own Production Code proscribed a variety of erotic matter including "indecent or undue exposure," "intimate sex scenes violating common standards of decency," "justification of illicit sex relationships," and "obscene speech, gestures, and movements."[4]

Not all censorial interest has been directed at erotic matter, however. Many boards could and did censor the portrayal of criminal behavior, of racial, religious, or class prejudice, and of anything which, in their opinion, could be an incitement to crime or lead to a disturbance of the peace. The Production Code cast an even wider net. Detailed and protracted acts of brutality, cruelty, physical violence, or torture were not to be shown, nor was excessive cruelty to animals. Religion was not to be demeaned, and words or symbols contemptuous of racial, religious, or national groups were not to be used in ways that might incite bigotry or hatred. And, lest there be any doubt, "evil, sin, crime and wrong-doing" were not to be justified.

It would be a mistake to suppose that these various censorial standards were the work of a few Mrs. Grundys. The state and local laws that created censor boards were deliberate decisions, publicly arrived at, reflecting a response to widespread popular concern with what was being shown on the nation's screens. Much the same can be said for the creation of the Production Code Administration and the formulation of the Code itself. In their breadth and scope the governmental and industry censorship standards reflected not only the awe in which the movies were held by most persons as a presumed shaper of ideas, attitudes, and even behavior, but also the range of concerns and values held by a large part of the nation.

The question of why there should be a censorship interest at all, that is, why certain content should be threatening or believed harmful, is less easily answered. Objections to obscenity, to take the most common object of censorship, are usually based on the assumption that it may lead to harmful results in the way of behavior, attitudes, or aesthetics. Through its supposed appeal to the prurient interest, obscenity is assumed to incite or at least encourage illegal and possibly antisocial acts of a highly aggressive sort. Exposure to obscenity is thought to affect an individual viewer's moral values and thus, indirectly, those of family or community. As an unsightly and unpleasant visual experience to many of those who may be exposed, obscenity is said to constitute an assault on aesthetics and taste and possibly an invasion of privacy and peace of mind in the case of involuntary exposure. Many who advocate censorship as a means of protecting against one or more of these alleged harms make distinctions based on the age of the person exposed, the degree to which the exposure

4. *The Motion Picture Code of Self-Regulation,* The Motion Picture Association of America (undated), pp. 5-6.

is unsought or unsuspecting, and whether or not the material is "pandered."

Some critics of censorship have maintained that dubious censorial motives lie behind concern about these alleged harms. Those who would keep certain matter from the sight of their fellow citizens are said to be psychologically disturbed Anthony Comstocks driven less by their professed rational concern for the public and common good than by their own personal fears and anxieties. And, indeed, some sophisticated criticism of the censorial disposition suggests that it may be explained as a projection of repressions tightly imposed upon oneself as a means of controlling powerful but deeply recessed drives toward sexual expression and aggression. By censoring, according to this theory, one reaffirms self-control and increases the distance between the conscious self and disturbing impulses or temptations within.

A more sociologically oriented criticism of motives suggests that the quest to censor often involves the desire to have one's own values, morals, or cultural standards or those of the group or class to which one belongs reflected in public policy and taste. Accordingly, the status of one's group or class and, indirectly, of oneself is enhanced or diminished by the degree to which its moral, ethical, or aesthetic standards or life style is "in force." In this view, censorial motives, whether conscious or unconscious, are not limited to concern about erotic depiction but go beyond it to include concern about the representation of social, political, economic, religious, and aesthetic ideas and values.

Clearly, censorship has always had a lunatic fringe where obscenity was seen in every unpunished adultery or in every four-letter word or décolletage. These censorial excesses and idiosyncrasies would seem to offer some confirmation of the psychological repression theory of censorial motives. Nor is there any lack of evidence of hypersensitivity to the depiction of status. Every year, the Production Code Administration and its successor, the Code and Rating Office, have received complaints, often running into the thousands, about the portrayal of some identifiable group of persons—lawyers, Hungarians, redheads, Moslems, glass blowers, South Carolinians, abstainers, men without undershirts, and so on. This steady outpouring of concern prompted one wit to observe that the only villain it was possible to portray safely in a movie was a white, Anglo-Saxon Protestant who was unemployed!

It would be unfair, however, to dismiss all censorial concern as a matter of repressed desires or the defense of particularist status values. Worry about erotica or the depiction of violence is a concern that also appears to be reasonably held by many reasonable persons. Unfortunately, there is no conclusive evidence that such portrayal in the movies has or does not have harmful effects; hence, it is impossible to say how justified or unjustified some of the fears may be. That judgment must await the comprehensive and definitive studies that would indicate whether a steady offering of sex and violence is actually damaging or merely offensive to conventional sensibilities.[5]

In the meantime, whether based on rational and "common sense" opinion or concerns about status or one's own libidinal and aggressive drives, censorship pressures are unlikely to abate. They probably will continue to be felt by public officials and by those who make, distribute, and exhibit motion pictures. In fact, even were conclusive evidence to be found that obscenity is not harmful, it would be unlikely to have much effect on irrational censorial concerns. The remainder of this chapter will deal with censorship interest since the *Miracle* case and with how public officials and those in the industry have responded to and been affected by it.

Obscenity and Censorship in the Law

Following the *Miracle* decision, not only did the Supreme Court invalidate every substantive censorship criterion except that of obscenity, but it also placed censor boards under a set of rigorous procedural requirements. Today, a board of censors requiring prior submission of films must be prompt in its review and, should it deny a permit because of alleged obscenity, must take the matter into court immediately. Once there, it must carry the burden of proving that the film is, in fact, obscene. This is an important procedural distinction since, in effect, it reverses the crucial burden of proof, taking it from the defendant film proprietor and placing it upon the censors. Previously, a proprietor could not exhibit a film denied a permit unless he himself sued the board of censors and proved the film not obscene. In order to prevent long, frequently delayed trials during which the film would, in effect, be suppressed, the Court has also required that the judicial decision be prompt.

The cumulative effect of the rulings cutting away the substantive ground of prior censorship and those imposing procedural rigor has been nearly to eliminate prior censorship as an institution. Denial of exhibition permits is now so difficult to sustain that many state legislatures and local

5. There have been many studies of the effects of erotica and violence in the media, including several involving movies, but the findings, though illuminating, are far from conclusive, at least as a basis for formulating definitive public policy on the matter. Among the more recent and systematic studies have been those conducted by the Commission on Obscenity and Pornography in 1969. The Commission also reviewed earlier studies and related them to the more recent work. See *Report of the Commission on Obscenity and Pornography* (Washington, D.C., 1970), pp. 139-263.

city councils have abandoned prior censorship altogether. At the time of the *Miracle* decision, seven states—Kansas, Maryland, Massachusetts, New York, Ohio, Pennsylvania, and Virginia—and as many as eighty cities and towns, including Chicago, Milwaukee, and Detroit among the larger ones, had prior censorship boards. Today, only Maryland and a handful of cities maintain them. Occasionally new boards are proposed, but such attempts are often made for their symbolic value or arise out of sheer frustration with other methods of control. Very few have gotten beyond the debating stage. If prior censorship has any future at all, it will probably be more in classifying films for children and adolescents than in censoring them for adults. In fact, one of the few operating boards left today, the Dallas Classification Board, has powers only to classify. An additional and perhaps somewhat paradoxical result of the demise of prior censorship is that the number of formal prosecutions of exhibitors for showing obscene films and the number of instances of informal harassment of exhibitors have both increased markedly, reflecting a new accommodation of censorship pressures.

The narrowing of what is legally proscribable as obscenity has had an even more profound effect on the movies. This doctrinal change is probably one of the true revolutions of our time and is, of course, part of a larger cultural change in sexual attitudes and behavior, which it unquestionably helped to bring about. Strange as it may seem, the Supreme Court had not considered the obscenity question itself in any definitive way until 1957. That year, in two cases heard together—one involving the mailing of allegedly obscene magazines, and the other the sale of similar material in a bookstore—the Court reaffirmed that obscenity, being "utterly without redeeming social importance," was outside the protection of the Constitution. But it added, pointedly, that "sex and obscenity are not synonymous," and that the portrayal of sex in art, literature, and scientific works was entitled to the constitutional protection of speech and press. The test to be used in determining whether a particular book, magazine, or film was obscene was "whether to the average person, applying contemporary community standards, the dominant theme of the material taken as a whole appeals to the prurient interest."[6] This formulation, known in constitutional law as the *Roth* test, after the name of one of the defendants in the two cases, is still the basic yardstick for obscenity today. Its application in specific cases has been tortuous, however, and it is significant that in no major obscenity cases have the nine justices of the Court been unanimous. In a few, a majority has not even been able to agree on a theory for deciding the case.

6. *Roth* v. *United States, Alberts* v. *California,* 354 U.S. 476,484 (1957).

In other cases following the 1957 decision, the Court appeared to add still another measure to be met before obscenity could be legally established—that of "patent offensiveness." Thus, in addition to the *Roth* test and the fact that a film, book, or magazine in question must be "utterly without redeeming social importance," it must also be "so offensive as to affront current community standards of decency."[7] With these tests, much of what was formerly thought to be obscene became constitutionally protected speech. Thus, speculation grew that the only proscribable obscenity left was so-called hardcore pornography.[8]

At the same time, the Court has spun out several exceptions to a hardcore standard. In one, involving prosecution of Ralph Ginzburg, publisher of the magazine *Eros,* the Court held that dealing with material that is not, in itself, hardcore pornography might nonetheless be punishable if the material were "pandered," that is, marketed as though it were legally obscene. In a second, the Court allowed that a different and broader test of obscenity might be applied where recipients of the communication were juveniles. These two exceptions to the hardcore standard introduce the important concept of "variable" obscenity—the idea that something may be obscene to one audience or in one mode of presentation but not another. A third exception was in the direction of further permissiveness and grew out of a prosecution of a man for possessing admittedly hardcore pornographic films discovered accidentally by police in a search of his home for evidence of illegal gambling. The Supreme Court held that mere private possession of hardcore pornography in one's home, in contrast to its public sale, exhibition, distribution, of dissemination, was not a punishable offense.

A major change in the obscenity doctrine and one having considerable bearing on the movies came in a set of decisions announced by a more conservative Supreme Court, led by Chief Justice Warren Burger, in 1973. In one case, involving the Paris Adult Theatre in Atlanta, the Court flatly rejected a position toward which many had thought it had been moving, namely, that even hardcore pornographic films might be shown publicly if the audience were consenting adults. The case involved *Magic Mirror* and

7. *Manual Enterprises* v. *Day,* 370 U.S. 478,482 (1962).

8. Exactly what constitutes hardcore pornography has never been established with much precision in the law or even in popular discussion, though it would appear to include depiction of actual and explicit sexual intercourse rather than suggested or simulated congress. It is also thought to include explicit depiction of various "perversions," such as masturbation, fellatio, cunnilingus, pedophilia, necrophilia, and bestiality. At least one Supreme Court justice, Potter Stewart, finds the hardcore concept a workable test for obscenity for the simplest of reasons: "I know it when I see it!" In the film trade, the distinction between hardcore and softcore content has considerable meaning in the marketing of many "sexploitation" films. More will be said of this later.

It All Comes out in the End, acknowledged to be obscene, which were shown to an audience of adults at a theater devoid of offensive advertising. A majority of the Court maintained that the right to have access to pornography was limited to the privacy of one's home and did not extend to commercial movie houses. According to Chief Justice Burger, a state could decide that "public exhibition of obscene material, or commerce in such material, has a tendency to injure the community as a whole, to endanger the public safety, or to jeopardize . . . the state's right to maintain a decent society."[9]

In a second case, *Miller* v. *California,* involving the mailing of pornographic illustrated books, the Court upheld the conviction of the sender and, in doing so, revised the test for obscenity in two important ways. First, it modified the requirement that proscribable obscenity must be "utterly without redeeming social importance," saying, instead, that "at a minimum, prurient, patently offensive depiction or description of sexual conduct must have serious literary, artistic, political, or scientific value to merit First Amendment protection."[10] Second, in a declaration that shook the entire film industry, the Court returned to an element in the original *Roth* test that had never been satisfactorily defined, "contemporary community standards," and held that "community" referred not to the national community, as many had supposed and as many civil libertarians had urged, but to the state or local community. Chief Justice Burger, again the spokesman for the majority of the Court, said that the nation was too large and too diverse for a single national standard to be "articulated for all fifty states in a single formulation, even assuming the prerequisite consensus exists." He added that it was unrealistic as well as constitutionally unsound to require that "the people of Maine or Mississippi accept public depiction of conduct found tolerable in Las Vegas or New York City. . . . People in different states vary in their tastes and attitudes, and this diversity is not to be strangled by the absolutism of imposed uniformity."[11] A corollary of establishing the state or locality as the "community" whose standards are to be applied is that the local trial judge or jury would be the agent for making that determination rather than the higher courts. The fact that different juries might reach different conclusions about the same material would not mean that constitutional rights had been abridged, according to the Chief Justice. Such a differential outcome is "one of the consequences we accept under our jury system."[12]

9. *Paris Adult Theatre* v. *Slaton,* 413 U.S. 49, 69 (1973).
10. *Miller* v. *California,* 413 U.S. 15, 24 (1973).
11. Ibid., 32.
12. Ibid., 26, fn. 9.

Though the Court was again badly divided, 5-4, in these two cases, the decisions still number among the few times when as many as five justices were able to agree on a clarification of a major substantive aspect of the obscenity test. Three of the dissenting justices thought pornographic communication should be free of restriction unless it were made available to juveniles or were given "obtrusive exposure to unconsenting adults." A fourth dissenter, Justice William O. Douglas, reiterated his long-held position that there should be no restrictions on pornography at all except where shown to present a clear and present danger of precipitating illegal acts.

The Court has achieved greater consensus on the procedural aspects of the obscenity problem than on the substantive ones discussed above. As in the case of governmental censor boards, the justices have been careful to hold prosecutors and police to certain standards of due process in order to protect material which is alleged to be obscene but which might possibly be found not obscene later in a trial. A book, magazine, or film, for example, may not be seized by police unless there has been some prior, though not necessarily conclusive, judicial finding that it may be obscene.

Erno Crisa and Danielle Darrieux in *Lady Chatterley's Lover,*
directed by Marc Allegret (1955)

As a practical matter, this has meant that before a film may be confiscated as allegedly obscene, a judge must view it, usually by paying his way into the theater where it is being shown, and then must issue a warrant for its seizure as a possibly obscene item. Police may not seize films on their own judgment that they are obscene. In a 1973 case involving *Blue Movie,* the Burger Court also clarified this aspect of the obscenity problem. New York City policemen saw the film and summoned a judge who viewed it and, at its conclusion, signed a warrant for the arrest of the theater manager, projectionist, and ticket taker, and for seizure of the film to preserve it as evidence. The Court upheld this action on the theory that the confiscated reels were not the only print of the film; hence, the seizure did not constitute a prior restraint that would prevent any exhibition of the film while the obscenity question was pending trial.

Despite these more restrictive recent decisions, libertarian evolution of the obscenity doctrine is dramatically evident in a comparison of films that have been the object of obscenity censorship at various times since the *Miracle* decision and formulation of the *Roth* test. The major movie obscenity cases of the fifties involved films like *Game of Love, The Lovers, Lady Chatterley's Lover,* and *La Ronde.* Objections to these films had largely to do with their themes of sexual immorality. Few of them contained any nudity, and none involved four-letter words. Their offense was that they appeared to advocate, or at least not condemn, certain transgressions against established sexual values, usually adultery. This kind of cinematic depiction, sometimes referred to as ideological obscenity, is clearly no longer proscribable. It is fair to say that all idea content and advocacy in movies are protected today against an allegation of obscenity, no matter how morally offensive the ideas may be to some persons. Though presenting different problems, the major cases of the 1960s seem almost as quaint now as those of the fifties. In the early sixties, the controversies involved limited erotic nudity, such as brief glimpses of female breasts or buttocks; nonerotic nudity in the "nudie" or nudist camp genre that quickly sprang up and almost as quickly disappeared (actually became passé as a result of films with detailed erotic nudity); particular words in the sound track like *shit,* as slang for heroin in *The Connection,* or *rape* and *contraceptive* in *Anatomy of a Murder;* and detailed simulated sexual violence as in the rape scene in *The Virgin Spring.* In the late sixties, the controversies more often than not involved simulated consensual sexual acts, as in the case of *A Stranger Knocks* and *491.* The latter, which includes a scene of a prostitute *about* to have intercourse with a large dog, was, like most of the controversial films preceding it, naively believed to approach the limits of cinematic freedom. None of these films and none of the objectionable categories of depiction—

advocacy of immorality, nudity, four-letter words or other frank dialogue, simulated sexual acts—are likely to constitute the hardcore pornography that would be constitutionally proscribable for an adult audience today. In fact, in the trade today, detailed erotic nudity and simulated sexual acts are known as softcore. Though this kind of cinematic depiction may occasionally provoke a prosecution or other censorial action today, it is unlikely that the Supreme Court would uphold a finding of obscenity based upon it.

Censorship cases in the mid-seventies are very likely to involve hardcore content, the kind represented in such films as *The Animal Lover* (where a woman actually has intercourse with a dog), *The Devil in Miss Jones, Behind the Green Door,* and *Deep Throat.* The last, the most financially successful pornographic film ever made, went into national distribution after a spectacular run in New York City. It became the object of obscenity actions in various cities and towns, including New York itself, where it was found obscene after a ten-day trial that accumulated more than a thousand pages of expert testimony and was covered on the front pages of the *New York Times.* The exhibitor was fined $100,000, which took most of his profits from a six-month booking. In its seventy-minute running span, the film encompasses fifteen nonsimulated sexual acts, including seven of fellatio, four of cunnilingus—one or both *de rigueur* in most hardcore films—and others requiring more imagination. The fact that *Deep Throat* has also been found *not* obscene in some trials in some communities is a striking indication of how radical an effect the evolving obscenity doctrine has had on movies.

It is not yet clear what long-run effects the 1973 Burger Court decisions will have. The requirement that depiction of sexual conduct must have "serious literary, artistic, political, or scientific value," may force producers of pornographic films to pay more attention to traditional story elements such as plot and character and may put an end to "loops"—pornographic shorts featuring sexual action only and totally lacking story and sometimes even credits or titles. Paradoxically, if the net result is to increase the quality of pornographic films, those films may become more widely attractive and have greater impact on viewers than anyone has yet imagined. The requirement that community standards be those of the state or local community could easily result in a film's being obscene in one city or state but not in another. This happened with *Deep Throat,* which was found not obscene in Binghamton, New York, and thus has been declared both obscene and not obscene in the same state! This "Balkanizing" effect would not be unlike that which prevailed in the days of unrestricted state and local prior censorship, where rulings on a film often differed from one state or locality to another. Such a possibility is a disturbing one for an industry that must rely on national distribution of its product and, therefore, on some uniformity of the marketplace. These economic imperatives could result in the production of films that would satisfy the lowest common denominator of standards, that is, those of the most restrictive communities. This would be particularly likely in the case of large-budget features. On the other hand, though the Supreme Court has given emphasis to state and local standards, it has reserved the right to conduct its own review of a film. It was through just such an independent review that the Court unanimously found *Carnal Knowledge* not obscene in 1974, even though it had been judged so in Georgia presumably through local application of local standards.

Self-Regulation—The Rating System

Self-regulation by the movie industry has always had a between-Scylla- and Charybdis status. It came into being and has continued in force in order to head off more restrictive governmental censorship and massive boycotts by organized groups. Yet, many people within the industry have never been happy with the economic burdens it often indirectly imposes, or with its limitations on creative energies. Before the antitrust decree of 1948, when the industry was still highly centralized, profits from the family film and the general economic power of the big companies helped to check dissident voices. These conditions ended in the fifties, and the Production Code gradually lost much of its power within the industry. Exhibitors, who could no longer be easily coerced into showing only films bearing the Code seal, opened their theaters to nonapproved films. On the production side, a major company, United Artists, successfully defied the Code by releasing Otto Preminger's *The Moon Is Blue* and *The Man with the Golden Arm* without seals. Tied to the censorship criteria of an earlier day, the Code office was also unable to give the seal to such later leading films as *The Pawnbroker* (because of nudity), *Who's Afraid of Virginia Woolf?* (profanity), and the British-made *Alfie* (subject of abortion). These decisions further weakened its standing, and many advocated dropping self-regulation altogether as unworkable. To do so, however, clearly would have invited massive efforts to enact new governmental censorship, possibly at the federal level.

Faced with this dilemma, the MPAA revised the Code in 1966, liberalizing its standards, and empowered the Code office to affix the label "Suggested for Mature Audiences" ("SMA") to certain films judged not suitable for children. The label marked a break in the industry's adamant opposition to any age classification of its films and was the forerunner of the present rating system. For those films affected, it appeared only in first-run advertising, and there was no arrangement at the exhibition level to give it effect at the box office. With these limitations, it soon proved unequal to the prime task of self-regulation, that of heading off outside censorship. Censorial pressures built up rapidly in the late sixties as an increasing number of films, including many of the widely distributed ones of the major companies, dealt with sexual themes and included nudity, detailed erotic behavior, and frank language. At the same time, the Supreme Court had expressly upheld the right of governmental censor boards to classify films for children and was exploring the concept of "variable" obscenity, with its implication that a film not obscene for adults might be proscribable if children and adolescents were in its audience. Thus, in 1968, two years after the Production Code had been revised and the "SMA" label established, the latter was dropped and, in near desperation, leaders of the industry embraced the idea of a full-scale rating system. Jack Valenti, the new president of the MPAA, and attorney Louis Nizer, the organization's respected general counsel, spent several months persuading major production, distribution, and exhibition elements to support a rating system and be willing to enforce it upon themselves. With a tentative consensus behind it, the MPAA inaugurated the system in November 1968, and the United States became the last major Western nation to have some kind of systematic age classification of motion pictures.

Under the system, American producers and the importers of foreign features submit their films before release to the MPAA's Code and Rating Office, successor to the Production Code Administration. The office, which has been headed successively by a former member of the Production Code staff, a psychiatrist, and a professor of mass communications, views each film and assigns one of four designations that have now become household symbols: "G" (general audience); "PG" (parental guidance suggested, indicating that some material may not be suitable for preteenagers); "R" (restricted, indicating that persons under seventeen may not be admitted unless accompanied by a parent or adult guardian); and "X" (no one under seventeen admitted). The specific criteria upon which these ratings are based have never been made public, and have apparently shifted over the years, mainly in the direction of greater permissiveness. Unsurprisingly, erotic content appears to be the chief concern in arriving at a rating, though violence may occasionally be taken into account. Of nearly three thousand films viewed and rated during the system's first six years, 1968-74, three-quarters were in the "PG" or "R" categories. The complete breakdown by percentage is "G", 20; "PG", 38; "R", 37; and "X", 5. Since the first years of the system, the percentage of "R" ratings has increased markedly and "X" ratings slightly. The percentage of "G" ratings has dropped considerably.

The enforcement responsibility, without which the system would be advisory only and probably largely ineffective in reducing censorship pressure, falls to exhibitors. Exhibitor cooperation with a system run mainly by production interests is voluntary and not always smooth. Attempts by the MPAA and production interests to coerce exhibitor cooperation through economic or other leverage would raise antitrust questions. The MPAA and the National Association of Theatre Owners, the largest exhibitor organization, estimate that about 80 percent of exhibitors work with the rating system. Among them are most of the large theater chains or circuits, many of which have enthusiastically supported the system from the beginning. Yet, even where exhibitors do cooperate, there are no reliable data today on the quality and thoroughness of box-office enforcement. Some evidence indicates the enforcement may be linked to the existence of local pressures.[13]

The extent to which the system covers films in commercial release also bears on its effectiveness. Just as exhibitors cannot be coerced into bringing their admission policies into conformance with the ratings of the films they are playing, so, too, producers and importers cannot be required to submit their films for rating. The system does provide that a film not submitted may, in release, bear an "X"—the so-called self-applied "X". But a film not submitted for rating may not bear any other rating letter. Independent studies indicate that about 80 percent of the films in commercial release have been submitted for rating. Because these include most of those of the major producing companies and major importers of foreign features, about 90 percent of the exhibition bookings or "playdates" involve rated films. Further, since most of the largest theaters and biggest circuits play mainly major, rated productions, probably as much as 98 percent of the American moviegoing audience on a given day or night views rated films.

Like the Production Code before it, the rating system faces two additional problems: one having to do with the degree of even-handedness with which it is administered within the industry, and the other the degree of credibility with the public at large. The first of these affects the amount of support attainable in a decentralized industry, the second the extent to which self-regulation is accepted as a substitute for other forms of censorship. Run by the MPAA, the trade association dominated by the major production companies, the rating system has been attacked by independent producers, importers of foreign films, and some other non-production elements in the industry as a tool by which major companies

13. See Richard S. Randall, "Classification in the Film Industry," *Technical Report of the Commission on Obscenity and Pornography* 5 (Washington, D.C., 1970), pp. 219-93.

can throttle or at least inhibit competition. Where charges of favoritism are made, they usually have to do with the Code and Rating Office having given an "R" or "X" to a film the proprietor of which thought it should have received a "PG" or "R", respectively. The economic consequences of a more restrictive rating can be formidable. The "PG" rating is usually the sought-after prize, since it involves no box-office restriction and, at the same time, avoids the sexless "Disney" stigma many believe associated with a "G" rating. Economically, an "X" is particularly restrictive, less so because the under-seventeen audience is excluded than because many theaters and some of the circuits do not book "X" films at all. With the rare exception of *Midnight Cowboy*, which had the advantage of being a major critical success, even a film with a medium-sized budget bearing an "X" is unlikely to turn a profit. With these prospects, many proprietors

Jon Voight and Dustin Hoffman in *Midnight Cowboy*, directed by
John Schlesinger. United Artists, 1969

are willing to alter a film in order to acquire the less restrictive "R". A large-budget film with an "R" may have difficulty as well, because of the relatively smaller audience from which it may draw and because of a smaller number of bookings, though the effect of an "R" on bookings is substantially less than that of the "X". Probably the most severe challenge the rating system has faced in its short history arose over an individual rating when James Aubrey, the president of MGM, threatened to release *Ryan's Daughter,* a film that had a reputed $14 million budget, without any rating if its designated rating were not changed from "R" to "GP" (the former designation for "PG"). On appeal to the Code and Rating Appeal Board, the rating was changed, a decision that may have headed off MGM's threatened withdrawal from the MPAA, which would have removed a major organizational support for the rating system.

Any proprietor who is not satisfied with the rating of the Code and Rating Office may take an appeal to the Code and Rating Appeal Board, a body of twenty-five members representing the three major segments of the industry—production, distribution, and exhibition. However, since twelve of its seats are filled by executives of member companies through appointment by the MPAA president, who is, himself, a member, the board tends to be dominated by MPAA interests. In about two-thirds of the cases it has heard, the board has sustained the original rating. In a few of these, the film in question did eventually receive a less restrictive rating after its proprietors agreed to make changes in it. Intraindustry charges of a "double standard" at the appeal or at the rating level are difficult to evaluate since overt evidence on the point is slim. However, the very structure of the rating system, with ratings administered by an agency responsible to a trade association representing the largest production interests, at least raises an organizational possibility that the raters could be more sensitive to the pleas of the large companies with big-budget productions than to others.

Another source of complaint, mainly from small producers and importers, is that the rating fee schedule discriminates against the small proprietor. However, the MPAA has, in fact, graduated the fee schedule for feature films, from $300 to $3,000, depending on the proprietor's aggregate domestic rentals during the previous year and on the cost of producing the negative of the film.

Credibility with the public at large has always been a major problem for a self-regulatory system. The Production Code was criticized by some who viewed it as a kind of sieve largely ineffective in keeping erotica and other sensationalism off the screen. At the same time, it was regarded by others, including many artists, critics, civil libertarians, and some film proprietors, as oppressive and a bar to honesty and maturity in the Hollywood film. The rating system runs the same hazards. Yet since the degree of freedom in the medium is much greater today than at any time in the past, the more frequently heard criticism tends to come from those who see it as not performing the function it is officially held out to do—informing parents of the content of films that may be harmful to youthful viewers. Specifically, the rating criteria are said to be too much concerned with sex, too little with violence, and related less to the psychological realities of child and adolescent development than to the legalistic aspects of obscenity. Language and visual elements are said to be weighed more heavily than general treatment or theme. In this view, many films should receive a more restrictive rating than they have, and a few, a less restrictive one. Further criticism alleges that the rating criteria frequently shift, possibly for reasons of expediency, and have become much more permissive since the system began. Reflecting these charges, two influential religious organizations, the United States Catholic Conference (formerly the Legion of Decency) and the Broadcasting and Film Commission of the Protestant Council of Churches, withdrew their support for the rating system in 1971. For its part, the MPAA has claimed, on the basis of studies it has periodically conducted, that the system is increasingly effective, in terms of both its general public acceptance and the advisory service it performs for parents.

Credibility within the industry and with the general public will probably remain a problem as long as the rating system is totally dependent on certain powers within the industry. The possibility of "double standards" and rulings of expediency could be minimized by some restructuring of the system so that it had greater independence from the MPAA and from the industry generally. Inclusion of outsiders both in the Code and Rating Office and on the Appeal Board and the creation of a largely public "blue ribbon" appeal board are two suggestions frequently made.

Other Censorships

Censorship of the movies cannot be fully comprehended unless the role of informal pressures and control is recognized. Unlike the relatively structured controls of governmental boards, obscenity prosecutions, and the industry's rating system, informal censorship ranges over a wide field of individual and collective behavior. Though these pressures are almost always brought to bear on local exhibitors, they can and often do affect production when they are "passed along" economically and psychologically. Local pressure, which is as old as the medium itself, involves attempts by authorities or private parties, or both, to influence exhibition through tactics ranging from friendly persuasion to outright coercion. In many cases, these pressures may be anticipated by the exhibitor who then, in effect, becomes the censor himself. This kind of self-regulation often leaves little or no public trace. In its more overt manifestations, however, informal censorship appears to have increased steadily and markedly since the days of the *Miracle* decision.

Much low-level informal pressure takes place by a simple visit to the theater or a telephone call by police or representatives of community groups. If these tactics are unsuccessful, the conflict may escalate and eventually precipitate other official action, including occasionally a formal obscenity prosecution. However, where there is little likelihood that the objectionable film could be proven obscene in court, which is often the case, escalation may take other forms and run in other directions. As a local entrepreneur and often a local resident as well, an exhibitor is vulnerable to threats of or actual attempts at interference with his property, reputation, convenience, and safety, as well as those of his customers and employees.

Since theaters in most communities are licensed for business like other commercial enterprises, an exhibitor may be refused a renewal of license, sometimes on a technicality, or be forced to agree to conditions being placed upon renewal, such as not playing "X" films. New "inspections" of the theater may be made by fire marshals or representatives of the board of health, who may discover violations under highly detailed and often antiquated fire and health codes. Obsolete curfew ordinances and Sunday blue laws may be capriciously enforced against a theater.

In many communities, movies and theaters have been the object of new restrictive legislation or threats of such legislation. Drive-ins in many rural and suburban areas have been required to construct high fences so that the screen is not visible from the surrounding highways, houses, or trees. Zoning laws have been changed to the disadvantage of theaters or to prevent the construction or the opening of new theaters. Many local and some state tax laws have been passed or proposed which place a large levy on tickets to "X" films or which adopt a sliding-scale levy coinciding with MPAA ratings. City and town councils have attempted to embarrass an exhibitor who is a local resident by passing resolutions of "censure." And, in a few communities, officials have made available municipal facilities for the showing of films in competition with an uncooperative exhibitor.

Other pressures have involved the harassment of theater patrons. At one Texas drive-in, police succeeded in getting a film removed by telling the manager they would otherwise begin arresting patrons for fornication. Elsewhere, police have threatened to arrest patrons of four-wall theaters showing allegedly obscene films, on charges of frequenting a disorderly house. In some communities, patrons have been photographed leaving the theater.

Where arrests and seizures have been made, police overkill is not uncommon. In such cases, not only the film but also the "instruments" or "fruits" of the alleged illegal activity may be confiscated, including the projectors, box-office receipts, and, in at least one reported case, a number of seats. Arrests may include various theater employees as well as the manager. A tactic used by New York City police in a periodic Times Square cleanup was arrest of the projectionist, not for the purpose of bringing charges against him—as a nonproprietor, his conviction would be difficult to obtain even if the film were proven obscene—but to force him to spend a night in jail among a collection of prostitutes, vagrants, and addicts picked up in an average night's roundup. This "experience" was calculated to provoke the militant projectionists' local to pressure theater owners either to discontinue hardcore films or face the threat of a walkout.

Many of the pressures on exhibitors, at least in the first instance, are the work of private groups of citizens rather than public authorities. In Milwaukee, a neighborhood organization waged a three-month fight against a local theater showing *Deep Throat* that included daily picketing of the theater and such tactics as infiltrating the admission line to purchase the three-dollar ticket with pennies or with hundred-dollar bills and painstakingly counting the change, or asking the ticket seller repeated questions—all designed to slow up or disrupt the admission of patrons. A tactic used with some success in New York City as well as in smaller towns was that of pressuring landlords of the theaters in question to find ways to break the exhibitor's lease or, where landlords were reluctant to do that, embarrassing them by publishing their names, as those of persons—often including members of the local establishment—leasing premises for exhibition of allegedly pornographic films.

Where local authorities have been reluctant to undertake an obscenity prosecution they might not be able to win, private citizens or groups have sometimes filed civil suits against exhibitors for maintaining common law "public nuisances." Even when such suits are unsuccessful, they force the exhibitor to undertake a legal defense and bear its costs. Exhibitors have also been subject to personal abuse of various sorts, such as being expelled from a local church congregation or receiving anonymous notes and, paradoxically, obscene telephone calls. Though actual violence and physical harassment are rare, instances of planted bombs have been reported, as well as at least one case of theater arson.

A special kind of informal censorship is that exercised by newspapers and occasionally other media on movie advertising. Many papers regularly alter ads and, in some cases, may refuse to accept them altogether. Provocative titles may be changed, descriptive phrases eliminated, and pictorial matter cut out or literally toned down. In one case, the country's largest newspaper, the *New York Daily News,* actually changed the name of the theater itself, from Tomcat to Thom. Since newspaper advertising is the chief means by which exhibition is publicized, refusal to accept an ad or a class of ads, such as for films with "X" ratings, can have severe economic consequences for the theater and the film in question.

Not all informal action and pressure against exhibitors is aimed at the banning or removal of a film. Some complaints have to do with classification, that is, with the admission of children or adolescents. The drive-in fencing requirements, for example, are aimed mainly at avoiding exposure to juveniles outside the theater, as well as preventing highway accidents. In some cases, the censorship interest has been satisfied by modification of an exhibition policy so that "X" films were shown only during certain weeks or days of the week. Other complaints have had to do with the "mixing" of films, especially of an "X" or "R" with a "PG" or "G" on a double bill, or the inclusion of an "X" trailer with a "PG" or "G" feature. In other cases, the pressure appears to have been focused on, or at least generated by, sensationalist ads or outer lobby displays, the discontinuance of which sometimes relieved the pressure. On the other hand, where actual removal of a film was the object of the censorship, pressures have occasionally intensified and have been directed against an entire hardcore exhibition policy, particularly where the theater was a suburban or neighborhood house. Such campaigns are apt to be marked by considerable hostility, since they often involve large segments of the community and actual closing of the theater may be among the censorship aims.

Exhibitors have responded to informal pressure in various ways. Limited resistance resulting in compromise with the censorship interest or in capitulation to it is common. Overt resistance, which may include bringing counter legal action, is not common but appears to have increased, particularly as profits from softcore and especially hardcore films increase. Exhibitors who play many types of films or who have large theaters may "pass along" the pressure through exhibitor organizations and call for a modification of content at the production level or for some other accommodation of censorship pressures. It was such pipelining of local pressure that helped to bring about the rating system.

The relationship of the rating system to informal censorship is complex and difficult to assess with any precision, especially with the latter censorship being as varied, diffuse, and often obscured from public view as it is. It does seem clear that the mere existence of the system, with its someone-minding-the-store appearance, has probably allayed some censorship interest. Though a few towns have tried to enact the rating system into law by making enforcement at "R" and "X" levels mandatory upon exhibitors, the system has probably been a major reason that neither Congress nor any state legislature has enacted official age classification of movies. Thus, the system tends to bear out the view of the MPAA and of many others in the industry who see ratings as a kind of preventive censorship and, therefore, the "least of the evils." Yet, it is also clear that the system, with its "X" category and label, does itself draw additional censorial attention to particular films. Since many persons and local authorities incorrectly assume an "X" rating indicates pornography, a film so labeled may become the object of pressure from those who know little about it except its rating. This, of course, is also one of the reasons that "X" films can expect fewer bookings than other-rated films. In those localities that have tried to make "X" and "R" films unprofitable by levying higher admission taxes on their bookings, the system, in effect, becomes an instrument of further censorship. Newspaper ad restriction is another instance where an "X" rating alone may place a film at a disadvantage, its particular content notwithstanding.

The chief difficulty in assessing the impact of the rating system on informal censorship is that the two types of control tend to address different types of films and to have different goals. A film submitted for rating is usually one aimed at a fairly large audience and wide distribution. Even one that receives an "X" rating is unlikely to be of the softcore or hardcore type that is the object of most censorship pressure today. Films of the latter sort, though occasionally bearing the self-applied "X", are almost never submitted for rating, since it is obvious which rating they would obtain. While the rating system aims at classification rather than prohibition, the pressures and goals of informal censorship, more often than not, seek to remove or ban the film. Finally, there seems to be little doubt that some of the censorship energy aroused by softcore and hardcore unrated films spills over in its reactive force to both "X" and "R" films and, in some cases, may be so undiscriminating as to cast its net of condemnation over the entire medium.

Conclusion

The censorship interest in movies seeks to keep certain content and depiction from being seen by some or all persons in the belief that harm may result to those exposed and, indirectly at least, to the community or society at large. Whether this assumption is valid is a factual question about which available evidence is inconclusive. Whether the censorship goal is desirable, given these factual uncertainties, is essentially a moral or philosophical question which tends to be answered differently by different persons.

Because censorship is an interest that is both strongly and widely held, it is also a source of considerable political energy and, like other activated political interests, tends to make public demands, including demands upon lawmakers. As such, it is a political and social force that cannot be realistically ignored or repressed by officials acting in a representative capacity. It should not be surprising, then, to see officials responsive to this interest and, at least to some degree, seeking to accommodate it, especially where it may appear to represent the will of the majority. Where *anti*-censorship policies have been made by government, they have invariably originated in the Supreme Court, a nonelected body, and have been applied by the lower judiciary, much of which is also nonelected and, in any case, bound by decisions of the highest court. We see, then, the phenomenon of elected and nonelected officials often being on different sides of the censorship question.

Although the censorship interest is a social and political force to be reckoned with, it would be incorrect to think of it as static or even necessarily permanent (though, to date at least, it is as old as the movies themselves). Levels of tolerance and popular acceptability change just as the content of movies does. Much cinematic depiction objectionable a few years ago is generally accepted today, and the sort that is now the object of censorship would have been considered altogether unthinkable for the commercial medium a few years ago. The trend of the last twenty years in all media of communication has clearly been in the direction of increasing acceptance of frankness and detail in both erotic and violent representation and greater ease with sexual themes. The desirability of this development may be debated, but it seems clear that some change of attitude in the general population has taken place. If not exactly glacial in pace, this change has at least been fairly gradual and has taken perhaps a generation to advance. As such, it is in marked contrast to the change in movies, which has been precipitated largely, though not entirely, by philosophical decisions about freedom of speech and by economic ones dictated by intermedia competition and the marketplace generally. The fact that the one change has run by a far different clock than the other is at the heart of much of the censorship tension surrounding the medium today.

It should also be understood that the operating (as opposed to the legal) degree of freedom in any medium of communication depends, to a large extent, on the nature of the audience for the particular medium. For years movies were a genuine mass medium, in the company of newspapers, mass circulation magazines, and radio. As such, their audience included the entire family and tended to cut across class, ethnic, educational, and social boundaries. Thus, the movies were very different from the "elite" media of hardcover books or the theater, the audience for which has always tended to be highly select, conspicuously adult, above average in education, and able to pay a relatively high "admission" price. The degree of functional freedom has always been greater in the elite than in the mass media, and the movies in the past were no exception to this rule.[14]

Today, however, movies present a special problem. Having been replaced by television as the chief medium of family entertainment and having been freed of many of their previous controls, the movies have developed, in terms of media sociology, a kind of split personality. In their content they have come to resemble closely the elite media; yet, continuing to address a large and still fairly heterogeneous audience, they remain in other respects a mass medium. For example, most major productions with their sizable budgets cannot hope even to recover costs without playing to a large audience. Most films are still advertised to the public at large, usually in the same space in the same newspapers as were the old family films. Their physical outlet often remains the same neighborhood theater or drive-in, and the price of admission is still modest compared to that of the older elite media. Though the moviegoing audience is much less the family one today than in the past, and though some audiences, such as those for certain foreign films, have always been small and select, it is still true that the larger audience for movies remains a fairly general and undifferentiated one.

Given this disequilibrium, it is not surprising that the movies should generate considerable censorial tension today and come under attack more frequently than any other medium of communication. The breakdown of the traditional division of labor among the media in the case of the movies makes clear why there is much concern about classification, on the one hand, and why, on the other, some hardcore films can be shown with little or no censorial attention beyond that of classification. The occasional tolerance of hardcore occurs where exhibition is unobtrusive—

14. It is true, of course, that some mass media—movies and magazines, for example— have had "underground" or, more accurately, under-the-counter segments that had illegal and limited distribution but also great freedom of content with regard to erotica. The old "stag" film was the segment in the movies. However, such freedom of content was possible, that is, tolerated, only to the extent that distribution of the product was clandestine and in numbers that were small. In effect, freedom of content was inversely related to freedom of dissemination. And it is not insignificant that the cost of access to or purchase of such clandestine communication was usually considerably higher than that of legitimate, aboveground expression in a medium.

usually low-key advertising or no advertising at all in the mass media and modest out-front displays at the theater—where the theater itself is located in a downtown restricted area, such as the "combat zone" in Boston, and where admission prices are fairly high. The concern with classification is, in effect, an attempt to restore the traditional audience-content balance. The "immune" exhibition of some hardcore films becomes possible where presentation is restricted in much the same way that it is in the elite media. Thus here, too, there is an attempt to restore, at least for the moment, the appearance of the traditional equilibrium.

It is where classification breaks down or seems ineffective, or where hardcore fare breaks out of its cinematic closet and is marketed like other films, that censorial tensions are apt to rise to a peak and also manifest far-reaching backlash potential. Because the film medium is no longer strictly a mass medium and yet is not fully or completely an elite medium, it will have a continuing censorship problem that may or may not be eased by further change in popular attitudes.

21

DAVID GORDON

Why the Movie Majors Are Major

Movie buffs tend to be as ignorant about the movie industry as they are knowledgeable about its products. The very word product is one they find distasteful, reminding them as it does of a manufacturing process churning out items for mass consumption. People who love films seem to need to bless the object of their affection with the sacred title of art. In so doing, they set up a whole mythology of how films come to be made which rests on a supposed opposition between art and industry. The directors and writers are the artists, the genuine film makers, the creators, and they are all on one side of the fence; the movie tycoons, the faceless executives, the studios, capriciously open and shut the golden gate and allow the artists to enter, forcing them to bend their talents to the philistine dictates of the money men. It is commonly assumed that good films are made in spite of the system, by some kind of a trick on a particularly good, or gullible, guard at the golden gate.

One does not have to be a particularly hidebound Marxist to realize that a capitalist world, with profit-motivated corporations, is not going to turn out films which often challenge the basis of that world. But it is dangerous nonsense to see the movie companies as natural enemies of film's creative talent. The major distributors, the old names like MGM, Paramount, and the rest, are still responsible for financing the bulk of the moviegoer's diet. They must take a share of the credit for the good films that are honest, true, genuine, and for the good films that are merely entertaining, and a

Sight and Sound 42 (Autumn 1973): 194-96.

share of the blame for the crap. But most of all, they must be seen to take the credit and the blame; the movie majors are still the dominant force in film production, in film financing, and in distribution. The film companies are important.

This statement of the obvious is long overdue. For too long, the movie buff has been allowed to get away with a version of film's industrial history which is as myth-ridden as the films the moguls were meant to turn out. Very briefly, Everyone's History of the Film Business goes as follows: In the beginning there was chaos, and everyone and his immigrant father-in-law owned a nickelodeon and showed one-reelers. Then the Motion Pictures Patent Company moved in and sewed the whole thing up, licensing the users of Edison-based patents. But the Trust simply churned film out by the reel, and sold it by the foot. Showmen, like Adolph Zukor and Carl Laemmle, understood that the public wanted stars, and longer films (which the Europeans had pioneered), and so managed to bust the Trust—with government help. In the 1920s, the film companies realized—Adolph Zukor first—that if you owned distributors, there was a much greater chance of your films being shown. And then they realized— Adolph Zukor first—that if you owned the cinemas as well, you were in a really strong position. Thus the movie companies vertically integrated. With a booming audience, they simply turned out films on an assembly line, and used studios (an arty word for a factory) as the most economic way of so doing.

But after the war, in 1948, the Antitrust Division of the Justice Department finally won a long battle to break the power of the movie majors, and compelled them to divorce production and distribution from cinema ownership. At the same time the stars and producers, the package and the packagers, broke away from the studios and asserted their independence by demanding more money for themselves, and declaring themselves independent because they were able to get more money. As television sucked more of the audience away, the studios stupidly thought the way to win them back was to spend more money on films (i.e., give more money to the independents). The power of the studios was broken. Then, during 1969-71, the studios themselves nearly went broke as a result of having spent too much money trying to photocopy the success of *The Sound of Music*. And now, the major film companies have all been taken over by conglomerates that are more interested in funeral parlors and life insurance than in films, and are no longer of any consequence. New low-budget films made by independents and financed by independents and independently distributed and shown in the new minicinemas have replaced the old powerhouses. A new era has begun since *Easy Rider* and *The Effect of Gamma Rays*, etc. Talent rises, is financed, and is shown to the new stratified audiences in the new stratified picture semi-detached palaces.

Unfortunately, the ending of the above caricature is particularly erroneous. In 1973 and 1974, many of the majors were or will be celebrating their fiftieth anniversary. It was in 1923 that Walt and Roy Disney signed the Alice Comedies contract. Warner Brothers, now Warner Communications, celebrates this year the half-century since a Wall Street bank helped it buy Vitagraph. It was in 1924 that Marcus Loew, who had bought Metro in 1920, bought Goldwyn Pictures (from which Sam Goldfish had already exited) and the production unit run by Louis B. Mayer; MGM became Loew's production and distribution arm serving, among others, the Loew cinemas. The business run by Cohn, Brandt, and Cohn adopted the name Columbia Pictures on January 10, 1924. Universal could celebrate its fiftieth birthday this year, taking the year that its parent company MCA was founded by Jules Stein, or its sixtieth birthday, dating from the year that Uncle Carl opened Universal City. Both Paramount and Fox can choose a range of anniversary dates from their confusing beginnings: for example, Paramount could rejoice this year in the fortieth year since being reorganized after bankruptcy. The movie companies are celebrating their birthdays with joy in their hearts, money in their coffers, and, still, muscle in their production and distribution arms.

It is not easy to prove the assertion that the movie companies are still a powerful world movie force. Facts are scarce; the absence of government assistance to the American film industry means that there is no government agency that collects figures on it, and the trade association, the Motion Picture Association of America, is secretive. However, the amount of money taken annually at the box office in American cinemas is estimated at some $1.3 billion by the U.S. Commerce Department. Something like two-thirds of that is kept by the exhibitors, leaving around $400 million to be shared by the distributors. *Variety* does an estimate of the market share of that distributors' gross by the majors, which is shown in the table below. All but 6 percent of the gross was collected by the majors in 1972—and the share appears to be growing. In 1970, National General, which distributed the films made by Cinema Center, the film-making subsidiary of the CBS television network company, and Cinerama, which was distributing the product of another network, ABC, managed to collect 10 percent of the market between them. Both the television networks have dropped out of movie financing. If anything, the grip of the major distributors is tightening in the American market. Why?

The reason is that the production, finance, and the distribution of films are irrevocably linked. It is not practicable simply to finance a roster of

TABLE 1
The Dominant Majors:
Percentage Share of US and Canadian Distributors' Grosses

Company	1972	1971	1970
Paramount	21.6	17.0	11.8
Warner Brothers	17.6	9.3	5.3
United Artists	15.0	7.4	8.7
Columbia	9.1	10.2	14.1
20th Century-Fox	9.1	11.5	19.4
MGM	6.0	9.3	3.4
Universal	5.0	5.2	13.1
Walt Disney	5.0	8.0	9.1
National General/Cinema Center	3.2	8.0	7.0
ABC/Cinerama	2.7	3.6	3.0

Source: *Variety*

films. And it is not possible simply to distribute films. (On a large scale, that is; there will always be room for small independents.) For one reason or another, those institutions that have gone into film financing and production without having control over a distribution organization outfit have not lasted (e.g., Cinema Center, ABC). Those distribution organizations that gave up film financing and production, such as the Rank Organisation in Britain, have ceased to be very significant world distributors.

There are a bunch of factors that explain the necessity of the finance/distribution conjunction. The first is that, in spite of their glaring blemishes, the distributors know their business, and part of this knowledge carries over from one function—distribution—to the other—production/financing. This is a lesson that Robert Altman learned not so long ago. Dissatisfied with the way that MGM handled *Brewster McCloud,* and the way that Warner handled *McCabe and Mrs. Miller,* he financed *Images* with the help of Hemdale, the young British showbiz company (now part of David Frost's Equity Enterprises). Seven months later: "The whole experience was not very pleasant. I now think it's probably a mistake not to have a distributor involved in a firm from the time you enter production. Columbia didn't even know until two months beforehand that they were going to handle *Images,* so they didn't have much time to formulate advertising and marketing."

On the whole, producers have found that the one thing worse than being involved with a major was not being involved with a major. They do, after all, have some helpful skills. Just as a good editor at a publishing house can make all the difference, a good movie executive can be useful to producers. They are not all the philistines of the cinéaste's mythology.

The second factor is that film distribution is necessarily expensive, and so risky that distributors have to exercise some control over what they

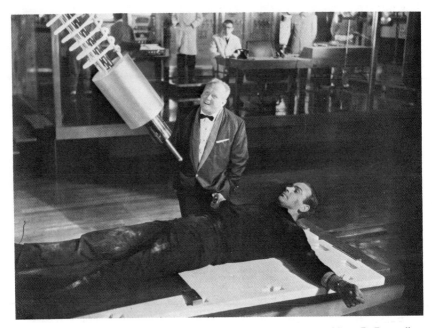

Goldfinger (United Artists, 1964), produced by Harry Saltzman and Albert R. Broccoli: Gert Frobe and Sean Connery

distribute. It is so expensive because the essence of film economics is that the unit of production costs millions of dollars, but the return comes back in millions of cents. It is gigantically expensive to get a film from studio to cinema. Very roughly, out of each $100 of cinema receipts, $60 is for the cinema costs and profit. Of the remaining $40, about $15 is available to cover the negative costs of the film, and the rest is for the overheads and profits of the distributor. In order to get the film into as many cinemas as possible, distributors have to have an international sales organization. Very roughly, the majors each spend in the region of $10 million in North America and $10 million in the rest of the world maintaining sales offices. In a way, big time distribution is like the steel industry; the costs of entry are very high. If you want your own world sales force, that is, which is why the newcomers to film production used the existing distributors. The newcomers tried to use the distributors as wholesalers. "Here are our films," they said, "which we have financed. You deduct a percentage from all you make by selling them, and pay the costs of prints and advertising, and hand over the balance to us." It didn't work.

They reckoned without the third factor. The distribution fee is not just the payment for marketing—it includes a reward for taking the risks of handling the picture. When a picture is a success, that reward is too high, and when it is a disaster, it is too low, for the individual pictures. The only way distributors can survive is by setting the super-profits of one production against the super-losses of another and the nothing-profits of the average picture. Only the film distributors have the cash flow to be able to do this risk-spreading, which is more akin to merchant banking than it is to wholesaling. Cash sticks to distributors; it has to. Those that merely make and finance pictures inevitably get an unfair percentage of the total take. This can be illustrated by the figures prepared by ABC when it pulled out of movies.

ABC financed, in whole or in part, some thirty-six films in the six years to 1972—putting its eggs in several baskets. The average budget was a moderate $2 million. The films included *Straw Dogs, Junior Bonner, Candy, The Killing of Sister George, They Shoot Horses, Don't They?, Song of Norway, Kotch,* and half of *Cabaret.* Before taking account of the full benefit of *Cabaret,* or of sales to television, or, on the other hand, of production company overheads, the loss at the end of the day was reckoned to be $47 million.

	$m.	*$m.*
Rentals from cinemas		107
Negative costs	81	
Distribution fee	27	
Prints and advertising	36	
Interest	10	
		154
Loss		47

A huge slice of the costs, the prints and advertising, was under the control of distributors. And the distribution fee inevitably represents more than the basic costs of distribution. Very possibly, had exactly the same program of films been financed at the same negative cost by the distributors, the total figure at the end of the day could be in the black, not in the red, thanks to lower real distribution costs and potentially higher revenues. As further evidence, there is the experience of the other powerful entertainment group that went into the movies, CBS's subsidiary Cinema Center Films. It also lost several tens of millions of dollars before learning that producing and financing films without control over distribution can be suicide.

So where does that leave us? In the laps of the distributors. For good economic reasons, the bulk of the films that get to the screen are financed by the distributors. They are the only people with the international sales force necessary to collar the cash; they alone have the cash flow to set off the inevitable losses against the much rarer successes; their knowledge of markets and experience at production, highly fallible though it is consistently proved to be, keeps a stream of films before our eyes that is tempting enough for us to want to dip hands in pockets.

It is in this broad context that the crisis of 1969-71 must be seen. Remember all those articles about the decline of Hollywood, about Fox's horrific loss of $65 million in 1969 and $81 million the following year, about problems at MGM and at all the majors? It was not the beginning of the end, but a painful adjustment to the facts of life. The basic fact of cinema's industrial life is that the market for films in the United States is $1.3 billion, and that American films can hope to take another $1 billion or so at cinemas in the rest of the world and, say, another $400 million from television distribution.

Since only $15 out of every $100 taken in revenue is available for the recoupment of negative costs, the market can support an investment in the region of $500 million (the figures are, of reluctant necessity, extremely rough and ready). In 1968 the movie majors, who were still busily following the false god of trying to lure the television audience back with very expensive superproductions, had invested for current release some $1.2 billion worth of films and projects. The result of such huge overstocking was that the companies had to take gigantic losses as they wrote off the values of the films and television rights down to a realistic level. But that is now over: for example, Fox's inventory of $238 million in 1968 is down to a mere $65 million now. (In an inflationary period, films are one of the products whose average cost has actually not increased—though rock bottom has probably now been reached, and the only future direction is up again.) All the majors, except Columbia, which was among the last to go down, are healthily back in the money—and in a mood to celebrate their fiftieth birthdays.

If this economic analysis of the role of the majors in world production and distribution is accurate, then there are certain significant—and disparate—conclusions to be drawn:

1. If the cinema audience continues to shrink (and there are hopeful signs of an upturn), either the number of films distributed, or their average cost, will have to fall again.

2. The economics of the industry determine that independent productions have a better chance of success if they are financed by a major distributor. It is possible to get films financed from other sources. In fact, hundreds of films are financed independently. According to Variety, 296 films were produced in 1972, and 170 were independents (although this includes independents wholly financed by the studios). However, only 96

Sunday Bloody Sunday (United Artists, 1971), directed by John Schlesinger;
Peter Finch, Murray Head, and Glenda Jackson

films made over $1 million for their distributors in North America. Some of them took much more, like *The Godfather,* which took $81 million. The figures show that the films that do well, do very well—and those that do not do very well, do very badly. The 200 films that did not even make the $1 million, had to share a tiny pool of some $50 million left over by those that did, which means that most of those 200 made a loss for their financiers. A disproportionate number of nonindependents avoided this fate. If for no other reason, it is because the big distributors have more muscle in getting movies into cinemas.

3. The power of the American distributors extends throughout Europe. It is because they make transnational films and have the transnational marketing outfit to handle them. The two things go together. The notion that French, or British, or Italian films would get a bigger showing if only there were a European film distribution network is wishful thinking. There has been nothing to stop the Europeans' building up a distribution network as powerful as that of the Americans. But it has not come to pass. With frequent exceptions—which do usually get on to the international circuit—European countries make films for their own and a neighbor or two's edification. Thus the idea of fostering European distribution power, as expounded in *Sight and Sound* (Spring 1973) by M. Claude Degand of the Centre National du Cinéma, is unrealistic.

Jaws (Universal, 1975), directed by Steven Spielberg: Robert Shaw and Richard Dreyfuss. From the motion picture *Jaws.* Courtesy of Univeral Pictures

4. There is no British film industry to speak of. Apart from the odd film made by Rank, EMI, or British Lion, the huge bulk of films made in Britain are financed by the American distributors. This is quite understandable. The British market is too small, and the costs of production are too high, for any but the most lucky or unimaginative (e.g., the films

TABLE 2
Film Markets, USA and the EEC:
Box Office Grosses in 1972, in Millions of Dollars

United States	1,300
Italy	364
France	202
West Germany	186
Britain	154
Belgium	33
The Netherlands	29
Denmark	23
	991

based on television programs) to make a profit in Britain alone. There is no way to increase true British production except by making films more cheaply than the film unions will allow, or by subsidy. Or by encouraging a British distributor to go multinational like the Americans. Rank tried and failed. With such a tiny home base—see the table—it is difficult. The total turnover of the British cinema, the money taken at the box office, is only 60 million pounds—or a fifth of the turnover of J. Sainsbury chain of grocery shops.

The major American film distributors combine international marketing with diversified risk-taking. It is a necessary combination. Since the total market for feature films shown in cinemas is, after adjustment for inflation, shrinking, the relative domination of the majors is likely to increase as fewer and fewer institutions find it worthwhile to get into the business of financing films or distributing them. The trend to smaller cinemas may not be the salvation it is cracked up to be. More cinemas might not bring in much more money in total at the box office—simply the same amount in smaller doses. But the increased number of screens increases the demands for films to show. Thus the effect of fragmentation might be to increase the total costs of the film industry (i.e., the costs of running the cinemas, plus distributing the films, plus making them). It is too soon to tell. But the major new source of revenue for feature films lies in their distribution on network television, or on cable television or cassettes. And who will benefit from this? Why, the major distributors. We should learn how to stop worrying and love them.

Contributors
Bibliography
Indexes

List of Contributors

JEANNE THOMAS ALLEN

is Assistant Professor of Communications Arts, University of Wisconsin-Madison.

TINO BALIO

is Professor of Communication Arts and Director, Wisconsin Center for Film and Theater Research, University of Wisconsin-Madison. He is author of *United Artists: The Company Built by the Stars* and co-author with Lee Norvelle of the *History of the National Theatre Conference.*

ERNEST BORNEMAN

was Director of Distribution for the National Film Board of Canada.

JOHN COGLEY

was Executive Editor of *The Commonweal* and prepared the two-volume *Report on Blacklisting* for The Fund for the Republic.

MICHAEL CONANT

is Professor of Business Administration at the University of California, Berkeley.

A. R. FULTON

taught film for many years in the Department of English at Purdue University. He now lives in Ann Arbor, Michigan.

J. DOUGLAS GOMERY

is Assistant Professor of Mass Communications, University of Wisconsin-Milwaukee. His dissertation topic was "The Coming of Sound to the American Cinema: The Transformation of an Industry" (University of Wisconsin-Madison, 1975).

471

DAVID GORDON

is Investment Editor of *The Economist* in London and a free-lance writer for film publications. His book on the economics of the film business will be published soon.

THOMAS H. GUBACK

is Research Associate Professor, Institute of Communications Research, University of Illinois, and author of *The International Film Industry: Western Europe and America since 1945.*

GORDON HENDRICKS

has done pioneering research on the origins of the American film. His latest contribution is *Eadweard Muybridge: The Father of the Motion Picture.* He resides in New York City.

MAE D. HUETTIG

received her Ph.D. from the University of Pennsylvania and conducted her industry study under a grant from the Rockefeller Foundation.

CARL LAEMMLE

was a motion picture pioneer who founded the Independent Motion Picture Company and helped establish the Universal Company.

FREEMAN LINCOLN

was a member of the Board of Editors of *Fortune.*

RUSSELL MERRITT

is Associate Professor of Communication Arts, University of Wisconsin-Madison. He has written several articles on motion picture history and is preparing a book-length study of D. W. Griffith's formative years.

GEORGE PRATT

is Associate Curator of Motion Pictures at George Eastman House, Rochester, and Editor of *Image.* He is the author of *Spellbound in Darkness: A History of the Silent Film.*

RICHARD S. RANDALL

is Associate Professor and Chairman, Department of Politics, New York University, and author of *Censorship of the Movies: The Social and Political Control of a Mass Medium.*

NORMA TALMADGE

was a star of the silent era.

Selected Bibliography

The following selected bibliography lists publications on the history of the American motion picture industry, its trade practices, and its leaders. A more comprehensive listing of the literature may be found in *Industrial Arts Index,* Vols. 1-45, 1913-1957; *Business Periodicals Index,* Vols. 1—, 1958—; *The New Film Index: A Bibliography of Magazine Articles in English, 1930-1970,* edited by Richard Dyer MacCann and Edward S. Perry (New York, 1975); and *The Critical Index: A Bibliography of Articles on Film in English, 1946-1973,* edited by John C. Gerlach and Lana Gerlach (New York, 1974).

The standard references on all aspects of the industry are *Film Daily Year Book of Motion Pictures,* published annually from 1917 to 1969, and *Motion Picture Almanac* and its successor, *International Motion Picture Almanac,* published annually from 1929.

The standard trade publications are *Variety,* published from 1905, and *Moving Picture World* (1907-1927), which merged into *Exhibitors' Herald* and later became known as *Motion Picture Herald.*

Special attention should be given to the *Journal of the Producers Guild of America* (known more familiarly as the *Journal of the Screen Producers Guild*), which since 1958 has analyzed contemporary conditions in the industry.

Aitken, Roy E. *The* Birth of a Nation *Story.* Middleburg, Va., 1965.

Allvine, Glendon. *The Greatest Fox of Them All.* New York, 1969.

Alpert, Hollis. *The Dreams and the Dreamers.* New York, 1962.

Arvidson, Linda. *When the Movies Were Young.* New York, 1925.

Baker, Fred, ed. *Movie People at Work in the Business of Film.* New York, 1972.

Balaban, Carrie. *Continuous Performance.* New York, 1942.

Balio, Tino. *United Artists: The Company Built by the Stars.* Madison, Wis., 1975.

Balshofer, Fred J., and Miller, Arthur C. *One Reel a Week.* Berkeley and Los Angeles, 1967.

Batman, Richard Dale. "The Founding of the Hollywood Motion Picture Industry." *Journal of the West* 10 (October 1971): 609-23.

Baumgarten, Paul A. *Legal and Business Problems of the Motion Picture Industry.* New York, 1973.

Beach, E. R. "Double Features in Motion-Picture Exhibition." *Harvard Business Review* 10 (July 1932): 505-15.

Bennett, R. C. "Merger Movement in the Motion Picture Industry." *Annals of the American Academy of Political and Social Science* 147 (January 1930): 89-94.

Bernheim, Alfred L. *Business of the Theatre.* New York, 1932.

Bernstein, Irving. *Hollywood at the Crossroads: An Economic Study of the Motion Picture Industry.* Hollywood, 1957.

Bluem, A. William, and Squire, Jason E., eds. *The Movie Business: American Film Industry Practice.* New York, 1972.

Borneman, Ernest. "Rebellion in Hollywood: A Case Study in Motion Picture Finance." *Harper's* 193 (October 1946): 337-43.

————. "United States versus Hollywood: The Case Study of an Antitrust Suit." *Sight and Sound* 19 (February 1951): 418-20+; (March 1951): 448-50. [reprinted herein]

Brady, Robert A. "Monopoly and the First Freedom." *Hollywood Quarterly* 2 (April 1947): 225-41.

Brown, Stanley. "That Old Villain TV Comes to the Rescue and Hollywood Rides Again." *Fortune* 74 (November 1966): 181-82+.

Brownlaw, Kevin. *The Parade's Gone By.* New York, 1969.

Campbell, Russell. "Warner Brothers in the Thirties." *Velvet Light Trap*, no. 1 (June 1971): 2-4.

Capra, Frank. "Breaking Hollywood's 'Pattern of Sameness'." *The New York Times Magazine,* May 5, 1946, p. 18+.

Carmen, Ira H. *Movies, Censorship and the Law.* Ann Arbor, Mich., 1966.

Cassady, Ralph, Jr. "Some Economic Aspects of Motion Picture Production and Marketing." *Journal of Business of the University of Chicago* 6 (April 1933): 113-31.

————. "Impact of the Paramount Decision on Motion Picture Distribution and Price Making." *Southern California Law Review* 31 (February 1958): 150-80.

————. "Monopoly in Motion Picture Production and Distribution: 1908-1915." *Southern California Law Review* 32 (Summer 1959): 325-90.

————, and Cassady, Ralph, III. *The Private Antitrust Suit in American Business Competition: A Motion-Picture Industry Case Analysis.* Los Angeles, 1964.

Chambers, R. "Double Features as a Sales Problem." *Harvard Business Review* 16 (Winter 1938): 226-36.

Champlin, Charles. "Can TV Save the Films?" *Saturday Review* 49 (December 24, 1966): 11-13.

Cogley, John. *Report on Blacklisting, I: The Movies.* New York, 1956. ["The Mass Hearings" reprinted herein]

Conant, Michael. *Antitrust in the Motion Picture Industry.* Berkeley and Los Angeles, 1960. [Chapter 6 abridged herein]

Coughlan, Robert. "Now It Is Trouble That Is Super Colossal in Hollywood." *Life* 31 (August 13, 1951): 102-14.

Crowther, Bosley. "The Movies," in Jack Goodman, ed., *While You Were Gone.* New York, 1946. Pp. 511-32.

————. *The Lion's Share: The Story of an Entertainment Empire.* New York, 1957.

————. *Hollywood Rajah: The Life and Times of Louis B. Mayer.* New York, 1960.

Danielian, N. R. *AT&T: The Story of Industrial Conquest.* New York, 1939.

Davis, John. "RKO: A Studio Chronology." *Velvet Light Trap,* no. 10 (Fall 1973): 6-12.

Dawson, Anthony H. "Motion Picture Economics." *Hollywood Quarterly* 3 (Spring 1948): 217-40.

_____. "Hollywood's Labor Troubles." *Industrial and Labor Relations Review* 1 (July 1948): 638-47.

_____. "Patterns of Production and Employment in Hollywood." *Hollywood Quarterly* 4 (Summer 1950): 338-53.

Dietrich, Noah, and Thomas, Bob. *Howard, the Amazing Mr. Hughes.* Greenwich, Conn., 1972.

Dowdy, Andrew. *"Movies Are Better Than Ever."* New York, 1973.

Drinkwater, John. *The Life and Adventures of Carl Laemmle.* New York, 1931.

Dunne, John Gregory. *The Studio.* New York, 1968.

Fernett, Gene. *Poverty Row.* Satellite Beach, Fla., 1973.

Fielding, Raymond. *A Technological History of Motion Pictures and Television.* Berkeley and Los Angeles, 1967.

Fortune. "The Case of William Fox." 1 (May 1930): 48-49+.

_____. *"Body and Soul* Is (Here) Put Together." 4 (August 1931): 26-34+.

_____. "Metro-Goldwyn-Mayer." 6 (December 1932): 51-58+. [reprinted herein]

_____. "The Big Bad Wolf." 10 (November 1934): 88-95+.

_____. "Twentieth Century-Fox." 12 (December 1935): 85-93+.

_____. "Paramount Pictures." 15 (March 1937): 87-96+.

_____. "Warner Brothers." 16 (December 1937): 110-13+.

_____. "The Hays Office." 18 (December 1938): 69-72+. [reprinted herein]

_____. "Loew's, Inc." 20 (August 1939): 25-30+. [reprinted herein]

_____. "United Artists: Final Shooting Script." 22 (December 1940): 95-102+.

_____. "Paramount: Oscar for Profits." 35 (June 1947): 90-94+.

_____. "What's Playing at the Grove?" 38 (August 1948): 94-99+.

_____. "Movies: End of an Era?" 39 (April 1949): 99-102+.

_____. "Cinerama—the Broad Picture." 47 (January 1953): 92-93+.

_____. "RKO: It's Only Money." 47 (May 1953): 122-27.

_____. "The Derring-Doers of Movie Business." 57 (May 1958): 137-41+.

French, Philip. *The Movie Moguls.* London, 1969.

Fulton, A. R. *Motion Pictures: The Development of an Art from Silent Pictures to the Age of Television.* Norman, Okla., 1960. [chapter 1 reprinted herein]

Geduld, Harry M. *The Birth of the Talkies: From Edison to Jolson.* Bloomington, Ind., 1975.

Gelman, Morris J. "The Hollywood Story." *Television Magazine* 20 (September 1963): entire issue.

Goodman, Ezra. *The Fifty-Year Decline and Fall of Hollywood.* New York, 1961.

Goodman, Walter. *The Committee: The Extraordinary Career of the House Committee on Un-American Activities.* New York, 1968.

Gordon, David. "Why the Movie Majors Are Major," *Sight and Sound* 42 (Autumn 1973): 194-96. [reprinted herein]

Grau, Robert. *The Business Man in the Amusement World.* New York, 1910.

_____. *The Stage in the Twentieth Century.* New York, 1912.

_____. *The Theatre of Science: A Volume of Progress and Achievement in the Motion Picture Industry.* New York, 1914.

Green, Fitzhugh. *The Film Finds Its Tongue.* New York, 1929.

Greenspan, Lou, *et al.* "The *Journal* Looks at Hollywood and the State of the Industry." *Journal of the Screen Producers Guild* 12 (March 1970): 1-32.

Greenwald, William I. "The Impact of Sound upon the Film Industry: A Case Study of Innovation," *Explorations in Entrepreneurial History* 4 (May 15, 1952): 178-92.

Griffith, Richard. *Samuel Goldwyn: The Producer and His Films.* New York, 1956.

_____. *The Movie Stars.* Garden City, N.Y., 1970.

_____, and Mayer, Arthur. *The Movies.* New York, 1957.

Guback, Thomas. *The International Film Industry: Western Europe and America since 1945.* Bloomington, Ind., 1969.

Gussow, Mel. *Don't Say Yes until I Finish Talking: A Biography of Darryl F. Zanuck.* Garden City, N.Y., 1971.

Hall, Ben M. *The Best Remaining Seats: The Story of the Golden Age of the Movie Palace.* New York, 1961.

Hampton, Benjamin B. *A History of the Movies.* New York, 1931.

Handel, Leo A. *Hollywood Looks at Its Audience.* Urbana, Ill., 1950.

Harlan, George C. "Putting Business Back into Show Business." *Magazine of Wall Street* 119 (Dec. 24, 1966): 341-44+.

Hays, Will H. *See and Hear.* New York, 1929.

Hellmuth, William F., Jr. "The Motion Picture Industry," in Walter Adams, ed., *The Structure of the American Industry: Some Case Studies.* New York, 1961. Pp. 393-429.

Henderson, Robert. *D. W. Griffith: His Life and Work.* New York, 1972.

Hendricks, Gordon. *The Edison Motion Picture Myth.* Berkeley and Los Angeles, 1961.

_____. *Beginnings of the Biograph.* New York, 1964.

_____. *The Kinetoscope.* New York, 1966. Abridged herein.

Heywood, Johnson. "How 'Movie' Industry Got on Sound Financial Basis." *Forbes* (March 1, 1927) pp. 13-16+.

Higham, Charles. *Warner Brothers.* New York, 1975.

Houseman, John. "Hollywood Faces the Fifties." *Harper's* 200 (April 1950): 50-59; (May 1950): 51-59.

Howard, Jack. "Hollywood and Television—Year of Decision." *Quarterly of Film, Radio and Television* 7 (Summer 1953): 359-69.

Howe, A. H. "A Banker Looks at the Picture Business." *Journal of the Screen Producers Guild* 7 (December 1965): 9-16.

_____. "How Movies Are Financed." *Films in Review* 7 (January 1966): 1-5.

_____. "A Banker Looks at the Picture Business." *Journal of the Screen Producers Guild* 11 (March 1969): 15-22.

_____. "A Banker Looks at the Picture Business—1971." *Journal of the Screen Producers Guild* 13 (June 1971): 3-10.

Huettig, Mae. *Economic Control of the Motion Picture Industry.* Philadelphia, 1944. [chapter 2 abridged herein]

Hughes, E. J. "M.G.M.: War Among the Lion Tamers." *Fortune* 56 (August 1957): 98-103.

Inglis, Ruth A. *Freedom of the Movies.* Chicago, 1947.

Irwin, William Henry. *The House That Shadows Built.* Garden City, N.Y., 1928.

Jacobs, Lewis. *The Rise of the American Film.* New York, 1939.

Jones, Dorothy. "Hollywood Goes to War." *Nation* 160 (Jan. 27, 1945): 93-95.

Jowett, Garth S. "The First Motion Picture Audiences." *Journal of Popular Film* 3 (Winter 1974): 39-54.

Kanfer, Stefan. *A Journal of the Plague Years.* New York, 1973.

Kennedy, Joseph P., ed. *The Story of the Films.* Chicago and New York, 1927.

King, Clyde C., and Tichener, Frank A., eds. "The Motion Picture in Its Economic and Social Aspects." *Annals of the American Academy of Political and Social Science* 127 (November 1926): entire issue.

Klingender, F. D., and Legg, Stuart. *Money behind the Screen.* London, 1937.

Knight, Arthur. *The Liveliest Art.* New York, 1959.

Knox, Donald. *The Magic Factory: How MGM Made* An American in Paris. New York, 1973.

Laemmle, Carl. "From the Inside." *Saturday Evening Post* 200 (Aug. 27, Sept. 3, and Sept. 10, 1927). [excerpted herein]

Lahue, Kalton C. *Continued Next Week: A History of the Moving Picture Serial.* Norman, Okla., 1964.

————. *World of Laughter: The Motion Picture Comedy Short, 1910-1930.* Norman, Okla., 1966.

————. *Bound and Gagged: The Story of the Silent Serials.* New York, 1968.

————. *Dreams for Sale: The Rise and Fall of the Triangle Film Corporation.* New York, 1971.

————. *Motion Picture Pioneer: The Selig Polyscope Company.* Cranbury, N.J., 1973.

———— and Brewer, Terry. *Kops and Custards: The Legend of Keystone Films.* Norman, Okla., 1968.

Lewis, Howard T. "Distributing Motion Pictures." *Harvard Business Review* 7 (April 1929): 267-79.

————. *Cases on the Motion Picture Industry.* Harvard Business Reports, no. 8. New York, 1930.

————. *The Motion Picture Industry.* New York, 1933.

Limbacher, James. *Four Aspects of Film.* New York, 1968.

Lincoln, Freeman. "The Comeback of the Movies." *Fortune* 51 (February 1955): 127-31+. [reprinted herein]

Lovell, Hugh, and Carter, Tasile. *Collective Bargaining in the Motion Picture Industry: A Struggle for Stability.* Berkeley, 1955.

Luther, Rodney. "Television and the Future of Motion Picture Exhibition." *Hollywood Quarterly* 5 (Winter 1950): 164-77.

————. "Drive-in Theaters: Rags to Riches in Five Years." *Hollywood Quarterly* 5 (Summer 1951): 401-11.

Lyons, Timothy J. *The Silent Partner: The History of the American Film Manufacturing Company, 1910-1921.* New York, 1974.
MacCann, Richard Dyer. *Hollywood in Transition.* Boston, 1962.
_____. "Independence with a Vengeance." *Film Quarterly* 15 (Summer 1962): 14-21.
McCarthy, Todd, and Flynn, Charles, eds. *Kings of the Bs.* New York, 1975.
McDonald, John. "Now the Bankers Come to Disney." *Fortune* 73 (May 1966): 139-41+.
Macgowan, Kenneth. *Behind the Screen: The History and Techniques of the Motion Picture.* New York, 1965.
McLaughlin, Robert. *Broadway and Hollywood: A History of Economic Interaction.* New York, 1974.
McWilliams, Carey. "The Island of Hollywood," in *Southern California Country: An Island on the Land.* New York, 1946. Pp. 330-49.
Martin, Olga J. *Hollywood's Movie Commandments.* New York, 1937.
Marx, Samuel. *Mayer and Thalberg: The Make-Believe Saints.* New York, 1975.
Mayer, Arthur. *Merely Colossal: The Story of the Movies from the Long Chase to the Chaise Longue.* New York, 1953.
_____. "Hollywood's Favorite Fable." *Film Quarterly* 12 (Winter 1958): 13-20.
_____. "Growing Pains of a Shrinking Industry." *Saturday Review* 44 (Feb. 25, 1961): 21-23+.
_____, et al. "The *Journal* Looks at Motion Picture Distribution." *Journal of the Screen Producers Guild* 3 (December 1961): 3-22.
Mayer, Michael F. *The Film Industries.* New York, 1973.
Moley, Raymond. *The Hays Office.* New York, 1945.
Munsun, Chris. *The Marketing of Motion Pictures.* Los Angeles, 1969.
Musson, Bennet, and Grau, Robert. "Fortunes in Films." *McClure's* 39 (December 1912): 193-202.
Niver, Kemp R. *The First Twenty Years: A Segment of Film History.* Los Angeles, 1968.
Nizer, Louis. *New Courts of Industry: Self-Regulation Under the Motion Picture Code.* New York, 1935.
_____. "Proxy Battle: The Struggle Over Loew's." In *My Life in Court.* Garden City, N.Y., 1961.
North, Joseph H. *The Early Development of the Motion Picture, 1887-1909.* New York, 1973.
Onosko, Tim. "Monogram: Its Rise and Fall in the Forties." *Velvet Light Trap,* no. 5 (Summer 1972): 5-9.
Paletz, David, and Noonan, Michael. "The Exhibitors." *Film Quarterly* 19 (Winter 1965-66): 14-40.
Partridge, J. H. "Tremendous Changes Coming in TV-Movies." *Magazine of Wall Street* 97 (Oct. 15, 1955): 78-81+.
Political and Economic Planning. *The British Film Industry.* London, 1952.
Powdermaker, Hortense. *Hollywood, the Dream Factory.* Boston, 1950.
Pratt, George. "No Magic, No Mystery, No Sleight of Hand." *Image* 8 (December 1959): 192-211. [reprinted herein]

Ramsaye, Terry. *A Million and One Nights: A History of the Motion Picture.* 2 vols. New York, 1926.

Randall, Richard S. *Censorship of the Movies: The Social and Political Control of a Mass Medium.* Madison, Wis., 1968.

Ricketson, Frank H. *The Management of Motion Picture Theatres.* New York, 1938.

Ringstad, Robert C. "The Great Transition in Motion Picture Industry." *Magazine of Wall Street* 103 (Oct. 25, 1958): 76-78+.

Ross, Lillian. *Picture.* New York, 1952.

Ross, Murray. *Stars and Strikes: Unionization of Hollywood.* New York, 1941.

Rosten, Leo C. *Hollywood: The Movie Colony, the Movie Makers.* New York, 1941.

Sanders, Terry B. "The Financing of Independent Feature Films." *Quarterly of Film, Radio and Television* 9 (Summer 1955): 380-89.

Sands, Pierre Norman. *A Historical Study of the Academy of Motion Picture Arts and Sciences (1927-1947).* New York, 1973.

Schary, Dore. *Case History of a Movie.* New York, 1950.

Schickel, Richard. *The Disney Version.* New York, 1968.

Schumach, Murray. *The Face on the Cutting Room Floor.* New York, 1964.

Seabury, William Marston. *The Public and the Motion Picture Industry.* New York, 1926.

———. *Motion Picture Problems.* New York, 1929.

Seldes, Gilbert. *Movies Come from America.* New York, 1937.

———. *The Great Audience.* New York, 1950.

Sheehan, R. "Cliff-hanger at M.G.M." *Fortune* 56 (October 1957): 134-35+.

Sinclair, Upton. *Upton Sinclair Presents William Fox.* Los Angeles, 1933.

Slide, Anthony. "The Evolution of the Film Star." *Films in Review* 25 (December 1974): 591-94.

Smith, Albert E., and Koury, Phil. *Two Reels and a Crank.* Garden City, N.Y., 1952.

Smith, Richard Austin. "RKO: A Crisis of Responsibility." In *Corporations in Crisis.* Garden City, N.Y., 1963.

Smythe, Dallas W., *et al.* "Portrait of an Art-Theater Audience." *The Quarterly of Film, Radio and Television* 8 (Fall 1953): 28-50.

———. "Portrait of a First-Run Audience." *Quarterly of Film, Radio and Television* 9 (Summer 1955): 390-409.

Stern, Seymour. "The Birth of a Nation." *Sight and Sound,* Index Series No. 4 (July 1945): 2-16.

Strauss, W. V. "Foreign Distribution of American Films." *Harvard Business Review* 8 (April 1930): 307-15.

Swenson, Joel. "The Entrepreneur's Role in Introducing the Sound Motion Picture." *Political Science Quarterly* 63 (September 1948): 404-23.

Talbot, Frederick A. *Moving Pictures: How They Are Made and Worked.* Philadelphia, 1912.

Talmadge, Norma. "Close-Ups." *Saturday Evening Post* 199 (March 12, 26, April 9, May 7, 21, June 25, 1927). [excerpted herein]

Thomas, Bob. *King Cohn: The Life and Times of Harry Cohn.* New York, 1967.
––––––. *Thalberg: Life and Legend.* Garden City, N.Y., 1969.
––––––. *Selznick.* Garden City, N.Y., 1970.
Thomas, Jeanne. "The Decay of the Motion Picture Patents Company." *Cinema Journal* 10 (Spring 1971): 34-40. [reprinted herein]
Thorp, Margaret Farrand. *America at the Movies.* New Haven, Conn., 1939.
U.S. Temporary National Economic Committee. *The Motion Picture Industry: A Pattern of Control.* Washington, D.C., 1941.
Vaughan, Floyd L. *Economics of Our Patent System.* New York, 1926.
Vaughan, Robert. *Only Victims: A Study of Show Business Blacklisting.* New York, 1972.
Walker, Alexander. *Hollywood UK: The British Film Industry in the Sixties.* New York, 1974.
Warner, Jack L. *My First Hundred Years in Hollywood.* New York, 1965.
Watkins, G. S., ed. "The Motion Picture Industry." *Annals of the American Academy of Political and Social Science* 256 (November 1947): entire issue.
Whitney, Simon N. *Antitrust Policies: American Experience in Twenty Industries.* 2 vols. New York, 1958.
Wood, Alan. *Mr. Rank: A Study of J. Arthur Rank and British Films.* London, 1952.
Yousling, George. "Bank Financing of the Independent Motion Picture Producer." Unpublished paper, Graduate School of Banking, Rutgers University, 1948.
Zierold, Norman. *The Moguls.* New York, 1969.
Zukor, Adolph. *The Public Is Never Wrong.* New York, 1953.

Index of Motion Picture Titles

General Index

ABC, 460, 463
Abe Lincoln in Illinois, 422
AB-PT Pictures Corporation, 324, 363
Abrams, Hiram, 150
Academy Awards, 287
Academy of Motion Picture Arts and Sciences, 208, 266
Acting, 17-18
Actophone, 133
Actors' Equity, 208-9
Addams, Jane, 63-64
Admission prices, 27, 39, 61, 67, 337
Admissions: during 1920s, 116; during Depression, 214-15; importance to majors, 233, 238-39; postwar drop in, 372; effect of TV on, 410; allocation of, 462; potential of domestic market, 464; mentioned, 460
Adolfi, John, 94
Adrian, 259, 260
Advertising: importance to star system, 106; campaign book, 161-63; in trade publications, 163; timing of, 164-65; truth in, 165-66; as a function of distribution, 180; annual expenditures for, 246; of production costs, 251-52; regulated by MPPDA, 309-10
Afram Films, Inc., 405
Agents, 217
Aitken, Harry, 141-42, 145
Aitken, Roy, 145
Alberteri, Monsieur, 94
Alexander, James S., 199
Alice Comedies, 460
Allied Artists Pictures Corporation, 320, 354, 359, 380
Allied States Association of Motion Picture Exhibitors, 368, 377
Altman, Robert, 461
American Broadcasting-Paramount Theatres, 348, 363, 378, 380
American Civil Liberties Union, 345
American Federation of Labor, 217
American Federation of Musicians, 208
American Film Manufacturing Company, 133
American Gramophone Company, 195
American Legion, 431

American Motion Picture Export Company (Africa), 405
American Mutoscope and Biograph Company: camera, 5, 10, 120; projector, 5, 52-55; studio, 8; attacked by Edison, 8, 16, 120; early history of, 10; vies for domestic market, 48; subjects, 52-55; film size, 53; inspired by Kinetoscope, 80; lighting techniques, 97-98; forms MPPC, 103, 121, 122; folds, 130; hires Pickford, 136; dependence on Griffith, 144-45; mentioned, 7, 87, 130, 133
American Mutoscope Company. *See* American Mutoscope and Biograph Company
American Optical Co., 385
American Telephone and Telegraph Co. (AT&T), 116-18, 194, 197-98, 207
Amvets, 430-31
Anderson, "Bronco Billy," 133
Angeles, Bert, 94
Anglo-American Film Agreement, 397
Annabella, 288
Antitrust: FTC investigation of Famous Players-Lasky, 131, 148, 333-35; suits of early independents, 132; RCA suit against AT&T, 207; monopolistic control of majors, 214, 247-48, 292-94; laws suspended by NIRA, 216; the *Paramount* case, 219, 300-301, 316-20, 332-45, 313; Loew's takeover by Fox, 265, 284; Loew's as a *Paramount* defendant, 278-79
Arbuckle, Fatty, 111, 302
Aristo arcs, 97
Armat, Thomas, 4, 28-29, 45, 49
Armat Moving Picture Company, 121, 122
Arnaz, Desi, 329
Arnold, Thurman, 279, 294, 332, 333
Art Cinema Corporation, 151
Artcraft Pictures Corp., 138, 143, 145-46
Art Theater, 319-20, 398
Associated Artists Productions, 322
Association of Cinematography, Television, and Allied Technicians, 407
Astaire, Fred, 285
Astor Theater, 131
AT&T. *See* American Telephone and Telegraph Co.
Attendance: in 1910, 63; in nickelodeon era,

Production (*cont.*)
433-34. *See also* Independent production; Labor; Production Code Administration —costs: 17, 110, 178-79, 287; control of, 189-90; effects of sound on, 215; during World War II, 226; budgets for majors, 251-52; in 1950, 352; in postwar decade, 356; affected by *Paramount* decrees, 357; relative profitability of big-budget pictures, 379

Production Code Administration (PCA): formed by MPPDA, 220-22, 308-9; operation of, 296-98, 301-2, 433; undermining of, 318-20, 349, 399, 435, 445; subject matter proscribed, 435-36; mentioned, 313

Projectors, 4-6, 19-20
Promotion, 74, 107, 161-63
Protection, 5-6, 182-83
Ptolemy, 20
Publicity, 95, 106, 153-57, 288-89
Publix Theatres Corporation, 114
Putnam, George, 259-60

Queen Victoria, 53

Rackmil, Milton R., 382
Radio Corporation of America (RCA), 118, 194, 206-9
Raff, Norman C., 3, 28, 38-39, 41-43
Raff & Gammon, 6, 7, 24, 45
Rainey, Paul, 156
Rank Organization, 461, 466
Ranous, William, 94, 95, 133
Rapf, Harry, 261
RCA. *See* Radio Corporation of America
Recording License Agreement, 206-7
Recruiting films, 64
Rector, Enoch, 25, 26, 41
Red Channels, 429
Reid, Wallace, 284
Reliance-Majestic, 145
Rembusch, Trueman, 368
Republic Pictures: sells films to TV, 322; affected by *Paramount* suit, 341, 359; releases AB-PT pictures, 363; mentioned, 235, 250, 252, 293, 301, 320, 354, 380
Rex Pictures, 105
Reynaud, Émile, 22
Rich, Walter, 200, 201, 203
Riesel, Victor, 414
Rin-Tin-Tin, 198
Rivoli Theater, 197
RKO: formation of, 118, 206-7; severs General Electric-Westinghouse connections, 209; effect of Depression on, 214, 218;

earnings, 227, 355, 360; theater holdings, 240*n*, 263; production budget, 251; Selznick production chief, 259; divorces theaters, 317, 342-44, 347; sells films to TV, 322; Hughes ownership, 329, 422; sells studio, 351; disbands stock company, 376; curtails production, 423; mentioned, 114, 213, 247, 260, 265

Roadshowing, 109
Robinson, Edward G., 413
Rock, William T., 6, 81-82, 95, 99
Rodgers, William, 290-93
Roeber, Ernest, 48
Rogers, Ginger, 327
Rogers, Lela, 327
Rogers v. U.S., 419
Roget, Peter, 173
Rooney, Mickey, 285
Roosevelt, Franklin Delano, 216, 217, 327
Rosenberg, Meta Reis, 426
Ross, Donald C., 48
Rossellini, Roberto, 432
Rossen, Robert, 420
Rowland, Richard A., 136, 146, 264, 283
Roxy Theater, 202, 205, 374
Royal Theater, 282
Rubin, J. Robert, 264, 281, 283, 286
Rudge, John, 28
Runaway production, 325-26, 400-402
Runs: trade advantages of, 79; established by General Film, 126; described, 181, 243, 334; changing the assignment of, 335-36; impact of *Paramount* decrees on, 364-66
Russell, Rosalind, 285
Russell Sage survey, 63

St. Denis, Ruth, 25
St. James Theater, 76
St. Louis, Monsieur, 94
Saltonstall, Nora, 78
Sandow the Strong Man, 25
San Juan Hill, 81
Santschi, Tom, 77
Sarnoff, David, 206-7, 209
Schary, Dore, 376, 428, 429
Schenck, Joseph M., 150-52, 293
Schenck, Nicholas M.: impressed with Vitaphone, 202; sells Loew's Stock, 210, 264-65, 284; negotiates for Louis B. Mayer Pictures, 264; administration of Loew's, 278-94 *passim;* mentioned, 267, 292, 294
Scott, Adrian, 328
Screen Actors Guild, 217, 422
Screen Directors Guild, 217
Screen Gems, 322, 362

DESIGNED BY GARY G. GORE
COMPOSED BY FOX VALLEY TYPESETTING, MENASHA, WISCONSIN
MANUFACTURED BY THOMSON-SHORE, INC., DEXTER, MICHIGAN
TEXT IS SET IN TIMES ROMAN, DISPLAY LINES IN HELVETICA, TIMES ROMAN

Library of Congress Cataloging in Publication Data
Main entry under title:
The American film industry.
Bibliography: pp. 475-80.
Includes index.
1. Moving-picture industry—United States—History.
I. Balio, Tino.
PN1993.5.U6A87   338.4'7'791430973   75-32070
ISBN 0-299-07000-X
ISBN 0-299-07004-2 (pbk.)